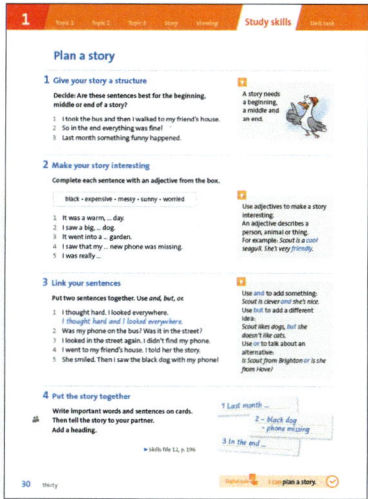

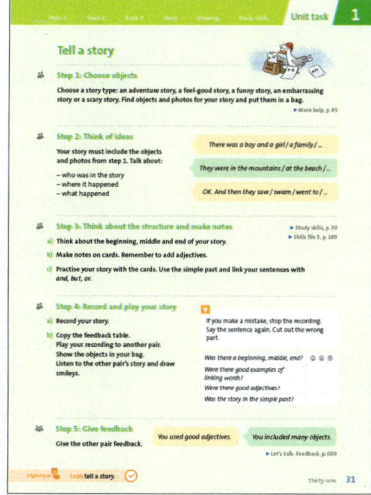

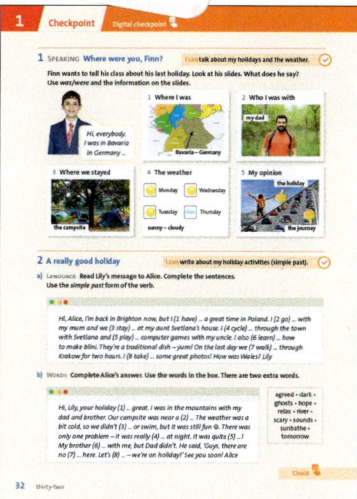

Lern- und Arbeitstechniken

Auf der *Study skills*-Seite übst du wichtige Lern- und Arbeitstechniken, z. B. wie du neue Wörter am besten lernst.

Eine Aufgabe am Unit-Ende

In der *Unit task* erstellst du ein größeres Produkt, z. B. eine Präsentation. Dabei wendest du das Gelernte aus der Unit an.

Im *Checkpoint* wiederholst du

Hier überprüfst du, wie gut du die Lernziele der Unit schon erreicht hast.

Im Anschluss findest du ein *Text file* mit interessanten Texten zum Thema der Unit.

Diese Verweise führen dich in die *Diff bank* am Ende der Unit

▶ More help

Hilfen zu den Aufgaben

▶ More practice

weitere Übungen

▶ Challenge

weitere Übungen mit höherem Schwierigkeitsgrad

Diese Lernangebote findest du im hinteren Teil des Buches

▶ Skills file

eine Übersicht über die Lern- und Arbeitstechniken

▶ Language file

die wichtigsten Sprachregeln

▶ Wordbank

zusätzliche Wörter zu bestimmten Themen

Let's talk

Redewendungen nach wichtigen Themen und Situationen geordnet

Vocabulary

eine Liste der neuen Vokabeln einer Unit mit hilfreichen Tipps

Dictionary

alphabetische Wörterlisten zum Nachschlagen (Englisch – Deutsch, Deutsch – Englisch)

ADVANCED
lighthouse 2

Im Auftrag des Verlages herausgegeben von
Martin Bastkowski, Schellerten;
Berit Schaarschmidt, Aschaffenburg *sowie*
Sonja Mahne, Basel; Ulrike Rath, Aachen

Erarbeitet von
Rebecca Kaplan, Mauer;
Rebecca Robb Benne, Kopenhagen;
Zoe Thorne, Royston *sowie*
Jennifer O'Hagan, Bristol *(Checkpoints)*;
Ulrike Rath, Aachen *(Skills file)*;
Ursula Fleischhauer, Hannover *(Vocabulary)*;
Dr. Philip Devlin und Ralph Williams *(Unit 6)*

In Zusammenarbeit mit der Englischredaktion
Klaus Unger (Projektleitung), Katrin Heinecke
(koordinierende Redakteurin), Doreen Arnold,
Lisa Ahmadi, Natalie Bernau, Michael Dunkel,
Franziska Gräbe, Chelsea Ledvinka-Heß, Jutta Seuren,
Silvia Wiedemann, Anja Zieschang *sowie*
Ingrid Raspe, Düsseldorf *(Vocabulary, Dictionary E–D)*

Beratende Mitwirkung
Nikolas Grote, Hannover; Christina McCrum, Köln;
Sandra Mercatoris, Ilvesheim; Stefanie Kelly, Villingen-
Schwenningen; Annette Müller, Kassel; Lara-Sophie
Räuschel, Hamburg; Christina Sieber, Schorndorf;
Andriana Zaroti, Krefeld *sowie*
Vertr.-Prof. Dr. Christian Ludwig, Berlin;
Prof. Dr. Bernd Rüschoff, Essen;
Prof. Dr. Michaela Sambanis, Berlin

Medienmanagement
Silke Kirchhoff

Illustrationen
Harald Ardeias, Schelklingen; Irina Zinner, Hamburg

Fotos
Anja Poehlmann, Brighton
Für die freundliche Unterstützung danken wir
der Varndean School, Brighton.

Umschlaggestaltung
Rosendahl, Berlin

Layoutkonzept
Klein & Halm, Berlin

Designberatung
designcollective, Berlin
Ungermeyer, Berlin

Layout und technische Umsetzung
designcollective, Berlin
Straive

Druck
Mohn Media Mohndruck, Gütersloh

PEFC zertifiziert
Dieses Produkt stammt aus nachhaltig
bewirtschafteten Wäldern und kontrollierten
Quellen.
PEFC
www.pefc.de
PEFC/04-31-1033

www.cornelsen.de

Soweit in diesem Lehrwerk Personen fotografisch
abgebildet sind und ihnen von der Redaktion fiktive
Namen, Berufe, Dialoge und Ähnliches zugeordnet
oder diese Personen in bestimmte Kontexte gesetzt
werden, dienen diese Zuordnungen und Darstellungen
ausschließlich der Veranschaulichung und dem
besseren Verständnis des Buchinhaltes.

Dieses Werk berücksichtigt die Regeln der reformierten
Rechtschreibung und Zeichensetzung.

Die Webseiten Dritter, deren Internetadressen in
diesem Lehrwerk angegeben sind, wurden vor
Drucklegung sorgfältig geprüft. Der Verlag übernimmt
keine Gewähr für die Aktualität und den Inhalt dieser
Seiten oder solcher, die mit ihnen verlinkt sind.

Die *Cornelsen Lernen App* ist eine fakultative Ergänzung
zu *Lighthouse Advanced*, die die inhaltliche Arbeit
begleitet und unterstützt. Als solche unterliegt sie nicht
der Genehmigungspflicht.

1. Auflage, 1. Druck 2023
ISBN 9783060358380 broschiert

1. Auflage, 1. Druck 2023
ISBN 9783060358397 gebunden

ISBN 9783060345854 E-Book

ADVANCED

lighthouse 2

Cornelsen

Inhalt

Inhalt

I can ...	Kompetenzen	Sprachliche Mittel	Seite

Unit 6
The treasure hunt

Story	... understand a story.	R/S Eine Geschichte verstehen · S Sich über die Geschichte austauschen · sich über Fairness austauschen · ein neues Ende der Geschichte schreiben und szenisch darstellen	Voc *outdoor activities*	176

Anhang

Die Angebote des Schülerbuchs sind nicht obligatorisch abzuarbeiten.
Die Auswahl der Übungen und Übungsteile richtet sich nach
den Schwerpunkten des schulinternen Curriculums.

Hello again!
The last day of the holidays

I'm so happy! It isn't raining today and this fish tastes delicious!

Hi, guys! What are you doing? We're enjoying the last day of the school holidays: We're hanging out at the beach with Alice. We don't want to go back to school – the summer holidays are too short! ☹

1 READING AND SPEAKING Ready for school

a) Look at the photos and read the Varndean kids' messages. Copy and complete the table.

Who?	Where?	What are they doing?	Happy or not happy? Why?
Lily and Zane	at the beach	They're …	They're (not) happy because …
Noah	…	He's …	…
Sunita	…		

▶ Language file 7, p. 203

b) WALK AROUND Are you happy or not happy to be back at school? Tell different partners.

> I'm happy to be back at school. I want to see my friends. / … What about you?

> I'm not happy to be back at school. I want to sleep late / have more free time / …

Really? I like school. 😃
I'm at home. I'm wearing my new school uniform.
I have a new school bag too.
Do you have new uniforms?
See you tomorrow! ✓

I'm in town with my mum.
We're buying my last school things.
I'm looking for a new pencil case.
What do you think? I can't wait to see all my friends at school. 😍 ✓

2 LISTENING AND SPEAKING A day at Brighton Beach

🔊 a) Lily and Zane are at the beach. Imagine you're there too. Close your eyes and listen.

🔊 b) Listen again. Draw a picture of you at the beach. You can use ideas from the audio.

👥 c) Show your picture to a partner and explain it.

> In my picture I'm sitting on the beach in ... / I'm looking at ...

> Some kids are playing / swimming / ...

> I can smell the sea / food / ...

> I can taste ice cream / ...

> I feel happy / sad / ...

> I can see the blue water / ...

> I can hear the seagulls / ...

▶ Language file Revision 3, p. 200 ▶ Workbook, pp. 6–7

 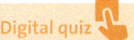

Unit 1
Travel and holidays

I was in Spain, in a hotel near the beach.

I wasn't away. I was at home in Brighton. It was a great holiday with some cool day trips with my parents and my dog.

Lily   Noah   Ms Bond

I was in Poland with my mum, but we weren't in a hotel. We were at my aunt and uncle's house.

1 LISTENING Where were they?

a) BEFORE YOU LISTEN Look at the holiday photos and read the speech bubbles on pages 12–13. Where do you think the people in pictures 1 and 2 were? Make notes.

Lily: ...   Noah: ...   Ms Bond: ...   Zane: ...   Alice: ...   Sunita: ...

b) Listen and check your answers from a).

c) Listen again. Complete the sentences about the weather.

1 In Poland it was ... and it wasn't ...
2 In Brighton it was ... and ... some days.
3 In France it was ... and ...
4 In Wales it was a bit ...

▶ More practice 1, p. 40

Nach dieser Unit kann ich ... ✓

- ✓ über meine Ferien sprechen
- ✓ über Ferienaktivitäten schreiben
- ✓ über das letzte Wochenende sprechen
- ✓ von neuen Erfahrungen berichten

Unit task ✓

- ✓ eine Geschichte erzählen

My mum, my big brother and I were in Prague, the capital of Czechia. We were in a hostel. My mum's partner Ben was at home with our parrot.

I was in the mountains with my dad and my brother. We were on a campsite in Wales.

I was in France with my parents and my little sister Holly. We were in a holiday apartment.

Alice   Sunita   Zane

2 SPEAKING Where were you?

a) Think and make notes about your summer holidays: the place, how it was and the weather.

👥 b) WALK AROUND Ask and answer holiday questions.

▶ More help, p. 41   ▶ Countries, inside back cover

Where were you?

How was it?

What was the weather like?

I was ... / We were ...

It was / wasn't great / ...

It was / wasn't hot / ...

▶ More practice 2, p. 41   ▶ Challenge 1, p. 41   ▶ Language file 1, pp. 200–201
▶ Workbook, p. 8

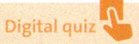

Digital quiz   **I can talk about my holidays and the weather.** ✓

Holiday stories

1 SONG **My summer holiday**

a) **Listen. Where was the singer? Was it a good holiday?**

b) **Listen again and write the correct words.**

> loved • moved • stayed • sunbathed • swam • was • watched • went • were

She ... (1) on holiday with her father and her brother.
They ... (2) in a hotel. The weather ... (3) hot.
They ... (4) and ... (5) every day.
They ... (6) dancers in the street and ... (7) their feet.
She ... (8) eating churros. The tapas ... (9) good.

churros

2 LOOKING AT LANGUAGE **The simple past**

a) **Look at the song. When was the holiday?**

b) **Look at the verbs in blue. Complete the rule.**

> Die einfache Vergangenheit *(simple past)* der regelmäßigen Verben bildest du durch Anhängen von ... an den Infinitiv. Die Vergangenheitsform der Verben ist für alle Personen gleich.

c) **Look at the verbs in green. Read the tip.**

> Manche Verben haben im *simple past* eine unregelmäßige Form, z. B.:
> *be – was/were, go – went, have – had, swim – swam.*
> Diese Formen musst du lernen.

d) **Close your books and listen to the song again. Stand up for every verb in the past.**

My summer holiday

I *had* a wonderful holiday last summer!
I *went* to Spain with my dad and my big
    brother.
We *stayed* in a hotel in Granada
and the weather, oh, it *was* hot, hot, hot!

We went to Spain and we went by train
and we *swam* and *sunbathed* every day.
It *was* so cool in the swimming pool!
It *was* the best ever holiday... ¡Olé!

We *watched* flamenco dancers in
    the street,
we *listened* and *danced* and *moved*
    our feet
I *loved* eating churros, hot and sweet
and the tapas, oh, they *were* oh-so good!

We *went* to Spain ...

▶ Irregular verbs, pp. 312–313

▶ Language file 1–2, pp. 200–201

3 GAME **Last summer**

Talk in groups. One student says a sentence about last summer with ideas from the box. The next student repeats the last sentence and adds a new sentence.

A   Last summer I played badminton.
B   Last summer I played badminton and I learned to skateboard.
C   Last summer I learned to skateboard and …

Ideas

cycled in the park / in my street / …
helped my parents / my grandparents / …
learned to code / skateboard / …
listened to music / some podcasts / …
played badminton / cards / with my pet / …
practised magic tricks / the guitar / …
watched lots of films / a football match / …
went on holiday by ferry / plane / train / …

4 Noah's summer

a)   **Complete Noah's sentences. Use the simple past form of a verb from the box.**

brush • hike • play • rest • visit • ~~work~~

My parents worked (1) some days. I … (2) on the beach a lot with Buddy and my cousin. I … (3) Buddy every day. He looks really nice now! One day I … (4) my grandma in Portsmouth. And another day my dad and I … (5) in the hills on a day trip. After our trip we … (6) for two days!

b)   **Now listen to Noah and check your answers.**

▶ More practice 3, p. 42

5 Sunita and Zane's summer

Look at the holiday pictures and find the correct caption for each picture from the box. There are two extra captions.

My family travelled to France by car. • I looked after my little sister. •
We went to the airport by taxi. • We swam in the river. • A guide showed us the old town. •
We had pizza by the river. • I watched TV with my little sister.

▶ Workbook, p. 9

6 READING A holiday story

a) BEFORE YOU READ **Answer the questions.**

1 Can you remember? Where was Sunita on holiday?
2 Look at the pictures. What sort of story do you think Sunita's story is?

> *I think Sunita's story is exciting / funny / sad / scary / ...*

b) **Read Sunita's story. Check your answers from a).**

1 When we were on holiday in Prague, my mum, my brother Nish and I went on a scary ghost tour in the old town. It was late at night and it was dark. Our guide was very old and he looked like a vampire! 5 He wore a costume and had vampire teeth.

2 The guide took us to an old underground place. It was cold and smelled bad. He told us a story about a vampire a 10 long time ago. The vampire did lots of horrible things. The guide was an amazing storyteller, and the story was very scary!

3 I wanted to tell Nish something, so I put my hand on his arm. He was really scared 15 and screamed. He was very loud! He thought that I was a vampire! Everybody in the group thought that it was funny, but Nish was really angry at me.

c) **Read Sunita's story again. Complete the summary.**

Sunita was on a ... (1) tour. They were in an old ... (2) place. The guide told a ... (3) story. Sunita touched ... (4) and he was really ... (5)! Everybody in the group thought that it was ... (6)

d) **Would you like to go on a scary ghost tour? Why or why not? Tell your partner.**

> *I'd like to go on a ghost tour like this. Ghost stories are exciting. / I like scary stories. / ... What about you?*

> *No thanks! I don't like scary stories / vampires / going out at night / ....*

7 WORDS **Past activities**

 a) Look at the story on **p. 16** again. Find the irregular simple past forms of *go, wear, take, tell, do, put* and *think*.

b) Check your answers on the irregular verbs pages **(pages 312–313)**. Which word has the same form in the past and the present?

c) Complete another story from Sunita's holiday with simple past forms from **a)**.

My family … **(1)** lots of other fun activities in Prague. We also … **(2)** on another kind of tour. Some people in our hostel … **(3)** us about it. Blind guides … **(4)** us on a journey through dark rooms in a big building. We all … **(5)** masks over our eyes. We … **(6)** our hands out to find the way. I … **(7)** it was an amazing experience, and I learned a lot. ► More practice 4, p. 42

8 WORDS **Travel and holiday words**

a) Collect words and phrases that you already know for the umbrella words. The words on **pages 12–16** can help you.

places	transport	activities
hotel, …	train, …	swim, …

 b) Compare with a partner. Add your partner's words and phrases to your umbrella words.

► More practice 5, p. 42   ► Challenge 2, p. 42   ► Skills file 1, p. 184

My task

9 **My summer holidays**

Read the postcard from your friend and write an answer. You can use your words from **8**.

Hi!
How were your summer holidays?
Were you at home or away on holiday?
I was in London with my parents. We went there by train. We went shopping and we visited lots of great places.
Tell me all about your summer activities!
Bye for now
Cameron

Hi, Cameron
London sounds great!
I was at home. / I was in …
We went there by …
I relaxed with friends / made pizza / …
Bye!
(your name)

► Digital help
► Countries, inside back cover
► Wordbank 1, p. 213

► Workbook, pp. 10–11

 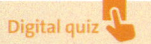

At home in the holidays

1 LISTENING Time to go to Pride

a) BEFORE YOU LISTEN **Lily had a busy day when she went to Pride.**
Match the pictures to the sentences.

> *Hi, Lily*
> *I hope the rest of the summer was good!*

> *Hi, Svetlana*
> *It was great, thanks! I went to Brighton Pride – it's a really big thing here!* 🙂 🏳️‍🌈

A

B

C

D

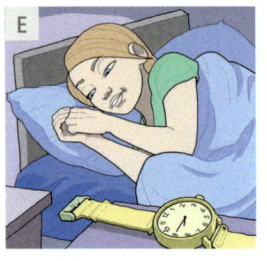
E

F

Good to know

Brighton is the LGBTQ capital of the UK. Brighton Pride is the city's biggest event and 160,000 people visit it in August every year.

1 Lily got up at seven twenty a.m.
2 She ate breakfast at seven thirty a.m.
3 She made Pride decorations at eight fifteen a.m.
4 Then she did her Pride make-up at nine o'clock.
5 She took the bus into town at nine twenty-seven a.m. to meet her friends at the station.
6 She went to bed at eight forty-five p.m. because she was so tired – it was a busy day!

b) **Lily, Noah and Zane waited for Sunita at the train station. Copy the table.**
Then listen to the station announcements and complete it.

From	Arrival time	Platform
Cambridge	*9.55*	...
Eastbourne	...	...
London Victoria	...	
Portsmouth	...	
Bristol		

c) **Listen to the dialogue and complete the information. Use the table in b) to help you.**

Sunita took the train from ... to Brighton. She arrived at platform ... at ...

▶ Skills file 6, p. 189

2 VIEWING **Buying a ticket**

a) Lots of tourists visit Brighton and they often travel by train. Watch the video and choose the correct buttons on the ticket machine.

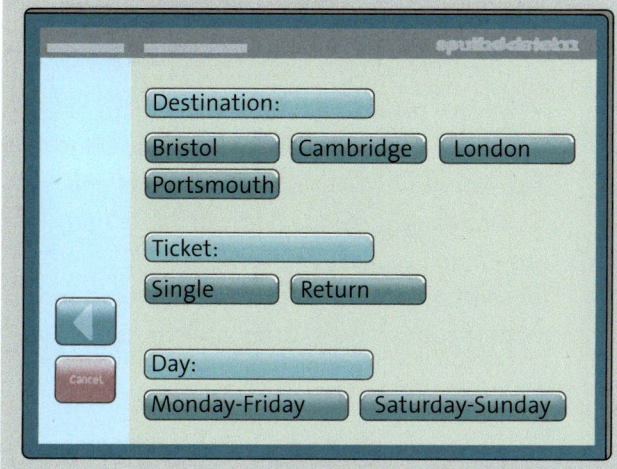

▶ More practice 6, p. 43

b) Read the dialogue on p. 43 with your partner.

c) Read the dialogue again. Use your own ideas for the words in blue.
ROLE-PLAY **Act out your dialogue for the class.**

Good to know

In the UK, the money is pounds (£) and pence (p). £1 is 100 pence (p).

You write:	You say:
50p	fifty p
£1.50	one pound fifty
£34.90	thirty-four pounds ninety

d) Look at these tickets (A–E) and say the prices.

Ticket A / B / ... costs ...

But I fly everywhere for free!

▶ Workbook, p. 12

3 READING Brighton Pride

Read Lily's messages to her aunt Svetlana about Pride and complete the information.

1   Lily went to Pride with …
2   Noah wore …
3   Lily loved …
4   In the parade they saw …
5   They ate …
6   They listened to …

Erklär-film

4 LOOKING AT LANGUAGE
The simple past: negatives

a) **Read Lily's messages again and look at the photos. Then read the list of top Pride activities.**
Tick ✓ the things Lily did and cross ✗ the things she didn't do: *1)* ✓

> **Top Pride activities:**
> 1 wear Pride make-up
> 2 watch the parade
> 3 go to the concert on Saturday night
> 4 buy a Pride flag
> 5 eat rainbow cake
> 6 take photos with friends

b) **Write the sentences for the things in a) that Lily didn't do ✗ . You can find them in the messages:** *Lily didn't …*

c) **Write the other sentences with didn't in Lily's messages.**
Then complete the rule.

> Du verneinst Aussagen im *simple past* mit … und dem Verb im Infinitiv. Eine Ausnahme ist *be*: Die verneinten Formen sind … und *weren't*.

Pride was amazing! I went with my friends, but Mum and Dad didn't go because they were at work. We went to the parade and Sunita bought a Pride flag, but I didn't buy anything because I made my own decorations. Noah wore his headphones so that the music wasn't too loud for him. ✓

We watched lots of different people in the parade and everyone was really happy. We were lucky with the weather: It didn't rain at all. I loved all the colours and rainbow clothes! We even saw our friend Willow in the parade with her girlfriend, but I didn't talk to them. ✓

Then we went to the Family Pride area and ate rainbow cake. Lots of children had Pride make-up. We didn't go to the concert after the parade, but we listened to street musicians and we had a great time! ✓

▶ Language file 3, p. 201

▶ Workbook, pp. 13–14

5 A message from Lily's aunt

Lily's aunt Svetlana texted her back. Complete her text with the correct positive ✓ or negative ✗ simple past forms.

▶ More practice 7, p. 43
▶ More practice 8, p. 44

That's wonderful, Lily! I love your photos. It looks as if you (1 ✓ have) had a great time!
We (2 ✗ have) didn't have a Pride festival here, but we (3 ✓ go) … to a music festival. The problem was, I (4 ✗ like) … the music at all! The bands (5 ✗ play) … my kind of music so I (6 ✗ want) … to dance. And your uncle (7 ✓ think) … the food was too expensive so he (8 ✗ buy) … anything to eat there. We (9 ✗ stay) … very long – we went home after an hour!

6 Julia didn't …

Start a sentence with a classmate's name and a verb in the negative simple past. Your partner completes the sentence and starts a new one.

A Julia didn't play …
B … tennis. Amir didn't watch …
A … TV. Laura didn't eat …

My task

7 Events in the holidays

a) Write five sentences about an event you went to or an activity that you did in the holidays: some true, some false. You can add photos.

▶ More help, p. 44
▶ Digital help

> *I went to a rock concert in my town.*
> *A singer played the piano.*

b) Swap with your partner. Find the false sentences and write sentences to correct them.

> *I think the singer didn't play the piano.*
> *She played the guitar.*

c) Swap again and check your partner's answers.

> *That's right! She didn't play piano.*
> *She played the guitar!*

▶ Workbook, p. 15

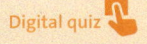

A weekend project

1 LISTENING Welcome, Finn!

a) BEFORE YOU LISTEN Look at the title of this exercise and the photo. Who do you think Finn is?

b) Copy the table. Listen and complete it. You don't need to understand everything. Add more details.

name	Finn Demir
from	...
pet	...
likes	...
why he's in Brighton	

c) Listen again and check.

He's really cute!

2 SONG Welcome to our school

a) Read the text of the song. Find words for the gaps that rhyme with the blue words.

b) Listen. Were your ideas right? Which words do you like more?

c) Listen and sing.

d) YOU CHOOSE Do task 1 or 2.

1 Write a note to Finn or a new student in your class to welcome him or her.

2 Write another verse for the song for Finn or a new student in your class.

WELCOME TO OUR SCHOOL

Welcome to our school

Welcome to our school!
You're new: That's really ...!

Our teacher is new here too.
Yeah, new now just like ...!
Hey Finn, don't worry.
There's really no big hurry
to meet the kids in here.
We're here all through the ...
Hey Finn, just wait:
Our school is really ...!

Welcome to our school!
You're new: That's really cool!

Yes, we can show you around
The school and Brighton ...
Hey Finn, come out
with us: Let's all ...!
Sleep late at the weekends
and then relax with ...
Hey Finn, was it
the same in Germany?

3 SPEAKING **Making friends**

a) Partner B: Look at p. 40.
Partner A: You're one of Finn's new classmates. Ask him questions about his summer.

1 What did you practise?
2 What did you put in boxes in Germany?
3 When did you look for a house in Brighton?

4 Who told you goodbye in Germany?
5 How did you travel to Brighton?
6 What did you buy for school?
7 Who showed you the way to school?

b) Swap roles. You're Finn. Answer your new classmate's questions about your summer. Use the ideas below or your own ideas and say complete sentences.

1 films: *I watched films.*
2 fish and chips
3 Brighton Pier, the i360 and Brighton Marina

4 by bus and bike
5 boxes
6 video games
7 8 a.m.
▶ Challenge 3, p. 44

4 MEDIATION **A silent disco beach clean-up**

a) Ms Bond tells class 8C about a class activity on Saturday. Read the flyer.

Come to our silent disco clean-up on Brighton Beach

Collect plastic bags, bottles and other rubbish.
Help make the beach and the water clean and safe for people and sea animals!

- Sing, dance and clean up.
- Wear cool clothes or a costume or a mask.
- Listen to music on headphones – you can borrow them for free.
- You don't need any equipment: We have rubbish pickers, rubbish bags and gloves.

b) During dinner at home, Finn told his mum about the beach clean-up. His mum asked questions. Act out the conversation with a partner.

Finn	Am Samstag wollen wir …
Mutter	Das klingt lustig. Was macht ihr genau?
Finn	…
Mutter	Was sollst du anziehen?
Finn	…
Mutter	Sollst du etwas mitbringen?
Finn	…

▶ Skills file 8, p. 191

5 LISTENING **On Monday**

🔊 **a)** After the beach clean-up, Ms Bond talks to the class. Look at the pictures and listen. Write the letters of the things that the kids found on the beach.

🔊 **b)** Listen again. Write who found each thing.

c) What was the message in the bottle? Write your idea.

▶ Digital help 🔽

⊠ **d)** Say what you think about the beach clean-up.

A 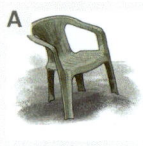 B  C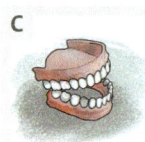

D 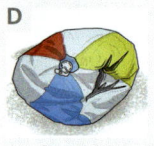 E  F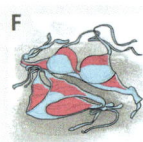

G  H 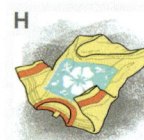 I

My task

6 Last weekend

a) In the break the kids talk about the rest of their weekend. Match Finn, Lily, Noah, Sunita and Zane to the correct activities.

1 At lunchtime on Saturday I cooked spaghetti for my mum and sister.

2 Last weekend I looked after our parrot. He was ill.

3 On Sunday morning I went for a long walk.

4 On Sunday afternoon my mum and I went on a Brighton bus tour.

5 Yesterday I had a parkour class.

b) SPEED DATING **Tell different partners about your last weekend.**

Last weekend / Yesterday / On Saturday / ... I ...
On Sunday morning / afternoon / evening I ...
At lunchtime / At 10.30 / At four o'clock / ... I ...

▶ More help, p. 45   ▶ More practice 9, p. 45

▶ Workbook, pp. 15–16

Digital quiz 🔽   **I can talk about last weekend.**

Background file

1 A tour of a British school

a) BEFORE YOU WATCH What are the important places in your school? Write down six places.

b) VIEWING Zane is giving Finn a tour of Varndean. Watch the video. While you watch, write down the six places Zane shows Finn. Are they the same places you wrote down for your school in a)?

c) What's one thing Zane says students do in each place?

d) What new facts about Varndean did you learn from the video?

e) VIEWING Watch the video again. What's different from your school? Write down three things. Talk about them with a partner. Did you write down the same things?

f) Are you a good detective? Answer these questions and find out!
You can find all the answers in the video.

1 What's Varndean's motto? It's on a sign next to the name of the school.
2 What colour is the board behind the students sitting in the classroom?
3 How much do the long sandwiches in bags in the canteen cost?
4 What animal is on the stage in the theatre? There are two of them!
5 A girl with brown hair is reading a book in the library. What scary thing is on the front of the book?
6 What animal is on a car under the words 'Sports fields'?
7 What instrument is at the front of the hall?

2 A tour of your school

There is a new student from Great Britain in your class.
What can you show him or her in your school?
What can you say about these places?
Share your ideas in class.
☒ You can also make a video tour.

> *This is the …*
> *You can … here.*
> *We … here every day.*

Noah's adventure

1 BEFORE YOU READ Noah's journey

Look at Noah's ticket and complete the sentences.

1   Noah travelled on …
2   He travelled from … to …
3   He travelled at …
4   He travelled by …
5   The ticket cost …

2 READING What happened?

a) **Read the story in Noah's journal. Who did he visit and what was the problem?**

Saturday, 5th October

1   Wow, what a day! Today I travelled out of Brighton alone for the first time. Go, me! I'm kind of proud!

2   I love seeing Grandma, but she lives two hours
5   away in Portsmouth, so we only see her once a month. Last week Sunita asked me, 'Do you want to go and see her alone? It's easy to get there by bus or train.' I thought about it a lot and I was a bit scared at first. We usually go by
10   car because I don't like it when there are lots of people.

3   But then I thought, 'I'm twelve now. I want to try this, even if it's scary.' So I asked Mum and Dad. They weren't sure, but they said yes in the end. And Grandma was really excited!

15   4   So this morning Buddy and I got on the train at Brighton station. We didn't take the bus because it's too slow – it takes nearly five hours! But the train only takes two hours and we didn't need to change trains. The journey was fine and Buddy loved being on the train.

5   I had a great day with Grandma in Portsmouth. It was sunny, so we went to
20   the beach. We had a picnic and Buddy swam in the sea – he was so happy in the water! We didn't go to the pier because it's very loud.

6   In the afternoon Grandma took me to Portsmouth station. You need a ticket to go on to the platforms, so I got on the train alone. But there was a problem – it was loud and I was tired and I took the wrong train! I heard the announcement that the train was

25 to Southampton, but it was too late. That was the wrong way!

7 I was really scared at first, but I was glad that Buddy was there: He helped me feel calm. I closed my eyes and hugged him. Then I texted

30 Sunita, Lily and Zane, and I got messages with lots of support from them. They told me to get off the train at Southampton and they helped me find the right train back to Brighton. So grateful for having them!

35 8 I texted Mum and Dad too and I told them what happened. They were at Brighton station and they were a bit worried. But they were really proud of me for trying something new, even if it was scary!

▶ Skills file 7, p. 190

b) **Put what happened in the correct order.**

a Buddy swam in the sea.
b Sunita talked to Noah about a trip.
c Noah's friends helped him.
d Noah got the train to Brighton.
e Noah got on the wrong train.
f Noah got the train to Portsmouth.

---

3 Feelings in the story

Copy the table. Find the words in the story for the pictures. Write who had each feeling and ⊠ why he / she felt this way.

	Where (part)?	How (adjective)?	Who (name)?	⊠ Why?
1	parts 1 and 8	proud	Noah, Noah's ...	Noah tried something new
2	parts 2 and 7	...	...	...
3	part 3	...	...	...
4	part 5	...	...	
5	part 7	...	...	
6	part 7	...		
7	part 8	...		

4 SHOWTIME **Scenes from Noah's story**

a) **Which character(s) in Noah's story maybe said or texted these sentences?**

1 *I want to see my grandma more, but she lives in Portsmouth.*

2 *Goodbye, love. Have a safe journey!*

3 *Do you want to go to the pier?*

4 *Thank you, Buddy. I feel calm now. I can do this.*

5 *You guys are awesome! Thanks!*

6 *Do you want to go and see her alone? It's easy to get there by bus or train.*

7 *Welcome to Portsmouth, Noah! It's so nice to see you!*

8 *Southampton? Oh no, I'm on the wrong train! I don't know what to do!*

9 *Don't worry, Noah. Get off the train at the next station.*

10 *We're so proud of you, Noah – that was scary, but you did it!*

b) **In groups, act out scenes from Noah's story. Use the sentences from a) and your own ideas.**

5 LIFE SKILLS **Try new things**

a) **Different things are scary to different people. How scary are the activities in the box to you?**
1 = not at all scary   6 = very scary

b) **Talk to your partner and compare your answers. What's the same? What's different?**

> **Scary?**
> a   singing to other people
> b   touching a snake
> c   travelling by plane
> d   walking around in a dark house
> e   talking to new people
> f   riding a horse

Riding a horse is (very / quite / not very / not at all) scary to me.

I agree. That's the same for me.

Really? For me, it's …

c) **What do you want to try this year? Write one thing. Use the list or your own ideas. Put it in an envelope and give it to your teacher. Don't open it until the end of the school year.**

▶ Workbook, p. 17

 Digital quiz 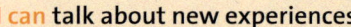 **I can talk about new experiences.**

Brighton stories: Summer holidays

Gloria · Daisy · Emir · Joe

1 Holiday places

BEFORE YOU WATCH **You can go on holiday anywhere[1] in the world[2]. Tell a partner where you would like to go and why.**

I'd like to go to … because there are amazing mountains / it's hot / you can surf there / … ▶ Countries, inside back cover

2 VIEWING **Three holiday experiences**

a) Watch the first part of the video. Match the four kids to the correct holiday places in the box. There are two extra places.

a Brighton • b Cornwall, England • c Edinburgh, Scotland • d Poland • e Portugal • f Spain

b) Watch the second part. What is Emir's great idea? Then look at the photos of three activities (A–C): What holiday experiences do you think they show?

c) Watch part three. True (T) or false (F)?

1 Daisy and Joe swim in a big pool.
2 Joe eats a Portuguese cake.
3 Emir shows Joe the caravan[3] where he stayed on holiday.
4 Emir went windsurfing and crab hunting[4].
5 Gloria shows Joe some pictures of Edinburgh's old town.
6 Joe tries a traditional Scottish cake.

d) Watch the last part. Which holiday experience did Joe think was the best? Why?

Joe thinks … is the best because he likes …

e) Which holiday experience do you think was the best? Why? Tell your group.

3 A fun experience

Share a fun experience with your class. Bring things and show photos.
We went to … last weekend / summer / night …   This is a photo of the park / the party / …
I bought / found / got this … in / at ….

---

[1] **anywhere** *irgendwo(hin), überall*   [2] **world** *die Welt*   [3] **caravan** *der Wohnwagen*   [4] **crab hunting** *Krebse fangen*

Plan a story

1 Give the story a structure

Before you tell a story, you have to plan it. Decide:
Are these sentences best for the beginning, middle
or end of a story?

1. I took the bus and then I walked to my friend's house.
2. So in the end everything was fine!
3. Last month something funny happened.

A story needs
a beginning,
a middle and
an end.

2 Make your story interesting

Read these sentences from the middle of the story.
Complete them with an adjective from the box.

1. It was a warm, … day.
2. I saw a big, … dog.
3. It went into a … garden.
4. I saw that my … new phone was missing.
5. I was really …

black • expensive • green • sunny • worried

Use adjectives to make a story
interesting.
An adjective describes a
person, animal or thing.
For example: *Scout is a cool
seagull. She's very friendly.*

3 Link your sentences

Read more sentences from the middle of the story.
Put two sentences together. Use *and, but, or.*

1. I thought hard. I looked everywhere.
   I thought hard and I looked everywhere.
2. Was my phone on the bus? Was it in the street?
3. I looked in the street again. I didn't find my phone.
4. I went to my friend's house. I told her the story.
5. She smiled. Then I saw the black dog with my phone!

Use *and* to add something:
Scout is clever and she's nice.
Use *but* to add a different idea:
*Scout likes dogs, but she doesn't
like cats.*
Use *or* to talk about an
alternative:
*Is Scout from Brighton or is she
from Hove?*

4 Put the story together

Write important words and sentences on cards.
Then tell the story to your partner.
Add a heading.

1 Last month …

2 - warm, sunny day
  - took the bus

3 In the end …

▶ Skills file 12, p. 195

 Digital quiz 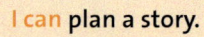 I can **plan a story.**

Tell a story

Step 1: Choose objects   ▶ Digital help

Choose a story type: an adventure story, a feel-good story, a funny story, an embarrassing story or a scary story. Find objects and photos for your story and put them in a bag.

▶ More help, p. 45

Step 2: Think of ideas

Your story must include the objects and photos from step 1. Show them and talk about:

– who was in the story
– where it happened
– what happened

> *There was a boy and a girl / a family / …*

> *They were in the mountains / at the beach / …*

> *OK. And then they saw / swam / went to / …*

Step 3: Think about the structure and make notes   ▶ Digital help    ▶ Study skills, p. 30

a) Think about the beginning, middle and end of your story.

b) Make notes on cards. Remember to add adjectives.   ▶ Skills file 5, p. 188

c) Practise your story with the cards. Use the simple past and link your sentences with *and, but, or.*

Step 4: Record and play your story

a) Record your story.

b) Copy the feedback table.
Play your recording to another pair.
Show the objects in your bag.
Listen to the other pair's story and draw smileys.

If you make a mistake, stop the recording. Say the sentence again. Cut out the wrong part.

Was there a beginning, middle, end?	☺ ☺ ☹
Were there good examples of linking words?	☺ ☺ ☹
Were there good adjectives?	☺ ☺ ☹
Was the story in the simple past?	☺ ☺ ☹

Step 5: Give feedback

Give the other pair feedback.

> *You used good adjectives.*

> *You included many objects.*

▶ Let's talk: Feedback, p. 227

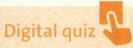 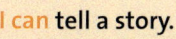

1 SPEAKING Where were you, Finn?

I can talk about my holidays and the weather.

Finn wants to tell his class about his last holiday. Look at his slides. What does he say?
Use *was/were* and the information on the slides to give Finn's talk.

*Hi, everybody.
I was in Bavaria
in Germany ...*

1 Where I was

Bavaria – Germany

2 Who I was with

my dad

3 Where we stayed

the campsite

4 The weather

☀ Monday   ☀ Wednesday

☀ Tuesday   ☁ Thursday

sunny – cloudy

5 My opinion

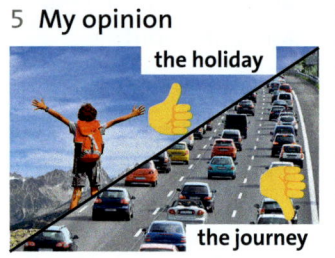

the holiday

the journey

2 A really good holiday

I can write about my holiday activities (simple past).

a) LANGUAGE Read Lily's email to Alice. Complete the sentences.
Use the simple past form of the verb.

● ● ●

Hi, Alice, I'm back in Brighton now, but I ... (1 have) a great time in Poland. I ... (2 go) with
my mum and we ... (3 stay) at my aunt Svetlana's house. I ... (4 cycle) through the town
with Svetlana and ... (5 play) computer games with my uncle. I also ... (6 learn) how
to make blini. They're a traditional dish – yum! On the last day we ... (7 walk) through
Krakow for two hours. I ... (8 take) some great photos! How was Wales? Lily

b) WORDS Complete Alice's answer. Use the words in the box. There are two extra words.

● ● ●

Hi, Lily, your holiday ... (1) great. I was in the mountains with my
dad and brother. Our campsite was near a ... (2) The weather was a
bit cold, so we didn't ... (3) or swim, but it was still fun ☺. There was
only one problem – it was really ... (4) at night. It was quite ... (5)!
My brother ... (6) with me, but Dad didn't. He said, 'Guys, there are
no ... (7) here. Let's ... (8) – we're on holiday!' See you soon! Alice

agreed • dark •
ghosts • hope •
relax • river •
scary • sounds •
sunbathe •
tomorrow

Check

3 LANGUAGE An interesting day

> I can talk about a special day in my holidays (simple past: negatives). ✓

Read Noah's conversation with his mum.
Complete the sentences with the negative simple past of the words in the box.

Mum	Hi, Noah, how was your day at Pride?
Noah	It was really interesting. It *wasn't* (1) like other Saturdays!
Mum	Which things were interesting?
Noah	Well, I … (2) sandwiches, I ate rainbow cake. I … (3) my old grey T-shirt, I wore the new green T-shirt and lots of other colours. I … (4) TV, I watched a parade. And people … (5) in the streets, they danced!
Mum	Wow, that really sounds different! Did you enjoy it?
Noah	Well, I liked the cake, but I … (6) all the people. And I wore my headphones because I … (7) to listen to the loud music and the people: They … (8), they screamed!
Mum	OK. Well, we can have a quiet Saturday next week! It sounds like you had fun, but you … (9) today!

> be • eat • like • relax •
> talk • walk • want •
> watch • wear

🔊 4 LISTENING The first day of my holidays

a) Read the sentences. Then listen to Zane. Which sentences are true? Choose three.

1 Zane ate sausages for breakfast.
2 In the morning the weather was good.
3 There were lots of people at Dover.

4 Zane was worried on the ferry.
5 After the ferry journey he read a book.
6 When they arrived, he went swimming.

b) Listen again and write the time for each picture: *1: 6.00*

Check 🔽

5 READING Evie's journal

I can **talk about last weekend.**

a) Read Evie's journal and sentences A–F. Put the sentences in the correct order: *1 D, ...*

Monday, 14th September

1 Wow, what a busy weekend! On Saturday morning I took Jimmy for a walk on the beach. There were three other dogs there. Jimmy ran around a lot and I took some cute pictures. It was fun!

2 But when I got home, my phone wasn't in my bag. It was a big problem because I use my phone every day and I have many very special photos on there.

3 I decided to go back to the beach, but then I saw my cousin Charlie at the door. I thought, 'That's weird, why is Charlie here on a Saturday morning?'

4 'Hi, Evie, I just got a message from a Varndean student,' said Charlie. 'He was at the beach clean-up and he found your phone there! His name is Noah.' Charlie had a big smile on his face.

5 I relaxed again and hugged him. 'Great news!' I said. 'Where does he live? And when can I come and get it?'

6 I got my phone yesterday evening. I gave Noah some chocolate to say thank you. Then I went home to check all my new messages!

A Evie's phone was missing.
B Charlie told her some good news.
C Evie got her phone back.
D Evie went to the beach.
E Charlie arrived at Evie's house.
F Evie asked Charlie for more information.

b) How did they feel? Write a feeling word for each paragraph. Use the words in the box.

1 Jimmy: ... 2 Evie: ... 3 Evie: ... 4 Charlie: ... 5 Evie: ... 6 Evie: ...

calm • excited • grateful • happy • surprised • worried

6 WRITING Last weekend

Imagine you found something last weekend. Write about it in your journal. Say what you found, where you found it and what you did next. You can use the ideas in the boxes.

Wow, what a weekend! I found ... Then ... In the end ...

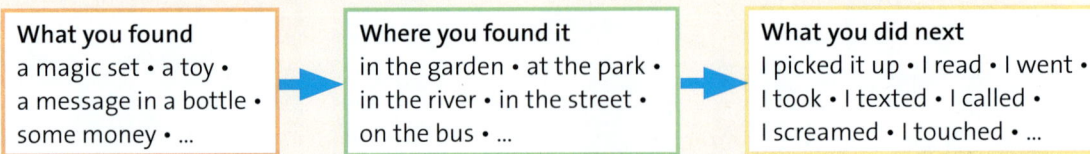

What you found
a magic set • a toy • a message in a bottle • some money • ...

Where you found it
in the garden • at the park • in the river • in the street • on the bus • ...

What you did next
I picked it up • I read • I went • I took • I texted • I called • I screamed • I touched • ...

Check

7 MEDIATION An interview with Finn

Read part of an interview in the school's online magazine.
Finn's grandpa asks him some questions on the phone. Complete Finn's answers.

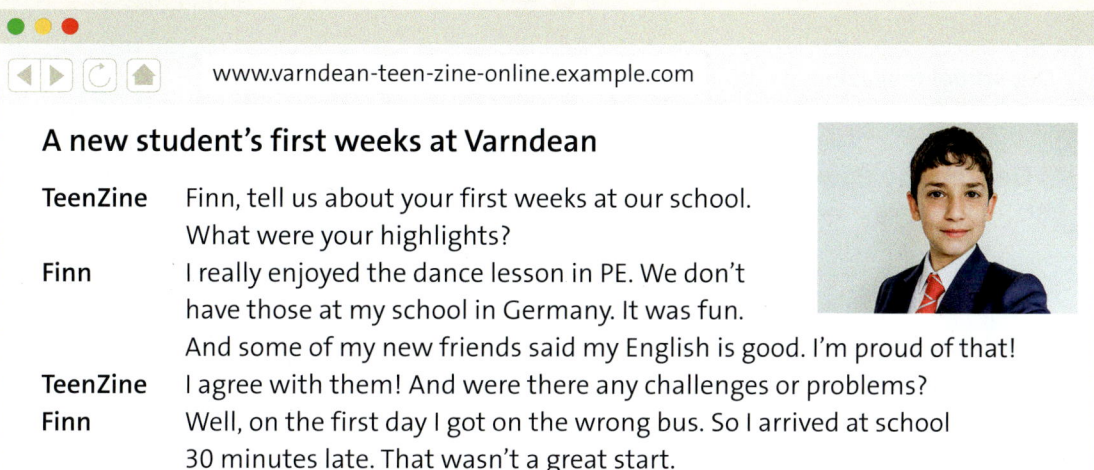

www.varndean-teen-zine-online.example.com

A new student's first weeks at Varndean

TeenZine	Finn, tell us about your first weeks at our school. What were your highlights?
Finn	I really enjoyed the dance lesson in PE. We don't have those at my school in Germany. It was fun. And some of my new friends said my English is good. I'm proud of that!
TeenZine	I agree with them! And were there any challenges or problems?
Finn	Well, on the first day I got on the wrong bus. So I arrived at school 30 minutes late. That wasn't a great start.

Opa	Gestern hast du mir ja dieses Interview mit dir geschickt. Worum ging es da?
Finn	Es ging um …
Opa	Und was hat dir bis jetzt am besten gefallen?
Finn	…
Opa	Es war aber bestimmt nicht alles einfach, oder?
Finn	Nein, zum Beispiel …

8 STUDY SKILLS Lena's story

a) **Read Lena's sentences for her scary story. Which sentence is the beginning? Which sentence is the end?**

A And the door opened, but nobody was there!
B I saw a cute cat with big, green eyes near an old house.
C It was a dark night in November.
D The cat looked scared, so I walked over to it.
E I didn't know and I didn't try to find out.
F I ran away and never went there again.
G Then I heard a loud noise from inside the house.
H How did it open? Was there a person in the house? Or maybe a ghost?

b) **Now put the sentences (A–H) in the correct order.**

c) **Lena uses adjectives to make her story more interesting. Write her adjectives.**

Check

VARNDEAN
Teen Zine

This month's topics: holidays and travel

Our school magazine: by students for students

George the Pavilion cat   *by Izzy*

In the summer holidays I went inside the Brighton Pavilion with my family. It was amazing!

I bought a book in the Pavilion shop about George the Pavilion cat. George walked into the Pavilion one day and stayed there for twelve years. He loved the beautiful rooms with their comfortable beds and chairs, but he didn't like the kitchen. Instead of[1] real food it had plastic food!

George had a terrible experience at the Pavilion one night: The Music Room caught fire! Poor George was very scared, but luckily the rest of the Pavilion didn't catch fire[2].

George also had lots of great experiences at the Pavilion. One day a nice man from a rug company[3] came to make new rugs for the Pavilion rooms. He liked George and made a special rug for him with his name on it. And one day George even met Queen Elizabeth when she came to visit!

After a long and happy life at the Pavilion, George died in 1980.

Funny signs

We asked students to send in funny signs from their holidays.
Which one do you like best?

---

[1] **instead of** *anstelle von*   [2] **(to) catch fire** *in Brand geraten*   [3] **rug company** *die Teppichfirma*
[4] **pasture** *die Weide*   [5] **dull** *langweilig*

Just for fun: Holiday jokes

> *Where did the sheep go on holiday?*

> *Where did the hamster go on holiday?*

> *The Baaahamas!*

> *Hamsterdam!*

Holiday games

Sad that you're back at school? Imagine that it's the summer holidays again and play these games with a friend.

The suitcase[1] game

Write down five things to put in this suitcase. Your friend can ask ten questions to guess what's in your suitcase.

Is / Are there …?

The holiday activities game

Play like this until you can't think of any more activities!

A *I went on holiday and I went swimming.*
B *I went on holiday, I went swimming and I ate ice cream.*

E-postcard from the USA

Lea from Varndean is on a school exchange[2] in the USA. She has a quiz about famous places for you. Find the answers on p. 313.

> *Hi from San Francisco!*
> *You all know the Golden Gate Bridge, right?*
> *But do you know the four famous attractions[3] in the other photos? Give yourself an extra point if you know where they are! And give yourself extra points if you can name other famous attractions in the USA.*

---

[1] **suitcase** *der Koffer*   [2] **school exchange** *der Schüleraustausch*   [3] **attraction** *die Sehenswürdigkeit*

Rock pooling

There are many **marine habitats** in the sea and on the beaches around Brighton. We can see a little of these underwater worlds in **rock pools**.

Tides and rock pools

There are two **high tides** and two **low tides** every day. That means that sometimes a lot of the beach has water on it, and sometimes the sea is a little far away from the beach. When the tide is low, some water stays in holes[1] and spaces in the rocks. Low tide is usually the best time to find interesting things on beaches and in the rock pools. You can read **tide tables** to find out when high and low tides are. The times are different every day.

Rock pools

Life in the rock pools

There are many animals in the rock pools. The piddock, a small animal with a soft body[2] and a hard **shell**, makes holes in the chalk rocks and lives in them. Small fish, **crabs** and **sea anemones** later hide[3] in the holes. Other animals that you can find are fish, **barnacles** and **starfish**. Barnacles look like rocks but they are animals. They can cut you, so be careful!

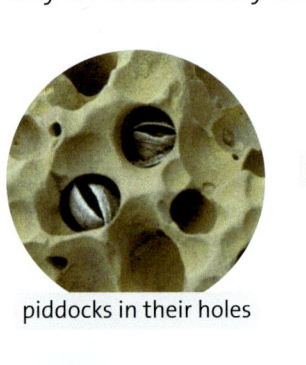
piddocks in their holes

spiny crab

strawberry anemone

starfish

barnacles

Key terms

Rockpooling
- barnacle *die Seepocke*
- chalk *die Kreide*
- cliff *die Felswand*
- crab *der Krebs / die Krabbe*
- high tide *die Flut*
- low tide *die Ebbe*
- marine habitat *der Meereslebensraum*
- net *das Netz*

- plant *die Pflanze*
- rock *der Stein*; rocky *steinig*
- rock pool *der Gezeitentümpel*
- sea anemone *die Seeanemone*
- shell *die Schale einer Muschel*
- starfish *der Seestern*
- tide *die Gezeit*;
  tide table *die Gezeitentabelle*

---

[1] **hole** *das Loch*   [2] **body** *der Körper*   [3] (to) **hide** *(sich) verstecken*

The Undercliff Walk

The five-kilometre Undercliff Walk starts at Brighton Marina. People can walk and cycle on it. On one side are high **chalk cliffs** and some shops and cafes; on the other side is the sea. In some places on the walk there are stairs[1] going down to the beach. There are some very good rock pools next to the Undercliff Walk.

Rock pooling: dos and dont's

Do ...
- Use your hands to look under rocks and in **plants** to find more animals.
- Listen: Can you hear fish or crabs?
- Wear shoes that don't slip[2] on rocks.
- Bring a camera to take pictures.
- Use a book or an app on your phone for information.
- Put rocks and animals back carefully.

Don't ...
- Don't pull[3] plants or animals off the rocks.
- Don't take plants or animals away with you.
- Don't use a **net**[4]: they can hurt[5] the plants and animals in rock pools.
- Don't go alone: Bring an adult[6] to watch the tide.
- Don't go when the tide is getting higher.
- Don't leave[7] rubbish in the rock pools.

1 Rock pools in Brighton

Read the text about rock pooling. Are the sentences true (T), false (F) or not in the text (NT)?

1 People in Brighton love swimming in the rock pools.
2 It's a good idea to go rock pooling at high tide.
3 The animals are usually swimming in the water: they're easy to see.
4 Barnacles can be dangerous[8].
5 You can take the Undercliff Walk to different parts of the beach.
6 It's OK to bring home cool animals.

2 Habitats near you

Go outside near your home or school, for example in a park. What animals and plants can you find? Take pictures. Show and tell your class what you saw. Look up words you don't know in the dictionary.

I saw two birds. They were white. I think they were seagulls. There were also some ...

Use your words and phrases	
I saw ...	a snake / a lot of mice / some fish / a tree / ...
They were ...	friendly / scary / big / small / red / ...
I think they were ...	seagulls / ...

---

[1] **stairs** *die Treppe*　[2] (to) **slip** *ausrutschen*　[3] (to) **pull** *(heraus)ziehen*　[4] **net** *das Netz*　[5] (to) **hurt** *verletzen*
[6] **adult** *der Erwachsene, die Erwachsene*　[7] (to) **leave** *zurücklassen*　[8] **dangerous** *gefährlich*

Partner page

▶ Page 23

👥 3 SPEAKING Making friends

a) Partner B: You're Finn. Answer your new classmate's questions about your summer. Use the ideas below or your own ideas and say complete sentences.

1 my English: *I practised my English.*
2 my books and favourite things
3 in June
4 my friends and family
5 by car
6 a uniform
7 my mum

b) Swap roles. You're one of Finn's new classmates. Ask him questions about his summer.

1 How did you practise your English?
2 What new food did you eat in Brighton?
3 What sights did you see in Brighton?
4 How did you travel round Brighton?
5 What did you help your mum with?
6 What did you play?
7 When did you get up every day?

Diff bank

▶ Page 12

More practice 1 | **I was …**

a) Make a list of different places on the board: *swimming pool, supermarket, …*

👥 b) Form groups and make a circle. Throw a ball and say where you were yesterday.

I was at the swimming pool. Where were you?

I wasn't at the swimming pool. I was at the supermarket. Where were you?

▸ Page 13

More help **2** SPEAKING **Where were you?**

a) **Think and make notes about your summer holidays: the place, how it was and the weather.**

I was We were	at home. at my friend's house / flat. at my grandparents' house / flat. at the swimming pool. at the park / skatepark. at the beach / by the sea. in the garden.	I was We were	on a campsite. on a farm. in a holiday apartment. in a hotel. in a hostel. in Germany / Austria / Turkey / …

It was It wasn't	amazing / boring / cool / fun / good / great / nice / OK / … cold / hot / rainy / sunny / warm / windy / …

More practice 2 WALK AROUND **Find someone who …**

**Find someone who was … Write down the name and the extra information.
When you have six different names, shout 'Here!'**

1 at their grandparents.
   (How long?)

2 at the cinema.
   (What film?)

3 in a hot country.
   (How hot?)

4 by the sea.
   (Where?)

5 on a day trip.
   (Where?)

6 in a place with animals.
   (What animals?)

Were you at your grandparents'?

Yes, I was. / No, I wasn't.

How long?

Two weeks / All summer / …

Challenge 1 **Summer travel**

a) **Write the conversation. Use *was / were* and *wasn't / weren't*.**

Lily Where … (1) you in the summer holidays?
      … (2) you in Brighton?
Beni No, I … (3) I … (4) in Albania with my family.
      We … (5) there for three weeks.
Lily How … (6) it?
Beni It … (7) cool. We … (8) in a hotel:
      We … (9) at my grandparents' house.
      It … (10) great to see them!

b) **Practise the conversation.**

▶ Page 15

More practice 3 **Saying simple past forms**

a) Read Scout's tip and copy the table.

Past -ed endings don't all sound the same!
We say 'wanted' [ɪd].
But we say 'liked' [t] and 'loved' [d].

	[ɪd] (wanted)	[t] (liked)	[d] (loved)
a)	...	...	...
c)	...		

Listen again to Noah. Which -ed endings sound like [ɪd] or [t]? Which endings sound like [d]? Write the words in the table.

b) Listen and repeat the past forms.

c) Listen to six other past forms. Write the words in your table.

d) Listen again and repeat.

▶ Page 17

More practice 4 **Irregular verbs tennis**

Play irregular verbs tennis: Say a word from the box.
Your partner says the simple past form. Take turns.

be • do • go • have • put • swim •
take • tell • think • wear

More practice 5 **What is it?**

Read the descriptions. What's the word?

1 It's a kind of transport. It's very fast. People get on it at a station.
2 It's a place to stay. It's like a hotel, but it isn't expensive.
3 It's an activity. You do it when you move your feet to music.
4 It's a place to stay. You don't sleep in a bed inside.
5 It's a kind of car. It takes you to places for money.
6 It's an activity. You do it when you walk in hills or mountains.

▶ Skills file 11, p. 194

Challenge 2 **Writing descriptions**

a) Choose three to five words from your umbrella words on p. 17.
Write descriptions of the words. (The descriptions in More practice 5 can help you.)

b) Swap your descriptions with a partner. Your partner says the word.

▶ Skills file 11, p. 194

▸Page 19

More practice 6 **Taking a train**

Complete the sentences with words from the box. In sentence 6 there are two answers.

> arrive • ~~big~~ • destination • platform • return ticket • single ticket • station • ticket machine

1 Brighton has a *big* train ...
2 The train's ... is London.
3 What time does the train ...?
4 I want to buy my ticket at the ...
5 My train is on ... 3.
6 I need a ... / ... to Eastbourne, please.

2 VIEWING **Buying a ticket**

b)
Mo Excuse me, hi!
Jarek Oh, hello!
Mo Do you need help?
Jarek Yes, please. I want to buy a ticket, but I don't understand the ticket machine.
Mo No problem, I can help you. Where are you going?
Jarek I need a ticket to London.
Mo OK. And do you want a single ticket or a return?
Jarek I'm coming back tomorrow, so I would like a return ticket, please.
Mo OK, it says here that a return ticket to London costs £34.90.
Jarek Oh, that's expensive!
Mo Yeah, trains to London are quite expensive. And this is a cheap ticket because it's the weekend! How do you want to pay? Cash or card?
Jarek Can I pay by card?
Mo Yes, sure! Just put it on the machine there.
Jarek Thank you for your help. Oh — when's the next train to London?
Mo It's in ten minutes. It's at 11.27. And it's a direct train.
Jarek Great! So I don't need to change trains?
Mo No.
Jarek Thank you so much!
Mo You're welcome. Have a nice day!

▸Page 21

More practice 7 **What I did**

GAME One student stands up and makes a sentence in the simple past. You can use the verbs from exercise 5, p. 21. Another student says the negative sentence and then a new sentence.

> I played the guitar.

> I didn't play the guitar.
> I ate a hot dog.

> I didn't eat a hot dog.
> I bought ...

More practice 8 ## Scout's day at Pride

Blue Bird thinks Scout did some bad things at Pride, but Scout says that she didn't do them. Write what Scout says.

Blue Bird	You ate all the chips!
Scout	No, I *didn't eat all the chips*. (1) Black Bird ate them!
Blue Bird	You played bad music on the beach!
Scout	No, I ... (2). Some teenagers played bad music.
Blue Bird	You wore my Pride hat! Now it's broken.
Scout	No, I ... (3). I wore my favourite red hat.
Blue Bird	You talked loudly at the concert!
Scout	No, I ... (4). That was Green Bird!
Blue Bird	You took a girl's Pride flag!
Scout	No, I ... (5). The wind took it.
Blue Bird	You went to bed too late after Pride!
Scout	No, I ... (6). I went to bed at eight o'clock.

OK, maybe I ate all the chips ...

More help **7** MY TASK **Events in the holidays**

I went to	a concert / a film festival / a market / a music festival / a show / ...	in my town. with my family / friends.
It was	amazing / boring / great / horrible / OK / ...	
I / we	ate bought listened to / saw / watched wore loved / enjoyed / liked / hated	hot dogs / popcorn / ... a hat / presents / ... a band / dancers / a film / ... clothes / a special T-shirt / ...
I / we didn't	buy / drink / eat / enjoy / hate / like / listen to / love / see / watch / wear	the food / the music / ...

▶ Page 23

Challenge 3 ROLE-PLAY **Nice to meet you!**

Do a role-play with a partner. One of you plays a new student. Ask and answer friendly questions. Then swap roles.

What's your name?
Where are you from? Where's that?
Do you like ...?
Do you have ...?

► Page 24

More help **6** MY TASK **Last weekend**

	I played	football / basketball / table tennis / handball / video games / …
Yesterday Last weekend / Sunday / … At lunchtime on Sunday At 10.30 / 3 p.m. / … On Saturday morning On Saturday afternoon On Saturday evening	I did	gymnastics / yoga / judo / my homework / a school project / …
	I went	horse riding / climbing / running / skateboarding / shopping / …
	I went to	the library / the market / the sports centre / my friend's house / …
	I cleaned	my room / my bike / the bathroom / …
	I had	a pizza / a barbecue / a karaoke night / …

It was amazing / a lot of work / boring / cool / exciting / fun / great / hard / horrible / scary / …

More practice 9 **Timeline**

a) **Get in a group. Look at the time phrases. Each student chooses a time phrase. Stand in a line in the correct order. Start with *today* at the front and go back in time. Each student says something he or she did at that time:** *I took a train to Hamburg last weekend. / …*

last month   last week   last weekend   last year   today   yesterday

b) **Write the time phrases from a) in the correct order.**

PAST   …   …   …   …   …   *today*   PRESENT

► Page 31

More help UNIT TASK **Tell a story, Step 1**

You can use this picture story for ideas.

want / not have the money

decide / sell / old things

sister / find / a bike / at a market

buy it / very happy

Unit 2
Friends and heroes

A

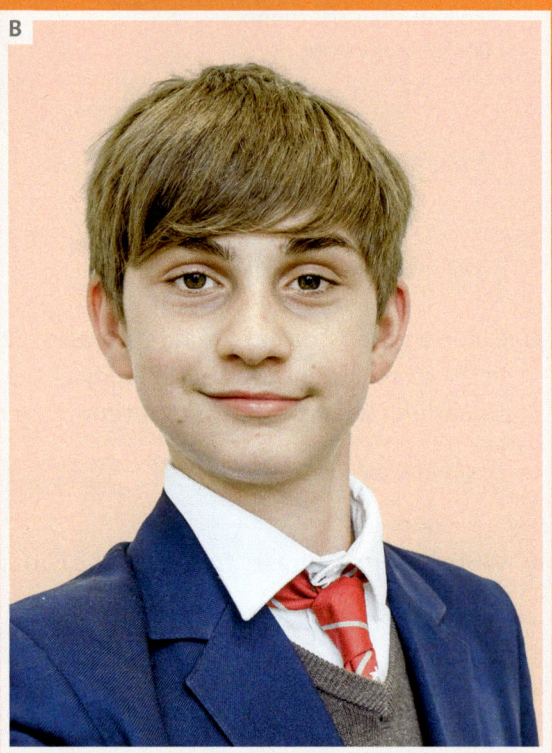

B

🔊 **1** LISTENING **The head students**

a) Copy the table. Listen and find the correct picture (A–D) for each head student.

Name	Picture	Hair	Tie	☒ Other
Mihai	...	...	...	...
Sofia	...	...	...	*braces*
Jodie	...	...	...	
Faye	...			

👥 b) Listen again. Complete the table with the words in the box. You can use some words more than once. Check your answers with a partner.

> blond • blue • blue-green • ~~braces~~ •
> brown • curly • eyes • glasses • long •
> purple • red • short • straight

Nach dieser Unit kann ich ...

⊙ Aussehen beschreiben
⊙ die Persönlichkeit meiner Freundinnen und Freunde beschreiben
⊙ über meine Vorbilder sprechen
⊙ einen Superhelden oder eine Superheldin beschreiben
⊙ über Zusammenarbeit sprechen

Unit task ⊙

⊙ Informationen recherchieren und ein Quiz erstellen

2 SPEAKING What do they look like?

GAME One student describes another student in class, but doesn't say the name. If the correct student stands up, he/she describes the next student. If not, try again. Your table from p. 46 and these phrases can help you.

This student has ... hair and ... eyes / glasses.

That's me! / Is it me? / Is that me?

Yes, it's you! / No, it isn't you. Let me try again: ...

Good to know

Many British schools have head students. They're students in year 11 and they help other students.

▶ Workbook, p. 25

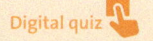

My friends

1 READING The poster competition

a) BEFORE YOU READ What's a good friend like? Make notes. Then collect words with the class.

A good friend is kind / understands me / ...

b) Read the two posters. Guess who they describe and who made them.

> **COMPETITION**
> Make a poster about your best friend. The best poster wins a prize! Give your poster to any head student.

A

My best friend

My best friend is amazing! He is kind and hard-working and he helps his family. He's very confident and funny – he always makes me laugh!

He's short and strong and good at sports. We often ride our bikes together. He has short, curly black hair and brown eyes.

He's my best friend because he's always there for me.

B

My best friend

My best friend is tall and she has long, straight black hair and brown eyes.

She's reliable and friendly and very clever too – she's really good with computers.

She's my best friend because she's very fair and patient with me, even when I'm too shy. I want to be brave like her!

c) Listen and check your answers.

d) Make a mind map in your VOCAB FILE with words to describe a person's looks and their personality. Use the blue words from the posters in b).

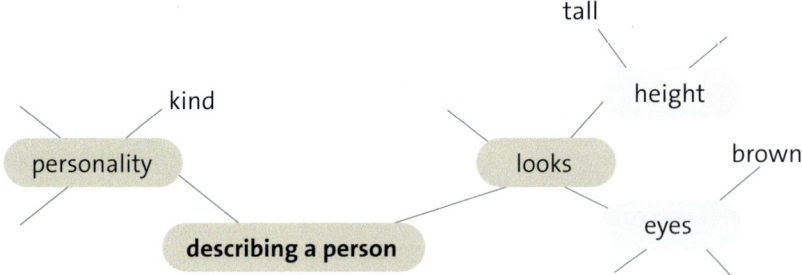

personality — kind

describing a person

looks — tall — height — brown — eyes

▶ Wordbank 2, p. 214

e) Describe someone in your class or at school. Be kind. Your partner guesses.

▶ Workbook, p. 26

2 SPEAKING I think you're ...

a) Think of at least five nice things that you can say to other people. Make notes.

👥 b) DOUBLE CIRCLE Say something nice to your partner.

> *I think you're very patient.*

> *Thank you! I think you're hard-working.*

> *Thanks.*

> *I'm clever! I'm funny! I'm good at flying!*

Be like Scout:
Be kind to yourself.

3 WORDS Personality words

👥 a) What's important to you in a friend?
Choose your top three personality words from the box.
Then discuss with your partner.

brave • clever • confident • fair •
friendly • funny • good at sports •
hard-working • honest • kind •
patient • reliable • shy

> *To me it's important that a friend is funny.
> What about you?*

> *I think it's important
> that a friend is patient.*

👥 b) What's important to you in a teacher, a head student, a sportsperson or a pop star?
Discuss and make a list with your partner.

👥 c) Make a wanted poster for your perfect head student, pop star, sportsperson or teacher.

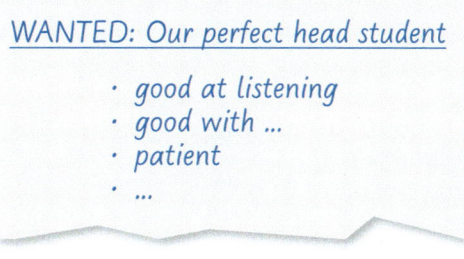

WANTED: Our perfect head student
· good at listening
· good with ...
· patient
· ...

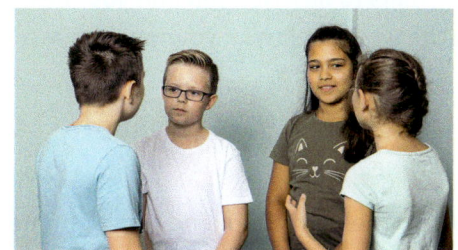

👥 d) Can you think of someone who fits this description?

▶ Workbook, p. 27

4 SONG No one else like you

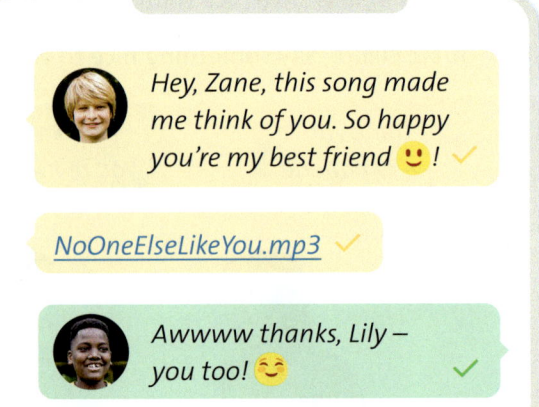

> *Hey, Zane, this song made me think of you. So happy you're my best friend* 🙂 *!* ✓
>
> *NoOneElseLikeYou.mp3* ✓
>
> *Awwww thanks, Lily — you too!* 😊 ✓

No one else like you

I want to tell you that you're my buddy.
You're always funny and ... (1).
And people know that when they see you
I'm never far behind.

'Cause I'm the bread and you're the ... (2).
You can't have one without the other.

You're left, I'm ... (3).
You're ... (4), I'm night.
You're the milk, I'm the ... (5).
It's always you and me.

I'm so glad that you're my best ... (6) —
There's no one else like you!

a) BEFORE YOU LISTEN **Look at the song text.**
Choose words from the box for 1–6.
There are two extra words.

> butter • day • friend • kind • light • nice • right • tea

b) **Listen to the song and write the correct words for 1–6.**
Which words from a) were correct?

c) **The singer uses a lot of pairs to describe him and his friend.**
Write pairs to describe you and your best friend.
Use the words below or your own ideas.

> *My best friend is Brahim.*
> *I'm the glove and he's the ...*
> *I'm the moon and he's the ...*   ▶ Challenge 1, p. 73

d) **Listen to the song again and sing or mime.**
Then have a competition with your class.
Who can mime the best?

5 MEDIATION A message from Finn

a) Read Finn's messages. Who are they for?

b) Look at Sunita's questions (1–4). Answer her questions in English.

A message from Finn! But it's in German.

1 'Freunde' means 'friends', I think. What does he say about friends?
2 What does Finn write about Noah?
3 I can see he talks about Buddy. Does Finn like him?
4 He talks about me too! What does he say about me?

▶ Challenge 2, p. 73
▶ Language file 6, p. 202

c) Check with a partner.

▶ Skills file 8, p. 191

Hi Suri, wie geht's dir? Ich hab schon viele Freunde an meiner neuen Schule. *Neben mir sitzt Noah. Etwas schüchtern, aber total nett. Er hat einen Therapiehund, der heißt Buddy* 🐕 *und ist sehr süß. In meiner Klasse ist auch ein cooles Mädchen, das richtig gut programmieren kann. Sie heißt Sunita und ist sehr witzig*
LG Finn

Sorry, Sunita, that message wasn't for you! It was for a friend in Germany.

You can use phrases like 'He says that ...' and 'She writes that ...' to report what someone else said or wrote.

My task

6 My favourite person

a) Make a poster about your favourite person. Don't say who it is! Use the posters in **1b)** and your mind map from **1d)** on **p. 48** to help you. You can also draw a picture.

My favourite person has red hair and a nice smile. She's very smart ...   ▶ Digital help 👆

b) GALLERY WALK Put your posters on the wall. Give feedback. Put your poster in your DOSSIER.

You used a lot of good adjectives. You described him very well.

Your picture is amazing! I think it's Leo! Remember to use more adjectives.

I think it's Leo!

▶ Let's talk: Feedback, p. 227

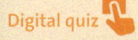 Digital quiz   **I can describe my friend's personality.**

My hero, your hero

1   LISTENING   Lily's neighbour

a) BEFORE YOU LISTEN   **Lily is at her neighbour Li-Jun's flat after school. Describe the picture.**

b) **Lily asks Li-Jun about the article. Listen and complete the sentences.**

Li-Jun saved the life of a little boy at the … (1). The boy went into the … (2) to get his … (3).

c) **Match Lily's questions (1–6) and Li-Jun's answers (a–h). Then listen again and check.**

1	Did you help somebody?	a	He was busy with the boy's sister.
2	Who did you save?	b	It happened at the beach.
3	Where did this happen?	c	No, he didn't. He was just cold.
4	Did the boy go underwater?	d	I saved a little boy.
5	Did the boy get hurt?	e	The boy's father told them the story.
6	When did it happen?	f	Yes, I did.
7	Why did his father leave the boy alone?	g	It happened two days ago.
8	How did the newspaper know?	h	Yes, he did.

d) **Take turns to read a question and an answer.**   ▶ Challenge 3, p. 73   ▶ Skills file 6, p. 189

---

2   LOOKING AT LANGUAGE   The simple past: yes/no questions and short answers

Erklär-
film

Look at the yes/no questions and the short answers below. Then complete the box.

Did you help somebody? – Yes, I did.   *Did the boy get hurt? – No, he didn't.*
Was the water cold? – Yes, it was. / No, it wasn't.
Were you scared? – Yes, we were. / No, we weren't.

> Fragen ohne Fragewort im *simple past* fangen meist mit … an.
> Nach dem Subjekt *(Sunita / it / you / …)* folgt die Grundform des Verbs (Infinitiv). **Positive**
> Kurzantworten *(yes)* bildest du mit dem Wort …, **negative** Kurzantworten *(no)* mit dem
> Wort … Eine Ausnahme bildet das Verb *to be*: Hier verwendest du … / *wasn't und* … / *weren't*.

▶ Language file 4, p. 202

3 SPEAKING **About Li-Jun**

a) **Partner B: Look at p. 72.**

**Partner A: Read about Li-Jun. Answer partner B's questions. Use *Yes, he did. / No, he didn't.*
☒ Give more information.** *He grew up in ...*

b) **Ask partner B these questions.**
1 Did Li-Jun get married?
2 Did he have children?
3 Did he always live on Whitehawk Estate?
4 Did he stop work a long time ago?

> **Li-Jun Chen**
> • grew up in a small village in China
> • didn't want to leave China, but wanted to help his family
> • lived in London, then in Brighton
> • got a job as a sports trainer

4 **When you were five years old**

a) **Put the words in the correct order to make questions in the simple past.**

1 to school / you / go / did / ?
2 your family / did / a pet / have / ?
3 like / you / did / football / ?
4 have / did / a garden / your flat or house / ?
5 share / a bedroom / did / you / ?
6 did / near you / your grandparents / live / ?

b) **Think about answers to a). Ask and answer the questions. Use short answers.**

▶ More practice 1, p. 73　▶ Challenge 4, p. 74

5 LOOKING AT LANGUAGE **The simple past: questions with question words**

Erklär-film

a) **Write questions 3 and 6–8 from 1c) into your table.**

b) **Complete the table headings 1–5 with the words below. Find the rule.**

1 ...	2 ...	3 ...	4 ...	5 ...
Who	did	you	save	✕ ?

Fragewort　Rest des Satzes　Subjekt　*did*　Infinitiv

▶ Language file 5, p. 202

6 **Lily's school day**

Complete Li-Jun's questions. Use a question word from the box and *did + you*.

> how • what • ~~when~~ • where • who • why

1 ... get out of school? – At 3.05, like every Monday.
   When did you get out of school?
2 ... come back late? – The chain came off my bike.
3 ... get home? – I took the bus.
4 ... leave your bike? – At school. It's OK there.
5 ... do at school today? – We did a science project.
6 ... choose as a partner? – Noah. He helped me a lot.

▶ More practice 2, p. 74
▶ Challenge 5, p. 74
▶ Workbook, pp. 28–30

7 LISTENING **Our heroes**

a) BEFORE YOU LISTEN **What sort of people are heroes for you? Add more ideas to the box. Say why.**

> activists • artists • influencers • teachers • tech people • …

b) **Lily asks four students about their heroes for the school's online magazine. Copy the table. Then listen and complete the answers for question 1.**

Student	Marek	Ivy	Cal	Dimitra
Name of hero	Jozef Krupa	Jade Woods	Sierra Evans	Otis King
1 Who is this hero?	*Marek's …*	*…*	*artist / …*	*…*
2 Why is he/she a hero?	*helps people is …*	*is … wants …*	*is … gives money …*	*is … is …*

c) **Listen again. Complete the answers for question 2. Add other notes.** ▶ Skills file 6, p. 189

---

8 WORDS **Opposites**

a) WORD BUILDING **Dimitra says that her brother's trainer is sometimes 'unkind'. Read the box about *un-*. What are the opposites of words 1–6? Write pairs.**

1	cool	3	friendly	5	helpful
2	fair	4	happy	6	tidy

b) **We can't always make opposites with *un-*. Match the adjectives (1–5) to their opposites (a–e).**

1	clever	a	shy
2	confident	b	rude
3	hard-working	c	horrible
4	nice	d	stupid
5	polite	e	lazy

c) YOU CHOOSE **Do 1 or 2.**

1 Mime a word from **a)** or **b).** Your partner says the word.
2 With your partner, mime a pair of opposites for the class. The class guesses the words.

d) **Make lists in your VOCAB FILE with opposites.**

▶ More practice 3, p. 75   ▶ Challenge 6, p. 75   ▶ Skills file 1, p. 184

When we add *un-* (= 'not') to the beginning of some adjectives, they have the opposite meaning.

Well done!

kind

You're too slow!

unkind (= not kind)

9 Two student heroes

a) **Partner B:** Look at p. 72.
Partner A: Read the article about Destiny.
Answer partner B's questions about her.

b) **Partner B has information about Jonah.**
Ask questions about him.

1 Why did Jonah spend a long time in hospital?
2 How did he feel in hospital?
3 What did Jonah want to do?
4 How did he do this?

c) **Write the blue words from the article and find their opposites in the box.**
There are two extra words in the box.

angry • old • sad • scary • uncool • unhappy

d) **Say a blue word to your partner:**
He or she tells you its opposite.

Destiny

Destiny's school football team needed new sports clothes for matches. But her school didn't have the money. So Destiny did something to help: She skateboarded for 10 kilometres in a superhero costume! Other kids from her team also skateboarded in funny or cool costumes. Her parents and friends gave her money for every kilometre, and people in the street gave her money too. Her team was very happy with its new football clothes!

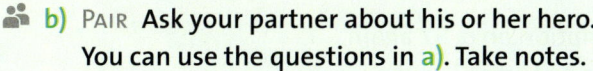

My task

10 My hero

a) THINK **Make notes about your hero. It can be somebody in your family, a friend or a famous person.**

• Who is your hero?
• What is or was he / she like?
• What good, brave or interesting thing did he or she do? ▶ Digital help ▶ More help, p. 75

My hero is George, Sunita's parrot. He's very funny. When he learned a bad word from Nish, he said it in front of Meera's friend!

b) PAIR **Ask your partner about his or her hero.**
You can use the questions in a). Take notes.

c) SHARE **Tell the class about your partner's hero.**

Adar's hero is his cousin Rashid. Rashid is very kind and clever. He collected old phones and gave them to families for free.

▶ Workbook, p. 30

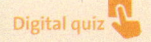 Digital quiz **I can ask and answer questions about my hero.**

Superheroes

1 READING Who is it?

a) BEFORE YOU READ In art class Lily, Sunita, Noah and Zane drew and described their own superheroes. Match the four students to pictures A–D. Say why.

I think Lily's superhero is picture ... because ...

b) Make groups of four students. Each student reads about one superhero on p. 57. Were your answers in a) correct? Check on p. 76.

c) Read about your superhero again and take notes.

name: ...
was born in ...
came to earth in ...
became a superhero in ...
has / wears ...
superpowers: can / has / knows ...

d) Tell your group about your superhero.

> **Good to know**
>
> You say years in dates like this:
> 1909: nineteen oh nine
> 1960: nineteen sixty
> 2006: two thousand and six
> 2021: twenty twenty-one

▶ More practice 4, p. 75

A

1
2

B

3
4

C

5
6

D

7

2 WORDS Clothes

a) Read the last sentence of each superhero description on p. 57 again. Match the clothes words to numbers 1–7 in the pictures. *1: cape, 2: ...*

b) Say which costume you like the best and why.

c) Make a page in your VOCAB FILE for clothes: You can make a mind map, draw pictures or write sentences. Add the words from these pages and other clothes words.

▶ More practice 5, p. 76   ▶ Wordbank 3, p. 215

▶ Workbook, p. 31

A My name is ComputerGirl. I was born on Voria, a small planet far away from earth, in 2006. I came to earth in 2021 when my planet became too hot. I'm very clever and I can get into any computer, but I only use my skills to help people. I fight online bullies. I get into their computers and stop them! I have a metal body and head and I'm very strong. I wear long black **boots** and a silver **helmet**.

C DolphinMan here! I was born in the sea in 2008. When people put chemicals in the water in 2020, I became part person and part dolphin. On land I'm a normal person, but in the water I'm a dolphin superhero! I can swim very fast. The police always ask me to help find villains! I don't have ears, but I can hear what people say from far away. I wear a silver **swimsuit**.

B I'm Superdog. I was born on earth in 2002. But in 2019 something weird happened: When I ate some dog food for a dare I became a superhero with a dog's face and four legs! I have very strong teeth and a good nose: I know people by their smell. Finding bad guys is no problem for me: I just need to smell their clothes. I wear a blue cape, blue **trousers** and a blue **eye mask**.

D I'm The Climber. I can climb everywhere. I was born on Planet Octo in 1960. I went away when bad lizards travelled to our planet and killed my family. After a very long journey I came to earth. I can run very fast and I use my eight arms to climb tall buildings and fight bad people. I wear a purple **dress** and a purple **cape**.

We use *when* to link two sentences. After *when* we use the normal word order: subject – verb – object.
When people put chemicals in the water, I became part dolphin.
I went away **when** lizards killed his family.

▶ More practice 6, p. 76   ▶ Language file 7, p. 203

3 Superpowers

a) **Superheroes always have superpowers. Which of the superpowers below do you think is best? Why? Talk with your group.**

being invisible

flying

talking to animals

being superstrong

I think being invisible is the best superpower. You can be safe / watch people / ...
I agree. You can also go to lots of places / ... – I disagree. I think ... is the best superpower.

b) **Think of one more superpower and tell your group about it. Why is it useful / cool / ...?**

Being superbig is cool because bad guys are scared of you / ...

▶ Workbook, pp. 32–33

4 WORDS **Superheroes and villains**

a) Every superhero fights villains. Copy the table and write
at least three things for superheroes and three for villains.
Use words from each box to describe superheroes and villains.

Superheroes ...	Villains ...
protect people	hurt ...
...	

Come back with my
pizza, you villain!

are • break • bring back • fight • get • help • hurt • protect • save • stop • want	+	bad guys • bullies • cities • fair • mean • money • people • power • superheroes • the planet • things • villains

b) Compare lists with a partner.

c) You can add *super-* to the beginning of many words to make new words. You already
know *superpower* and *superhero*. Find five other words with *super-* at the beginning.
You can use a dictionary. Tell your class about the words and what they mean.
Are they like words in German and other languages that you know?

▶ Skills file 2, p. 185

My task

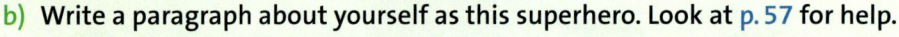

5 Me as a superhero

a) Create your superhero and make notes:
name, story, superpower(s), looks, clothes.   ▶ More help, p. 77   ▶ Wordbanks 2–4, pp. 214–216

b) Write a paragraph about yourself as this superhero. Look at **p. 57** for help.   ▶ Digital help

- What's your superhero name? *My name is ... / I'm ... / ... here!*
- Tell your story. How did you become a superhero? Use the simple past.
  I was born in ... I became a superhero when ...
- Describe yourself as a superhero (looks, clothes). *I wear ... / I have ... / I'm ...*
- What's your superpower? *I can ...*
- ☒ Who do you fight? *I fight Rubbishman / the Snowwoman / ...*

c) Check and correct your work. Did you tell your superhero's story and
describe your superhero? Are spelling and language correct?   ▶ Digital help

d) Present your superhero to a partner. Say what you like about your partner's superhero.
Put your paragraph in your DOSSIER.

Digital quiz 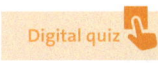   **I can write about superheroes.**

Background file

1 READING Varndean heroes

a) Each of Varndean's five small schools has the name of a hero. Read about them and answer the questions with complete sentences.

Maya Angelou (born 1928 • died 2014)
Maya Angelou was born in the USA. She was hard-working, brave and creative. Her favourite activities were writing, singing, dancing and acting, and she won many prizes for her books. Maya Angelou fought for more rights for black people in the USA.

Ethel Ellis (born 1874 • died 1961)
Ethel Ellis was born to British parents in New Zealand. The family returned to England when Ellis was a teen. She became head teacher of Varndean in 1926. She thought it was important to teach girls and she was very interested in sports and art. Ellis was clever, hard-working, reliable and creative.

Annie Lennox (born 1954)
Born in Scotland, Annie Lennox is a singer and activist. She was in a popular band called *Eurythmics* in the 1980s. She fights for women and LGBTQ rights, for a healthy planet and against diseases. She got a special award from Queen Elizabeth for this work. Annie Lennox is strong, confident and kind.

Bertrand Russell (born 1872 • died 1970)
Philosophy, maths, computers, languages, history: Bertrand Russell was interested in a lot of things! He was born in Wales. There were two world wars during his life, but he worked for peace. Russell was very clever and thought that it's important to give your opinion and to be fair.

Alan Turing (born 1912 • died 1954)
He is famous for the 'bombe': a machine that learned a German code in World War Two. Alan Turing was good at programming, codes and maths. He was also very clever, honest and brave. Every year a Turing prize goes to a person who does important computer work. Turing was born in London.

1 Who got prizes for her books?
   ... got prizes for her books.
2 What is Lennox like?
3 Where was Ellis born?
4 When did Ellis become head teacher?
5 Why did Lennox get an award from the Queen?
6 How did Turing help England in a war?

7 Which two people were very good at maths?
8 Whose name do you find in the name of an important prize?
9 Who was born first?
10 Who tried to help black people have better lives?

b) **Which hero do you like most? Explain why.**

▶ Workbook, p. 33

A great team!

1 READING An accident

a) BEFORE YOU READ **Read the title of the story in 1 and look at the pictures. Say what you think happened.**

The kids were at …   Lily …   Then I think Finn …

b) **Read the story. Choose the correct summary: A, B or C.** ▶ Skills file 7, p. 190

A The friends helped Finn after an accident. They didn't need the ambulance in the end.
B Finn's friends helped him after he fell. He was hurt and needed to go to hospital.
C Finn had an accident. He was hurt and his friends didn't know what to do.

Last Saturday the four friends and Finn were at Lily's estate. They were tired after the school week. They wanted to hang out together and talk.

5 Finn wanted to know more about the friends' free-time activities. Noah told Finn about his circus skills and Zane told him about the swimming team and how much he liked cooking.

10 **Finn**   I know you like coding, Sunita. What about you, Lily? What do you do in your free time?

Lily   I do parkour. Do you know what that is?

Finn   It's the same word in German, but I'm
15   not sure what people do. Do you jump from walls and climb things?

Lily   Yes, that's right. Look, let me show you.

Lily   I can walk on the wall like this. Then from this wall I can jump over to the
20   other side and … land on my feet like this!

Finn   Wow, that was cool, Lily. It looked really easy. Let me try …

Lily   No, Finn! It looks easy, but it isn't.
25   You need lots of practice.

But Finn didn't listen …

Lily	Get down, Finn! It's dangerous.
Finn	No, it isn't. The wall isn't very high and I'm really good at jumping. OK ... ready – and go!

Finn jumped ... and fell. The kids were really shocked. Finn's face was very white.

Lily	Finn, are you OK? Finn, talk to us!
Finn	My ankle hurts. And I hit my head.
Lily	Right, let's make a plan.
Sunita	OK, first let's call 999. ... Hello, I need an ambulance, please. Yes, my name's Sunita Chandra. My friend Finn fell off a wall. He hit his head and his ankle hurts. ... Yes, Finn Demir, he's twelve. We're on Whitehawk Estate in Brighton, near Kingfisher Court ... Yes, thanks.

Sunita	Don't move your legs, Finn. Just stay on your back. ... We must keep him warm and not let him fall asleep.
Noah	We need to stay calm. I can help.

Noah showed everybody some breathing exercises. Then Lily ran to get a warm blanket. Zane told Finn some funny stories and jokes and Finn tried to be brave. Sunita called Finn's mum.

Finn	Is the ambulance coming? I feel bad.
Lily	Yes, it's coming. Just a minute ... Oh, wait, I can hear something!
Noah	The ambulance is here. It's OK, Finn.
Man	Hello, Finn, I need to check you out. Right ... Let me put this on your neck ... Now let's get you in the ambulance!

The man and woman put Finn in the ambulance. At that moment Finn's mum arrived. She was very upset. She talked to the ambulance people and to Finn. Then the doors closed and the ambulance drove to the hospital. Finn's mum and the four friends got in her car and drove behind the ambulance.

They all looked worried.

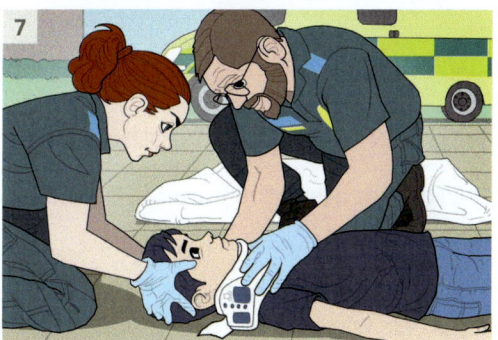

Good to know

In Britain you call 999 for an ambulance, a fire engine, or the police. Always say WHO you are and WHO is hurt, WHAT happened and WHERE you are.

2 What did they do?

a) Read the story again. Say who did what.

1   ... called 999 and Finn's mum.
2   ... showed the others some exercises to relax.
3   ... got a warm blanket.
4   ... tried to make Finn laugh.
5   ... wanted to be brave.

b) Say how they felt in the story.

1   At the beginning, the kids were ...
2   When Finn fell, the four friends were ...
3   After the breathing exercises, they felt ...
4   When Finn's mum arrived, she was ...
5   When the kids went to the hospital, they were ...

3 Words   Parts of the body

a) The words for 1–6 are in the story. Write the words. You can also draw a picture.

 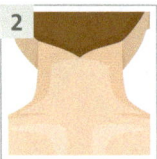 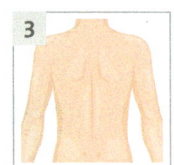 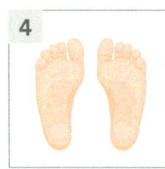 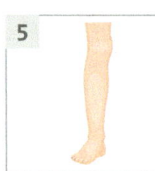 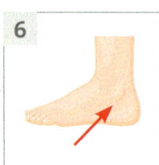

b) Write the words for 7–12. Check with Wordbank 4.

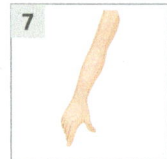 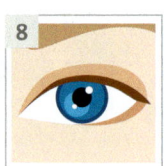 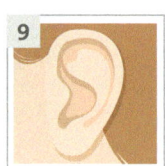 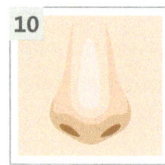 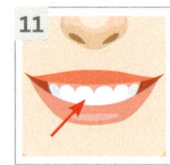 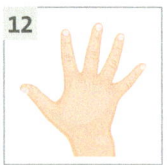

► More practice 7, p. 77   ► Wordbank 4, p. 216

4 Listening   The end of the story

The kids are at the hospital. Listen. True or false? Correct the false sentences.

1   Finn feels fine.
2   He has a broken leg.
3   He wants to see his friends.
4   Lily thinks Finn was stupid.
5   Finn wants a promise from Lily.
6   Finn thought Zane's jokes were funny.

5 Life skills   Teamwork

The kids worked as a team when Finn had an accident. Brainstorm other situations when teamwork is important. ☒ Say why.

► Workbook, p. 34

Digital quiz 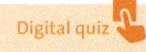   **I can** understand a story about teamwork. ✓

Brighton stories: Special people

👥 1 A present for Gloria's uncle

BEFORE YOU WATCH Gloria's favourite uncle is going to get married.
What can she give him and his new wife as a special present?
Think of some ideas.

🖥 2 VIEWING Gloria's present

a) Watch the first part. Answer the questions with notes.

1 Where are Gloria and Joe and what are they doing?
2 What doesn't Gloria want to do in front of a lot
of people?
3 What's Joe's idea for a present?
4 What does Gloria think of the idea?

b) Watch the second part and match the kids to
their roles.

1 Daisy   A plays the girlfriend.
2 Emir   B plays the uncle.
3 Gloria   C films the scene.
4 Joe   D manages the scene and props.

c) Watch the video again. Choose the best answers for 1–6 and complete sentence 7.

1 Daisy's uncle Tim is   A *a doctor* B *a nurse*[1] C *a hospital cleaner*.
2 Tim and his girlfriend Claire met   A *in the canteen* B *in the corridor* C *at the bus stop*.
3 Tim asked about Claire's   A *book* B *bag* C *job*.
4 Tim hit Claire with his   A *rucksack* B *umbrella* C *arm*.
5 Tim and Claire   A *got on the bus together* B *went back into the hospital*
  C *shared the umbrella*.
6 Tim and Claire thought the video was   A *funny* B *exciting* C *embarrassing*[2].
7 Gloria said 'Oh no' at the end because her uncle and aunt want her to …

👥 3 SHOWTIME Now you

a) Write a short scene for a first meeting between two best friends. Think about:
   – the place where they met
   – what they said
   – what they did together after the meeting.

b) Act out the scene with a partner. Put your scene in your DOSSIER.

---

[1] **nurse** *der Krankenpfleger, die Krankenpflegerin*   [2] **embarrassing** *peinlich*

Work out meaning

You don't understand a word? Stay calm and work out the meaning.

1 WORD BUILDING Use word families

👥 **a)** What do the words in blue mean? Think of their word family.

1 Finn showed great bravery when he had the accident.
2 Finn plays video games with other players. He's usually the winner.
3 Finn thinks some English food is unhealthy.
4 Happiness for Finn is a computer and his cat!

b) Copy and complete the table with the blue words in a). Add other words for each family.

	noun (person)	noun (thing)	verb	positive adjective	negative adjective
1		bravery		...	
2	...		...		
3		...		...	...
4		...		...	...

☒ **c)** Add more word families to your table – for example for the verbs *work* or *help*.

2 Use German and other languages

a) Finn speaks German, Turkish and English. He understands a lot of English words because they're like German:
English: *arm* – German: *Arm*

Some English words aren't like German, but they're like Turkish:
English: *ambulance* – German: *Krankenwagen* – Turkish: *ambulans*

💡 Some words look the same in some languages and have the same meaning.

👥 Say what the blue words below mean. Use German or other languages to help you.

1 Finn has a German and a Turkish passport.
2 In Germany, Finn loves to buy cakes from the bakery.
3 Finn's favourite sea animals are whales.
4 He doesn't like worms!

b) Sometimes Finn makes mistakes:
Some English words look like German words,
but they have a different meaning.
Choose the correct English words from the box.
There are two extra words.

💡 **False friends** look the same in some languages, but they have a **different** meaning.

> bad • find • get • good • hall • menu

1 I ~~become~~ some money from my dad every month.
2 In our new flat, there isn't a ~~floor~~ when you come in the front door.
3 In a cafe: Can I have the ~~card~~, please?
4 Buddy is a very ~~brave~~ dog. He always listens to Noah.

▶ Skills file 2, p. 185

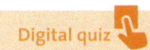 Digital quiz **I can work out the meaning of new words.** ✓

Make a quiz about heroes

Step 1: Think of people

a) Make teams. Together think of heroes (real or fictional). Choose heroes that everybody knows. The box can help you.

b) Choose two or more heroes.

> activist • artist •
> hero in a film, video game or on TV •
> influencer • scientist • singer •
> sportsperson • TV presenter

Step 2: Check facts

Think about important things that your heroes did. Then use the internet to research the answers.

When / Where was this hero born?
When did this hero become an activist / ...?
What did this hero discover / do / win / ...?

Check that the information is correct:
Use at least two different websites.

▶ Skills file 4, p. 187

Step 3: Write quiz questions

a) Write five quiz questions about each of your heroes' past. Use the simple past.

▶ More help, p. 77

b) For each question write the correct answer and two wrong answers.

> Where did Malala Yousafzai start her work as an activist?
> A   Pakistan
> B   Afghanistan
> C   Poland

Step 4: Do the quiz

a) Do the quiz in two teams. Teams take turns to ask and answer questions. Each team gets two points for a correct answer.

> I think it's B. What about you?

> I think so too.

> I think it's C.

> OK, so we think it's ...

> That's right! Two points to you. / Sorry, that's wrong. It's ...

b) Give feedback: Which questions were easy or hard? Which were fun or exciting questions? Which questions had new information for you?

1 SPEAKING Who is it?

I can describe what someone looks like.

Describe a Varndean student, but don't say his or her name. Your partner says who it is. Take turns. Tip: Think about hair, eyes, braces, glasses and tie colour.

 Noah
 Sunita
 Zane
 Lily

This student has long, black hair and brown eyes.

That's Sunita!

 Sofia
 Mihai
 Faye
 Jodie

2 LISTENING A group project

I can describe my friend's personality.

a) Noah, Sunita, Lily and Zane are working on a presentation about the history of Brighton. Copy the table. Then listen. Write the correct picture (A–D) for each student.

Name	Picture (A–D)	Personality
Noah	...	...
Sunita	...	...
Lily	...	
Zane		

b) Listen again. Write the personality words for each student. There are two extra words.

clever • confident • funny • hard-working • kind • patient

Check

3 LANGUAGE **Sports heroes** I can ask and answer questions about my hero (simple past).

a) Read Lily's message to her friends. Then write their questions in the simple past.

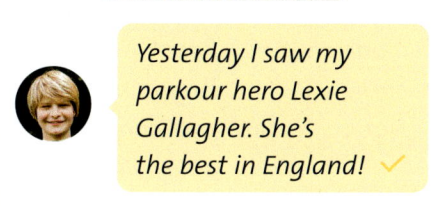

Yesterday I saw my parkour hero Lexie Gallagher. She's the best in England! ✓

1 ... see her / in Brighton / you / ?
   Did you see her in Brighton?
2 ... / have / you / a good time / ?
3 ... / take / some photos / you / ?
4 ... / to you / she / talk / ?
5 ... / any new skills / show you / she / ?
6 ... / do / you / some parkour together / ?

b) Now write Lily's short answers to her friends' questions.

1 Yes, *I did.*   2 Yes, ...   3 Yes, ...   4 No, ...   5 No, ...   6 Yes, ...

c) Read Zane's message. Complete his friends' questions with the correct question word from the box.

How • What • When • Where • Who

I saw my heroes too – Albion FC! ✓

1 ... did you see them? – On Saturday afternoon.
2 ... did you see them? – At the Amex, of course!
3 ... did they play? – They were great. They played 3:0!
4 ... did you watch the game with? – With Holly.
5 ... did you do after the game? – I went swimming.

4 WORDS **Noah's hero**

Some words on Noah's poster are missing. Complete the sentences with the correct words from the box.

climbed • grew • high • hurt • lazy • lives • police • positive • spend • wife

My hero

This is my uncle Chris. He's my hero! He ... (1) up in London, but now he lives in Hove with his ... (2) Sarah. She's my aunt.

My uncle works for the ... (3). Last year, after an accident, he helped people who were ... (4).

Once a boy ... (5) a tree that was too ... (6) Chris helped him to come down again. Sometimes he even saves ... (7).

I really like to ... (8) time with him. He has lots of hobbies and interests – he's never ... (9). He's a happy and ... (10) person.

Check

5 WRITING **Finn's superhero**

Look at Finn's notes and picture for his art project. Then write a paragraph about RoboGull. You can use the phrases in the box and your own ideas.

name:	RoboGull
born:	Brighton, 2023
story:	was hungry
	ate a phone
	...
description:	four feet
	...
superpowers:	play music with feet
	...

His / Her	name / ... is ... eyes / feet / ... are ...
He / She	was born in ... became a superhero when ... can / has / is / wears / ...

6 MEDIATION **A message from Suri**

Read the message from Finn's friend Suri in Dresden. Answer Zane's questions in English.

Zane   Hey, Finn, you're smiling. What's your message about?

Finn   My friend Suri is telling me about ...

Zane   Cool. How did SkateGirl become a superhero?

Finn   ...

Zane   What does she look like?

Finn   ...

Zane   And what can she do?

Finn   ...

Hi, Finn!
Dein RoboGull klingt witzig! Ich habe mir auch mal eine Superheldin ausgedacht. SkateGirl heißt sie. Sie hat zu viel Zeit im Skatepark verbracht und sich eines Tages in SkateGirl verwandelt. Sie sieht aus wie jedes beliebige Mädchen, aber anstelle von Füßen hat sie ein Skateboard. Sie kann superschnell fahren und sehr hoch springen.
LG, Suri

Check

7 READING **An interview**

a) Read the interview with the head students in the school's online magazine. Choose the correct summary (A, B or C).

A   A student was ill. Some teachers and students went to hospital to see him.

B   The head students planned a special present for a Varndean student in hospital.

C   A student was ill. He went to a special assembly at school and then felt better.

www.varndean-teen-zine-online.example.com

Teen Zine	Mihai, can you tell us how your week started?
Mihai	Well, we heard about Jake in assembly. Jake is in year 7 and he's in hospital at the moment.
Teen Zine	And you wanted to help him?
Jodie	Yes. So we talked at lunchtime and made a plan.
Sofia	The next day, Jodie and I made a big card. Over a hundred students wrote something in it, and some teachers did too.
Mihai	And then Faye had a great idea …
Faye	Yes. I like to play the guitar and write songs. So I wrote a song for Jake.
Mihai	And then we thought: Let's sing this in assembly.
Faye	It was amazing – all the students singing Jake's song together.
Teen Zine	I was there too. It sounded great. And Mihai, what did you do?
Mihai	I made a video of the song and took it to Jake in hospital with the card.
Teen Zine	I'm sure Jake was very happy. Well done, guys. We're proud of you!

b) Say who did what.

1   … collected messages.
2   … wrote a song.

3   … filmed the song.
4   … went to the hospital.

8 STUDY SKILLS **Instructions at school**

Fill in the gap. Use the word at the end of each line to form a word of the same word family.

1 Don't run in the corridor! It's not …	SAFETY
2 Always be polite! Even if you don't …	DISAGREE
3 Be … and help other people.	KINDNESS
4 … each other's work. This can help you learn.	CORRECTIONS
5 Please … only on the cycle lanes.	CYCLING

Check

VARNDEAN
Teen Zine

This month's topics: friends and heroes

Our school magazine: by students for students

My favourite friend poem

Hug O'War   *by Shel Silverstein (1930–1999)*

I will not play at tug o'war.
I'd rather play at hug o'war,
Where everyone hugs
Instead of tugs,
Where everyone giggles
And rolls on the rug,
Where everyone kisses,
And everyone grins,
And everyone cuddles,
And everyone wins.

I love this poem because I don't like fighting or competitions. It's a bit cheesy, but you get a nice feeling when you read it. Do you like it? **Silas**

tug o'war

giggles

kisses

grins and cuddles

Fergal's reading tip

My favourite book this year is 'A Brighton mystery' about five friends and their hero dog. It's an exciting story and the puzzles are fun too. What happens? Lily, Noah, Sunita, Zane and Finn are at the Royal Pavilion. There are so many police officers that the children are curious. Something mysterious has happened and they want to know what it is. Can you help solve the mystery?

Teen Zine's team wrote a top ten list of the things that we like to do with our friends. Here it is!

1. have a sleepover[1]
2. make pizza
3. look at photos on our phones
4. have a film night
5. listen to music
6. play video games
7. play card games
8. have a picnic in the park
9. play mini golf
10. prank[2] each other

Send us your top ten lists!

---

[1] **sleepover** *die Übernachtungsparty*   [2] **(to) prank** *einen Streich spielen*

Black heroes

October is Black History Month and *Teen Zine* wants to celebrate it!
Here are two of our favourite black heroes. Do you know more?

Lewis Hamilton
Formula 1 racing driver

Lewis Hamilton was born in the UK in 1985. A world champion seven times, he has over a hundred Formula 1 Grand Prix wins. As the first black driver in Formula 1, he experienced (and still experiences) terrible racism[1].
As an activist he fights for diversity[2] in motorsport and against[3] racism.

Doreen Lawrence
Anti-racist activist

Doreen Lawrence came to the UK from Jamaica when she was nine and later became a bank worker.
In 1993 Doreen's son Stephen died in a racist attack at a bus stop when he was 18 years old. Doreen fought for justice[4] for her son for many years and continues to fight for help for other black people.

E-postcard from the USA

This month Lea tells us about friends and clubs at her school in San Francisco.

Hi, everyone!

I'm really missing all my friends at Varndean. But luckily I have some new friends at my school here. It's easy to make friends because there are a lot of clubs. There's a club for dance, film, climbing, photography, Japanese, frisbee, cooking, computers, ... everything!
I'm in the science club and the jazz band.

One of my best friends is Luisa. She was born in the USA, but her parents are from Mexico, the country to the south[5] of the USA. They speak Spanish at home and Luisa is teaching me some Spanish – it's the second language in the USA because in the past Spanish explorers[6] came to the USA. Later a lot of people moved here from Cuba, Mexico, Puerto Rico and other Latin American countries.

¡Hola!

---

[1] **racism** *der Rassismus* [2] **diversity** *die Vielfalt* [3] **against** *gegen* [4] **justice** *die Gerechtigkeit*
[5] **to the south of** *südlich von* [6] **explorer** *der Forscher, die Forscherin*

Partner page

▶Page 53

3 SPEAKING **About Li-Jun**

a) **Partner B:** Ask partner A these questions.

1 Did Li-Jun grow up in China?
2 Did he want to leave China?
3 Did he always live in Brighton?
4 Did he get a job in the UK?

b) **Partner B:** Read about Li-Jun. Answer partner A's questions. Use *Yes, he did. / No, he didn't.* Give more information. *He got married to …*

> **Li-Jun Chen**
> • got married to Betty
> • didn't have children
> • came to Whitehawk Estate four years ago
> • stopped work two months ago

▶Page 55

9 **Two student heroes**

a) **Partner B:** Partner A has information about Destiny. Ask questions about her.

1 Why did Destiny need money?
2 What did she do?
3 Who did she get money from?
4 How did her team feel?

b) **Partner B:** Read the article about Jonah. Answer partner A's questions about him.

c) **Partner B:** Write the blue words from the article and find their opposites in the box. There are two extra words in the box.

> negative • nice • short • small • tall • unfriendly

When Jonah was ten years old, he was very ill. He spent a long time in hospital, but he always stayed positive. The doctors, nurses and other kids were very friendly and helped him a lot. Before his accident, Jonah loved doing magic tricks. When he came out of hospital, he wanted to say a big thank you to everyone there. So he did a magic show in the hospital.

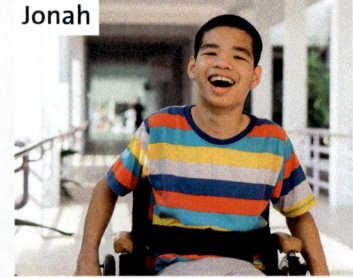

Jonah

d) **Partner B:** Say a blue word to your partner. He or she tells you the opposite.

Diff bank

▶ Page 50

Challenge 1 **Pairs**

What words go with the words in the box?
Find pairs.

cloud • fish • macaroni • pen • question • salt • shoes • summer

I'm the fish …

… and I'm the chips!

▶ Page 51

Challenge 2

Read the conversation between Finn and Sunita and tell a friend about it.

1 **Finn:** 'Suri is one of my best friends in Dresden.' *Finn said that Suri is …*
2 **Sunita:** 'I like her name!'
3 **Finn:** 'I like the name Sunita!'
4 **Sunita:** 'My name is a Hindi name.' ▶ Language file 6, p. 202

▶ Page 52

Challenge 3 SHOWTIME **What happened?**

Write what Li-Jun, the father and the boy said at the beach. Act it out.

▶ Page 53

More practice 1 **When Noah got Buddy**

Lily is asking Noah about Buddy. Complete the conversation. Use the answers to help you.

Lily   … (1 you / get) Buddy when he was small?
Noah   No, we didn't. He was a year old.
Lily   … (2 your parents / help) you look after him?
Noah   Yes, they did at first. But now I usually look after him.
Lily   … (3 come) from another home?
Noah   No, he didn't. He had training before we got him.
Lily   … (4 learn) to be quiet and patient?
Noah   Yes, he did. He's never scared or mean.
Lily   … (5 love) him when you got him?
Noah   Yes, I did. He's so cute and friendly!

▶ Page 53

Challenge 4 **The accident**

The newspaper reporter is talking to the lifeguard about the accident. Look at the lifeguard's answers and write the reporter's questions. The words in blue can help you.

Reporter (1) Did you see the boy fall into the water?

Lifeguard Yes, I did. I saw the boy fall into the water and I ran to him, but Li-Jun was already there.

Reporter (2) …?

Lifeguard No, he didn't. Li-Jun was very fast, so he didn't stay underwater for a long time.

Reporter The boy's father was on the beach with the sister. (3) …?

Lifeguard No, she didn't. The mother didn't go to the beach with her family because she was at work.

Reporter (4) …?

Lifeguard Yes, we did. The lifeguards talked about the accident: we want to stop them!

Reporter (5) …? We always need a phone number for people we interview.

Lifeguard Yes, you did. You already asked for my phone number a few minutes ago.

More practice 2 **Who did what?**

a) **Make questions for sentences 1–5.**

What time did you get up yesterday?

b) WALK AROUND **Ask different partners and write a name for each question.**

c) **Tell the class who did what.**

Slava got up at six a.m. yesterday.

> Find someone who … ──────
>
> 1 got up at six a.m. yesterday.
> 2 went to school by bike yesterday.
> 3 saw a friend on the way to school.
> 4 went to a club after school yesterday.
> 5 had pasta for dinner yesterday.

Challenge 5 **Last weekend**

a) **Write five questions with question words to ask somebody about last weekend.**

Who did you meet last weekend?

b) **Find a partner and ask your questions. Answer your partner's questions.**

Who did you meet last weekend? – I met my grandma last weekend.

▶ Page 54

More practice 3 **Sunita is clever**

a) Write two sentences to describe Lily, Sunita, Noah, Zane and Scout. Write pairs of opposites.

Lily is .... She isn't ...

b) Compare your sentences with a partner.

Sunita is clever. She isn't stupid.

Challenge 6 **More opposites**

a) How many opposite pairs of verbs can you think of? Make a list.

listen – talk   *sit – ...*

b) Compare your list with a partner.

▶ Page 55

More help **10** MY TASK **My hero**

My hero ...
... is *(name)* ... / is a neighbour / star / ...
... is kind / brave / cool / interesting ...
... saved somebody's life / my pet / had a great idea / started a club / started a business / ...
... helped a friend / a neighbour / animals / the planet / somebody in the street / ...
... worked hard / stayed positive when he or she was ill or had a big problem / got a prize / ...

▶ Page 56

More practice 4 **Years and dates**

a) Say the dates. Take turns. Then listen and check.

1 6th June
2 12th September
3 20th May
4 3rd July
5 22nd February
6 21st March
7 5th May
8 19th November

The first day of the year is the first of January. The last day of the year is the thirty-first of December. My favourite day is the first of April. That's my birthday!

b) Now say the years. Take turns. Then listen and check.

1 2022   2 1968   3 1750   4 1895   5 1999   6 2009   7 2015   8 1983

▶Page 56

1 READING **Who is it?**

Answers: A The Climber: Lily • B Computer Girl: Sunita • C Superdog: Noah •
D DolphinMan: Zane

More practice 5 **Lady Cool and Mr Brave**

Describe the superheroes and what they're wearing. *Lady Cool is wearing a red ...*

Lady Cool

Mr Brave

▶Page 57

More practice 6 **A superhero from planet Oolala**

a) **Link the two sentences. Start with *when*.**

1 I was a kid. I lived on planet Oolala.
2 The Zoogs killed my parents. They took me to planet Zoog.

b) **Link the two sentences with *when* in the middle.**

1 I went away. It got really hard.
2 I was happy. I came to earth.

c) **Link the two sentences with *so* in the middle.**

1 I saw that people looked different (on earth).
I changed my body.
2 People needed my help. I became a superhero.

⊠ d) **Complete the sentences for you.**

1 When I was little, ...
2 I was happy when ...

▶ Page 58

More help **5** MY TASK **Me as a superhero**

My story

- I was born in … (year) / in … (country / city) / on … (Planet …).
- I came to earth when
  bad people / animals came to the planet / country / city / …
  the city / country / planet became too hot / cold / …
- I ate a snake / drank a chemical / … and became a superhero.

My superpowers

- I'm very clever / fast / strong / brave / …
- I have good eyes / a good nose / …
- I can become a different person or animal / can become invisible / can fly / can see through things and people / can swim underwater / can travel in time / can walk through walls / can talk to animals / can make people healthy / can see at night / can stop bad weather / …
- I know what other people think or feel / speak many languages / can't get hurt / …

▶ Page 62

More practice 7 **Parts of your body**

Write the correct parts of the body.

1 It's at the end of your arm.
2 It's between your leg and your foot.
3 It's at the top of your body.
4 You hear with them.

5 You see with them.
6 You smell with it.
7 Numbers 5 and 6 are on this.
8 It goes from your neck to the top of your legs. It isn't at the front of your body.

▶ Page 65

More help UNIT TASK **Make a quiz about heroes, Step 3**

When			
Where	was	…	born?
When	did	…	become a … / die / start to … / …?
What	did	…	discover / win / write / …?
Who	did	…	help / talk to / …?
How many prizes / …	did	…	get?
In which city / country / year / …	did	…	fight for / against … / sing … / win … / …?

Unit 3
Activities and games

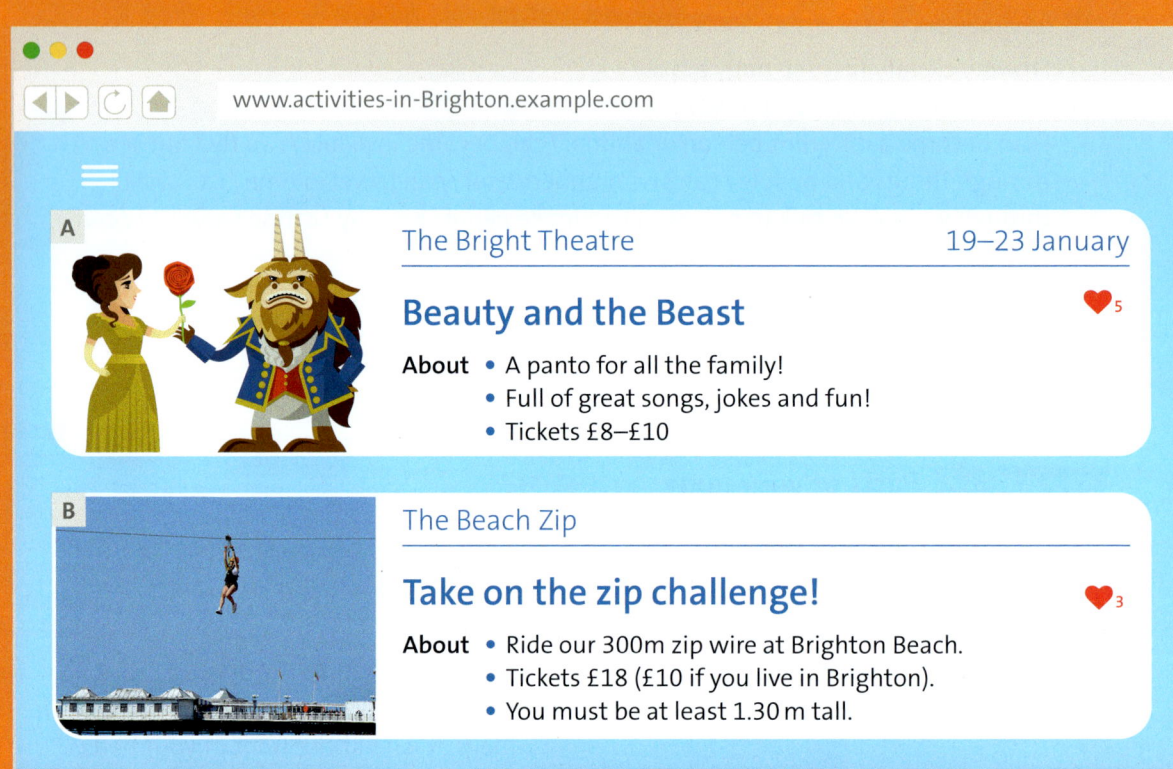

www.activities-in-Brighton.example.com

A

The Bright Theatre   19–23 January

Beauty and the Beast   ♥ 5

About • A panto for all the family!
         • Full of great songs, jokes and fun!
         • Tickets £8–£10

B

The Beach Zip

Take on the zip challenge!   ♥ 3

About • Ride our 300m zip wire at Brighton Beach.
         • Tickets £18 (£10 if you live in Brighton).
         • You must be at least 1.30 m tall.

1 LISTENING What's on in Brighton

a) BEFORE YOU LISTEN **Look at the four activities in Brighton. Say which one looks interesting and why. Why aren't you interested in the other activities?**

I think … looks interesting because I like cooking / exciting activities / making things / singing / …
I'm not interested in … because it's boring / … I don't enjoy … / I don't like …

b) **Listen to Zane and his family. Say which activity they choose together.**

c) **Listen again. Say who doesn't want to or can't do the other three activities. Say why.**

▶ Challenge 1, p. 106

Good to know

In Britain, a pantomime or 'panto' is a funny musical show. The audience sings the songs and talks to the actors.

🔍 EN ⌄

C

Brighton Cook and Bake   19 January

Learn to cook Thai food!   ❤2

About • Make delicious food and take it home!
        • Two-hour class.
        • Cost: £40   • Location: Brighton Cooking School

D

Get creative at the Family Arts Centre

Make your own insect hotel!   ❤0

About • A family activity where you make little homes for insects.
        • You can also see lots of different insects in special boxes.
        • You don't need to book a time or tickets: it's free.

🔊 **2** LISTENING **Booking tickets online**

a) **Listen to Zane. He is booking tickets online. Answer the questions.**

1 When does the first show start?   3 What show do they choose and why?
2 When does the second show start?

b) **Listen again.**

1 Where does Zane's mother / father / sister like to sit?
2 Where in the theatre are the family's seats?

▶ Skills file 6, p. 189
▶ Workbook, p. 42

What are your plans?

1 READING **School activity week in year 8**

a) BEFORE YOU READ **This is the programme for activity week next month. Look at the activity titles and the photos. Which activities do you know?**

b) **Say which three activities look interesting and which don't look interesting. Say why.**
I (don't) like … because it looks …

Activity week –

Dungeons and Dragons
Discover this wonderful role-playing world and play other exciting games at school. Everyone can try it!

Football with pros
Train with a team of professional trainers here at school and visit a professional football stadium.

Goats and other animals
Find out more about the school goats and take them for walks! We also visit a Brighton farm and see more animals there.

and new skills!

History in Brighton
Discover Brighton's amazing history. Visit Brighton Pavilion, Lewes Castle, Newhaven Fort and more!

Knitting
In this creative course at school, you can knit a toy animal or a blanket and make amazing decorations.

Karate and fitness
Practise karate with a professional trainer. We also play team sports and do fitness training in the sports hall.

a week of fun

Tea party and show
Plan a summer tea party for Brighton people at Varndean and prepare a show with singing and acting.

Photography
Learn new photography skills. Take photos of the beach, buildings in the town and artists' street art.

c) **Now read about the activities. Which activities …**

1 are creative?
2 are sporty?
3 can you do alone?
4 do you do with a partner or team?
5 take place at school?
6 take place in other places in Brighton?

Some activities happen at school and in other places.

► More practice 1, p. 106
► Workbook, p. 43

2 LISTENING What are you going to choose?

a) BEFORE YOU LISTEN After class Noah, Sunita, Lily and Zane talk about activity week next month. With a partner, talk about the best activity from 1b) for each student.

*I think the best activity for Zane is …
because he likes / is good at … / is …*

▶ More help, p. 107

b) Listen and complete the correct activities. Then match them to the reasons a–d. Were your ideas in a) correct?

1 Lily: I'm going to choose …	a because I love role-playing games.
2 Noah: I'm going to choose …	b because I like creative activities.
3 Zane: I'm going to choose …	c because street art is really interesting.
4 Sunita: I'm going to choose …	d because it looks fun.

c) Listen again. Complete the sentences with the activities that the students <u>aren't</u> going to choose and the reason why.

1 Lily: I'm not going to choose … because I already do a lot of …
2 Noah: I'm not going to choose … because I know all those …
3 Zane: I'm not going to choose … because the camera on my phone is …
4 Sunita: I'm not going to choose … because there are always so many animals at …!

d) WALK AROUND You're a student at Varndean. Tell different partners your top activity and one activity you aren't going to do. Say why.

I'm going to choose the tea party and show because I'm good at singing. I'm not going to choose the goats because I don't like them. What about you?

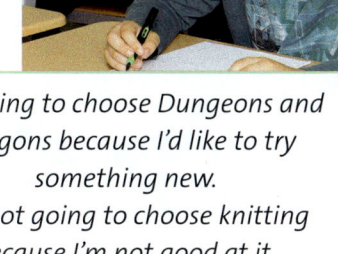

*I'm going to choose Dungeons and Dragons because I'd like to try something new.
I'm not going to choose knitting because I'm not good at it.*

▶ Workbook, p. 43

Erklär-film

3 LOOKING AT LANGUAGE **The going to-future**

a) Read the conversation between Zane and Lily. Copy and complete the examples in the table.

Lily   Yay, it's nearly the weekend! Do you have any plans?

Zane   Yes, I'm going to go to swimming training today after school. And at the weekend I'm really busy. I'm going to help my dad at the cafe. What about you?

Lily   I'm not going to do anything special this evening. Tomorrow Mum and Dad aren't going to work. Mum is going to make a cake and we're going to have a relaxing day.

subject	*be*	*going to*	verb	object
I	'm	going to	...	my dad at the cafe.
Mum (She)	...	going to	make	a cake.
We	...	going to	have	a relaxing day at home.
I	'm not	going to	...	anything special.
Mum and Dad (They)	...	going to	work.	

b) Copy and complete the box.

Mit dem *going to-future* sprechen wir über Pläne für die Zukunft (*after school, at the weekend, tomorrow, next week, next month, ...*).
Wir bilden das *going to-future* mit einer Form von ... + *going to* + Verb.

▶ Language file 8, p. 203

---

4 Zane's weekend

Complete the sentences with *'m, are / 're or is / 's + going to + (verb)*.

1   On Saturday morning Holly ... (play) with a friend.
2   On Saturday afternoon I ... (swim) in a competition.
3   On Saturday evening Mum and Dad ... (have) dinner in town.
4   Grandma ... (look) after us and she ... (make) dinner.
5   On Sunday I ... (make) lunch.
6   On Sunday afternoon we ... (go) to the theatre.

---

5 Plans for the weekend

a) Take turns. Say what the students are going to do or not do at the weekend. Use the verbs in the box.

do • eat • go • listen to • play • watch

She isn't going to do her homework. – That's Poppy.

b) Tell your partner about your plans for the weekend.

▶ More help, p. 107   ▶ Challenge 2, p. 107

✓ Sunita and Nish   ✗ Noah   ✗ Amir

✓ Edek and Kyle   ✗ Poppy   ✓ Livia

▶ Workbook, p. 44

6 LOOKING AT LANGUAGE The going to-future (yes/no questions)

Erklär-film

a) Read Scout's conversation with George.
Copy and complete the table with the questions.

Are	you	going to	stay	at home tonight?
...	...	...	...	...

b) Look at your table in a) and the table in 3a).
Complete the sentence.

Going to-Fragen, auf die man mit *yes / no* antwortet, beginnen mit einer Form von ...

▶ Language file 9, p. 204

George Are you going to stay at home tonight?
Scout No, I'm not.
George Are you going to go on a date?
Scout Yes, I am.
George Is your friend going to meet you here?
Scout No, he isn't.
George Am I going to meet him?
Scout Yes, you are.

7 More questions for Scout

a) ROLE-PLAY Put George's questions in the correct order. Then act out the conversation.
For Scout's answers use your own ideas.

1 buy / going to / a new hat / are / you / ?
2 going to / fly / your friend / to the date / is / ?
3 somewhere / going to / you / eat / are / ?
4 you / dance / are / together / going to / ?

b) Write Scout's answers. Use your own ideas. Then practise the questions and answers.

1 Who are you going to meet?
2 What time are you going to meet?
3 Where are you going to go?
4 What are you going to wear?

▶ More practice 2–3, p. 108   ▶ Language file 9–10, p. 204

My task

8 What are you going to do at the weekend?

Partner B: Look at page 106.
Partner A:

a) You have plans for the weekend. Use the notes below to answer your parent's questions.
Partner B starts.
swimming with Nelly: Saturday 10.45 a.m., pool

b) Swap roles: You're the parent. Ask questions. You start the conversation.

1 Who ... meet? *Who are you going to meet?*
2 What ... do?
3 Where ... meet?
4 When ... meet?

▶ Digital help

▶ Workbook, p. 45

Digital quiz   I can make plans and talk about them.

Music, films and shows

1 LISTENING What kind of music do you like?

a) BEFORE YOU LISTEN **Look at these kinds of music. Which words look like words in German or another language that you know? Tell your partner.**

A   classical music
B   acoustic music
C   pop
D   rap
E   rock
F   electro

'Rap' is the same in German.

b) **Listen to six music clips (1–6). Match them to the kinds of music (A–F) in a).**

c) **Listen to the conversation at Noah's house. Who is it: Lily (L), Noah (N), Sunita (S) or Zane (Z)? Sometimes you need more than one person. Write** *1 Z, 2 …*

1   Who loves rock?
2   Who doesn't like rock?
3   Who listens to classical music?
4   Who doesn't like pop?

5   Who likes rap?
6   Who doesn't like rap?
7   Who thinks acoustic music is boring?
8   Who likes electro?

d) **Which kinds of music do you like or don't you like? Tell your partner. Use the words in a) or your own ideas. Say why or why not.**

I like electro, but I don't like acoustic music because I think it's boring. What about you?

I agree. / I don't agree. I love pop music because it's cool.

▶ Workbook, p. 15

Erklär-
film

2 LOOKING AT LANGUAGE **Comparatives**

a) Look at these sentences. Copy the adjectives (1–9) and add their comparatives from the sentences.

It's even louder than their last one.
Can you play something a bit quieter?
It's slower and more relaxing than other kinds of music.

Pop is a bit happier.
It's cooler. The lyrics are more interesting.
It's faster and more energetic than acoustic music.

1	loud → *louder*	3	slow	5	happy	7	interesting	9 energetic
2	quiet	4	relaxing	6	cool	8	fast	

b) Look at the comparatives from a) again. Highlight the two kinds of comparatives in different colours.

c) Copy and complete the rules with 1, 2 or 3.

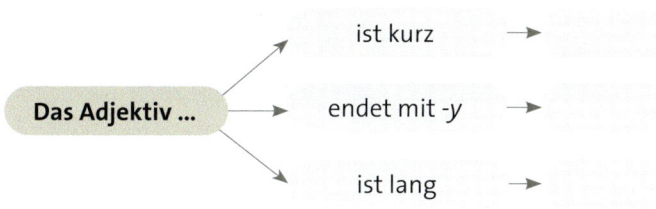

ist kurz →

Das Adjektiv ... → endet mit -y →

ist lang →

1 *more* + Adjektiv
2 Adjektiv + *-ier*
3 Adjektiv + *-er*

Manche Komparative sind unregelmäßig:
good → better   bad → worse

Wenn zwei Dinge gleich sind, benutzt du *as* [Adjektiv] *as*.

Chips are better than sandwiches!
And cheese is worse than fruit!

Chips are as good as fish!

▶ Language file 11, p. 205

3 Comparing music

a) Complete the sentences with comparatives. Listen to the conversation in 1c) again and check.

1 Noah thinks classical music is ... (slow) and ... (relaxing) than rock.
2 Zane thinks pop is ... (bad) than classical music.
3 Lily thinks rap is ... (cool) than pop.
4 Sunita says electro is ... (fast) and ... (energetic) than acoustic music.

b) WALK AROUND **Compare two kinds of music from a) with a partner. If your partner agrees, he or she continues. If your partner doesn't agree, find a new partner.**

I think rock is cooler than pop. – Yes, I agree. / No, I don't agree. I think ...

▶ More help, p. 108   ▶ More practice 4 + 5, p. 109

▶ Workbook, p. 46

4 READING What do you want to watch?

a) BEFORE YOU READ The kids want to watch a film or show online.
Match the three pictures (A–C) to the kinds of film and show in the box.

an action film •
a cartoon •
a sci-fi film

The funniest show of the year! Doctor Meow is the most clever cat in town – but Doctor Woof thinks he's more clever ...
Rating: ★★★

Winner of the Best Special Effects prize last year. Dex 3000 is the worst robot ever – but also the kindest. Can he find a friend?
Rating: ★★★★★

Agent Green is back for her most exciting adventure! She's the coolest, fastest hero – but is she stronger than the terrible 'Lizards'?
Rating: ★★★★

b) Read the reviews in a) and look at what the kids say. Choose a film or show for each one. Say why.

I want to watch the film with the best rating so we know it's good. And I love films about space or robots.

I want to watch something funny. I don't like scary films!

I don't like cartoons – I want to watch something more exciting!

I think the best film / show for Sunita / Zane / Lily is ... because it's ...

Erklär-film

5 LOOKING AT LANGUAGE Superlatives

a) Look at these adjectives.
Copy the table and write the missing comparatives and superlatives. Find the superlatives in 4a).

b) Copy and complete the rules.

Adjective	Comparative	Superlative
funny	funnier	
cool / fast		
clever	more clever	
exciting	more exciting	
good		
bad		

Wenn der Komparativ mit *-er* oder *-ier* gebildet wird, endet der Superlativ mit ...
Wenn der Komparativ mit *more* gebildet wird, verwendet man im Superlativ ...

▶ Language file 12, p. 205

▶ Workbook, p. 47

6 SPEAKING **The best film**

Which film from 4a) do you think is best and why? Tell a partner. Use the adjectives from 5a).

I think ... is best because it's ...

▶ More practice 6, p. 110

7 VIEWING **Film time**

a) **The kids watched one of the films from 4a). Which film did they choose? Watch the trailer to find out.**

b) **Watch the trailer again and choose the correct answers.**

1 The main character is an alien / a robot / a scientist.
2 He's clever / fast / friendly.
3 The film takes place in Brighton / Liverpool / London.
4 The film is about friends / war / space.
5 People think that the film is scary / sad / funny.
6 It has great actors / special effects / music.

My task

8 **A film trailer**

a) **Work in a small group. Choose a film that you all like.**

b) **Write the voice-over for a trailer of this film. You can use the trailer in 7) and these sentences to help you.**

[Studio name] presents: [Film name]
This is a ... film about ...
The film takes place in ...
The main character is ...
[Website / Magazine] says it's ...

SuperScout *is the best action film this year. She's cooler than all the other superheroes!*

▶ More help, p. 110   ▶ Wordbank 5, p. 217

c) YOU CHOOSE **Do task A or B below to present your film trailer.**

A SHOWTIME Act out your film trailer in front of the class. One student reads the voice-over and the others mime the actions. You can record it if everyone agrees.

B Make a video of your film trailer. Use a slide show of photos or film video clips with your group. Add music and record your voice-over. Play your trailer to your class.

d) **Have a prize ceremony in your class. Which film trailer was:**

★ the funniest?   ★ the scariest?   ★ the most exciting?   ★ the best?

▶ Digital help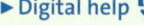

▶ Workbook, p. 47

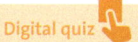

Gaming

1 What do you think?

Your teacher reads a sentence. Stand up if you agree, sit down if you don't.
☒ Explain why or why not.

1 Video games are boring.
2 Computer gaming is better than console gaming.

3 Puzzle games aren't real games.
4 Adventure games are the best.

2 LISTENING Where do I go next?

a) BEFORE YOU LISTEN Finn and Sunita are playing an online game. Look at the game map. Tell your partner what you can see.

b) Sunita is helping Finn with the game. Listen and complete the directions.

To find the key 🔑, Finn must go through the ... (1) and turn left at the ... (2).
He keeps going straight on, past a small ... (3) and then turns ... (4).
He goes across the ... (5) and then up the ... (6) to a ... (7).

c) Listen again and check. Where's the key? Describe it or point.

► More practice 7, p. 110   ► More practice 8, p. 111

3 READING Sunita's trophies

 a) Sunita has a lot of trophies from the game. Read her chat with Finn and point to the trophies that they talk about.

b) Read the descriptions of some of Sunita's other trophies. Write the letter of the trophy.

1 It's the one to the right of the eye trophy.
2 It's the one on the top left.
3 It's the one above the eye trophy.
4 It's the biggest one.
5 It's the one between the bird trophy and the fire trophy.

 c) Choose a trophy and describe it. Your partner guesses.

It's the one over / under / next to / between …
It's the one to the right / left of …
It's the big / small / round / square / long / blue / red / yellow / … one.

💡

You can use **one** so that you don't say or write the same noun every time.

FinnD	Oh wow, you have so many trophies!
SuperNita	Haha, thx!
FinnD	What's the big square one for? I don't have that one.
SuperNita	You mean the one next to the smiley? That's for a perfect score.
FinnD	Coooooool … And what about the one on the bottom right?
SuperNita	That's my favourite one! I got it when I found a secret level!
FinnD	😍😍😍
SuperNita	😊

▶ Vocabulary, p. 254   ▶ More practice 9, p. 111   ▶ Skills file 7, p. 190

4 Class trophies

a) What's the best thing about your partner? Draw a trophy for him or her. Use a special symbol, like a green flower or an orange cat. Explain why you picked the trophy.

It's a cake / … because you make the best cakes / …!

b) Show the trophy from your partner to a new partner and describe it.

It's a car / … because I'm the fastest / … person in our class.
… gave me a camera / … because I like taking pictures / …

c) GALLERY WALK Hang the trophies in rows on the wall. Ask about a trophy.

Whose trophy is the cat in the top / middle / bottom row on the left / right?
What's it for? Who drew it?

▶ Workbook, pp. 48–49

5 Meeting online

a) BEFORE YOU LISTEN   Look at the clock. Point to 15, 30 and 45 minutes past the hour.

b) Listen to Finn and Sunita. They want to meet online to play video games together. Complete the sentences.

Finn wants to meet online at … (1), but Sunita has her dancing class until … (2). Sunita suggests … (3), but Finn's family is going to eat dinner at … (4). They agree to meet online at … (5).

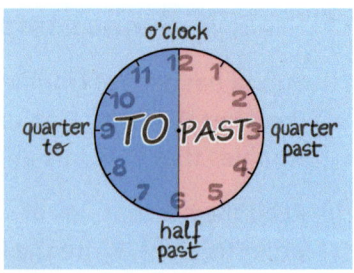

half past twelve = 12.30
half past one = 1.30

6 Match the times

Match the times on the left (1–8) to the times on the right (a–h). Then listen and check.

1	10.45	5	2.45
2	7.30	6	5.30
3	3.15	7	11.15
4	8.30	8	4.30

a   half past eight   e   quarter past three
b   half past five   f   half past seven
c   quarter past eleven   g   half past four
d   quarter to three   h   quarter to eleven

▶ Challenge 3, p. 111

7 SPEAKING   Timetable expert

Use *half past* and *quarter to / quarter past* to test your partner about your timetable.

What subject do we have on Mondays / … at half past nine / …?

You can also say times in the middle of a lesson!

My task

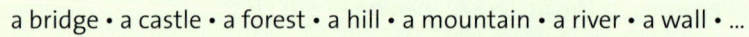

8 Game designer

a) Draw a game map like the one in 2. Include lots of different places:

> a bridge • a castle • a forest • a hill • a mountain • a river • a wall • …

b) Draw where the character starts. Write directions to a secret place on the map. Use the directions in 2 to help you.   ▶ More help, p. 111

Go left / right / straight on at the …   *Go across / down / past / through / up the …*

c) Swap with your partner and follow his or her directions to find the secret place.   ▶ Digital help

▶ Workbook, p. 50

Digital quiz   **I can** give directions and talk about the time.

Background file

1 READING The international language of computers

a) BEFORE YOU READ Sunita likes action-adventure video games. Match the picture from each game to its description from the box. There are two extra descriptions.

> A simulation • B quiz •
> C sports • D puzzle •
> E role-playing • F snake

 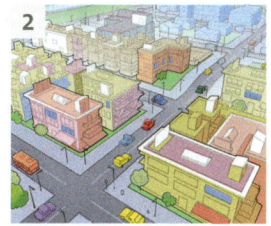  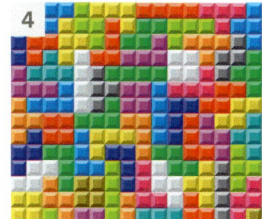

b) Read the text.

Like most kids, you probably surf the web, watch videos on social media or play video games. What language do you often need for these activities? English, of course. All over the world, people use English on their screens.

Why English?
People speak English nearly everywhere, often as a lingua franca: When two people speak different languages, they use English together. English is also the international language of computers: More computer programs and websites are in English than in other languages.

Gaming
You can play a lot of computer games in German, but some are only in English. And in some games you can talk or write to other players around the world. Usually players use English together. That's a good reason to learn new words! The pictures and the situations in video games can help you to understand their meaning. In some games you see the same words often: It makes it easier to remember them.

Gaming streamers are also popular: You can watch them play games online. They're very good players, and most streamers speak English in their videos.

> **Good to know**
>
> Be safe! When you're online, never give your real name or other information about you to another person. You don't know who the other person really is.

c) What kind of (computer) games do you play? Do you need English for them?

d) Where do you see, hear, read and use English in your life? Keep a journal about English in your life for a week. Share with a partner or with your class. Put your text in your DOSSIER.

► Workbook, p. 50

Zane online

1 READING Too much of a good thing?

a) BEFORE YOU READ **Tell a partner how much time you spend online every day and what you do.**

> *How much time do you spend online?*

> *I usually spend about ... minutes / hours every day.*

> *What do you do?*

> *I usually chat with friends / play games / send messages / watch videos / ...*

▶ Wordbank 6, p. 218

b) **Look at the pictures. What can you see? What do you think the story is about?**

c) **Now read the story. Check your answers from b).**

▶ Skills file 7, p. 190

'Oh, I'm so bored!' thought Zane. 'What am I going to do all day?'
It was Friday morning, but Zane was at home because he was ill. He had a bad cough and a headache.

5 'I can't go out. I can't talk to my friends because they're at school. And I can't do homework because my head hurts!'
'PING!' Zane checked his messages. It was break time at school. The message was from Finn and it had a link

10 to a video. 'Watch this, Zane! And get better soon!'
'OK,' thought Zane. 'Why not?' He clicked on the link.

The video was really funny. Zane laughed out loud. He clicked on the next one ... and the next one ... Then it was lunchtime.

15 'How are you feeling, Zane?' asked his mum.
'OK, Mum, thanks. I just need to rest a bit more.'
'Your dad is going to get Holly from school today. And I have a meeting in town until quarter past two. Are you going to be OK?'

20 'Sure, Mum,' said Zane. 'I'm going to lie down on the sofa for a while.'
After lunch Zane watched videos again. When his dad came home with Holly, Zane was still on his phone. He was tired and his headache was worse.

25 'No more screen time today, Zane!' said his dad.
'You know the rules – one hour a day!'

The next week Zane went back to school, but he watched videos every evening – often until very late. 'You look tired, Zane,' his mum said on Thursday. 'And
30 you spend a lot of time in your room. What's wrong?' Zane smiled. 'I'm just tired from when I was ill.' 'Hmm,' said his mum. 'You have a maths test on Monday – it's on the calendar. Do you need help?' 'A maths test? Oh, yes, right. No, I don't need help,
35 thanks. Everything is fine.'

The next weekend, his friends went swimming, but Zane didn't go. 'Sorry, I still have a cough,' he said to Lily on the phone. 'And I need to study for the maths test.'
40 'I can come round and help you,' said Lily. 'Thanks, but my mum is going to help me,' Zane said. 'I must go now. Bye!'

Lily was puzzled. Zane didn't have a cough now and he always went swimming with them.
45 'Something is wrong,' she said. 'Zane didn't come for brunch at Noah's last weekend, and he got a bad mark for his history homework – Noah told me.' 'Finn said Zane watches lots of videos now,' answered Sunita. ... 'You know, Nish had a problem with screen
50 time last year.' 'Right,' said Lily. 'I'm going to visit Zane.'

Lily went to Zane's house after swimming. 'Good to see you,' Zane's mum said. 'Zane is in his room.' Zane was surprised and not very happy. 'You know
55 I'm busy.' 'Too busy for your friends, Zane?' asked Lily. Zane looked angry. 'Please go, Lily.'

2 Zane's problem

Read the story again. Match the sentence parts. *1g, 2 ...*

1 Zane's problem started when ...
2 He got a link to ...
3 He watched ...
4 The next week ...
5 His mum was worried and ...
6 Lily knew that ...
7 Lily went to see Zane, but ...

a she asked Zane if he needed help.
b he didn't want to see her.
c something was wrong.
d videos all day.
e a video from Finn.
f he watched videos every evening.
g he was ill.

3 The story ending

Look at the three possible story endings. Which one do you think is the best? ☒ Say why.

I think ending A / B / C is the best (because ...)

A Lily looked sad, but she went down the stairs and out of the door.
'Wait, Lily!' Zane ran after her. 'I'm sorry, I can't stop watching videos,' he said. 'It isn't fun now. I think I need help.'

B Lily didn't move. 'No, Zane! I'm not going to leave! You're my best friend and I'm worried about you. Sunita, Noah and Finn are worried too. Don't you think friends are more important than stupid videos?'

C 'OK, Zane, I'm going to leave,' said Lily. 'I want to help you, but you're too stupid! I don't want to be your friend any more.'
'But Lily ...,' Zane looked shocked.
'Bye, Zane.'

4 Words and phrases in the story

Work out the meaning of these words and phrases. Check in the Dictionary on **pages 277–298**.

1 bored (line 1)
2 cough (line 4)
3 headache (line 4)
4 Get better soon! (line 10)
5 What's wrong? (line 30)
6 puzzled (line 43)
7 mark (line 46)
8 screen (line 49)

Remember:
• You can use pictures and word families to understand the meaning of words.
• You can also use German and other languages.
• Look at the meaning of the word in the sentence.

▶ Study skills, p. 64   ▶ Skills file 2–3, pp. 185–186

5 LIFE SKILLS Plan your screen time

a) Discuss these questions. The tips in the box can help you.

1 What happens when you spend too much time online?

*I forget to do my homework / see my friends / ...
I get lazy / tired / a headache / ...*

Tips
• Go outside.
• Meet your friends.
• Go swimming.
• Use a timer app.
• Put your phone in the living room at night.

2 Which tip do you think is best for Zane?
3 Do you know any other good tips?
4 Does your family have rules about screen time? What rules?

b) Plan your screen time for next week and tell a partner.

I'm going to spend / use / ...   *I'm not going to ...*

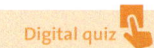 Digital quiz 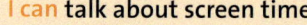 **I can talk about screen time.**

Brighton stories: After-school fun

👥 1 After-school activities

BEFORE YOU WATCH The kids are talking about after-school activities.

a) Put the activities in the box in order from your most favourite (1) to your least favourite (4).

> gardening[1] • photography • sewing[2] •
> street dancing

b) Talk to your partner about your list.

My number one / two / … is …
I like … because I like plants[3] / clothes / …
I don't like … so much because it's hard / boring …
I think … is creative / exciting / fun / relaxing / …

💻 2 VIEWING A group activity

a) Watch part 1 of the video and complete the sentences.

1 Daisy wants her friends to go to …
2 The others want to …

3 The person who learns the most and dances well will …!

b) Watch part 2. Choose the best adjectives from the box to describe:

> easy • fun • good • surprised and tired •
> unplanned[4]

1 how Daisy finds the dancing at first
2 what type of dancing 'freestyle' is
3 Gloria's freestyle moves
4 how Emir describes the dancing after they stop
5 how Daisy feels after the dancing

c) Watch the last part. Who learned the most? Who was the winner? Say if you agree with Joe and why or why not.

👥 3 Now you

Think about activities, sports or languages that you do now or tried in the past. Tell a partner about them.

At first I thought handball was hard. After some practice I found it … In the end …

---

[1] **gardening** *die Gartenarbeit* [2] **sewing** *das Nähen* [3] **plant** *die Pflanze* ▶ Workbook, p. 51
[4] **unplanned** *ungeplant*

Give your opinion

1 LISTENING **What do you think?**

a) The five friends are talking about a new show. Listen and answer the questions.

1 What's Zane's opinion of *Scout's world*?
2 Who agrees with Zane?
3 Who doesn't agree?

b) Copy the table. Write the phrases from the box in the correct place. Then listen again and check.

Give an opinion	Ask for an opinion	Agree	Don't agree
I think ...	...	...	...

Phrases
- I agree. / I don't agree.
- In my opinion, ...
- For me that isn't true.
- You're right.
- I don't think so. / I think ...
- What do you think?

Always give your opinion politely, especially if you don't agree.

2 SPEAKING **I think ...**

Choose a topic from the box or use your own idea. Give your opinion. The adjectives in the box can help you. Your partner agrees or doesn't agree. ☒ Say why.

I think cats are horrible!

I don't agree. Cats are really cute! I think mice aren't nice.

I agree.

Topics

cats • cold weather • dogs • football • gaming • mice • onions • pizza • school • school uniforms • shopping • the colour pink • vegan food • zoos

Adjectives

boring • cool • cute • delicious • easy • exciting • fun • hard • horrible • interesting • nice • scary • unhealthy • useful

3 OPINION LINE **'Is learning English easy?'**

What do you think: Is learning English easy? In groups form an opinion line. ☒ Say why.

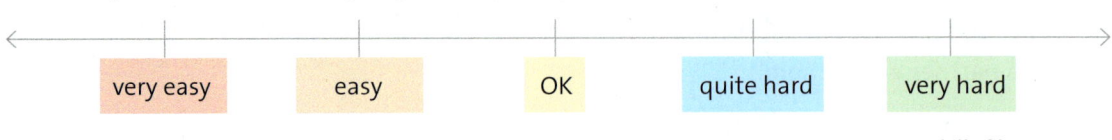

very easy   easy   OK   quite hard   very hard

▶ Skills file 10, p. 194

Digital quiz    **I can** ask for opinions and give my opinion.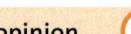

Plan and present an activity day

Step 1: Think of ideas for an activity day

You're going to plan an activity day at school in a group.
First brainstorm with a partner and make a list. The ideas in the box can help you.

▶ Digital help

Ideas

- sports and games (a match or a competition)
- making things (costumes, decorations, …)
- a party or a show (a musical, concert or disco)
- collecting money (for your school or town)
- activities to help people in your town or village

Step 2: Discuss your ideas

Join another pair. Compare and discuss your ideas. Agree on two activities.

You have some great ideas!
I think a fun run is the best activity.
I think a disco is more exciting than a concert.
I agree. / I don't agree. I think …

▶ Study skills, p. 96

What about a cooking competition?
I can test everything!

Step 3: Plan your day

a) Make notes for a plan with two activities. Think about people, times and places. Give directions. Don't forget to add a break.

b) Make a flyer for your activities.   ▶ Digital help

Your flyer should get attention! Make the text easy to read and not too long. Use colours and an interesting picture.

Step 4: Present your activity day

a) Tell another group or the class about your day.

At half past eight we're going to have breakfast together in the canteen.
Then at … we're going to …
That's going to be in … To get there, go …

b) Give the other group feedback on their ideas and on their flyer. Then choose the best activities for an activity day at your school.

Digital quiz   **I can plan and present an activity day.**

1 SPEAKING At the family arts centre

I can talk about plans for a family activity. ✓

a) Look at the posters. Which two activities do you want to do?

b) Agree on two or three activities. Say when and where they take place.

IN THE **GARDEN**
9.15 – 9.45
Meet our new fish and give them some breakfast!
10.30 – 11.30
Go on an insect tour.

IN THE **ART ROOM**
9.30 – 10.30
Make an insect hotel for your garden.
10.45 – 11.30
Design a tree house for our centre. Prizes for the best designs!

— IN THE — **CAFE**
9.00 – 9.30
Hungry? Try some eggs from our chickens.
10.15 – 11.15
Decorate and eat a cake.

> At nine fifteen I want to … in the …

> Good idea! It ends at …, so we can … at …

> OK, then let's first … and then …

2 LANGUAGE After school

I can make plans and talk about them (going to-future). ✓

Read the conversation. Complete the sentences. Use the going to-future.

Finn What a long day! What are you going to do after school?

Sunita I *'m going to have* (1 have) dinner with my family, and then I … (2 play) some computer games: After that Nish … (3 help) me with the French homework, I hope! What about you?

Finn It's my grandpa's birthday, so we … (4 have) a video call. He … (5 open) his present from me and Mum. Then we … (6 make) a pizza. And after that I … (7 play) some computer games with my friends from Germany! They … (8 meet) online tonight.

Sunita I think you … (9 have) a great time!

3 LANGUAGE Lily's trip

a) **Lily is going to go to Scotland for the weekend. Put Zane's questions in the correct order.**

1 travel / going to / by car / are / you /?
2 going to / read / are / you / on the trip /?
3 the weather / going to / is / be / cold /?
4 you / go / are / skiing / going to /?

b) **Look at Lily's things. Write her answers. Use short answers: *Yes/No, I/it …***

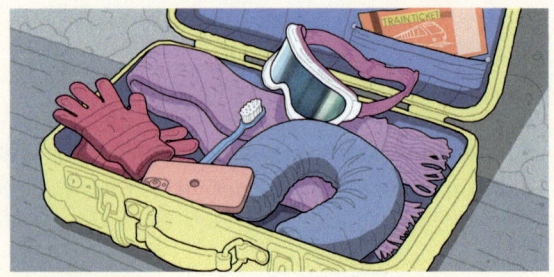

Check

4 READING **Comments about a new song**

> **I can** compare music, shows and films (comparatives and superlatives).

a) Read the online comments about a new song. Choose the correct text for each person:

PopQueen   Calm_Cal   Electro*Guy   Rock_4eva

 www.what's-new-in-rock-music.example.net

1 *Oh no. My favourite band isn't cool any more 😞 . Their last album was amazing, but this song is ... not good at all. It's their worst song. Rock music needs to be louder than this! I think I'm going to fall asleep 😴 .*

2 *Wow! What a great song. I don't usually listen to rock music (pop is my thing), but this sounds so good. It's much cooler than my dad's old rock songs 😜 . I love the video too. I want to have a house on the beach like that!*

3 *Interesting lyrics, but the guitars are too loud for me. Songs sound so much better when you can hear what the singer is saying! I'm going to listen to some quieter music now – it's more relaxing ...*

4 *Cool song! I'm not really a fan of rock music because sometimes I think it sounds angry. But this is perfect for me: It's energetic and it makes me want to dance 😊 !*

b) Look at the comments in **a)** again. Choose the correct word(s) in each sentence (1–4).

1 The new song is A quieter B louder C more exciting than the band's other songs.
2 The music video is A as good as B better than C worse than the new song.
3 The singing is as A relaxing B important C loud as the music.
4 The new song doesn't sound as A cool B energetic C angry as other rock songs.

5 LANGUAGE **Which show do you want to see?**

Look at the flyers. Complete the sentences. Use the comparative or the superlative form of the word in blue.

1 *Mary Poppins* is ... (funny) than *Oliver!*
2 *Oliver!* is ... (energetic) than *Mary Poppins*.
3 *Mary Poppins* is ... (short) than *Billy Elliot*.
4 *Oliver!* is the ... (long) show.
5 *Billy Elliot* is the ... (expensive) show.
6 *Mary Poppins* is the ... (short) show.

BILLY ELLIOT

A boy wants to dance!

90 minutes | Tickets: £20

OLIVER!

A musical with lots of energy

120 minutes
Tickets: **£15**

Mary Poppins

A funny show for all the family

75 minutes
Tickets: **£12**

Check

6 WORDS **A secret level**

Sunita tells Finn how to find a secret level in the computer game. Look at the pictures and complete her sentences with the correct word from the box. There are three extra words.

> above • across • between • come • into • keep • past • right • straight • through • turn • up

I can give directions and talk about the time. ✓

Go ... the forest.

Go ... the silver bridge.

When you're on the other side, ... right.

... going straight on.

Go ... the castle.

Stop ... the two weird trees.

The key is ... your head in a gold bag.

Look ...

🔊 7 LISTENING **Playing online**

The five friends want to play online together. Listen to them and complete the sentences with the correct times.

1. Finn wants to meet at *quarter past two.*
2. Zane gets back to his house at ...
3. He has time at ...
4. Noah is going out to eat at ...
5. Lily asks about Sunday at ...
6. Sunita doesn't want to start until ...
7. Zane comes online at ...
8. Finn and Lily were online at ...
9. Noah and Sunita come online at ...
10. Finn's dad wants to call him at ...

Check

8 WRITING **Sunita's screen time**

For her computing homework Sunita needs to write a plan for her screen time next week. Look at her notes and write her plan. You can use the phrases in the box.

> I'm going to spend / use … on Monday / … •
> I'm not going to … •
> I think it's going to be quite easy / hard / …

You can start like this: *This is my plan for my screen time next week: I'm going to use my computer on Monday. I'm going to spend 45 minutes gaming. …*

> *Monday: computer – gaming – 45 min*
> *Tuesday: no screen time*
> *Wednesday: computer – homework – 30 min*
> *Thursday: no screen time*
> *Friday: phone – watch videos – 25 min*
> *Saturday: no screen time*
> *Sunday: phone – chat with friends – 30 min*

9 STUDY SKILLS **Talking about films**

I can ask for opinions and give my opinion.

a) You're talking to your British friend Millie about films. Tell her what you think about her favourite kinds of film. Say why. You can use the phrases in the box.

> I agree. / I don't agree. • You're right. •
> In my opinion, … • For me, … • I think … /
> I don't think so. • … because … • … but …

I think sci-fi films are the best.

Action films are great too – they're exciting.

And scary films are much better than cartoons.

b) Ask Millie for her opinion about your favourite film or kind of film.

Check

VARNDEAN
Teen Zine

This month's topic: activities

Our school magazine: by students for students

Game review

TopRacer   *by Sunita Chandra in 8C*

I don't usually play car racing games because I like adventure games better – they're more interesting and exciting! But my friend Finn likes a game called TopRacer, so I tried it and it was much better than I thought. (Especially when I won! 🙂)

You drive different cars to see who is the best. When you win, you get points so you can buy faster and more beautiful cars.

My favourite car is the Tomahawk because it's the coolest one! This game is fun to play with friends and I recommend[1] it, even if you don't normally like sports or car games.

Send us a review of your favourite game!

What's the best sports or music event?

Zeina

Asim

Laura

My favourite sports event is Wimbledon because I love tennis. I want to see it live in London next summer!

I think Glastonbury Festival is the coolest music event. I went with my family last year and we stayed on a campsite. It was amazing – even though[2] it rained!

I love going to Latitude Festival because it has the most amazing bands. And the best sports event? I think it's the London Marathon – I want to run it one day!

What do YOU think is the best sports or music event?

We love music jokes!

Cool music!

I'm a moo-sician!

---

[1] (to) **recommend** *empfehlen*   [2] **even though** *obwohl*

The best friends game

Write your answers to these questions. Your partner guesses your answers.
How well does your partner know you? Then swap!

1 What's your favourite sport?
2 Which football team is the best?
3 Who is your favourite band or singer?
4 Can you sing or play an instrument?
5 What was the last album or playlist that you listened to?

6 What song makes you feel happiest?
7 What kind of films or shows do you like?
8 What was the last film that you watched?
9 What's your favourite game?
10 PC, console or phone: Which is the best for games?

I think your favourite sport is basketball!

No, sorry – I wrote badminton!

E-postcard from the USA

This month Lea writes about the sports at her new school.
Write Lea a postcard and tell her about the sports at your school.

Hi, everyone!

I loved PE lessons at Varndean, especially when we played cricket or football (or, as they call it here in the USA, 'soccer'). But the PE lessons here are very different!

Here they play American football, which is kind of like rugby, but a little bit calmer. There are eleven players on the team. This is my friend Jung in his special football clothes to keep him safe! He loves watching sport on TV too, especially the Super Bowl. It's like our World Cup, but for American football.

They also play baseball, which is really fun. It's a bit like cricket, but a lot faster!

What's your favourite sport?

Getting to know Sussex

The City of Brighton and Hove is in a part of England called Sussex. It's in the **south** of the country. Sussex has two parts: the **counties** of **East** Sussex and **West** Sussex. Brighton and Hove are in East Sussex.

1 VIEWING **Out and about in Sussex**

a) **Match the names in the box with the photos on the map at the bottom of the page. Say why.** *I think this is / these are … because …*

📺 b) **Watch the video. Were you right?**

📺 c) **Watch the video again. Write the order of the places you see:** *1 D, 2 …*

> Houseboats[1] •
> The Old Town Hall[2] •
> Stanmer Park •
> Seven Sisters

2 **Working with a map**

a) **Read the box on the right. Look at the map below.
In which square[3] is each of the places: Brighton, Shoreham-by-Sea, Stanmer, Steyning?** *Brighton is in C3 …*

b) **Choose the correct direction[4] in each sentence.**

1 Shoreham-by-Sea is to the A west B east C south of Brighton.
2 Steyning is to the A south B north C east of Shoreham-by-Sea.
3 Brighton is to the A east B north C south of Stanmer.

💡 A map helps you find places and describe where they are. Many maps have squares. Each square has a letter and a number. The top left square is A1, the square next to it is A2 and the square under A1 is B1. Usually **north** is at the top of a map.

Key terms

Working with a map
- county *der Landkreis*
- east *der Osten; östlich; Ost-*
- north *der Norden; nördlich; Nord-*
- south *der Süden; südlich; Süd-*
- west *der Westen; westlich; West-*

---

[1] **houseboat** *das Hausboot*   [2] **town hall** *das Rathaus*   [3] **square** *das Quadrat*   [4] **direction** *die Richtung*

3 LISTENING **Back in Brighton**

a) BEFORE YOU LISTEN **Look at the map. What sights can you find? What do you already know about them?**

b) **Listen to the tour guide. Follow the directions with your finger on the map.**

c) **Listen again. What places does the tour go to? What new facts do you learn about these places?**

d) **Each of you chooses a place on the map. Don't say where! Ask your partner where he or she is. Then give directions to your place. Can your partner find the correct place? Take turns.**

> **Good to know**
>
> You pronounce -*cester* at the end of names (Gloucester, Leicester) like -*ster*: for example, Gloucester is pronounced 'gloster' [ˈɡlɒstə]. Lots of cities and towns end in -*cester*, even in the USA[1].

> **Use your words and phrases**

Where are you at the moment?

I'm ...	at / in front of / next to / near / between ... / on (the corner[2] of) ... Street (and ...).
Go ...	through / down / up / past / across / into ... / straight on.
Turn ...	left / right.
Can you see ...?	a small / big / red / ... bridge / building / house / park / pier / river / shop ...?

---

[1] **USA** *USA (= die Vereinigten Staaten von Amerika)*   [2] **corner** *die Ecke*

Partner page

▶ Page 83

8 MY TASK **What are you going to do at the weekend?**

a) Partner B: You're the parent. Ask questions. You start the conversation.

1 Who ... meet? *Who are you going to meet?*   3 Where ... meet?
2 What ... do?   4 When ... meet?

b) Swap roles: You have plans for the weekend. Use the notes below to answer your parent's questions: *playing games with Oscar: Sunday 2 p.m., Oscar's house*

Diff bank

▶ Page 78

Challenge 1 **Weekend activities in Brighton**

READING **Match each type of activity on the left to the description on the right. There are two types of activities with no match: Write X for those.** *1F, 2 ...*

1 art
2 concert
3 family
4 science
5 food
6 history
7 library
8 market

A This weekend only: Taste delicious dishes from around the world!
B The Phurries play their cool rock at their show on Friday at 8 p.m.
C Take a walk and learn about our city's past and hear exciting stories about it.
D Hear Jarvis Lee read from his new book about a group of brave teens.
E Fruit, vegetables, eggs and meat from farms around town every weekend!
F Beautiful animal drawings by Sierra Evans are in the Brighton Picture Gallery until the end of the week.

▶ Page 80

More practice 1 **Photos of the town**

Rewrite the sentences with the possessive form (*'s* or *s'*) or an *of*-phrase.

1 All the (students – photos) were amazing.
   All the students' photos were amazing.
2 One photo showed the (lights – pier).
3 Another photo showed a (little boy – dog).
4 Mia took photos of some (skateboarders – tricks).
5 Tim took photos of the (top – i360).
6 The best photo showed the (different colours – sea).

Remember:
• the girl's dog =
  der Hund des Mädchens
• the girls' dog =
  der Hund der Mädchen
• the end of the game =
  das Ende des Spiels

▶ Page 81

More help **2 LISTENING What are you going to choose?**

a) BEFORE YOU LISTEN **After class Zane, Sunita, Noah and Lily talk about activity week next month. With a partner, talk about the best activity for each student. You can look at 1b) on p. 80 again.**

I think the best activity for	Lily Noah Zane Sunita	is …	because he / she	likes animals / games / history / sport / … is good at art / cooking / photography / … is brave / creative / sporty / …

▶ Page 82

More help **5 Plans for the weekend**

b) **Tell your partner about your plans for the weekend.**

I'm going to … / I'm not going to …

- eat ice cream / pizza / sushi / …
- do my homework
- listen to music
- go to the cinema / the swimming pool / …
- go shopping

- look after my brother / sister / pet / …
- meet my friends
- watch a film / a show
- play basketball / football / table
- tennis / computer games / …

Challenge 2 **What's going to happen?**

Zane and his family are talking before the panto begins. Finish the sentences with *am / is / are + going to* and the words in the box.

We can also use *going to* to talk about future events that are already clear.

see the panto • be loud • get wet • like it too • start

1 There were clouds in the sky when we got here and it's very dark: *I think it's going to rain.*
2 We didn't bring our umbrellas: We …
3 There are a lot of people here: I think it …
4 My friend saw the panto yesterday and said it was great: I think I …
5 Holly, don't stand up during the show! Nobody …
6 They're turning the lights off: The panto …

▶ Page 83

More practice 2 **Next Friday evening**

SPEED DATING Ask different partners what they're going to do next Friday evening. Find students for three activities in the table.
⊠ Ask for more information.

Activity	Name	⊠ More information:
do a sport	...	...
watch a film	...	...
cook	...	
go to a club	...	
do homework	...	
meet friends		

A Are you going to do a sport on Friday evening?
B No, I'm not.
A Are you going to watch a film?
B Yes, I am.
(A What / Where / When / ...?)

More practice 3 MEDIATION **A phone call**

a) BEFORE YOU LISTEN Look at the picture. Say what you can see.

Finn is ...   Finn's mum is ...

b) Listen. Finn's mum wants to know what Zane is saying. Complete Finn's answers.

Mutter	Was ist schade? Hat er etwas vor?
Finn	Ja, er ... Und heute Abend ...
Mutter	Und morgen?
Finn	Morgen ...
Mutter	Was ist mit seiner Oma?
Finn	...
Mutter	Habt ihr doch etwas ausgemacht?
Finn	...

▶ Skills file 8, p. 191

▶ Page 85

More help **3 Comparing music**

b) WALK AROUND Compare two kinds of music from a) with a partner. If your partner agrees, he or she continues. If your partner doesn't agree, find a new partner.

I think	acoustic music / classical music / electro / pop / rap / rock	is	cooler / faster / happier / louder / quieter / slower / ... more energetic / more interesting / more relaxing / ... better / worse	than ...

More practice 4 **Scout's favourite band**

a) **Write the comparative form of the adjectives.**

1 Ellis has ... (long) hair than Alex.
2 Alex is ... (tall) than Sam, but ... (short) than Charlie.
3 Ellis is ... (popular) than Charlie.
4 Sam's guitar is ... (small), but ... (modern) than Charlie's guitar.
5 Charlie's guitar is ... (expensive) than Sam's guitar.
6 Alex is ... (strong) than Ellis.

b) **Look at the picture and write the names of the four people in the band (A–D).**

More practice 5 **The singer and the guitar player**

Look at the pictures. Copy and complete the sentences. Use *as ... as* and an adjective from the box. There are three extra adjectives.

> ~~cool~~ • creative • fast • happy •
> loud • sad • strong • tall • tired

The singer is *as cool as* the guitar player.

The singer is ... the guitar player.

The singer is ... the guitar player.

The guitar player is ...

The guitar player is ...

The guitar player is ...

▶ Page 87

More practice 6   **Good, better, best!**

a) Put these kinds of music and films in the correct order for you. Begin with your least favourite and end with your favourite.

1 classical music • rock • electro   3 action films • cartoons • sci-fi films
2 acoustic music • pop • rap

b) Write sentences and compare the kinds of music, films and shows. The words in the box can help you.

I think electro is cooler than classical music, but rock is the coolest.

> bad • boring • cool • exciting • fast • good • interesting • relaxing • slow

More help   **8** MY TASK   **A film trailer**

b) Write the voice-over for a trailer of this film.

[Studio name] presents	[Film name]		
This is	an action film / a cartoon / a sci-fi film / …	about	animals / friends / music / space / superheroes / …
It takes place in	London / New York / a school / space / …		
The main character is	a dog / a football player / a robot / a singer / a superhero / …		
[Website / Magazine] says it's	the best / funniest / most exciting / …	film	this summer / this year / …
	better / funnier / more exciting / …	than	[another film]

▶ Page 88

More practice 7   **Scout's sandwich**

**Help Scout get the sandwich.
Complete the directions.**

Scout, you need to go … (1) and turn … (2) at the grey bin. Turn … (3) and go … (4) past the family with the dog. Then turn … (5) again at the sandcastle. The sandwich is … (6) the green bin.

More practice 8 **Where do I go?**

Match these prepositions to the pictures below.

across • down • into • past • through • up

... the stairs

... the stairs

... the tree

... the street

... the forest

... the shop

▶ Page 89

More practice 9 **Buying gaming equipment**

Make this conversation sound better – change the nouns (1–7) to one or ones.

Finn	Look at these keyboards! Which (1) ~~keyboard~~ *one* do you like best, Sunita?
Sunita	I think the black (2) keyboard looks cool, but I like the big grey (3) keyboard too.
Finn	Me too. That's my favourite (4) keyboard. And I need some headphones! Which (5) headphones do you have?
Sunita	I have blue (6) headphones, but I really want some red (7) headphones.

▶ Page 90

Challenge 3 **What time is it?**

a) **Listen and write the times (1–6).**

1 *5.40*   2 ...

b) **Think of and say five times. Your partner writes them.**

 Remember: The UK usually uses the twelve-hour clock:
9 a.m. = 9 o'clock in the morning
9 p.m. = 9 o'clock in the evening

More help **8** MY TASK **Game designer**

| Go / Turn | left / right / straight on | at the | dragon / house / tree / wall / ... |
| Go | across / down / into / past / through | the | bridge / castle / forest / mountain / river / ... |

Unit 4
Celebrate!

1 LISTENING Celebrations in Britain

a) BEFORE YOU LISTEN **Choose a photo (A–D). What can you see? Your partner guesses.**

b) **Copy the table. Listen and complete. Listen again and check. Add more information.**

Name	Photo	When?	More information
Holi (Festival of colours)	…	… or …	*Indian festival*
Eid al-Fitr (Festival of breaking the fast)	…	*… month of …*	…
Notting Hill Carnival	…	…	
Guy Fawkes Night (Bonfire Night)	…	*… November*	

▶ Skills file 6, p. 189

Nach dieser Unit kann ich ...

- ⊘ über Feste in Großbritannien und anderen Ländern sprechen
- ⊘ ein Festessen beschreiben
- ⊘ über Festvorbereitungen und Familienfeiern reden
- ⊘ Präsentationen planen und üben

Unit task ⊘

- ⊘ ein Fest präsentieren

fireworks and bonfire

2 SPEAKING Your celebrations

a) THINK **First brainstorm celebrations in your class. Then choose one and think about:**

1 Name of the celebration? When?
2 Costumes or special clothes?
3 A parade or music?

4 Lights, candles or fireworks?
5 Special food?
6 Presents or money?

▶ More practice 1, p. 138

b) PAIR **Tell a partner about your celebration.**

c) SHARE **Tell the class.**

▶ Workbook, p. 59

Special meals

1 READING **Ramadan and Eid al-Fitr**

a) BEFORE YOU READ **What do you know about Ramadan and Eid al-Fitr?**
Make notes.

▶ Skills file 5, p. 188

b) **Read the conversation. True (T), false (F) or not in the text (NT)? Correct the false statements.**

1 Zane can't eat lunch with Noah.
2 Zane thinks fasting is hard for his dad.
3 Muslims can't eat or drink during the month of Ramadan.
4 Zane loves celebrating Eid al-Fitr.
5 Zane's dad helps other people at Eid al-Fitr.
6 Zane gets money at Eid al-Fitr.

	Noah	Hi Zane! Can I have lunch with you?
	Zane	Sure!
	Noah	How are you? I see you aren't fasting. You know, for the month of Ramadan.
5	**Zane**	No, my dad fasts, and the rest of the family doesn't.
	Noah	Ah, OK. Can I ask you – is it hard for your dad when he is working in the cafe?
10	**Zane**	Yes, I think so. But he's a practising Muslim, so it's important to him. He often gets thirsty because he can't have any food or drink between sunrise and sunset.
15	**Noah**	Do you all celebrate Eid al-Fitr?
	Zane	Yes, we all go to the celebration meal.
	Noah	But Eid al-Fitr isn't just about food, right?
20	**Zane**	No, it isn't. Dad prays and thanks Allah, and he gives money to charity. Children usually get presents from their parents and grandparents. We decorate our home with lots of lights, flowers, moons and stars.

c) **Find words for these definitions in the text in b).**

1 not eat, especially for religious reasons (line 3)
2 when you need to drink something (line 12)
3 when the sun comes up (line 14)
4 when the sun goes down (line 14)
5 talks to or thanks his / her god (line 19)
6 help for people (line 20)

d) **Add new information about Eid al-Fitr and Ramadan to your notes from a).**
You can add your new words to a 'celebrations' page in your VOCAB FILE.

2 WORDS **Food**

a) REVISION **Think of the food words that you know. Make lists in your VOCAB FILE with fruit, vegetables, food from animals, sweet things and other foods.**

b) Zane went shopping and bought the things in pictures A–H. Which words are:
1 countable (have a plural form)?
2 uncountable (don't have a plural form)?
Add the new words to your VOCAB FILE.

c) Match the phrases in the box with the correct words in the pictures.   *1G, 2 …*

> 1 a bottle of • 2 a pot of • 3 a carton of •
> 4 a packet of • 5 a jar of • 6 a tin of •
> 7 a piece of • 8 a box of

A biscuits	B chocolates
C honey	D cheese
E milk	F baked beans
G orange juice	H yoghurt

d) Close your books. How many things in the pictures can you remember?

e) Make a shopping list for a meal. Write ten things. Use the words in c).

A bottle of …   ▶ More practice 2 + 3, p. 139   ▶ Skills file 1, p. 184   ▶ Wordbank 7, p. 219

3 MEDIATION **An invitation to Eid al-Fitr**

It's now nearly the end of Ramadan. Zane invites his friends to the Eid celebration. Finn writes to his dad and tells him about the invitation. Complete his message.

*Lieber Papa,
Zane hat mich zu … eingeladen.
Er feiert mit …
Das Fest findet am …, um …, im … statt. Zane hat geschrieben, dass wir …
Es ist Tradition, dass man …
Ich freue mich schon darauf!
Liebe Grüße aus Brighton
Finn*

*Dear friends,
I'd like to invite you to celebrate Eid al-Fitr with my family and other people in our neighbourhood.*

*Date: Sunday 1st May
Time: 1 p.m.
Place: garden behind the mosque*

We're going to wish each other 'Eid Mubarak' and eat a delicious meal together.

It's traditional to take a bath and wear clean clothes for the celebration.

*I hope you can come!
Best wishes from Zane*

▶ Skills file 8, p. 191

▶ Workbook, p. 60

4 LISTENING **Before the celebration**

a) BEFORE YOU LISTEN **You have an invitation to a celebration. What questions do you want to ask? Think about activities / clothes and costumes / presents / how long the celebration is / …**

b) **Listen. What four topics do Zane and his friends talk about? Choose from the box.**

> charity • clothes • food • games and activities • Zane's invitation • presents

c) **Listen again. Choose the correct answers.**

1 Lily says thank you to …
   A Zane. B Zane's dad. C the people at the mosque.
2 Zane asks his friends not to bring …
   A presents. B food. C cake.
3 At the meal there's usually …
   A beef, lamb and chicken. B pork. C no meat.
4 At the meal some people give …
   A money. B toys. C other things for children.
5 Zane asks his friends to …
   A look smart. B show respect. C enjoy their meal.

Erklär-
film

5 LOOKING AT LANGUAGE *some* and *any*, *a little* and *a few*

a) **Look at the sentences and the picture with Scout.**
   Then complete the rule in the box with *some* and *any*.

There are some salads.
There is some cake and some bread.
Don't bring any food!
There isn't any pork.

Would you like some chips?

Yes, please. Can I have some fish, too?

In bejahten Sätzen verwenden wir für eine unbestimmte Menge …
Dies gilt auch für Fragen (wenn wir etwas anbieten oder um etwas bitten).
In verneinten Sätzen verwenden wir …

b) **Now look at these sentences. Then complete the rule in the box with *a little* and *a few*.**

People give a little money – not a lot.
My favourite bread has a little sugar on it.
People can buy a few meals – or a few toys or other things.

Wir verwenden für eine kleine Menge
• mit zählbaren Wörtern: …
• mit nicht zählbaren Wörtern: …

▶ Language file 13–14, p. 206
▶ Workbook, p. 60

6 Ready for Eid al-Fitr

Zane and his family are getting ready for the Eid meal. Complete the speech bubbles with *some*, *any*, *a little* or *a few*. Sometimes there are two possible answers.

> Zane, would you like ... (1) water?

> No thanks, Mum. I still have ... (2) juice.

> Mum, can I have ... (3) biscuits?

> No, you can't have ... (4) food before the meal, Holly.

> Dad, I don't have ... (5) money.

> I can give you ... (6) pounds for the Eid collection, Zane.

▶ More practice 4, p. 140

7 SPEAKING What would you like?

a) Zane is giving food to Finn at the Eid meal. Complete the conversation. Then listen and check.

Zane	Would you like ... (1) potato curry?
Finn	Yes, ... (2). I'd like some rice and some yoghurt too.
Zane	OK, ... (3) you are. Would you like a lamb kebab?
Finn	No, ... (4). Could I have a little salad, please?
Zane	... (5) course. What about some fruit?
Finn	Yes, please. May I ... (6) some melon?
Zane	Yes, here you are. ... (7) your meal!

b) Practise the conversation. Then change the words in blue and practise it again.

▶ More practice 5, p. 140

My task

8 An invitation to a special meal

a) You invite an English exchange student to a special meal at your home.
Change the words in blue in the invitation.

▶ More help, p. 140   ▶ Wordbank 7, p. 219

b) Check your text.
☐ Does it have all the information?
☐ Are your descriptions of the food clear?
☐ Is your spelling correct?
Check in a dictionary.

c) GALLERY WALK Read all the invitations. Which meal sounds best? Tell the class.
☒ Say why.   ▶ Digital help

> Dear Charlie
> I'd like to invite you to a special meal at my home on Sunday at 6 p.m.
> First we're going to have some soup with pancakes in it. That sounds strange, but it tastes great!
> After that we're going to have some 'Maultaschen' – they're a bit like big ravioli with a little meat inside.
> For dessert we're going to eat apple cake with cream. It's my aunt's recipe.
> I hope you can come!
> Sasha

▶ Workbook, p. 61

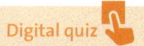

Meera ♥ Ben

1 LISTENING A big celebration

a) BEFORE YOU LISTEN **Look at the title of this topic. Who are Meera and Ben? What celebration do you think Sunita and Lily are discussing?**

> a birthday • Christmas • a festival • Halloween • a new job • Valentine's Day • a wedding

b) **Listen and check your ideas.**

c) **Listen again. Choose the correct answers.**

1   Sunita has / doesn't have new clothes for the celebration.
2   Lily, Zane and Noah can come / can't come to the celebration.
3   The bandstand is perfect because it's near Sunita's house / it's romantic.
4   Sunita wants an idea for a present / surprise for her mum and Ben.
5   Lily talks about the presentation / song on Zane's birthday.
6   Lily, Zane and Noah can help with music / special effects.
7   The wedding is / isn't next Saturday.

2 READING Sunita's surprise

a) BEFORE YOU READ **Can you remember what Sunita's surprise for Ben and Meera is? What do you think Sunita must prepare?**

I think she must find / make / practise / prepare / think of / …

b) **Read Sunita's checklist. Say what she's happy about ✓ and what she isn't happy about ✗. Use *has* or *hasn't*.**

Sunita is happy that …
1   she has asked Willow for help.
2   she … thought of some nice stories.
3   she … found photos of her mum and Ben.
4   she … made a photo slide show.

Sunita isn't happy that …
5   she hasn't found any good music.
6   she … talked to Finn about special effects.
7   she … practised the presentation.
8   she … asked her friends what they think.

1   Ask Willow for help ✓
2   Think of some nice stories ✓
3   Find photos of Mum and Ben ✓
4   Make a photo slide show ✓
5   Find some good music ✗
6   Talk to Finn about special effects ✗
7   Practise the presentation ✗
8   Ask my friends what they think ✗

3 WALK AROUND How do you feel?

Tell different partners how you feel: Choose an adjective and a reason from the boxes. Say at least three different sentences.

> angry • bored • happy • hungry • proud • sad • thirsty • tired • unhappy • worried

I'm happy because I've just had my favourite lesson. What about you?

I'm worried because I haven't finished my homework yet.

I haven't had enough sleep.
I've just talked to my best friend.
I haven't studied for a test.
I've just helped somebody.
I've just had a fight with my friend.
I've had a good day so far.
I've forgotten my water bottle.
I've had a nice message from a friend.
I haven't done any interesting things yet.
I've just found something I lost.
I haven't eaten enough today.

4 LOOKING AT LANGUAGE The present perfect

Erklär-
film

a) Look at the sentences in 2b) and 3. Complete the box below.

Why are you sad?

I've lost my favourite hat. It has blown away.

Wir verwenden das *present perfect* für etwas, das bereits (irgend-wann mal) geschehen ist und Folgen in der Gegenwart hat.

PAST   PRESENT
I've just talked to my best friend. → *I'm happy.*

Wir bilden das *present perfect* mit *have ('ve)* oder ... und einer besonderen Verbform, dem *past participle*.
Regelmäßige *past participles* enden auf ... *(talked, played)*.
Manche *past participles* haben eine unregelmäßige Form *(had, done)*. Die musst du lernen!

b) Find three regular and three irregular past participles in 2b) and 3. Write the infinitives.
regular: asked – ask, ...   ▶ Language file 15, p. 207   ▶ Irregular verbs, pp. 312–313

5 How do they feel?

Complete the sentences with past participles. All the verbs are regular.

Ben feels proud because Meera has ... (1 ask) him to marry her. Meera feels excited because Ben has ... (2 prepare) something special for her. Lily is tired because she and Sunita have ... (3 work) on the presentation. Willow feels angry because her girlfriend hasn't ... (4 call) her. Sunita is really happy because her mum has ... (5 invite) Finn to the wedding. George the parrot is sad because no one has ... (6 talk) to him – everybody is busy!

▶ Workbook, p. 62

6 Poor George!

Complete the sentences with irregular past participles. Find them in the list on **pages 312–313**.

George I'm tired. I haven't … (1 sleep) well. Everybody is stressed.
Scout Yes, I've just … (2 hear) about the wedding.
They haven't … (3 send) me an invitation yet, but
I've already … (4 buy) a new hat. Do you like it?
George Hmm, very nice. Is that fruit? I'm hungry!
They've … (5 forget) to feed me.
Scout I've … (6 see) some fruit in the garden. I can get some.
George Thanks, Scout! You're a good friend.

▶ More practice 6–7, p. 141   ▶ Irregular verbs, pp. 312–313

7 Getting ready

a) **Partner B:** Look at **p. 138.**
Partner A: Write what Sunita says to Nish.
Use **'ve / haven't** and the past participle.

> *I haven't found (1 not find) any clothes for the wedding yet.
> And I … (2 not finish) my presentation. I … (3 invite) my friends.
> But I … (4 not get) the invitations from Mum yet. I … (5 buy)
> a present for Mum and Ben. But I … (6 not make) a card yet.*

b) **Your partner tells you what Nish has done. Tell your partner
what Sunita has done. Say what they've both done.**
Sunita has / hasn't … They've both …

▶ Challenge 1–2, p. 141

8 READING Sunita's family

a) **Willow is calling Sunita. Who is at Sunita's house?**

Willow Hi, Sunita. Have your grandparents arrived from India?
Sunita Yes, they have. They've just got here.
Willow Has your family from Birmingham come too?
Sunita Yes, my aunt and uncle and cousins are here. Our house
is full of people! Willow, have you bought your clothes
for the wedding yet?
Willow No, I haven't. I'm going shopping tomorrow morning – you can come with me.
Sunita Great, thanks! Oh, my cousins want to play with me again. Don't laugh, Willow!
They're going to be your cousins soon!

b) **Do you have a big or small family? What's good or bad about it?**

▶ Workbook, p. 63

9 LOOKING AT LANGUAGE **The present perfect: yes/no questions**

Erklär-film

a) Write the three questions from **8a** in your exercise book.
Highlight the parts of the questions in different colours:

auxiliary verb	people or thing (subject)	past participle	rest of the sentence
Have	your grandparents	arrived	from India?

b) Sunita has some questions for Willow. Put them in the correct order.
Then match them to Willow's answers.

1 invited / a lot of / has / friends / Ben / ?   a No, they haven't.
2 with / you / Ben / have / the wedding / helped / ?   b Yes, he has.
3 hard / the preparations / been / have / for you / ?   c Yes, I have.   ▶ Language file 16, p. 208

---

10 SPEAKING **Today**

a) Ask your partner the questions about today. Your partner answers with *Yes, I have.* or
No, I haven't. Write ✓ or ✗ for your partner's answers. Then swap roles.

1 Have you had breakfast?
2 Have you made your bed?
3 Have you smiled at a teacher?
4 Have you texted a friend?
5 Have you listened to music?
6 Have you eaten spaghetti?

b) Compare your answers and make notes: Which are the same? Which are different?

We've both had breakfast and listened to music. You have ..., but I haven't done that.

▶ Challenge 3, p. 142

My task

11 QUIZ **Have you ever ...?**

a) Write at least eight quiz questions about amazing
experiences. Use *Have you ever ...?*
▶ More help, p. 142   ▶ Irregular verbs, pp. 312–313

Have you ever ridden a horse?

Yes, I have / No, I haven't.

b) Ask your partner your questions and take notes.
Answer your partner's questions.

*Bijan has ridden a horse, but
he hasn't ever seen a rainbow.*

c) Tell the class about your partner.

▶ Digital help ⬇   ▶ More practice 8, p. 142

▶ Workbook, pp. 64–65

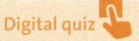
Digital quiz   **I can** talk about preparations and experiences.

Family celebrations

1 LISTENING Ben and Willow's song

Sunita's family has come together for sangeet, the day before an Indian wedding.

Ben's songs are so cheesy!

a) BEFORE YOU LISTEN **Who is in the picture? What are they doing? Tell a partner.**

b) **Listen to the song and answer the questions.**

1   What are Ben and Willow singing about?
2   How do they feel?

c) **Listen again and find word pairs in the song that rhyme.**

easy / cheesy, ...

d) WORDS **Look at the song lyrics and find:**

1   a phrase that means 'very happy'
2   three family members
3   three words that mean 'really good'
4   two words about parties

e) **What do you think about the song? Tell your partner.**

I think it's boring / cheesy / cool / fun / ...
I like / don't like the lyrics / music / rap / ...

The day that I've waited for ♫

I have something to say, but it isn't easy.
I hope it doesn't sound too cheesy,
but I'm feeling over the moon
'cause we're getting married soon.
And I don't think that anyone
could be a better stepdaughter or
* stepson.*
And someone amazing is gonna be my wife,
so that's why this is gonna be the best day
* of my life!*

It's the day that I've waited for.
I have everything I want and more.
There's nowhere else I wanna be
than right here with my new family
on this day that I've waited for.

Is everyone ready to throw that confetti?
I feel like I've joined the family already.
I can't wait to celebrate this awesome date.
Dad, don't be late!
Ha, don't worry – it's gonna be great!

It's the day that I've waited for ...

2 LOOKING AT LANGUAGE At the sangeet celebration

a) Copy and complete the table with the words in blue from the song.

	some	every	no	any
person	…	…	*no one*	…
thing	…	…	*nothing*	*anything*
place	*somewhere*	*everywhere*	…	*anywhere*

b) Look at the first part of the song in 1 again and complete the rules with *some* and *any*.

> 1 In verneinten Aussagen und Fragen verwenden wir … und seine Zusammensetzungen für „jemand", „etwas", „irgendwo" bzw. „niemand", „nichts", „nirgendwo".
> 2 In bejahten Aussagen verwenden wir … und seine Zusammensetzungen für „jemand", „etwas", „irgendwo".

▶ Language file 17, p. 208

c) Sunita shows a picture of the sangeet to a friend.
Complete the sentences with the highlighted words from **a)**.

1 There are flowers and decorations …
2 … is very colourful.
3 George the parrot is … in a tree.
4 … looks like they are having fun.
5 … looks sad or bored.
6 … is dancing.
7 Willow is holding … in her hand.
8 There isn't … sitting at the table.

▶ More practice 9, p. 143

▶ Workbook, pp. 66–67

👥 ✉ **3** GAME **Hot potato**

Stand in a circle. Student 1 holds a 'hot potato' (for example a soft ball). He or she throws it to student 2 and says one of the words from 2a). Student 2 says a true sentence about a celebration with that word. Then he or she throws the hot potato to another student and says another word from 2a).

Someone always makes a cake for my birthday. – Everything!

I liked everything at Christmas this year.

My task

4 Our favourite family parties

👥 **a)** **Brainstorm family celebrations.**
a birthday, a christening, ...

b) **Read the messages. Which party sounds the most fun to you? Think about a party your family celebrated and make notes.**

name day – last year – disco – cake – ...

c) **Write three questions about a family party.** ▶ More help, p. 143

👥 **d)** WALK AROUND **Ask your questions and make notes. Find at least three partners.**

What did you celebrate?

We celebrated my name day.

When/What/... did you ...?

e) **Tell the class about your results.**
Some students celebrated in a hall.
Everyone ate cake and most people ... No one ...

Thanks for the photo, Sunita! Ben's song was soo romantic 😍 *At my big sister Chloe's house-warming party we sang karaoke and then we watched fireworks in the garden.*

Buddy doesn't like fireworks because they scare him. My best party ever was my birthday party in the park last year – remember we wore funny costumes? 😄

Yeah, that was cool. My family also had a great party two years ago when my dad opened his cafe. It was in a hall and we had a disco. I loved the music, but my dad's dancing is soo embarrassing! 😳

▶ Digital help

Digital quiz 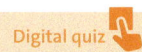 **I can** talk about family celebrations.

Background file

1 READING Traditional British weddings

a) The photo below is from a traditional British wedding. Describe what you see.

b) Read the text below. What's the same as in Germany and other countries you know? What's different?

In traditional British weddings, the bride wears a white dress and the groom wears a suit. Weddings usually take place at noon. At a big wedding, friends, cousins, nieces or nephews of the bride and groom are bridesmaids or groomsmen. The bridesmaids all wear the same dresses and the groomsmen wear the same suits. At the wedding, the bride and groom give each other the rings. Afterwards, they sometimes travel to the wedding party in a nice car. There's usually a beautiful cake, music and dancing.

c) Read the poem. Brides often wear these things on their wedding day for luck. Think of four good things to wear for this tradition.

> ♡
> *Something old,*
> ♡ *Something new,*
> *Something borrowed,* ♡
> *Something blue.*

2 Modern British weddings

In Britain, you can get married in lots of different places, not just in an office.
Look at the photos. Tell a partner what you like and what you don't like about these places.
What place do you like most? Say why or why not.

The big day

1 READING What's going to happen?

a) BEFORE YOU READ **Complete the sentences.**
The phrases in the box can help you. You can use one or more phrases to complete each sentence.

> a blue suit • calm • late • on time •
> a red sari • smart clothes • stressed •
> the wrong clothes • untidy clothes •
> a white dress

1 I think Meera is going to be ...
2 I think Ben is going to be ...
3 I think Ben is going to wear ...
4 I think Meera is going to wear ...

b) **Then read the story and check if you were right.**

▶ Skills file 7, p. 190

1

It's nine o'clock on Saturday morning and everyone is excited because it's Ben and Meera's big day!
Sunita is helping her mum to put on her
5 beautiful red sari while Nish is checking the flowers.
'Mum,' says Sunita, looking worried. 'Do you think Ben is going to be late today? He's great, but, erm, you know: He's a bit
10 disorganized ...'
Meera smiles. 'Don't worry, Sunita. This is an important day for him too. It's all going to be fine.' 'OK,' says Sunita, but she texts Willow.

Hey, Willow, is Ben awake yet? I'm worried he's going to be late!

😄 You're joking, right? He's been awake for hours! He set five alarms this morning!

2

15 Willow is helping her dad to put on his tie.
'Do you think I look OK?' he asks. 'I haven't worn a suit for a long time!'
He looks at himself in the mirror.

You look amazing!

'OK, I'm nearly ready,' says Ben. 'I just need to clean my shoes, then it's time to go. Have you called the

20 taxi yet, Willow?'

'We don't need a taxi, Dad,' smiles Willow. 'Look out of the window.'

Ben looks down at the street. 'You've decorated our bikes! Oh, Willow – they're perfect, thank you!'

3

25 But while Ben and Willow are looking out of the window, they suddenly see two men – they're stealing the bikes!

'Hey! Stop!' Ben and Willow run downstairs, but when they run out into the street, the two men have

30 left – with Ben and Willow's bikes! And then they hear the door close behind them ...

'I can't believe they've taken our bikes! And – oh no, we're locked out!' Ben checks his pockets. 'My keys and phone are still in the flat!'

4

35 Willow looks down at Ben's feet. 'And that's not all, Dad – your shoes are in the flat too. You're still wearing your slippers!'

'I can't wear slippers to my wedding! What are we going to do? We can't call anyone because we don't

40 have our phones. And my money is in the flat too, so I can't buy new shoes.'

Ben looks at a clock in a shop window. 'It's half past nine! We really need to go now.'

5

As they walk, Ben says sadly, 'I can't believe it. I tried

45 so hard to be organized and on time. And now I'm going to be late and untidy. Meera's going to be so disappointed in me ...'

'No, she isn't,' says Willow. 'Look, here's the bandstand. And look at Meera!'

50 Meera is smiling at Ben. She's surprised that he looks so smart – and then she laughs as she sees his slippers!

'Sorry,' says Ben, embarrassed. 'I can explain later ...'

'Don't worry,' laughs Meera. 'Just like our wedding

55 promise, I'm going to marry you for better, for worse, in sickness, in health – and in slippers!'

2 What happened?

Complete the sentences.

1 Sunita worried about Ben being ...
2 Ben and Meera both looked ...
3 Two men stole ...
4 Ben and Willow left their ...
5 Ben wore ...
6 When Meera saw Ben, she ...

▶ Challenge 4, p. 143

3 Words in the text

Find the words in the story with these meanings.

1 when you often forget things (part 1)
2 a very smart jacket and trousers (part 2)
3 when you can't get inside your house (part 3)
4 shoes that you wear inside (part 4)
5 sad because something you hoped for is different (part 5)

4 A multicultural wedding

Choose a person in the wedding picture and describe him or her. Your partner points.

> She's on the left. She's wearing a yellow dress and a red scarf. She has long black hair.

> That's Meera / Sunita / this woman here / ...

5 LIFE SKILLS Be a global citizen

a) **Meera and Ben have a wedding with Indian and British traditions. Can you think of people and things from different countries and cultures in your life? Think about:**

family and friends   favourite foods   favourite music, films and shows   things in your home

b) **Compare your ideas with the class.**

> My best friend is from Ukraine and I love Chinese food.

> I listen to American music and watch Japanese cartoons.

▶ Workbook, p. 68

 Digital quiz   **I can** talk about different cultures in my life.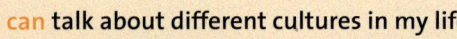

Brighton stories: Family and heritage[1]

1 Two truths[2] and a lie[3]

BEFORE YOU WATCH **Look at the sentences for Gloria, Emir and Daisy. Guess: Which sentence for each person is a lie?**

1 **Gloria**
   A Her dad is from Jamaica.
   B Her parents met in a skating[4] club.
   C Her mum is a hairdresser.

2 **Emir**
   A His sister only eats yellow food.
   B His mum has a tattoo on her foot.
   C His dad is Kurdish.

3 **Daisy**
   A Her great-great-grandma's name was Daisy.
   B Daisy and her mum both have blue eyes.
   C All her family has always lived in Brighton.

2 VIEWING Family people and places

a) **Watch the first part of the video. Check your answers from 1.**

b) **Watch part 2, Daisy's tour. Write the names of the four places that the kids visit. Add extra details if you can.**

c) **Watch part 2 again and check. Answer the questions.**

   1 What do Emir, Joe and Gloria say about Daisy's family history and her tour?
   2 What does Daisy think?

   She thought ..., but now she thinks ...

3 Now you

a) **Play the game 'Two truths and a lie'. Write three sentences about your family for your partner: One must be a lie. Your sentences can be about family, pets, food, hobbies, school, films, music, holidays, ... The sentences in 1 can help you.**

b) **Read out your sentences to your partner. Your partner guesses the lie!**

---

[1] **heritage** *die Vorfahren, die Familiengeschichte*   [2] **truth** *die Wahrheit*   [3] **lie** *die Lüge*   [4] **skating** *das Schlittschuhlaufen*

Prepare and practise a presentation

1 Make your slides

Finn has collected ideas for a presentation on the Elbhangfest. Now he is making his slides. Look at slide 1 and Scout's tips and help Finn make slide 2 better.

Remember: First collect ideas and put them in order. Then prepare your slides. Use:
- a big title
- big pictures and some colour
- short notes

1 **The Elbhangfest**
- big festival
- every summer
- hills of River Elbe, Dresden

2 At the Elbhangfest there are lots of cool activities and shows and great music concerts. You can eat lots of great food too.

2 Make cards with keywords

a) Finn has made a card with keywords to present slide 1 in class. What is he going to say?

b) Make a card with keywords for slide 2.

Slide 1
- *usually 20,000 – 50,000 people*
- *on (!) the last weekend in June*
- *Elbe area: big river, beautiful*
- *hills, castles (don't say the 't'!)*

3 Practise, practise, practise!

a) Decide which tips in the box are useful. Do you know other good tips?

▶ Wordbank 8, p. 220 ▶ Let's talk: Feedback, p. 227

b) You're presenting Finn's two slides. Practise with a partner. Your partner gives you feedback.

First, I'd like to talk about … Next …

Sorry, that's the wrong word. I mean …

Sorry, I've forgotten the word. It's when …

The picture shows …

c) Work on your presentation with your partner. Make it even better! ▶ Skills file 9 + 11, pp. 192 + 194

Good or bad tips?
1 Look at your cards all the time.
2 Don't look at your group.
3 Structure your presentation with useful phrases.
4 Speak loudly and clearly.
5 Don't smile.
6 Explain your pictures.
7 Practise your presentation in the mirror at home or record it: How do you look and sound?
8 Correct mistakes while you're speaking.
9 If you've forgotten a word, explain it.

Digital quiz  I can **prepare and practise a presentation.**

Present a celebration

Step 1: Think of a celebration

Think of a celebration in your area, your country or your family. The ideas in the box can help you.

> a birthday • Christmas • Halloween • Hanukkah • Oktoberfest • a school party or ceremony

Step 2: Collect ideas and organize them

Make notes about your celebration and organize them. Then think how to say them in class. ▶ Digital help 🔧

We have a party at school every year on 31 October.
I've worn a lot of different costumes: I've been a ghost, a …

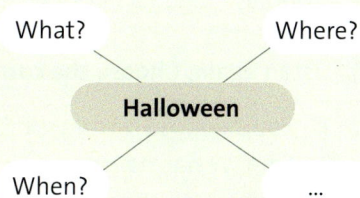

What?   Where?

Halloween

When?   …

Step 3: Make your slides and cards

a) **Make and design your slides.**
   Then make your cards with keywords.
   ▶ Study skills, p.130

💡 Add audio and visual effects to your slides: music, maybe a video, text effects, …

b) **Look at the checklist. Have you thought of everything? Think of useful phrases for your presentation.**

I'm going to talk about …
In this photo you can see …
▶ Digital help 🔧   ▶ Wordbank 8, p.220

Have you …
- put pictures on your slides?
- used short notes on your slides?
- made the text big enough?
- checked your spelling?
- made cards with keywords, tips and extra information?

Step 4: Practise your presentation

a) **Practise your presentation with a partner.**
   Give feedback.   ▶Let's talk: Feedback, p.227

You've done a great job! I've learned about a new celebration. But the text on your slides was a bit small.

b) **Use your partner's feedback to make your presentation better.**

Step 5: Present your celebration

a) **Present your celebration to a group.**

Have you ever seen the 'Karneval der Kulturen'?

b) **Talk about the celebrations in the presentations.**

No, I haven't. But it sounds really fun! I'd like to go there.

 Digital quiz 🔧   I can **present a celebration.** ✓

1 LISTENING A winter celebration

I can talk about celebrations.

a) BEFORE YOU LISTEN **Look at Zane's picture. What is he celebrating?**

Halloween   Bonfire night   a birthday

b) **Now listen. What do Finn and Zane talk about? Choose three topics from the box.**

clothes • food • games • history • music • weather

c) **Listen again. Choose the correct answers.**

1 Zane's photo is from A October B November C December.
2 Finn A has never heard B wants to know more C knows quite a lot about Bonfire Night.
3 Zane A always B sometimes C never celebrates at the same park.
4 Zane usually celebrates with A his friends B his sister C his mum, dad and sister.
5 When the weather is really cold, Zane A stays at home B still celebrates C doesn't enjoy it.

d) SPEAKING **What do you celebrate in the winter? Tell your partner about it. You can use the ideas below.**

I celebrate Christmas / Diwali / my dad's birthday / New Year's Eve / ... • We eat ... • I wear ...

I don't celebrate ..., but I celebrate ... • I also celebrate ... • We eat ... • I wear ...

2 LANGUAGE On the phone

I can describe a special meal (*some* and *any*, *a little* and *a few*).

Complete the sentences with *some*, *any*, *a little* or *a few*. Sometimes there are two possible answers.

Caller	Hi, we'd like ... (1) pizzas, please: one cheese, two vegetarian and two ham and tomatoes. Can we please also get ... (2) chips?
Restaurant	Sure! Would you like ... (3) sauces? And would you like ... (4) drinks?
Caller	We don't want ... (5) drinks, thank you. But we'd like ... (6) mayo.
Restaurant	Great. It will be ready in half an hour.

Check

3 MEDIATION **A message from Leon**

Read the message from Finn's friend Leon in Dresden. Answer Sunita's questions in English.

Hey Finn, tut mir leid, aber ich kann heute doch nicht mit dir und Sunita Computer spielen. 🙁 Meine Familie organisiert ein besonderes Essen für meine Schwester, da sie für einen Monat nach Frankreich fährt. Wir machen ein Picknick mit all ihren Lieblingsgerichten – Hühnercurry, Salat (ohne Tomaten!), verschiedene Käsesorten und Chips. Danach gibt's Obst mit Joghurt 😕 . Morgen Abend habe ich Zeit, oder am Wochenende. Wie sieht's bei euch aus?
Bis dann, Leon ✓

Sunita	Is Leon going to play with us tonight?
Finn	He can't because (1) …
Sunita	Ah, OK. Is it someone's birthday?
Finn	No, his sister is going (2) …
Sunita	What are they going to do?
Finn	They're going to have a picnic with (3) …
Sunita	Sounds nice! Can he play another time?
Finn	Yes, he can (4) …

4 LANGUAGE **Before the meal** | I can talk about preparations and experiences (present perfect).

a) It's the afternoon before the Eid meal. What have Zane and his family done?
Complete the sentences with past participles. The **green** verbs are irregular.

1 Zane's dad has … (pray).
2 And he has … (buy) some more rice.
3 Zane has … (prepare) a salad.
4 Holly has … (help) with the salad.

5 Holly and Zane have … (clean) some garden chairs.
6 Zane's parents have … (say) 'Eid Mubarak' to each other.

b) Complete the conversation. Use *have / haven't* and the past participle. The **green** verbs are irregular.

Dad	Zane, Holly, why are you watching TV?
Zane	We *'ve finished* (1 finish) all of the jobs, Dad! We're ready to go.
Holly	Yeah, Zane and I … (2 make) a really big salad!
Dad	We … (3 not finish) everything! The salad looks good, but we … (4 not make) the curry. Holly, you … (5 not clean) your shoes, and Zane, you … (6 not text) Grandpa to say thanks for the present.
Zane	I … (7 text) him! I can show you!
Holly	And I'm going to clean my shoes now!

Check 👆

5 READING Welcome to Brighton!

I can **talk about family celebrations.**

1

LILY *Hey, guys. I've had a busy afternoon. Check out the garden area near our flat.* ✓

SUNITA *Love it!! 😍 Are you having a party?* ✓

2

LILY *Yes, my aunt and uncle from Poland are coming to stay with us, so we're having a surprise party. They haven't visited us for a long time. A lot of family members are going to be there and we've invited some neighbours too.* ✓

ZANE *That's really cool. Surprise parties are the best. How are they going to find out about the party?* ✓

3

LILY *Well, Dad's going to meet them at the train station, and then he's going to take them back to the flat. He's going to say 'Oh no, I've lost my key! I think I left it in the garden.' When they get there, everyone is going to jump up and shout 'Welcome to Brighton!' I hope no one scares them too much!* ✓

ZANE *Great! You should take a photo of that moment!* ✓

NOAH *Have you made a cake, Lily?* ✓

4

LILY *My sister Chloe has made a cake. My job was to decorate the garden. And I need to find some good music.* ✓

SUNITA *Oh, for a disco?* ✓

5

LILY *Yes! We're going to have a silent disco. We want to dance, but we want our party to be quiet!* ✓

a) **Read the messages about Lily's party. True (T), false (F) or not in the text (NT)?**

1 Lily's aunt and uncle have never been to Brighton.
2 Lily's dad is going to tell them about the party.
3 The party is going to be in the flat.
4 Noah doesn't like surprise parties.
5 Lily is going to choose some songs.
6 Lily's party is going to be very loud.

b) WORDS **Complete the sentences with words from Lily's messages (1–5).**

1 When someone doesn't know about a party, it's a … (message 2)
2 When you're part of a family, you're a … of it. (message 2)
3 When you've asked someone to come to a party, you've … him/her. (message 2)
4 When you don't have something anymore, you've … it (message 3)
5 When you make someone feel shocked and worried, you … him/her. (message 3)

Check

6 WRITING A special thing

 I can talk about different cultures in my life.

a) Your English class is doing a project about different countries and cultures.
Think about a special thing from another country. Make notes first. You can use the ideas in the boxes.

What is it?	**Where is it from?**	**Why is it special?**
a book • a letter • a photo • a magazine • a song • a T-shirt • …	America • England • France • Japan • Poland • Turkey • …	beautiful • expensive • old • a present • …

b) Write your post for the project. You can start like this:

I'd like to tell you about a special person/thing …

7 STUDY SKILLS My dream festival

 I can prepare and practise a presentation.

a) Zeynep has made two slides and cards with keywords, tips and extra information for a presentation.
Partner A: Present slide A to your partner.
Partner B: Present slide B to your partner.

A

FunFest
- small garden party
- 1st August
- cool activities

– around 40 people (friends and family)
– under trees – perfect when hot
– on (!) the (!) first of (!) August
– We can do these activities:
  – dance competition (competISCHen)
  – yoga
  – henna painting

B

What we need
- decorations
- food and drink
- music

– decorations: floWers (no V sound!), ballOOns
– food: salad, sandwiches, sausages, cake, fruit
– drink: lemonade, juice, water
– cool music for party and dance competition (competISCHen)

b) Give feedback. You can use the ideas below.

	☺	☹
You looked …	at me.	at your cards.
You …	smiled.	didn't smile.
You spoke …	clearly / loudly.	very quietly / quickly / slowly.
I understood …	everything that you said.	most / some of what you said.

Check

VARNDEAN
Teen Zine

This month's topics: celebrations and food

Our school magazine: by students for students

Burning[1] the clocks

There's nothing more 'Brighton' than the *Burning the Clocks* festival! Every year on 21st December (the shortest day of the year) more than 20,000 people celebrate because the days start to get longer again. There are parades and music, and people have paper lanterns[2] in different shapes[3], especially clocks.

Kieron in 8B says, 'When I was little, I loved making a lantern and walking in the special children's parade. But now I just go with my friends to watch. I love the lights and, of course, drinking hot chocolate to keep warm!'

And the most beautiful part of the festival? At the end everybody goes to the beach and puts their lanterns on a big fire. Then there is an amazing firework show. Don't forget to send us your photos this year!

What languages do Varndean students and teachers speak?

Make a language cloud for your friends, family and neighbours!

French
Turkish
Hindi   Spanish
Polish   Arabic   Urdu
Romanian   English   German
Bengali   Mandarin

Healthy eating challenge

Can you tick all five boxes every day this week?
Then check out the video about English breakfasts.
What's your favourite breakfast?

- I have eaten **three** meals today: breakfast, lunch and dinner.
- I have eaten food of **four** different colours today.
- I have eaten **five** portions[4] of fruit and vegetables today.
- I have drunk **six** glasses of water today.
- I **haven't** had too much sugar today.

---

[1] (to) **burn** *(ver)brennen*   [2] **lantern** *die Laterne*   [3] **shape** *die Form*   [4] **portion** *die Portion*

Varndean students' special meals

Sarah: For Hanukkah my grandma makes these amazing latkes – they're special potato pancakes and we eat them with apple sauce.

Mei-Lin: In my family it's not a party if my dad hasn't cooked Chinese food! His special rice with chicken, egg and vegetables is just the best!

Puzzle time

Match the English words to the languages where they come from. What other English words do you know that come from other languages? Find the answers on p. 313.

1c, …

1 broccoli   2 sushi   3 marmalade   a German   b French   c Italian

4 restaurant   5 cookie   6 coffee   d Turkish   e Japanese   f Dutch

E-postcard from the USA

This month Lea writes about American food. Find the answers on p. 313.

Hi, everyone!

I miss British food sometimes (especially fish and chips on the beach), but wow – the food here is amazing! Before I thought American food was just burgers, but people eat food from lots of different cultures. I think my favourite is Mexican food. There's a small restaurant near our house which sells the best tacos and guacamole ever!

American restaurants are a bit different to British ones. You usually get free water with lots of ice. And it's very important to give the waiter[1] or waitress some extra money, called a 'tip'[2].

Can you solve my maths puzzle?
It's polite to tip 20% of the total bill[3]. So:
1) bill = $30   tip = $???   2) bill = $55   tip = $???

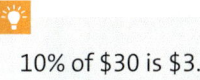

10% of $30 is $3.

---

[1] **waiter, waitress** *der Kellner, die Kellnerin*   [2] **tip** *das Trinkgeld*   [3] **bill** *die Rechnung*

Partner page

▶ Page 120

👥 7 Getting ready

a) **Partner B:** Write what Nish says to Sunita. Use **'ve / haven't** and the past participle.

> I (1 find) *have found* some nice clothes for the wedding. But I (2 not get) … a tie yet. I (3 invite) … my girlfriend. But I (4 not talk) … to her about it yet. I (5 find) … some great music for the wedding. I (6 buy) … a present for Mum and Ben.

b) Your partner tells you what Sunita has done. Tell your partner what Nish has done. Say what they've both done. *Nish has / hasn't … They've both …*

Diff bank

▶ Page 113

More practice 1 **Celebration words**

a) Write the celebration words for the pictures.

b) Start a 'celebrations' page in your Vocab file. Decide how to organize it: Make lists under umbrella words (*decorations, food, activities …*), a mind map or example sentences. Add more words from the unit.

▶ Skills file 11, p. 194

▶ Page 115

More practice 2 **Two dishes**

a) **Look at the pictures and complete the description of the two dishes. Use the words in the boxes. There are three extra words in each box.**

bread • ham • noodles • peas • potatoes • sauce • spices • tomatoes • whipped cream

A This is a delicious curry with ... (1) and ... (2). You make the ... (3) with a tin of ... (4) and lots of ... (5). Eat it with rice or ... (6).

carrot • chicken • lemon • melon • noodles • oil • pepper • salad • yoghurt

B You make this ... (7) with a pot of ... (8) and some ... (9). It tastes great with a green ... (10) with some ... (11) and salt and ... (12).

b) **Talk to your partner about food.**
Which dish in a) would you like to eat? Why?
What kinds of food do you often eat? Why?
What don't you eat or like? Why?

Phrases

I'd like to try ... because I like ... •
I often eat ... because I like ... •
I don't eat/like ... because I don't like ... /
I'm allergic to ...

▶ Wordbank 7, p. 219

More practice 3 **Odd word out**

a) **Which is the odd word in the group?**

1 a bottle of ice cream / water / cola / lemonade
2 a pot of cream / milk / soup / yoghurt
3 a carton of eggs / juice / milk / chicken
4 a packet of popcorn / bread / pasta / water
5 a jar of butter / honey / tomato sauce / jam
6 a tin of tomatoes / cheese / fish / fruit
7 a piece of cake / bread / meat / rice

b) **Write another 'odd word out' group for a partner.**

▶ Page 117

More practice 4 **Thanks, Black Bird!**

Look at the picture. Complete what Scout says to Black Bird. Use *some, any, a little* **or** *a few.*

1 I'd like … sausages – not many, only two or three.
2 I'd like … orange juice – a small carton of orange juice, please.
3 I don't want … salad. I don't like salad.
4 The fruit looks nice – I'd like … strawberries. A lot of strawberries, please.
5 And can I have … cheese? Not much.
6 And I'd like … cake – lots of cake! I love cake!

Are you hungry? What would you like?

More practice 5 SHOWTIME **A dinner talk**

With one or more partners, practise a conversation like the one in 7a). Add to the dialogue: welcome the guests, tell them a little about the meal, etc. You can use weird or horrible foods and funny reactions. Act it out for the class.

Use props like knives and forks or draw pictures of your food.

A Welcome to our Halloween / … dinner. We have …, … and … Would you like some chicken eyes with chocolate sauce?
B No, thank you!!!
   …

More help **8** MY TASK **An invitation to a special meal**

It's	my favourite food / a family recipe / a famous dish from Syria / …	
It's a kind of	pasta / rice / vegetable / meat / … dish.	
It's a	hot / cold / German / Indian / vegan / … dish.	
There's	a little / a lot of	cheese / cream / fruit / sauce / … in it.
There are	a few / a lot of	spices / vegetables / … in it.
You eat it with	bread / cheese / chocolate sauce / potatoes / rice / salad / yoghurt / …	
It's	delicious / spicy / sweet / …	

▶Page 120

More practice 6 **be – was – been**

🔊 a) Look at the forms of the irregular verbs in the box and listen.

🔊 b) Listen again. Clap the rhythm and repeat.

💡

Learn the three forms of an irregular verb together.
Learn forms with similar sounds or similar spelling together.
Say them out loud.

be – was – been
see – saw – seen

come – came – come
do – did – done

buy – bought – bought
think – thought – thought

get – got – got
lose – lost – lost

More practice 7 **Run and say**

a) Your teacher has put notes with some sentences on the walls. Partner A runs to a note, tries to remember the sentence and then tells partner B. Partner B writes the sentence on a piece of paper. Take turns.

b) Together, put the sentences in the correct order and practise the conversation.

That's a cool activity! You can cut the paper into pieces and move the sentences around!

Challenge 1 **The happiest student**

a) Think of reasons why you're happy – they can be true or false.

I've won a competition. My sister has left home and I've got her room./...

b) Tell the group. The group decides on the happiest student.

Challenge 2 **My day so far**

a) Look at the cartoon and Scout's speech bubble. Then write three sentences about your day so far. Use the present perfect and *just*, *already* and *yet*.

b) Make a cartoon with a speech bubble with your sentences.

*I've just had breakfast.
I've already brushed my feathers.
But I haven't picked a hat yet.*

▶ Page 121

Challenge 3   **Yes, I have!**

a) Write as many questions with *Have you ever …?* as you can. You want your partner to say *Yes, I have.* to all your questions.

b) Ask your questions. Write a tick ✓ or a cross ✗ for the answers. Answer your partner's questions.

c) Count your ticks. The partner with the most *yes*-answers is the winner!

> Have you ever eaten cheese?

> Yes, I have. / No, I haven't.

More help   **11**   QUIZ   **Have you ever …?**

Have you ever	been	skiing?
	eaten	chips with cheese?
	had	an amazing dream?
	found	an exciting thing?
	given	money to charity?
	met	your hero?
	ridden	a horse?
	seen	a whale?
	swum	in the sea?
	won	a competition?

> Have you ever ridden a horse?

> No, I haven't.

> Have you ever swum in the sea?

> Yes, I have.

More practice 8   SONG   **Have you ever, ever, ever …?**

a) Look at the words of a traditional English children's song. Then listen and sing.

> I have you ever, ever, ever in your long-legged life
> seen a long-legged sailor with a long-legged wife?
> – No, I've never, never, never in my long-legged life
> seen a long-legged sailor with a long-legged wife.

b) In a group, think of a new verse. Change the words in blue.

c) Sing your new verse to the class.

► Page 123

More practice 9 **I've looked everywhere!**

Complete what Scout says. Use the words in the box.

> anyone • anywhere • ~~everywhere~~ • nothing •
> someone • somewhere

Oh no, I've looked *everywhere* (1), but I can't find my invitation to the party ... (2). Has ... (3) seen it? It must be here ... (4). I've looked in my bag, but there's ... (5) in there. You see, ... (6) has invited me to a party, but I can't remember where it is. And I still need to buy a present!

► Page 124

More help **4** MY TASK **Our favourite family parties**

Why did you have a party? / What did you celebrate?
What did you do / eat / wear?
Where was the party? Was it in a hall / at home / at a restaurant?
Did you dance / eat cake / play games / sing karaoke / watch fireworks / wear a costume?
Who came to the party?

► Page 128

Challenge 4 **Ben's story**

Read the story again on pages 126–127.
Help Ben explain to Meera what happened.

Meera	Well, we did it! So come on, now you can tell me why you're wearing your slippers.
Ben	Oh, it's so embarrassing!
Meera	Haha, you can't keep any secrets from your wife!
Ben	That's true!
	OK, well, first of all, I didn't get up late! I ...
	Willow showed me ...
	Then suddenly, ...
	But the problem was ...
	So then ...
	But in the end ...

Unit 5
Getting ready for the future

1 LISTENING **After the year 8 assembly**

a) BEFORE YOU LISTEN **Some Varndean parents talked about their jobs at assembly. Match photos A–H to the jobs in the box. Then check in class.**

> artist • builder • cook •
> firefighter • hairdresser • mechanic •
> nurse • programmer

b) **Listen to the conversation between the kids and put the photos in the correct order:** *1C, 2 …*

c) **Listen again and take notes. Give as much information as you can.**

Sunita: liked firefighter, …   *Lily: aunt is a …*   *Zane: …*   *Noah: …*

▶ Skills file 6, p. 189

Nach dieser Unit kann ich ...

- über verschiedene Berufe sprechen
- meine Zukunft beschreiben
- über Arbeiten im Haushalt sprechen
- über Geld und Einkaufen sprechen
- geschriebene Texte überprüfen

Unit task

- Spaß-Horoskope schreiben

2 My friends' and family's jobs

a) **Who do you know with one of the jobs in 1? Tell your partner.**

I know a / an ...
My cousin / neighbour / ... is a / an ...
My uncle / friend / ... works in a / an ...
I don't know any cooks / ... What about you? ▶ Wordbank 9, p. 221

 Always use a or an
with jobs:
My cousin is a dancer.
My mum is an artist.

b) **Make small groups. One student mimes a job. The other students guess.**

Are you a / an ...?   *Yes, that's right! / No, that's wrong.*

▶ Workbook, p. 76

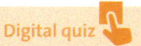 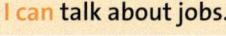

Future jobs and plans

1 READING Then and now

a) BEFORE YOU READ The kids are talking to their friend Ava at school.
Say which jobs you think Sunita, Lily, Zane and Noah want to do. Then read and check.

Lily Hey, Ava, how's it going? We're just talking about what we wanted to be when we were little. I remember you wanted to be a nurse, right?

Ava Ha, yes: You're right! I wanted to look after people. But now I think that I want to work for an animal charity. What about you?

Lily I wanted to be a police officer. But now I want to be a firefighter like my aunt.

Ava Oh yeah, you're really strong and good at climbing! And you, Noah?

Noah Well, I've always loved trains so I wanted to be a train driver. But now I think it's better to be a vet because I love animals – especially my dog.

Sunita That's true, but it's a lot of work too – ask my mum! When I was little, I wanted to be an architect, but now I want to be a gamer so I can play games all day.

Zane Cool! Well, when I was little, I really wanted to be a famous footballer. But it's no surprise that I want to be a cook now.

Sunita Well, I hope we can eat for free in your restaurant, Zane!

b) **Read the text again and choose the correct person for each question.**

1 Who wanted to work in a hospital?
2 Who wants to do the same job as somebody in her family?
3 Who loves trains?
4 Who says that being a vet is hard work?
5 Who wanted to be a sportsperson?

▶ More practice 1, p. 171

2 WORDS Secret sentences

a) **Copy and complete the sentences on a piece of paper. You can also use a dictionary.**

When I was little, I wanted to be a / an ... Now I want to be a / an ...

▶ Skills file 3, p. 186
▶ Wordbank 9, p. 221

b) **Your teacher collects the sentences and reads one out. Guess who wrote it. The student who wrote the sentence reads the next one.**

▶ Workbook, p. 77

3 SONG **Hey, world!**

a) BEFORE YOU LISTEN Look at the song lyrics with the pictures of five jobs on the right. What do you think these jobs are? Write the jobs.

b) Listen to the song. Did you write the correct jobs?   ▶ Skills file 6, p. 189

c) Look at the lyrics. Choose the best new title for the song.

1 I know what I want to be
2 I can do anything
3 I'm scared about my future

d) Look at the five jobs from the song again. What strengths must you have for these jobs? The words in the box can help you.

> be brave • be creative • be strong • be good at biology • be good at maths • be good at planning • be good with language • have good ideas • like animals • like designing things • like machines • work well in a team • …

A / An … must …

In the future maybe I'll be a … *(1)*.
My friends, they won't believe it
when I'm a famous … *(2)*.
Maybe I'll be a star!
If I work hard, I'll go far.
Or maybe I'll be a … *(3)*.
I haven't made my mind up yet.

But I'll be, yeah, I'll be anything I want to be.
So you'll see:
Hey, world — look out for me!

Oh, the girl who is cool and rules the school —
She'll show me respect.
When I'm a business owner or an … *(4)*.
I'm also strong and good at maths —
I'll make a great … *(5)*.
And if things go wrong sometimes,
I won't panic.

No, 'cause I'll be, yeah, I'll be
anything I want to be.
Everyone, they'll see:
Hey, world — look out for me!

Good to know

Lots of jobs end in *-er*:

build ▶ builder	game ▶ gamer
drive ▶ drive	sing ▶ singer
football ▶ footballer	write ▶ writer

In English you usually use the same words for jobs for men and women:

She's a firefighter.
He's a firefighter.
They're both firefighters!

For some jobs, there are different words for men and women, but these days people often try to use the same word for everyone:
policeman / policewoman ▶ police officer

▶ Workbook, p. 77

Erklär-film

4 LOOKING AT LANGUAGE **The will-future**

a) Listen to the song from **3** again. Put up your hand when you hear a word ending with the short form *'ll* or the word *won't*.

> *The other birds say I won't be a famous singer, but they'll see. I'll earn a lot of money. George will be my biggest fan and Black Bird will work as my manager!*

b) Find phrases with *'ll* and *won't* in the song on **p. 147** and with *will* in Scout's speech bubble. Complete the rules.

Wir verwenden das *will-future*, um Vorhersagen oder Handlungen in der ... zu beschreiben.

Das *will-future* bilden wir mit:

I
you
he / she / it ➕ ... / ... (bejahte Sätze) ➕ Grundform (Infinitiv)
we   ... (verneinte Sätze)   des Verbs *(be / do / go /*
you   *have / like / live /*
they   *show / ...)*

Die Langform *(will)* und die Kurzform *('ll)* bedeuten dasselbe.

Die Langform verwendet man meist mit Namen und Nomen:
George will be ...

In verneinten Sätzen verwendet man meist die Kurzform *won't (= will not).*

▶ Language file 18, p. 209

---

5 Crazy predictions

a) Write an example of:

| 1 | a job | 3 | a number | 5 | a colour | 7 | a day of the week |
| 2 | a city | 4 | someone in your class | 6 | an adjective | 8 | a verb |

1 firefighter   2 ...

▶ Grammatical terms, p. 211

b) Add your answers from **a)** to the text on **p. 170** and read it to your partner. Who has the funnier prediction?

▶ More practice 2, p. 171   ▶ Challenge 1, p. 171

▶ Workbook, p. 78

6 READING Finn's poster

be (2x) • go • hang out • have • have children • live (2x) • make • surf • work (2x)

a) Class 8C has made posters about their dream future. Complete Finn's poster. Use the words from the box with *'ll* or *won't*.

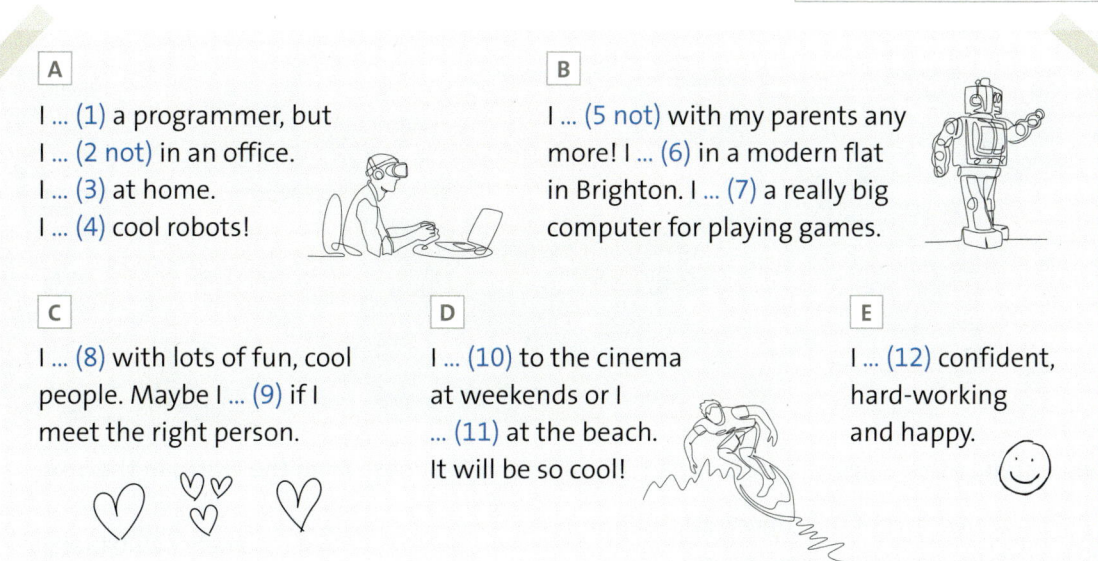

A
I ... (1) a programmer, but
I ... (2 not) in an office.
I ... (3) at home.
I ... (4) cool robots!

B
I ... (5 not) with my parents any more! I ... (6) in a modern flat in Brighton. I ... (7) a really big computer for playing games.

C
I ... (8) with lots of fun, cool people. Maybe I ... (9) if I meet the right person.

D
I ... (10) to the cinema at weekends or I ... (11) at the beach. It will be so cool!

E
I ... (12) confident, hard-working and happy.

b) Match the headings to the correct letters (A–E) in Finn's poster. There are two extra headings.

Family and friends   Hobbies   Home   Job   Personality   Pets   Travels

My task

7 A poster about my dream future

a) WRITING Make a poster about your dream future like Finn's poster in 6. Write sentences and draw pictures for each heading.

I'll be / go / have / live / work / ...
I won't be / go / have / live / work / ...
Maybe / I think I'll / I think / I won't / ... ► More help, p. 172

b) GALLERY WALK Look at all the posters. Write feedback and positive comments. Put your poster in your DOSSIER.

Yes, you can do it!   *I think you'll be famous!*   *I love the pictures.*

If you imagine being successful, maybe it will come true! Put your poster on your wall at home and imagine your dream future.

► Digital help

► Workbook, pp. 78–79

Jobs at home

1 LISTENING Look at this room!

a) BEFORE YOU LISTEN **Look at the picture. What can you see?**

b) **Listen to the conversation. Complete the sentences. Choose from the words in the box.**

1 At the start of the conversation, Sunita is …
2 Willow is … at the beginning.
3 After Sunita's explanation, Willow feels …
4 When Sunita asks her about chores, Willow is …
5 At the end, Sunita feels …

> angry • embarrassed •
> happy • surprised •
> unhappy

c) **Listen again. Say who …**

1 … folds jeans, T-shirts and other things.
2 … washes clothes.
3 … looks after the family's pet.
4 … takes out the rubbish.
5 … cleans the toilet and shower.
6 … does the shopping and works in the garden.

2 WORDS More chores

Complete each chore with the correct verb from the box. There are two extra words.

> babysit • empty • make • set •
> take out • vacuum • wash

1 … my little brother
2 … my bed
3 … the table
4 … the dishwasher
5 … the floors

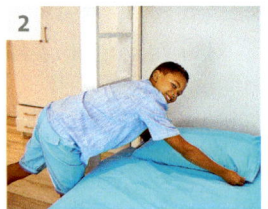

▶ More practice 3, p. 172
▶ Workbook, p. 80

3 SPEAKING **Chores in class 8C**

a) **Look at the chart.**
What does it show?

It shows the number of … in class …
and the … that they have to do.

b) **How many students have to**
do each chore?

24 students have to make their bed.
24 students have to …
One student has to fold clean clothes.
One student has to …

c) **There are 30 students in 8C.**
How many students *don't have to*
do each chore?

Six students don't have to make …
Eleven students don't have to set …

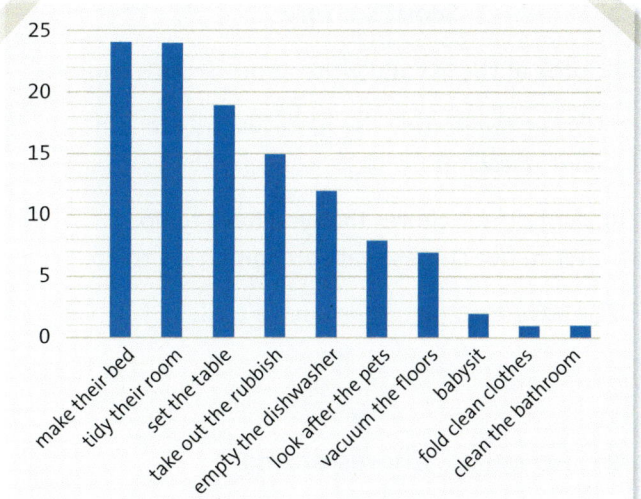

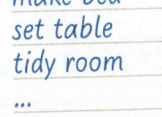 *(lightbulb icon)*

You have to eat / go / … = Du **musst** essen / gehen / …
You don't have to eat / go / … = Du **musst nicht** …
(= Du **brauchst nicht** zu …)

 (lightbulb icon)

A bar chart has a horizontal axis (also called the X-axis) at the bottom and a vertical axis (the
Y-axis) on the left.
A longer bar means a larger number of the thing on the bar. You can look at a bar chart and see
what things are larger and what things are smaller.

4 **A chore chart**

a) **Make a list of the chores from the chart in 3a).**

b) **How many students in your class do each chore?**
Write the number next to each chore.

make bed
set table
tidy room
…

Do you have to set the table?
Put up your hands.

… students have to …
One student has to …

c) **Make a chart as in 3 for your class. Use paper with squares.**
The highest number on the Y-axis is the number of students in your class.

d) **Add bars to each chore. Each bar shows the number of students from 4b).**

e) **Talk about your chart. What is the chore that the most students have to do?**
How many students don't have to do each chore? Put the charts in your DOSSIER.

▶ Workbook, pp. 81–82

5 WRITING Scout's chores

a) Look at the list and write about Scout's chores.

Scout has to tidy her nest. She has to …
She doesn't have to …

b) Write three chores that you have to do.
Write five chores that you don't have to do.

I have to …   I don't have to …

- tidy my nest ✓
- take out the rubbish ✓
- find food ✓
- go to the supermarket ✗
- make dinner ✗
- set the table ✗

▶ More practice 4, p. 172   ▶ Challenge 2, p. 173   ▶ Wordbank 10, p. 222

---

6 SHOWTIME Chores drama

a) WRITING With a partner, write a dialogue between a parent and a child about chores.
Use the phrases below. Be careful: Use the correct form of the verbs.
Find a good ending for the dialogue: Do parent and child agree?

Partner A (parent)	Partner B (child)
• Can you please …?	• Why do I have to …?
• It's your turn to …	I'm reading / playing / … now!
• Yes, but your brother / sister has to …	• I … yesterday. I also …
and … today.	• I'll … in an hour / tonight / tomorrow / …!
• You won't have time to …	• No, I don't have to … tomorrow:
You have to …	That's on Tuesday.

b) Act out your role-play for the class. Use your voice and face to show how your character feels:
friendly, tired, angry …

My task

7 My chores

a) Tell a partner about your chores at home. Use your sentences from 5b).

I have to … / I don't have to …

b) WALK AROUND Your teacher says a number. Make groups with that number of students.
Tell your group what chores you don't mind and what chores you hate.

I have to empty the dishwasher, but I don't mind that.
I have to take out the rubbish. I hate that!

c) Make a top three each of the chores that you like and hate most.   ▶ Digital help

Digital quiz 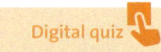   **I can talk about chores.** ✓

Background file

1 READING Typical British shops

a) BEFORE YOU READ **With a partner, talk about the shops in the photos. Describe what you see.**

b) **Read the texts.**

1 Corner shops

Sometimes you have to buy things at the last moment: milk, pens, birthday cards, bananas, magazines, bread, umbrellas, pet food. That's when corner shops can be really useful. They sell lots of different things, there's always one near you, and they're open from early till late.

2 Sweet shops

Is this a dream? No, it's a sweet shop. Every British town has them and they're very special. Inside you can see hundreds of big glass jars with sweets in different colours and sizes. Some sweets are round, some look like fruit, others are like mice or little cola bottles. The shop assistant mixes them just for you and puts them in a little bag: three of these and two of those. That makes shopping here a really fun experience.

3 Charity shops

Most British towns have a lot of charity shops. Each shop makes money for one charity, for example to help animals or children. They sell clothes, games, books and many other things. Nearly everything is second-hand and doesn't cost much, so a visit to a charity shop is always an adventure. What can you find today? A nice jacket? A special present for someone? You never know.

c) **Where can you hear these sentences? Match each sentence below to one of the shops above.**

A Five of those green snakes, please.
B Excuse me, how much does this skirt cost?
C I'm glad you have rice! I need some for a recipe.

D Do you have any cheaper cat food?
E This is nice. It looks as good as new.
F They're in the jar at the left on the top shelf.

▶ Workbook, p. 82

Spend or save?

1 READING UK kids and money

 **a)** BEFORE YOU READ **How do you get money or treats?**
Tell a partner three ways. Use the box or your own ideas.

I sell old video games and trainers.
I get a treat like a film night when I help at home.

b) **Read the left part of the article.**
Say what's interesting or surprising for you.

It's interesting / surprising that a lot of kids
buy / save / shop / use …

> **Money**
> - on birthday / holiday
> - sell old things
> - do chores / babysit

> **Treats**
> - parents pay for phone
> - grandparents buy snacks
> - extra screen time
> - stay up late

---

www.pocket-money-uk.example.com

Top 3 things that UK kids buy
1 video / online games
2 sweets and chocolates
3 books and magazines

How UK kids shop
online with parents 40%
in shops 60%

How much UK kids save
UK kids save 39% of their money.

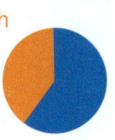

Pocket money apps
61% of UK kids use a pocket money app.
Sources: NatWest Rooster Money,
The Fintech Times

Spotlight on Molly (14)
My parents put pocket money for
me on a card every month. I use the
card to pay in shops and to get
cash at a cash machine. I also walk
my neighbour's dog for extra money.

I can see what I spend on the card's app. I buy a lot
of second-hand clothes. When they're too small or
I don't like them any more, I sell them. I also spend
money on books and swimming and going to
cafes with my friends.

My parents say it's my money, but I mustn't
buy too much fast food and I mustn't spend
it all: I have to save something every month.
I put some money in a savings account at the
bank and I also put some coins in a piggy bank at home.

Sources: https://roostermoney.com/pocket-money-index-uk (10.11.2022)
https://thefintechtimes.com/61-of-uk-children-use-an-app-to-manage-pocket-money (10.11.22)

---

c) **Read 'Spotlight on Molly'. True or false? Correct the false sentences.**

1　Molly gets pocket money and extra money.
2　Molly's parents give her the pocket money in cash.
3　She uses a card to buy things to wear.
4　They don't want her to spend a lot on fast food.
5　Molly saves all of her money in the bank.

d) WORDS **Find all the money words in the article:** *buy, save …*
Make a 'money' page in your VOCAB FILE.

▶ More practice 5, p. 173
▶ Workbook, p. 83

2 SPEAKING **Your money**

a) THINK **You get €20 for your birthday. What do you do with it?**

▶ More help, p. 173

I spend the €20 on … / I buy … / I save some of it / a little / …
My parents say I mustn't buy … / spend it on …

b) PAIR **Tell a partner. Listen to your partner and take notes.**

c) SHARE **Tell the class what your partner does with the €20.**

Leonie loves painting and she spends most of her money on that.

3 WORDS **Shops and shopping**

a) **You buy shoes at a shoe shop and a clock at a clock shop. What are the names of the shops for the things in the box?**

bikes • clothes • pets • sweets • toys

b) **Choose the correct names from the box for each shop.**

bakery • bookshop • charity shop •
electronics shop • gift shop • newsagent's

c) **What are your favourite shops? What do they sell?**

My favourite shop is a newsagent's near me. It sells magazines and chocolate.

d) **Choose the best words and phrases for you in sentences 1–5. Tell your partner.** ☒ **Add more information.**

1 I go to a bakery every day / every week / every month.
2 I like / don't like / hate shopping.
3 I often / sometimes / never go shopping with my friends.
4 I / My parents / My friends choose my clothes.
5 I dress smartly / comfortably / expensively.

▶ More practice 6 + 7, p. 174   ▶ Language file 19 + 20, pp. 209–210

Place before time:

I go to a pet shop every week.

I often buy something at the bakery after school.

▶ Workbook, pp. 83–84

4 VIEWING Shopping

a) BEFORE YOU WATCH **Look at the box.
Then take turns and say prices 1–6.**

1	£9.99	3	£12.95	5	£4.50
2	32p	4	£6.75	6	£38.99

b) Lily's cousin Theo is looking for some clothes.
Watch the video. What kind of shop is it?

A a sports shop
B a second-hand clothes shop
C a clothes shop with expensive brands

c) Watch again and say what Theo buys: size, colour, price.

d) Copy phrases 1–10 below. Watch the video again and complete the phrases.
Who says the sentences and questions: the customer or the shop assistant?

Starting to shop
1 Hello, can I ... you?   2 I'm just ...

Asking for help and trying on
3 Could you ... me, please?
4 Can I ... it on?
5 The changing ... is over there.
6 How ... is it?   7 I'll ... this.

Paying and leaving
8 Do you want to buy a ...?
9 Would you like to pay by ... or cash?
10 ... your change and your receipt.

*That donut is sixty-five pence –
or sixty-five 'p'. And that sandwich is
two pounds twenty.*

5 That T-shirt is too big

a) **Look at the picture. Which words in blue
do we use when something is near?
And when something is further away?**

b) **Theo has found a shirt and some trousers in
another shop. Complete his questions with
this, *that*, *these* and *those*.**

1 What size is ... shirt?
2 Can I try on ... trousers?
3 How much is ... blue jacket over there?
4 Do you have ... shoes over there in black?

▶ More practice 8, p.174

*This T-shirt is your size.
These trainers are £15.*

*That T-shirt is too big.
Those trainers are £30.*

6 MEDIATION AND SPEAKING In a gift shop

a) Finn is helping a German tourist in a shop in Brighton. Complete the conversation.

Assistant	Hello, can I help you?
Tourist	Hallo, äh, ich meine hello. Äh …
Finn	Kann ich Ihnen helfen? Ich spreche Englisch.
Tourist	Danke, gern. Ich hätte gern dieses T-Shirt, aber in einer kleineren Größe, für meine Frau.
Finn	She'd like to buy …
Assistant	We only have this T-shirt in M and L.
Finn	Sie haben …
Tourist	Dann nehme ich es in M. Was kostet das?
Finn	…

Assistant	It's £14.99. Does she want to pay by card or cash?
Finn	Es … £14.99. Möchten Sie …?
Tourist	Alles klar. Ich möchte mit Karte zahlen. Und ich möchte bitte eine Tüte kaufen.
Finn	That's fine. She'd like to … and …

▶ Skills file 8, p. 191

b) SPEAKING **Partner B: Look at p. 170.**
Partner A: You're an assistant in a gift shop. Read the card and think how to say your parts. Then have a conversation with your customer (partner B).
You start.

Say hello and ask if you can help.
Say the price of the postcards is 40p each.
Say the shorts cost £16.50.
Say you're sorry, you don't have the orange shorts in M. But you have size M in red.
Ask how the customer wants to pay.
Give the customer the change. Say goodbye.

My task

7 GAME Buy and sell

a) Make two groups: buyers and sellers.
Sellers: Look at p. 170.
Buyers: Choose a shopping list.

b) WALK AROUND You have £30. To win, you have to buy everything on your list and have the most money left.

Hello. / Excuse me. Do you have …?
How much is it? / How much are they?
Sorry, that's too expensive. I'll give you …

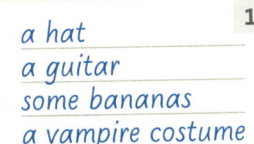

1
a hat
a guitar
some bananas
a vampire costume

2
a mirror
a skateboard
a packet of biscuits
some shoes

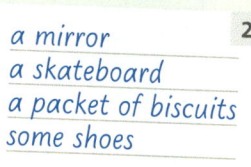

3
a swimsuit
a robot
some headphones
a bottle of water

4
a drone
some sunglasses
a bike helmet
a cushion

▶ Workbook, p. 84

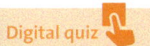 Digital quiz **I can** talk about money and shopping.

Goodbye, everybody!

1 READING Ava's great idea

a) BEFORE YOU READ **Look at the pictures and make notes: Which students can you see? Describe what they are doing. What's Ava's great idea?** ▶ Skills file 5, p. 188

In the first / second / ... picture I can see ...
Ava and Sunita are ... Finn is ...
I think Ava's great idea is to ...

b) **Read the story. Check your ideas from a).** ▶ Skills file 7, p. 190

1 Ava wants to make money for an animal charity. But what can she do? She's creative and good at baking. She's good at listening to people too.

I know – I'll sell cupcakes! Maybe Zane will help me to bake them.

2

On Saturday Ava's dad takes her to the park. Sunita helps Ava to sell the cupcakes. A friendly woman in a blue dress buys two ... and then comes back and buys two more.

3 After an hour Ava has already sold a lot of cupcakes. Her dad has gone back home to bring some more and Ava is waiting for him.

It's me, Ava! When will you be here?

What? I can't hear you. Could you say that again?

OK, Dad. See you soon!

4 The other friends come to the park too. Finn has to go back to Germany soon. Sunita will miss him a lot.

I'll miss everybody in Brighton – especially you, Sunita.

Lily comes with big news. **5**

My dad has a new job in London. We have to move.

Lily's dad doesn't have to work such long hours in the new job, but Lily doesn't want to leave her friends.

6

Don't be sad. It will be an adventure. And I'll come and visit you.

Ava's dad has come back with more cupcakes. Just then Zane arrives at the park. Ava gives him a cupcake to say thank you. **7**

Thanks for your help with the cupcakes, Zane.

You're welcome! It was fun.

8

Are you OK, Noah?

Not really. My parents follow me everywhere – so annoying!

My parents do that too. Look, there's my father now! But they also help me when I need it. Have a cupcake!

Noah wants to be more independent.

The woman in the blue dress buys ten more cupcakes and puts £100 into Ava's bowl. She gives Ava her business card. **9**

I have a bakery. Maybe you'd like to learn more about baking?

10

Well done, Ava! You've made £137.20 for the charity!

Everyone is happy for Ava, but a little worried about all of the changes in their lives. How will their summer holidays be? What will things be like in the new school year?

2 The students in the story

a) Match the six students in the story and their situations.

1 ... has to move to a new city.
2 ... wants to do things alone.
3 ... has to go back to another city.

4 ... enjoyed helping a friend.
5 ... wants to help a charity.
6 ... will miss two good friends.

▶ More practice 9, p. 175

b) Complete Ava's phone call with her dad. Use picture 3 on p. 158 to help you. Then read it with your partner.

Dad	Hello.
Ava	Hi, Dad. ...
Dad	In about five minutes.
Ava	What? ...
Dad	I'll be there in five minutes, Ava.
Ava	OK, Dad, ...

When you make a phone call
Say hello and who you are:
Hi / Hello! It's ...
If the connection is bad, say:
I can't hear you. / Can you hear me?
Ask for the other person to repeat something:
Could you say that again, please?
Say goodbye:
Bye! / See you soon! / See you later!

3 Ava's phone call

Read the first part of the phone call. Put the rest (a–h) in the correct order: *1h, 2...*
Then read the call together.

	Sara	Hello, this is Sara Osman.
	Ava	Hello, Ms Osman. This is Ava Burt. You bought some cupcakes from me.
a	Ava	Sorry, I can't hear you. Could you say that again, please?
b	Sara	I'd love to help, Ava! Can ... bakery ... Tuesday?
c	Ava	I'm fine, thank you. I'd like to learn more about baking – can you help me?
d	Sara	OK, see you on Tuesday. Bye, Ava.
e	Sara	I said that I'd love to help. Can you come to my bakery after school on Tuesday?
f	Ava	Goodbye.
g	Ava	Yes, I can. Tuesday is fine.
h	Sara	Yes, I remember. Hello, Ava. How are you?

▶ More practice 10, p. 175

4 LIFE SKILLS Know your strengths

a) Ava is creative and good at baking and listening to people. On a piece of paper, make a list of things that you're good at. You can use a dictionary.

▶ Wordbank 2, p. 214

b) In groups, each student reads out a different list. The group says who it is. Say more strengths for each student.

You're also clever and good at solving problems.

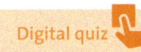 Digital quiz   **I can understand and talk about people's strengths.**

Brighton stories: Chores

1 Emir's chores

BEFORE YOU WATCH **Gloria, Daisy
and Joe want to watch a marathon[1]
with Emir, but Emir has to finish his
chores.
What do you think he has to do?
You have one minute: Write a list.**

2 VIEWING **Help with chores**

a) **Watch the video and answer the questions:**

1   What's Emir's first chore?
2   How do they make the chores fun?
3   What's the second chore?
4   Who helps Emir do his chores?

b) **Copy the notes for chores 1 and 2 below. Then watch the video again and complete them.**

Chore 1
aim[2]: …
timekeeper[3]: …
will get extra points if …
winner: …
reason: …

Chore 2
winner so far: …
will lose if …

c) **What does Emir think would be another good idea?**

3 My opinion

a) **Daisy, Emir, Gloria and Joe did three competitions:
holiday experiences (p. 29), street dancing (p. 63) and chores (this page).
Say which one you liked best and why.**

b) **Brainstorm other competitions for the kids. Then choose the best one.**

---

[1] **marathon** *der Marathon(lauf)*   [2] **aim** *das Ziel*   [3] **timekeeper** *der Zeitnehmer, die Zeitnehmerin*

▶ Workbook, p. 85

Check your writing

1 Use a checklist

a) Finn is back in Germany. Read his letter to Sunita. What will Finn miss in Brighton?

b) Correct or make the underlined parts better. Use the checklists.

> **The letter**
> • Does the letter have the date?
> • Does the letter start correctly?
> • Is the letter personal and friendly?
> • Does the letter end correctly?

> **The language**
> • Are there linking words *(and, or, but, when, …)*?
> • Is the spelling correct?
> • Is the word order correct?
> • Are the tenses correct?

Dresden, 25th June

Sunita

How are you? I hope that everything in Brighton OK is.

I'm happy to be home. I've really missed my dad. I haven't seen my German friends for a year. I can't wait to see them this week.

I'll miss my Brighton friends, but I don't forget them. I'll also miss the beech and the sea in Brighton too, but I won't miss the school uniform!

I'm sending you some of my favourite treats with this letter. Tell me how you like them! Please write soon.

Finn

▶ Language file 18 + 20, pp. 209 + 210,
▶ Dictionary, p. 277

2 Use linking words

Texts are easier to read if they have linking words. Look at two sentences from Finn's letter. Then link sentences 1–4 with *because* or *so*.

I'm happy to be home because I've really missed my dad.
I haven't seen my German friends for a year, so I can't wait to see them again.

1   I'm writing you a letter … I want to send you something from Germany.
2   I've also missed German food … I'm looking forward to that too.
3   England is great … the people are so friendly.
4   Luckily our internet is very fast … we can play online games together.

3 Write and check your letter

a) Write a letter to Sunita, Noah, Zane or Lily about your plans for the summer.

b) Check your letter with the checklists in 1.

c) Swap letters with a partner and check your partner's letter.

d) Correct or rewrite your letter. Put your letter in your DOSSIER.

Have a great summer!

▶ Skills file 13, p. 196

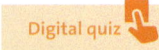 Digital quiz   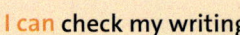 I can **check my writing.**

Write fun horoscopes

Step 1: Read about star signs   ▶ Digital help

a) **Find your star sign in the chart. Do you agree with the adjectives? Tell the class.**

 If you don't know a word or its pronunciation, check in a dictionary.

b) **Make twelve groups. Your teacher will give you a star sign. Read about it in the chart.**

Step 2: Write predictions

Write two or three positive horoscope predictions for your star sign.

You'll get great marks in your English test because you're so hard-working.

▶ More help, p. 175

CAPRICORN
Dec 22 – Jan 19
calm and hard-working

AQUARIUS
Jan 20 – Feb 18
clever and imaginative

PISCES
Feb 19 – Mar 20
artistic and romantic

ARIES
Mar 21 – Apr 19
fast and organized

TAURUS
Apr 20 – May 20
shy and strong

GEMINI
May 21 – Jun 20
kind and curious

CANCER
Jun 21 – Jul 22
friendly and tolerant

LEO
Jul 23 – Aug 22
dramatic and confident

VIRGO
Aug 23 – Sep 22
helpful and practical

LIBRA
Sep 23 – Oct 22
fair and sociable

SCORPIO
Oct 23 – Nov 21
brave and creative

SAGITTARIUS
Nov 22 – Dec 21
funny and generous

Step 3: Check!

a) **Check your own sentences with the checklist. Then check the sentences of another pair.**   ▶ Study skills, p. 162

b) **Rewrite your predictions on a piece of paper. You can also add drawings.**   ▶ Digital help

- Is the spelling correct?
- Is the word order correct?
- Are the tenses correct?
- Are your predictions positive?

Step 4: Read and give feedback

a) GALLERY WALK **Read the predictions for your own star sign.**

b) **Read out a prediction and give feedback on it to the class.**

I liked this prediction because …   *I think this prediction won't happen because …*

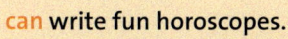

1 WORDS What do you want to be?

Some Varndean students are talking about their dream jobs. Complete the sentences with the correct jobs from the box. There are three extra jobs.

> architect • builder • firefighter • footballer • gamer • hairdresser • mechanic • programmer • train driver

Lewis   I want to be a ... (1) because I love coding and I want to make websites.

Evie   That sounds cool. I want to work with computers too, but I want to be a ... (2) because I want to play on my computer every day.

Sam   That's not a real job! It's too fun. I want to do so something with cars – maybe I'll be a ... (3).

Shakiel   I think it's amazing to design houses, so I want to be an ... (4).

Alex   We can work together, Shakiel! I want to be a ... (5) like my uncle. He's strong and really practical.

Mia   I don't have a dream job yet. I just know that I want to help people in trouble.

Lewis   There are lots of jobs for you then! Maybe a ... (6) or a nurse?

Mia   Maybe!

2 LANGUAGE My dream home

a) **Sunita is writing an email to Finn about her dream home. Complete the sentences. Use *will*, *'ll* or *won't* and the correct verb from the box.**

> be (2 x) • come • do • get up • have • leave • need • play • swim • visit

---

To   Finn

From   Sunita

Hi, Finn

You asked me about my dream home. It ... (1) in Brighton, but it ... (2 not) like other houses! It ... (3) ten bedrooms, a swimming pool and a cinema. I ... (4 not) my house at the weekend because all of my friends ... (5) me. I hope you ... (6) too! On Saturdays we ... (7) in the pool and watch films together. On Sundays we ... (8) yoga in my beautiful studio and then we ... (9) computer games. On Mondays I ... (10) early and go to work. I ... (11) to have a good job to pay for this house!

Best wishes from Sunita

---

b) **WRITING Write a message to your British friend about your dream home. Use the will-future. The text from a) can help you.**

3 MEDIATION Finn's friends in Germany

 I can **talk about chores.**

Finn wants to tell his class in Brighton about the chores that kids in Germany do.
He asked ten of his friends in Dresden what they have to do at home. Look at the chart.
Then complete Finn's sentences.

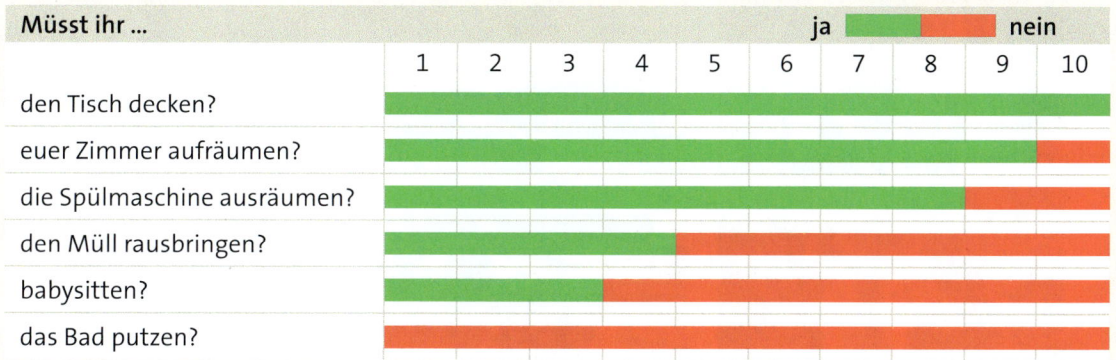

Müsst ihr …	1	2	3	4	5	6	7	8	9	10
den Tisch decken?	ja	ja	ja	ja	ja	ja	ja	ja	ja	ja
euer Zimmer aufräumen?	ja	ja	ja	ja	ja	ja	ja	ja	ja	nein
die Spülmaschine ausräumen?	ja	ja	ja	ja	ja	ja	ja	ja	nein	nein
den Müll rausbringen?	ja	ja	ja	ja	ja	nein	nein	nein	nein	nein
babysitten?	ja	ja	ja	nein	nein	nein	nein	nein	nein	nein
das Bad putzen?	nein	nein	nein	nein	nein	nein	nein	nein	nein	nein

1 I asked my friends in Germany about …
2 Everybody has to …
3 Most people have to … and …
4 Some people have to … and …
5 Nobody …

4 SPEAKING The worst chores!

Look at pictures 1–6. Who has the worst chores? Why? Talk to a partner.

I think … has the worst chores because she / he has to … I think this chore is boring / dirty / …

I agree, that's …

I don't mind that. I think … has the worst chores because …

 Check

🔊 **5** LISTENING **A shopping trip**

I can **talk about money and shopping.** ✓

a) Lily and her dad are doing some shopping. Which shops are they going to?
Listen and put the pictures (A–F) in the correct order (1–4). There are two extra pictures.

A gift shop

B newsagent's

C electronics shop

D clothes shop

E bakery

F fish and chip shop

b) The receipts have rain on them. Listen again. Copy and complete the missing information.

Product:
j _ _ _ _ _
Price: £19._ _

Product:
c _ _ _ _ _ _
Price: £ _ .45

Product:
_ _ _ _ _ _ cleaner
Price: £ _ _ .00

Product:
chocolate _ _ _ _
Price: £8._ _

👥 **6** SPEAKING **In the second-hand shop**

Partner A: You're the shop assistant. In your exercise book, write a price between 50p and £6 for each thing below, but don't show your partner.

Partner B: You have £10. Choose three things. Ask for the price and decide what you want to buy. Partner A starts. Then swap roles.

- Hello. Can I help you?
- Yes, please.
- How much is / are the ...?
- The ... costs / cost ...
- That's great / too expensive.
- What about this / these ...?
- I'll take the ... and the ...
- Thank you very much.
- You're welcome.
- Goodbye.

trainers

helmet

basketball

robot

jacket

headphones

skateboard

hoodie

rucksack

Check

7 READING **Finn's last week**

Finn is getting ready to go back to Germany, but there's a problem: He has too many things! Finn's mum goes into his room and says: 'Finn! We can't take all of this back to Dresden.' A few hours later, Finn has an idea. He sends a message to his friends: 'Hi, guys. I want to sell some of my things at the weekend. Do you want to help me?? Finn 😊'.

On Saturday morning, Lily and Noah arrive early. Noah finds some tables and puts them in the garage. Lily finds some nice paper to put on the tables. She also writes down the prices.

The first people arrive at 9 a.m. Zane patiently answers all of their questions and helps them to choose what to buy. At 3 p.m., everything is gone. Sunita has good news. 'OK guys, I've counted the money. Finn, you now have £53!' Finn smiles at Sunita: 'Thanks, Sunita, but that money isn't for me. It's for our pizzas!'

a) **Read the story. Who is it? Write the correct name or names.**

1   … has to find a solution for a problem.
2   … help with the preparations.
3   … talks to the customers.
4   … knows how much Finn has earned.
5   … are going to have a special meal.
6   … is probably happy that Finn sold his things.

b) **What are their strengths? Complete the text with words from the box.**

When Finn wants to sell his things, Noah shows that he's really … (1). Lily has a … (2) for decorating. Zane is very … (3) with the customers. Sunita looks after the money because she's … (4) maths. In the end Finn invites his friends for pizzas: That's very … (5).

> friendly • generous • gift • good at • practical

8 STUDY SKILLS **Mina's weekend plans**

a) **Read Mina's message to her British friend Arlo. Correct the underlined parts. You can use the checklist for language on** p. 162.

b) **Write a message to your British friend about your weekend plans. The message from a) can help you.**
Check your text and / or a partner's text.

> Hi, Arlo
> How are you? I'm really happy because it finally Friday is 😊.
> I have some exciting plans for the Weekend. Tomorrow I'm going to see a film at the cinema with some frends. Then I go to visit my cousins. They lives near the sea. What are your weekend plans? Will you in Brighton be? Have a great weekend!   Mina

Check

VARNDEAN
Teen Zine

This month's topics: jobs and money

Our school magazine: by students for students

An interesting job

Ash from 9C interviewed his uncle Jude about his job for *Teen Zine*. Would you like to do this job?

Ash   You have a cool job. What is it?

Jude   I'm a ghostwriter[1]. I write books, but I write them for other people.

Ash   What sort of people?

Jude   Well, sometimes famous people want to write a book about their life and they don't have time. Or sometimes they need help to tell their story.

Ash   What famous people have you helped?

Jude   I can't say their names, but I've just written books for a footballer and a singer.

Ash   But is that OK? I mean, you do the work and they get the money!

Jude   I earn money too. And it's their story and their ideas – I just find the right words.

Money on my mind[2] by Sam Smith

This song by Sam Smith is about the job of a singer / songwriter. Money isn't the most important thing about this job: Love for music and the fans is more important. Find the official lyrics video on the internet and sing along!

When I signed my deal, I felt pressure[3].
Don't want to see the numbers, I want to see heaven[4].
You say, 'Could you write a song for me?'
I say, 'I'm sorry, I won't do that happily'.

When I go home, I tend[5] to close the door.
I never wanted more, so sing with me, can't you see?
I don't have money on my mind,
money on my mind.
I do it for, I do it for the love.
I don't have money on my mind,
money on my mind.
I do it for, I do it for the love. [...]

Sam Smith is an award-winning singer / songwriter from London.

---

[1] **ghostwriter** *der Auftragsschreiber, die Auftragsschreiberin*   [2] **on my mind** *im Kopf, in meinen Gedanken*

[3] **pressure** *der Druck*   [4] **heaven** *der Himmel*   [5] (to) **tend to do sth.** *dazu neigen, etwas zu tun*

We love shopping jokes!

Which is your favourite joke?

> **Customer:** *Can I try on that jacket in the window?*

> **Girl:** *I bought a new pen. It can write underwater.*

> **Mum:** *Please put ketchup on the shopping list.*

> **Assistant:** *No, sorry. Please use the changing room.*

> **Boy:** *Can it write other words too?*

> **Dad:** *OK, I've done that, but now I can't read it.*

Pocket money puzzle *by Rose*

I'm 14 and I have a twin sister[1]. I also have a brother (10 years old) and another sister (8 years old). We all get pocket money every week: 50 p for each year of our life. How much pocket money do I get? How much pocket money do our parents give us four children every week?

Find the answers on p. 313.

E-postcard from the USA

This month Lea writes about chores and money.
Find the answers for the money puzzle on p. 313.

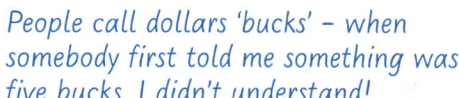

In my host family[2] chores are a big deal[3]! I have to tidy my room and vacuum the floors. I also have to help set the table and empty the dishwasher.

My family has a really big yard (that's the American word for 'garden'). My host brother Curtis keeps the yard clean and tidy. He also has to wash his car – he's only 17, but he already has a car, so the family has three cars! Curtis has a job too. At weekends he works in a fast food restaurant to earn money.

It was strange at first using dollars and cents instead of[4] pounds and pence.

People call dollars 'bucks' – when somebody first told me something was five bucks, I didn't understand!

Can you solve my money puzzle? Antonella had $50. Hudson has $10. Diego will have $25.
Who has the most money?

---

[1] **twin sister** *die Zwillingsschwester* [2] **host family** *die Gastfamilie* [3] **big deal** *eine große Sache, sehr wichtig*
[4] **instead of** *anstatt*

Partner page

▶Page 148

5 Crazy predictions

b) You'll be a ... (1 job) in ... (2 city) and you'll earn ... (3 number) euros an hour.
... (4 someone in your class) will be your boss and you'll wear a ... (5 colour) uniform at work.
You'll think your job is really ... (6 adjective). You won't work on ... (7 day of the week).
Lucky you: You won't need to ... (8 verb)!

▶Page 157

6 In a gift shop

b) SPEAKING **Partner B: You're a customer in a gift shop. Read the card and think how to say your parts. Then have a conversation with the shop assistant (partner A).**

Partner B (customer): Your partner starts.
Greet the assistant. Ask the price of the postcards.
You would like to have three postcards. Ask how much the orange shorts in the window cost.
Say you'd like size M.
Say that's fine. You'd like the red shorts in M.
Say you want to pay cash. Give the assistant £20.
Say thank you and goodbye.

7 MY TASK   Buy and sell

a) **Sellers: Choose a card.**

b) **Stand at a desk. Buyers come and ask for things.**
Sell your things to the buyers – at a good price! To win, sell everything on your card and have the most money.

Sorry, I don't have that / those.
Yes, I have that / those.
It's / They're ....
Sorry, that isn't enough. How about ...?

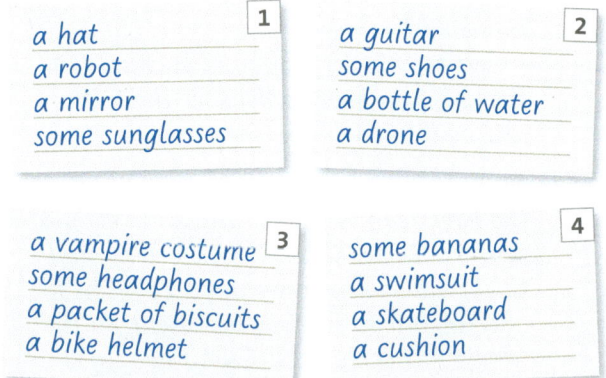

1
a hat
a robot
a mirror
some sunglasses

2
a guitar
some shoes
a bottle of water
a drone

3
a vampire costume
some headphones
a packet of biscuits
a bike helmet

4
some bananas
a swimsuit
a skateboard
a cushion

Diff bank

▶ Page 146

More practice 1 **Jobs**

Complete the job descriptions on the left with the endings on the right. *1g, 2...*

1	A firefighter stops fires and saves	a	cars or bikes.
2	A train driver drives	b	computers to build websites, apps and games.
3	A hairdresser cuts	c	bad guys.
4	An architect designs	d	delicious food.
5	A police officer finds	e	new buildings.
6	A mechanic fixes	f	people's hair.
7	A cook prepares	g	people's lives.
8	A programmer works with	h	people and things from station to station.

▶ Page 148

More practice 2 **Scout's friends**

Complete Scout's sentences. Use '*ll / will* or *won't* and a verb.

Tomorrow I think I ... (1 🚶) to Hove Beach with Blue Bird and maybe we ... (2 👂) to the street musicians. Then we ... (3 👁) for some lunch. Blue Bird ... (4 🍴) lots of chips and then she ... (5 🎵) really badly. In the afternoon I ... (6 🏃) home because I have a date with Black Bird.

Challenge 1 **If I work hard ...**

a) **Look at the lines below from the song on p. 147. Complete the rule for conditional sentences (type 1) in the box. Write 'will-future' and 'simple present' in the correct places.**

If I work hard, I'll go far.
If things go wrong sometimes,
I won't panic.
▶ Language file 21, p. 210

Bedingungssätze *(conditional sentences)* haben zwei Teile.

– Im Nebensatz verwenden wir *if* + ...   Der *if*-Satz kann auch
– Im Hauptsatz verwenden wir ...   hinten stehen.

b) **Complete the sentences. Use the correct form of the verb.**

1 If I work in a restaurant, I ... (be) happy.
2 If my friend ... (work) hard, she'll get a good job.
3 If you ... (play) your guitar every day, maybe you ... (be) famous one day.
4 If he ... (be) always late, he ... (not get) the job he wants.
5 If I ... (not earn) lots of money, I ... (not have) any problem with it.

▶Page 149

More help   **7** MY TASK **A poster about my dream future**

Maybe I'll I'll / I will I think I'll I won't	be	famous / a gamer / happy / hard-working / successful / …
	live	alone / in a big house / in London / with my family / …
	work in	a bank / a different country / a hospital / Paris / …
	have	a dog / a nice car / children / lots of friends / …
	go	on holiday / swimming / to the moon / …

▶Page 150

More practice 3   **A robot for chores**

a) THINK Sunita's robot Robbie is cool, but he can't do chores. Design a robot: Give it a name, decide what it looks like and what chores it can do.
You can also draw a picture.

b) PAIR **Tell your partner about your robot.**

My robot's name is …
It's brown and it looks like a dog. It has four legs and …
It can tidy my room, …

c) SHARE **Tell the class. Who has the coolest robot?**

▶Page 152

More practice 4   **Chores at Noah's home**

a) **Noah's family has a cleaner, Adam. Read the box on the right and complete sentences 1–8.**
Use *has to*, *have to* or *doesn't have to*, *don't have to*.

1 Adam *has to* vacuum all the floors.
2 Adam … do the shopping.
3 Noah's mum and dad … do any cleaning in the house.
4 Noah … walk Buddy.
5 Noah's mum and dad … look after the garden.
6 Adam … tidy Noah's room.
7 Noah's mum and dad … wash the car.
8 Noah … fold the clean clothes.

b) **Use the list of chores and write three more sentences with *has to*, *have to* or *doesn't have to*, *don't have to*.**

Adam:
– vacuum all the floors
– clean all the floors
– clean the bathroom and the kitchen

Noah's mum and dad:
– look after the garden
– wash the car
– do the shopping
– fold clean clothes

Noah:
– take out the rubbish
– tidy his room
– walk Buddy

▸Page 152

Challenge 2 **When Zane was little**

a) Read what Zane says. Then look at the pictures and write what else he had to do or didn't have to do.

When he was little, Zane didn't have to ... He had to ...

When I was little, I had to put away my toys, but I didn't have to clean my room.

b) Write what you had to do and didn't have to do when you were little.

▸ Wordbank 10, p. 222

▸Page 154

More practice 5 **Money**

Complete the conversation with money words or phrases from the box.

> app • buy • cash •
> cash machine • piggy bank •
> pocket money • save •
> savings account • sell •
> spend

Sunita Do you get ... (1) from your parents, Noah?
Noah Yes, I do. I get £10 every week.
Sunita That's a lot! I don't get that much. But I babysit for extra money. And I ... (2) old video games.
Noah Well, I have to ... (3) some money. I put some money in a ... (4) at the bank and I put coins in my ... (5) – it's yellow and looks like a pig.
Sunita Cute! I use a pocket money ... (6). It's really cool because I get a card and I can ... (7) things with that. I can get money from the ... (8) at the bank with the card too.
Noah My parents give me the money in ... (9). But they say I mustn't ... (10) it on unhealthy fast food like burgers and chips. Healthy food is really important to them.

▸Page 155

More help **2** SPEAKING **Your money**

I spend the €20 on / I buy	books / the cinema / clothes / free-time activities / games / magazines / snacks / sports equipment / sweets / video games / ...
I save (some of) it in	a piggy bank / a savings account / ...
My parents say I mustn't spend	(any / too much) money on fast food / snacks / ... all my money every month / ...

▶Page 155

More practice 6 | **Place and time**

a) **Put the sentences in the correct order.**

1 goes shopping / my family / every weekend / at the supermarket
   My family goes shopping at the supermarket every weekend.
2 to school / every day / take / I / my little brother
3 the dog / I / after school / in the park / walk
4 to the ice rink / went / yesterday / my friends and I
5 at 6 o'clock / at the cinema / you / I'll / meet
6 at school / see / tomorrow / I'll / you

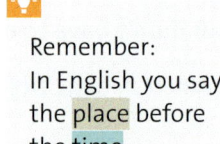

Remember:
In English you say
the place before
the time.

b) **Write two more jumbled sentences like the ones in a) for a partner. Include a time and a place.**

More practice 7 | **At the chip shop**

Scout is talking to Black Bird.
Choose the best adverb for each sentence.

Scout	A man outside the chip shop today ate his chips very (1) sadly / slowly / safely, so I (2) stupidly / kindly / badly helped him to eat them. But he screamed at me very (3) calmly / patiently / angrily.
Black Bird	He acted very (4) rudely / politely / happily, Scout. You just wanted to help! What did you do then?
Scout	I screamed very (5) quietly / nicely / loudly in his ear and he ran away (6) shyly / unhappily / lazily – without his chips!

An adverb of
manner describes
how you do
something:
I dress comfortably.
Listen carefully.

▶Page 156

More practice 8 | **In a clothes shop**

Look at the pictures. Complete the conversation
with *this*, *that*, *these* or *those*.

Lily	Do you like … (1) white trainers, Zane?
Zane	They're OK. But I like … (2) black trainers better.
Lily	Yeah, they're nice, but I want white ones.
Zane	Oh, right. Oh, … (3) red hoodie is cool. I like red – … (4) red T-shirt is my favourite.
Lily	I like red too. The hoodie looks good with … (5) yellow jeans.
Zane	Mm, I don't like yellow. I usually wear black or blue jeans – or white jeans like … (6) ones.

▸ Page 160

More practice 9 What will they do?

Make predictions about the students in the story on pages 158–159.

1   Will Sunita and Finn stay friends? How?
2   How will Lily feel in London?
3   Will Noah become more independent? How?
4   Will Ava call the woman in the blue dress? What will the woman / Ava say?

More practice 10 Your phone call

You want to meet a friend (your partner). Think of an activity, a place and a time. Then phone your partner and make a plan. Use some of the phrases in the box. Take turns starting the call.

Phrases

Hello! It's …
Are you free this afternoon / evening?
Would you like to …?
Let's meet at … on …
I can't hear you. / Can you hear me?
Can you say that again, please?
Bye! / See you soon! / See you later!

▸ Page 163

More help UNIT TASK Write fun horoscopes, Step 2

You			(and / because / so)
	'll	meet an amazing / interesting person / …	
		go on a wonderful trip / …	
		have an exciting / a lucky day / …	
		find something important / useful / …	
		get a surprise / a present / a phone call / …	
	'll have to / must	look after your health / a good friend / …	
		be kind to your family / pet / …	
		be careful with money / work hard / …	
	won't	lose your phone / keys / …	
		have to do any homework / chores / …	

The treasure hunt

1 READING School trips

a) BEFORE YOU READ **Year 8 is on a day trip to Stanmer Park.
Tell your class where you have gone on school trips.**

I've / We've gone swimming / to the theatre / to a museum …

b) GAME **Your class is also going on a day trip to a park!
What are you taking with you?**

A I'm taking a hat.   B I'm taking a hat and an apple.   C I'm taking a hat, an apple and …

> **Good to know**
>
> You can see Stanmer Park in the video from the bilingual module 'Getting to know Sussex' on p. 104.

It was a sunny day in April. Year 8 was
excited: It was the day of their trip to the
Stanmer Park Nature Reserve. They
walked from the bus to the park with
5 their teachers.

"I'm glad we're here," said Camilla at the
park. "My feet hurt!"
"We've only walked half a mile from the
bus, Camilla!" answered Ms Bond. "We're
10 going to walk a lot more today. But you'll
enjoy it, I promise."

Zane looked around at the empty park.
"It's so quiet. I haven't seen anyone."
"Yes," agreed Sunita. "It's very green and
15 pretty. I like it."

"It's beautiful here," said Mr Pancake.
"And it's not far from our school."

Alice took a picture of some flowers. "I've
never been here before," she said. "It's
20 great!"

Ms Bond stopped. "OK, everyone," she
called. "We've prepared an activity for you
– a treasure hunt."
"Cool!" shouted Zane. "How does it
25 work?"
"First, we're going to put you into teams
of four," explained Ms Bond. "Each team
follows a trail through the park. At the
end of each trail, I've left some cards.
30 Each card has a letter on it. The letters
spell the name of a character from a
British children's book. Each team has a
different character. You have to work out
his or her name."

35 Ms Bond divided the class. "Team 1: Alice, Zane, Ravi and Sunita. Team 2: ..." The students joined their teams and waited for more instructions.

"We've hidden four clue cards along the
40 trails. Each clue tells you how to find the next one," said Mr Pancake. "I'm going to hand out the first clue now. And each team gets a map. We'll meet at the tea rooms at quarter to eleven. Good luck,
45 everyone!"

Sunita held team 1's first card in her hand. "Who's going to read it?" she asked. "You choose!" said Zane. "Do a counting-out rhyme."
50 "Hmm," said Sunita. "OK. I'll do 'One potato, two potato'. Hold out your hands!"

Each team member made one hand into a 'potato' and held it out. Sunita touched each hand with hers and chanted: "One
55 potato, two potato, three potato, four. Five potato, six potato, seven potato, more." Her hand landed on Ravi's hand. He took it out of the circle.

Sunita began again. "One potato, two
60 potato, ..." She continued until only Alice's hand was in the circle. "You're it, Alice. Read it out!"

Alice read the card slowly:

> I go up and down. I don't move.
> Find me and see some ducks.

Sunita thought for a second and then
65 asked, "Where can you see ducks?"

> One potato, two potato, three potato, four.
> Five potato, six potato, seven potato, more.

Good to know

Counting-out rhymes are used to decide who is 'it' (You're 'it'. = It's your turn.) or who is 'out' (who can't play any more).
The plural of 'potato' is 'potatoes', but the rhyme sounds better without an 's'.
Say the rhyme with 'potatoes':
What do you think?

Zane pointed at the map. "Look, here's a pond. Ducks like ponds, right?"

Alice looked around. "I can see the pond – over there. Look, those steps go down
70 to it."

Sunita stared at the steps. "Guys, that's the answer!"

"How do you know?" asked Alice.

Sunita began to explain. "Steps lead up
75 and down, but ..."

Alice finished her sentence. "... they don't move. Great, Sunita. Let's go!"

*

"OK, here are the steps," Ravi said. "But where's the next clue?"
80 The kids began to look around.

"Here's a bag. There's a clue inside!" called Zane. "Ravi, do you want to read this one?"

"Sure," said Ravi. He opened the bag and
85 took out the clue:

> **I'm a colour and a fruit.**

Ravi smiled. "That's pretty easy. Orange is a colour and a fruit. But where do we look for it?"

Sunita still had the map. "Look," she said.
90 "There are three marks on the map: a red one, a yellow one and an orange one."

Zane looked at the map. "The orange mark is on the other side of the pond. That's a long walk. Let's move!"

*

95 The four kids arrived at the other side of the pond fifteen minutes later.

Ravi discovered a bag under a bush. "Here's clue number three!" he announced. "Sunita, do you want to read
100 this one?"

Sunita took the card and read it out loud:

> **I have a lot of rings, but no fingers.**

She looked at the other three kids. "A bell rings. Is that it?"

"Planets have rings and no fingers," said
105 Zane.

Alice laughed. "That's true. But our teachers haven't hidden the clue on another planet, Zane. This is a park with trees and grass ..."
110 "That's it!" shouted Zane. "Trees have rings too, right?"

"We're under a tree now," said Sunita. "Look up – there's a bag! Alice, you're the tallest. Can you jump up and get it?"

115 Alice jumped. "I've got it!" She opened the bag and took out the clue card. "This is our last clue. Zane, you can read this one."

There's a bag!

In a loud voice, Zane read:

> First I'm yellow, then I'm white and then I fly away.

120 "Do some birds change colour?" Alice asked.
"Baby chickens are yellow," said Zane.
"But I don't think there are chickens in the park. And they don't fly away."

125 "I know!" shouted Ravi.
"Ravi, quiet!" said Sunita. "Team 3 is over there."
Ravi looked. "That's OK. They have different clues. And I know the answer to
130 our clue. Dandelions! First they're yellow, then they're white. You can blow on them and they fly away. And look around the bench: lots of dandelions!"

The team ran to the bench. Under the
135 bench was a bag! Alice picked it up and looked inside. There were eleven cards in the bag, and each card had a letter on it. She picked up the cards and put them on the ground.

140 "Careful, Alice," said Sunita. "It's windy." Too late! The wind blew the cards in the direction of team 3. Sunita, Zane, Ravi and Alice ran after them, but they weren't fast enough to catch them all ... and
145 team 3 was fast enough! Marek and Camilla picked up five of the cards and put them in their bags.

"Hey, Camilla, Marek!" Alice cried. "Can you please give back our cards?"

150 "Cards?" asked Camilla. "I didn't see any cards. Marek, did you see any cards?"

"No, no cards here," said Marek, laughing. "Sorry, team 1: I guess you lose!" Marek, Camilla and
155 the other members of team 3 ran away.

"I don't believe it!" shouted Alice angrily. "That's really mean! Let's
160 go tell the teachers."

"Wait," said Sunita. "Let's be smart. They're all running away ... and I don't think they've found their own letter cards yet. I think we can guess the name of our character without all the letters. And we'll be faster than team 3! We can tell the teachers later."

"We've lost five letters," said Zane. "How many letters did we catch?"

"We still have six letters. We can guess the name!" Sunita said. She held the letters in her hand and showed them to the others.

> **!**
>
> Do you want to work out the name of the character? Look at the letters in Sunita's hand below and then at the names at the bottom of this page. Which name is the right one?

"Let's think," said Ravi. "Ms Bond said it has to be a character from a British children's book. What characters do we know?"

"Tom Gates!" shouted Zane.
"Tom Gates is really cool," agreed Alice.
"But too short. We need a name with eleven letters because we lost five and we still have six."

"Willy Wonka is long! You know, the guy from *Charlie and the Chocolate Factory*," said Zane.
"Not long enough," said Ravi. "And it doesn't have the right letters: No 'R' or 'P'. But it was a good guess!"
"George the Pavilion Cat!" laughed Sunita.
"I loved that book when I was little," said Alice. "It's so fun to see Brighton in a book. But that's too long ..."

The kids thought. "I can think of lots of American characters, but what's British?" asked Zane.
"Peter Pan is a British character," said Ravi. "But it's too short. And it doesn't have all of the letters."

"Harry Potter!" shouted Alice. "It has eleven letters! There's an 'A', an 'R', a 'P', an 'O' and a 'Y'. Oh no – but no 'I'! I really thought I had the right answer." She looked very disappointed. "Maybe this isn't so easy."

Tom Gates   Mary Poppins   Peter Pan   Harry Potter   George the Pavilion Cat   Willy Wonka

Sunita gave them a big smile. "Yes, it is, guys! I've just worked it out. Our character is Mary Poppins. The five missing letters are 'M', 'N', 'S' and 210 two 'P's."

Zane pointed at Sunita. "Meet Sunita Chandra – the cleverest student at Varndean!"

Sunita looked a little embarrassed, but 215 she smiled again. "I'm just lucky, Zane. I love Mary Poppins – the book and the film. I've seen the film about twenty times!"

It was quarter to eleven and the treasure 220 hunt was over. All the teams met with the teachers in front of the tea rooms. Mr Pancake held the solutions in his hand.

> **Good to know**
>
> A tea room is a small restaurant where you can have tea, cakes and sandwiches. Stanmer Park has a special Alice in Wonderland tea room!

"Well, year 8," he said. "Only one team 225 didn't work out their character's name: Sorry, team 3! Congratulations to the other teams. Team 1 had Mary Poppins, team 2 had Alice in Wonderland, team 3 had Hermione Granger ..."

230 There were a lot of teams, but he finally got to the results. "And the fastest team was ... team 1!"

Sunita and the other members of team 1 clapped and shouted. "We did it! Cool! 235 Well done, guys!"

The members of team 3 looked very unhappy. Ravi heard Oscar say, "It was your idea!" in a loud and angry voice to Camilla.

240 Zane smiled at his teammates. "Team 3 was too busy running and hiding from us: They didn't have time to work out their character's name!"

"I wanted to tell the teachers that team 3 245 cheated," said Alice. "But I think the results were fair. Let's go have some cake!"

2 SPEAKING **Talking about the story**

a) **What did or didn't you like about the story? Say why or why not.**

> *I liked the clues because they were fun to work out.*

> *I didn't like the ending because team 1 didn't tell the teachers that team 3 cheated.*

b) **Was the story easy or hard to read? Give reasons.**

> *It was easy / hard because...*

> *I didn't know some words / understand ... / ...*

> *The dictionary / pictures / ... helped me.*

c) **What words didn't you know? How did you work out their meaning?**

I didn't know the word ... I looked in the dictionary / asked the teacher / guessed / ...

3 **School clues**

a) **Write one or more clues about places in your school. Read your clue(s) to the class: They guess the places.**

> **We go through here many times a day, but never to learn, sit or stay.**

☒ b) **Make a treasure hunt for a friend. You can hide a small treasure (some sweets or a nice note, for example) at the end.**

> *The corridor!*

4 LIFE SKILLS **Being honest and fair**

a) **Team 1 doesn't tell the teachers that team 3 cheated. Do you think this was right? Why or why not?**

b) **In the story, team 3 cheats at a game. In what other situations do people cheat?**

c) **What do you think about cheating at games? Is it OK? Why or why not?**

5 SHOWTIME **A new ending**

a) **Make groups with four to six students.**

b) **Write a scene with a new ending for the story. Here are some questions to think about.**
   - **Does team 1 talk to team 3 about cheating?**
   - **Does team 1 tell the teachers about the cheating?**
   - **What do the people say?**
   - **Who is happy at the end? Who isn't happy?**

c) **Act out your scene for the class.**

▶ Workbook, pp. 91–93

Auf den **Skills file**-Seiten findest du Methoden und Tipps, die dir helfen, z. B. Wortschatz zu lernen, Informationen zu sammeln, Texte zu überprüfen oder kleine Vorträge zu halten.

Inhalt

Die mit diesem Symbol gekennzeichneten Abschnitte enthalten Hinweise und Tipps, die dir dabei helfen, elektronische Medien beim Englischlernen einzusetzen.

Erklär-film Dieses Symbol zeigt dir, dass du einen Erklärfilm zu diesem Thema in der App findest.

Lösungen der Merkaufgaben

SF 2, Merkaufgabe:
a) ähnliches Wort im Deutschen: (Luft-)Ballon; Wörter aus anderen Sprachen: balon, ballon, بالون [baːˈlɔːn]
b) Wortfamilie und Wortbildungsgesetze: (to) write + Nachsilbe -er: writer
c) Wortfamilie und Wortbildungsgesetze: safe + Vorsilbe un-: unsafe

SF 3, Merkaufgabe:
a) der Buchstabe
b) der Brief

SF 4, Merkaufgabe:
b) school + routine + UK

SF 7, Merkaufgabe:
Es geht um eine Woche mit Freizeitaktivitäten, z. B. Fußball, Karate und Fotografieren.

SF 8, Merkaufgabe:
a) Hier kann man für unterschiedliche Tage Hin- und Rückfahrkarten in verschiedene Städte kaufen.

SF 9, Merkaufgabe:
(zwei Tipps von diesen:) Sortiere vor dem Vortrag deine Kärtchen.; Übe deinen Vortrag, lies nicht alles ab.; Schaue das Publikum an.; Sprich laut und deutlich.; Bedanke dich bei deinen Zuhörern.; Erkundige dich, ob jemand Fragen hat.

SF 10, Merkaufgabe:
b) For me that isn't true. I like to spend my time on other things.

SF 11, Merkaufgabe:
a) sport
b) places

SF 1

Erklär-
film

Vokabeln lernen

▶ Unit 1 | p. 17   ▶ Unit 2 | p. 54   ▶ Unit 4 | p. 115

Führe dein VOCAB FILE aus Klasse 5 weiter.

Neue Vokabeln lernst du am besten an einem ruhigen und aufgeräumten Platz, an dem du nicht abgelenkt wirst.

Wiederholen kannst du sie überall – beim Warten, im Bus, im Bett etc. Für unterwegs kannst du sie dir aufs Handy sprechen oder per Vokabeltrainer-App üben. Je öfter du die Vokabeln wiederholst, desto besser wirst du sie dir merken können.

Wie merke ich mir neue Wörter besser?

Erstelle Wortfelder

- Ordne die Wörter unter einem Oberbegriff *(umbrella word)*. Du kannst eine Liste machen oder eine Mindmap anlegen, die du immer weiter ergänzt.

- Oder du arbeitest mit Karteikarten. Schreibe den Oberbegriff in Großbuchstaben auf die Vorderseite einer Karteikarte und die dazu passenden Wörter auf die Rückseite. Später kannst du neue Wörter ergänzen.

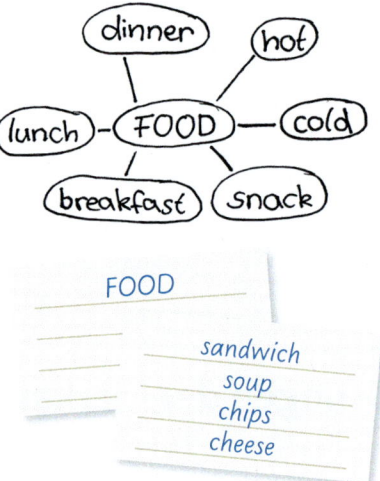

Finde Gegensatzpaare

Sammle Gegensatzpaare und schreibe sie z. B. auf die letzte Seite von deinem VOCAB FILE. Füge Bilder hinzu. Das hilft dir beim Lernen.

Lerne *phrases* statt Einzelwörter

Phrases sind Ausdrücke, die aus mehreren Wörtern bestehen, z. B. *a bottle of water = eine Flasche Wasser*. Lerne also nicht *bottle* und *water* als Einzelwörter, sondern den ganzen Ausdruck: *a bottle of water*.

Weitere Beispiele:
lunchtime → at lunchtime
listen → listen to music
sad → feel sad

Merkaufgabe 1

Gehe dein VOCAB FILE aus den Klassen 5 und 6 durch. Erstelle eine Liste mit Gegensatzpaaren.

Checkliste Vokabeln lernen
- ✓ Lerne nur 5–10 Vokabeln auf einmal.
- ✓ Lerne jeden Tag 10 Minuten.
- ✓ Lerne zusammen mit Freunden. Das macht mehr Spaß.
- ✓ Lerne unterwegs mit einer Vokabellern-App.
- ✓ Schreibe schwierige Wörter auf (mehrmals!).
- ✓ Sprich die Wörter und nimm dich mit dem Handy auf.

Unbekannte Wörter erschließen

▶ Unit 2 | p. 58   ▶ Unit 3 | p. 94

Du kannst englische Texte verstehen, auch wenn du nicht alle Wörter kennst. So kannst du die Bedeutung herausfinden:

Bilder

Bilder zeigen oft Dinge in einem Text, die du nicht verstehst. Schaue sie deshalb genau an.

He has long, black hair. He's wearing it in plaits. He has an earring in his left ear.

Ähnliche Wörter im Deutschen oder in anderen Sprachen

Viele englische Wörter klingen ähnlich wie im Deutschen, werden ähnlich geschrieben, oder du kennst sie vielleicht aus anderen Sprachen und kannst sie deshalb verstehen.

🇬🇧 garage
🇩🇪 die Garage
🇫🇷 le garage
🇷🇺 гараж
🇹🇷 garaj

Wortfamilien und Wortbildungsgesetze

Ein Wort gehört immer zu einer Wortfamilie. Kennst du ein Wort aus der Wortfamilie, z. B. das Verb *act*, hilft es dir, auch die Nomen *action* und *activity* und das Adjektiv *active* zu verstehen. Mit Regeln zur Wortbildung kannst du die Bedeutung ableiten:

Vorsilben		
un-	Aus einem positiven Adjektiv wird ein negatives.	friendly → unfriendly happy → unhappy
Nachsilben		
-ful	Aus einem Nomen wird ein Adjektiv.	colour → colourful use → useful
-er	Aus einem Tätigkeitsverb wird eine Person.	listen → listener sing → singer
-ness	Aus einem Adjektiv wird ein Nomen.	happy → happiness kind → kindness

Kontextsätze

Manchmal helfen dir die Sätze vor und nach einem Wort, es zu verstehen.

Please turn up the volume. I can't hear the song.

Was soll ich hochdrehen? Sie kann das Lied nicht hören? Ah! Die Lautstärke.

Merkaufgabe 2

Schaue dir die Wörter an. Mit welcher Strategie kannst du ihre Bedeutung herausfinden?

a) balloon   **b)** writer   **c)** unsafe

(Die Lösung findest du auf Seite 183.)

SF 3

Erklär-
film

Im Wörterbuch nachschlagen

▶ Unit 3 | p. 94   ▶ Unit 5 | p. 146

Wie finde ich Wörter und Ausdrücke im *Dictionary*?

Die Wörter im Wörterbuch sind alphabetisch aufgelistet:

- k kommt vor l   • ka kommt vor ke   • karao kommt vor karat

In Online-Wörterbüchern stellst du nur die Suchrichtung (Englisch-Deutsch oder Deutsch-Englisch) ein und tippst dann das Wort ein.

Der Haupteintrag (z. B. *name*) steht **fett** und ggf. farbig am Anfang. Daneben oder darunter findest du oft zusammengesetzte Wörter oder Redewendungen (z. B. *first name*).

K

karaoke [ˌkæriˈəʊki] das Karaoke 1
karate [kəˈrɑːti] das Karate 2: 3 (80)
kebab [kɪˈbæb] der Kebab 1
keep [kiːp], kept, kept:
  1. halten; behalten; aufbewahren
  2: 2 (61)
  °keep a diary Tagebuch führen
  2. keep doing sth. etwas dauernd/
  immer wieder tun 2: 3 (88)
  keep going (immer) weiter gehen
  2: 3 (88)

N

name [neɪm] der Name 1 first name
  der Vorname 1 What's your name?
  Wie heißt du? 1

Was erfahre ich aus dem *Dictionary*?

Rechtschreibung und Aussprache

Du erfährst, wie das Wort geschrieben und ausgesprochen wird. Schaue dir für die richtige Aussprache die Lautschrift hinter dem Wort an: *sound* [saʊnd].

Wenn du ein Online-Wörterbuch verwendest, kannst du dir das Wort anhören.

▶ English sounds, p. 229

Unregelmäßigkeiten

Hat ein Wort einen unregelmäßigen Plural oder eine unregelmäßige Zeitform, findest du diese Form vor oder hinter der Lautschrift.

---

knew [njuː] *siehe* know
knife [naɪf], *pl* knives das Messer 1

Unterschiedliche Bedeutungen und unterschiedliche Wortarten

Die Ziffern 1, 2 usw. zeigen, dass ein Wort mehrere Bedeutungen hat oder sogar als unterschiedliche Wortarten vorkommt. Lies also immer den ganzen Eintrag und entscheide dann, welche Bedeutung die richtige ist.

---

love [lʌv]:
  1. der Liebling 1
  2. die Liebe 1
  3. lieben, sehr mögen 1
  I'd (= I would) love … Ich hätte
  liebend gern … / Ich möchte liebend
  gern … 1 I'd (= I would) love to
  meet … Ich würde mich liebend
  gerne mit … treffen. 1

Merkaufgabe 3

Was heißt *letter* in diesen Sätzen?

a) Let's write the texts on our poster with big letters so everyone can read them well.

b) Adalet wrote me a long letter when she was in Turkey last summer.

(Die Lösung findest du auf Seite 183.)

Im Internet recherchieren

▶ Unit 2 | p. 65

Im Internet kannst du dir schnell Informationen aus aller Welt besorgen. Mit ein paar Tricks behältst du den Überblick.

Suchen

- Überlege dir Suchbegriffe, die zu deinem Thema passen.

- Gib nicht nur einen Suchbegriff ein, sondern zwei oder mehrere. Du suchst z. B. Informationen zum englischen König. Wenn du nur *king* eingibst, wirst du zunächst wenig Passendes finden. Wenn du aber eingibst *king + England* oder *king + UK*, hast du schon bessere Ergebnisse.

Nicht alle Informationen, die du findest, sind richtig und wichtig. Prüfe sie sorgfältig und verlasse dich nicht nur auf eine einzige Internetseite als Quelle.

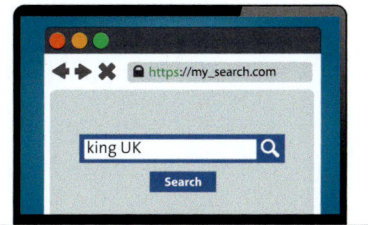

Auswählen

Beschäftige dich nur mit den Seiten und Links, die wirklich zu deinem Thema oder deiner Aufgabe passen. Prüfe:

- Von wem stammt die Seite? Wie verlässlich ist die Information? Ist es z. B. ein Online-Lexikon oder ein Chat-Forum? Achte auf die Endung der Internetadresse oder URL: Sie kann dir wichtige Hinweise geben:
  - .com bedeutet, es ist eine kommerzielle Webseite, die auch Werbung enthalten kann.
  - .gov weist auf eine offizielle Webseite der amerikanischen Regierung hin.
  - .uk bedeutet, dass es sich um eine britische Seite handelt.

- Passen die Informationen zu deinem Thema? Überfliege die Seite und achte auf Überschriften und Bilder.

Vorsicht bei Wikipedia: Das Onlinelexikon wird von freiwilligen Helfern geschrieben und kann Fehler enthalten.

Sichern

- Setze *bookmarks* (digitale Lesezeichen), um bestimmte Seiten später schnell wieder aufzurufen. Mache dir Notizen oder drucke wichtige Seiten aus und markiere wichtige Stellen.

- Schreibe die Texte nicht wörtlich ab, sondern gib die Inhalte in deinen eigenen Worten wieder.

Wenn du Inhalte einer Webseite verwendest, nenne immer die Autorin oder den Autor der Seite und die dazugehörige Internetadresse, die du direkt in dein Dokument hineinkopieren kannst. Schreibe auch das Datum dazu, an dem du die Webseite zuletzt aufgerufen hast.

Merkaufgabe 4

Was sind die besten Suchbegriffe zum Thema „A school day in the UK"?

a) school + day   **b)** school + routine + UK   **c)** school + UK

(Die Lösung findest du auf Seite 183.)

SF 5

Notizen erstellen

▶ Unit 1 | p. 31   ▶ Unit 4 | p. 114   ▶ Unit 5 | p. 158

In vielen Situationen ist es hilfreich, wenn du deine Gedanken sammelst und Notizen machst, z. B. wenn du eine Geschichte planst oder wenn du den Inhalt eines Textes zusammenfassen oder eine Geschichte nacherzählen möchtest.

Wie erstelle ich Notizen?

- Verwende für deine Notizen kleine Zettel oder Karteikarten.

- Schreibe Stichpunkte auf, keine ganzen Sätze.

- Schreibe nicht alles auf. Sammle nur die Punkte, die besonders wichtig sind.

- Strukturiere deine Notizen optisch, z. B. durch Überschriften und Absätze. Du kannst beispielsweise *wh*-Fragewörter *(what, where, when, who, why)* als Zwischenüberschriften verwenden.

- Schreibe deine Notizen gleich in der Reihenfolge auf, in der du deine Gedanken vortragen möchtest. Verwendest du kleine Zettel oder Karteikarten, kannst du diese am Ende leicht sortieren und nummerieren.

Worauf muss ich achten?

Fasse dich kurz:
- Schreibe Ziffern anstelle von Zahlwörtern, z. B. „15" statt *fifteen*.
- Verwende Abkürzungen, z. B. *veg* statt *vegetable*, „+" statt *and* oder einen Schrägstrich statt des Worts *or*.
- Verwende Symbole und Zeichnungen anstelle von Stichwörtern, z. B. Smileys für Gefühle, Flaggen für Länder, Strichzeichnungen für Personen usw.

Merkaufgabe 5

Probiere es gleich aus. Stelle dir vor, du möchtest jemandem über deine letzte Geburtstagsparty berichten. Mache dir Notizen dazu.

favourite family party → 1
Grandma's 70th birthday

when: 15/8
where: Grandma's garden

favourite family party → 2
Grandma's 70th birthday

what: all my family
barbecue
play with cousins ☺
pool 👍

💡 Es gibt auch Apps, mit denen du deine Notizen anfertigen kannst. Denke aber daran, mit deinen Eltern zu sprechen, bevor du eine kostenpflichtige App herunterlädst.

Hörtexte verstehen

▶ Unit 1 | p. 18   ▶ Unit 2 | p. 52   ▶ Unit 3 | p. 79
▶ Unit 4 | p. 112   ▶ Unit 5 | p. 144

Nicht nur im Englischunterricht, sondern auch im Alltag oder im Urlaub kommt es darauf an, einen englischen Hörtext zu verstehen, z. B. in Gesprächen, Filmen, im Hotel oder am Flughafen. Mit ein paar Tipps lassen sich Hörtexte gut bewältigen.

Vor dem Hören

Lies dir die Aufgabenstellung genau durch und überlege, was du tun sollst. Wenn du etwas nicht verstehst, frage nach. Finde die Schlüsselwörter in der Aufgabenstellung. Diese zeigen dir, worauf du beim Hören achten musst.

Im Alltag gibt es viele Hinweise, die sich aus der Situation ergeben, in der du dich gerade befindest, z. B. bei einer Durchsage an einem Bahnhof Wörter wie *platform* oder *destination*.

Nutze unterschiedliche Möglichkeiten, um englische Texte zu hören. Wähle etwas aus, was dir gefällt, z. B. dein Lieblingslied oder dein Lieblingsbuch als Hörbuch auf Englisch. Schaue Filme und Serien auf Englisch. Blende Untertitel ein, falls du Probleme beim Verstehen hast. Blende sie aus, wenn du dich sicherer fühlst oder eine Episode schon mehrfach gesehen hast.

Beim Hören

Versuche, zunächst grob zu verstehen, worum es in dem Text geht. Konzentriere dich auf die Schlüsselwörter aus der Aufgabenstellung.

Achte auf den Kontext. Manchmal liefert der Text weitere Informationen, die klar machen, was gemeint ist. So kannst du Wörter erschließen, die du nicht kennst.

Mache dir kurze Notizen auf einem Notizzettel oder mit Bleistift auf deinem Aufgabenblatt. Bleibe ruhig, wenn du beim ersten Mal nicht alles verstehst. Du hörst den Text meist zweimal.

Die Aufgaben stehen in der Regel in der gleichen Reihenfolge, in der die entsprechenden Stellen im Text vorkommen.

▶ Skills file 5, p. 188

Nach dem Hören

Vervollständige deine Notizen direkt nach dem Hören.

Lies noch einmal genau durch, was du geschrieben hast. Passen deine Antworten zu den Fragen?

Konzentriere dich beim zweiten Hören auf das, was du beim ersten Mal nicht verstanden hast.

Auch wenn du es nicht geschafft hast, alles aufzuschreiben, sind die Informationen wahrscheinlich noch in deinem Gedächtnis.

Merkaufgabe 6

Höre dir ein englisches Lied an. Versuche zuerst, den Refrain zu verstehen, um das Thema herauszufinden. Höre das Lied dann noch einmal und versuche, Details zu verstehen.

SF 7

Lesetexte verstehen

▶ Unit 1 | p. 26   ▶ Unit 2 | p. 60   ▶ Unit 3 | p. 92
▶ Unit 4 | p. 126   ▶ Unit 5 | p. 158

In diesem Buch findest du viele verschiedene Texte, z. B. Dialoge, Bildergeschichten und Tagebucheinträge. Die Strategien auf dieser Seite helfen dir sie zu verstehen.

Je mehr englische Texte du liest, desto größer wird dein Wortschatz und desto schneller und besser verstehst du Texte.

Vor dem Lesen

Schaue dir die Überschrift und die Bilder, die zum Text gehören, mit ihrer Bildunterschrift an. Sie geben dir Hinweise zum Inhalt des Textes.

Lies dir auch die Aufgaben zum Text gut durch und achte auf Schlüsselwörter. So weißt du, worauf du beim Lesen achten musst.

Beim Lesen

Lies den Text einmal ganz durch und versuche, ihn insgesamt zu verstehen. Lasse unbekannte Wörter erst einmal beiseite.

Versuche, die fünf *wh*-Fragen zum Text zu beantworten: *Who? What? Where? When? Why?* (Wer macht was, wo, wann und warum?) So siehst du, ob du den Text verstanden hast.

Zerteile längere Texte in Abschnitte und gib den Abschnitten Überschriften. Das hilft dir beim Verstehen, und du kannst so den gesamten Text später einfacher zusammenfassen.

Überlege, ob du die Aufgaben schon beantworten kannst. Falls nicht, lies den Text noch einmal mit den Aufgaben im Hinterkopf. Wenn nötig, mache dir Notizen. Triffst du auf ein unbekanntes Wort, versuche, dir die Bedeutung zu erschließen.

Du musst nicht jedes Wort in einem Text verstehen, um den Inhalt zu verstehen. Erst wenn du merkst, dass du ein Wort wirklich brauchst, um eine Aufgabe zu beantworten, solltest du es nachschlagen oder erfragen.

▶ Skills file 5, p. 188
▶ Skills file 2, p. 185

Nach dem Lesen

Beantworte nun die Fragen zum Text. Wenn möglich, vergleiche deine Ergebnisse mit einem Partner oder einer Partnerin.

Merkaufgabe 7

Schaue dir die Broschüre auf Seite 80 in Unit 3 an. Lies die Überschriften und sieh dir die Bilder an. Was weißt du nun schon über den Inhalt der Broschüre?

(Die Lösung findest du auf S. 183.)

Mediation

▶ Unit 1 | p. 23   ▶ Unit 2 | p. 51   ▶ Unit 3 | p. 108
▶ Unit 4 | p. 115   ▶ Unit 5 | p. 157

In manchen Situationen musst du zwischen zwei Sprachen vermitteln. Dies nennt man Mediation. Du überträgst die wichtigsten Informationen von der einen Sprache in die andere.

Wann vermitteln?

 → 🇩🇪

- Du möchtest jemandem z. B. englische Spielregeln oder einen englischen Artikel auf Deutsch erläutern.
- Du bist mit deiner Familie in England. Dein kleiner Bruder will z. B. Süßigkeiten kaufen oder wissen, was in einer Broschüre oder auf einem Schild steht.

🇩🇪 → 🇬🇧

- Jemand spricht dich in deinem Wohnort an der Bushaltestelle auf Englisch an, weil er oder sie den Anzeigetext nicht versteht.
- Ein Austauschschüler oder eine Austauschschülerin besucht dich und spricht nicht sehr gut Deutsch.

Worauf muss ich achten?

Keine Panik vor unbekannten Wörtern

Du musst nicht 1:1 übersetzen. Deshalb ist es auch in Ordnung, wenn du nicht jedes Wort verstehst. Es reicht aus, dass du die zentrale Aussage verstehst.

Gib nur die wichtigsten Informationen weiter

Lasse unwichtige Wörter und Satzteile weg. In der Broschüre deines Urlaubshotels z. B. heißt es: *Play football on our great football field behind our hotel with the wonderful view.* Du erklärst deinem kleinen Bruder: *Es gibt einen Fußballplatz hinter dem Hotel.*

Sage es anders

Wenn du ein Wort nicht kennst, versuche es mit anderen Wörtern zu umschreiben. Beispiele:

außer dienstags	→ *but not on Tuesdays*
Mindestalter 14 Jahre	→ *you must be 14 or older*
ermäßigte Eintrittskarten	→ *cheaper tickets*

Sage es kurz

Bilde kurze und einfache Sätze, um Fehler zu vermeiden.

Checkliste Mediation
- ✓ Gib nur die wichtigsten Infos weiter.
- ✓ Umschreibe unbekannte Wörter.
- ✓ Verwende kurze und einfache Sätze.
- ✓ Achte auf Pronomen.

▶ Skills file 11, p. 194

Achte in Gesprächen auf die Pronomen

Überlege immer, an wen du dich gerade wendest: Wenn sich die Perspektive ändert, ändern sich meist auch die Pronomen.

Achte auf kulturelle Unterschiede

Versetze dich in dein Gegenüber und überlege, was für diese Person wichtig ist, um die Situation oder die Inhalte verstehen zu können.

Merkaufgabe 8

Du bist mit deiner Familie in Brighton und deine kleine Schwester möchte wissen, was auf dem Bildschirm des Fahrkartenautomaten von S. 19 steht. Was sagst du ihr?

a) Hier kann man für unterschiedliche Tage Hin- und Rückfahrkarten in verschiedene Städte kaufen.

b) Oben wählst du „London" aus, in der Mitte eine Fahrkarte für die Hinfahrt und unten einen Tag.

c) Wenn du eine Fahrkarte kaufen möchtest, musst du das hier am Automaten tun.

(Die Lösung findest du auf Seite 183.)

Eis essen war eine super Idee, oder? Frag Jane doch mal, wie ihr ihr Eis schmeckt.

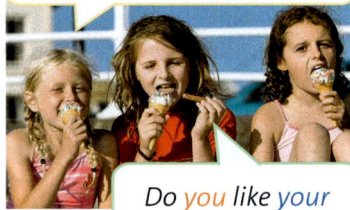

Do you like your ice cream, Jane?

SF 9

Einen Kurzvortrag halten

▶ Unit 4 | p. 130

Um einen guten Kurzvortrag halten zu können, musst du ihn gut vorbereiten und üben.

Einen Kurzvortrag vorbereiten

Schritt 1: Informationen sammeln

Nutze verschiedene Medien als Quellen.

 Nutze das Internet, Bücher, Zeitschriften und Zeitungen.

▶ Skills file 4, p. 187

Schritt 2: Strukturieren und ordnen

Ein Kurzvortrag sollte folgendermaßen aufgebaut sein:

- **Einleitung:** Hier nennst du das Thema.

- **Hauptteil:** Nun nennst du deine Hauptpunkte. Dann erzählst du mehr zu jedem Punkt.

- **Schluss:** Du bedankst dich fürs Zuhören und erkundigst dich, ob jemand Fragen hat.

I'd like to talk about …

First I'd like to tell you about … Then … This picture shows …

Thank you for listening. Do you have any questions?

Schritt 3: Veranschaulichen

Veranschauliche deinen Vortrag mit Bildern oder Gegenständen. Achte darauf, dass die Verwendung der Bilder erlaubt ist. Nutze daher z. B. Bilder von *Creative Commons*.

Beachte bei einer Präsentation am Computer:

- Wähle ein einfaches Folienlayout.
- Verwende eine Schriftgröße von mindestens 16 Punkt.
- Beschränke dich auf wenig Text.
- Wähle nur ein Bild pro Folie. Schreibe dazu, woher du dein Bild hast, z. B. die genaue Internetadresse und das Datum.

Suchst du Bilder im Internet, kannst du im Suchfeld nach *Creative Commons*-Lizenzen filtern.

My favourite animal is a seagull

© jobikoe.example.com

Schritt 4: Notizen machen

Mache dir kurze Notizen auf Karteikarten. Strukturiere deine Notizen genauso wie deine Präsentation. Hebe die wichtigsten Begriffe mit verschiedenen Farben hervor. Du kannst auch kleine Erinnerungen zum Ablauf deines Vortrags notieren, z. B. wann du welches Bild zeigst.

▶ Skills file 5, p. 188

Schritt 5: Den Kurzvortrag üben

Übe deinen Vortrag mehrmals vor einem Spiegel oder mit einem Partner oder einer Partnerin. Gebt euch gegenseitig Tipps, wie ihr euch verbessern könnt. Du kannst dich auch selbst mit dem Smartphone aufnehmen. Achte auf die Zeit.

Den Kurzvortrag halten

Überprüfe zu Beginn, ob alles vorbereitet ist: Ist das Poster aufgehängt? Ist der Computer bereit? Liegen die Vortragskarten richtig sortiert? Dann beginne deinen Vortrag:

- Schaue dein Publikum an und warte, bis es ruhig ist.
- Sprich langsam, laut und deutlich.
- Zeige während deines Vortrags auf Bilder oder dein Poster.

Merkaufgabe 9

Schaue dir Video 1 von Kats Vortrag an. Gib ihr zwei Tipps, wie sie es beim nächsten Mal besser machen kann.

(Die Lösung findest du auf Seite 183 und in Video 2 von Kats Vortrag.)

SF 10

Die eigene Meinung äußern

► Unit 3 | p. 96

Wie drücke ich aus, was ich denke?

Zu Beginn einer Diskussion sagst du, was du über ein Thema denkst.

> In my opinion, …
> I think that …
> I'm sure that …

Wie frage ich nach der Meinung anderer?

In Diskussionen geht es nicht nur um die eigene Meinung. Daher fragst du die anderen auch nach ihrer Meinung.

> What do you think?

Wie reagiere ich angemessen?

Gehe auf die Beiträge anderer ein und respektiere sie. Sei auch bei Meinungsverschiedenheiten sachlich und höflich.

> I agree.
> You're right.
> For me that's true.
> I think so too.

Merkaufgabe 10

Welche Aussage ist in einer Diskussion angemessen?

a) I don't agree. It's stupid to spend hours on your phone.

b) For me that isn't true. I like to spend my time on other things.

(Die Lösung findest du auf Seite 183.)

> I'm not sure here.
> Well, I don't agree.
> I don't think so.
> I don't think that's true.
> For me that isn't true.

SF 11

Wörter umschreiben

► Unit 1 | p. 42   ► Unit 4 | p. 130

Fehlt dir beim Sprechen ein Wort oder fällt es dir nicht ein, kannst du es umschreiben.

Finde zunächst einen passenden **Oberbegriff** *(umbrella word)*. **Umschreibe**, indem du weitere Details nennst.

> It's a kind of …
> It's a person …
> It's a place …
> It's an activity …

	Beispiele für *umbrella words*	Beispiele für Umschreibungen
waitress	It's a person.	She works in a restaurant.
kitchen	It's a room in the house.	You make food there.

	umbrella words
Personen	person • man • woman • boy • girl • child • …
Orte	place • building • room • country • …
Dinge	food • drink • game • musical instrument • sport • thing • …

Merkaufgabe 11

Finde das richtige *umbrella word* für die Begriffe.

a) rugby • tennis • football • cricket

b) school • park • town hall • supermarket

(Die Lösung findest du auf Seite 183.)

Eine Geschichte planen

► Unit 1 | p. 30

Schritt 1: Ideen sammeln

Sammle zuerst wichtige Ideen und Wörter, z. B. in einer Mindmap. Beantworte dafür die *wh*-Fragen: *Who? When? Where? What? Why?*

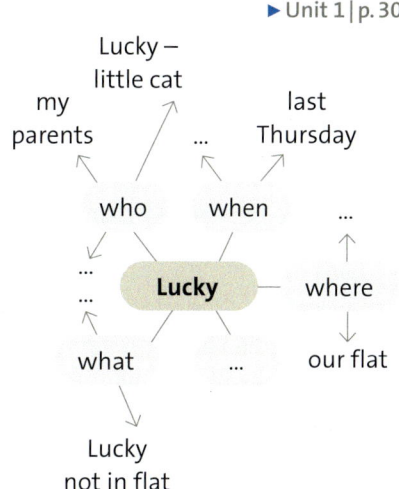

Schritt 2: Die Geschichte strukturieren

Deine Geschichte ist viel besser zu verstehen, wenn du sie gliederst. Unterteile sie deshalb in:

- **Anfang** *(beginning)*: In einem einleitenden Satz sagst du, worum es in deiner Geschichte geht.

- **Mittelteil** *(middle)*: Im Mittelteil beschreibst du die Umstände und Ereignisse deiner Geschichte.

- **Schluss** *(end)*: Schließe deine Geschichte mit einer kleinen Zusammenfassung ab.

Schritt 3: Einen Textentwurf erstellen

Möchtest du die Geschichte mündlich vortragen, mache dir nun Stichpunkte. Schreibe dafür wichtige Wörter auf Kartei-karten und übe, sie frei sprechend vorzutragen.

Möchtest du die Geschichte aufschreiben, erstelle einen Textentwurf – auf einem Blatt Papier oder am Computer.

Überlege dir eine sinnvolle Reihenfolge und beginne bei neuen Punkten mit einer neuen Zeile, z.B. nach deiner Einleitung und vor deinem Schluss.

Schritt 4: Deine Geschichte interessant klingen lassen

Deine Geschichte klingt interessanter, wenn du Adjektive und linking words verwendest: Beschreibe Personen, Orte oder Dinge mit Adjektiven. So kann sich dein Publikum deine Geschichte besser vorstellen. Verbinde deine Sätze mithilfe von *linking words*, z.B. *and, or, but, because, so, then.*

Merkaufgabe 12

Beantworte für eine Geschichte zum Thema „My last weekend" die *wh*-Fragen. Sammle die Antworten in einer kleinen Mindmap wie oben im Beispiel.

---

beginning

Last week something bad happened.

middle

When I came home from school last Thursday, I wanted to play with my cute little cat, Lucky. I looked for her everywhere in the flat, but she wasn't there. Then I saw the open window. I was scared because I thought Lucky fell out of the window. When my parents came home from work, I was very sad. Then we had an idea. We wrote a note with a nice picture of Lucky and my dad's phone number. We put up the note in our neighbourhood. Two days later a man called my dad. There was a little cat in his small garden, so my dad and I went to his house. When the man opened his door, there she was: Lucky!

end

My parents and I were very happy that Lucky was back.

SF 13

Texte überprüfen und verbessern

▶ Unit 5 | p. 162

Ein Text ist noch nicht fertig, wenn du ihn zu Ende geschrieben hast. Du solltest ihn noch mehrmals durchlesen bzw. in Partnerkorrektur durchlesen lassen und auf folgende Punkte achten:

Erstes Lesen: Ist der Text vollständig und verständlich?

Lies den Text und prüfe:
- Hast du irgendwo ein Wort oder Satzzeichen vergessen?
- Sind die Sätze gut verständlich?
- Ist die Reihenfolge der Sätze sinnvoll?
- Hast du Absätze gemacht?
- Hast du *linking words* benutzt?
- Hast du Personen, Orte oder Dinge mithilfe von Adjektiven beschrieben?

Zweites Lesen: Findest du noch Fehler?

Groß- und Kleinschreibung

- Im Englischen schreibt man fast alles klein. Prüfe also: Hast du Wörter wie *football*, *cinema*, *train*, … kleingeschrieben?

- In manchen Fällen schreibt man aber groß – prüfe also: Hast du alle Satzanfänge großgeschrieben?
  Our school starts at 8 o'clock.
  Hast du das Wort *I* (= ich) immer großgeschrieben?
  Maybe I'll play football.

Die richtige Zeitform

- Schreibst du über die Gegenwart? Oder über Dinge, die du regelmäßig machst? (Signalwörter: *today*, *often*, *always*) Dann brauchst du das *simple present*:
  I often go to the swimming pool.

- Oder schreibst du über Sachen, die schon passiert sind? (Signalwörter: *yesterday*, *last Friday*) Dann brauchst du das *simple past*:
  Yesterday I went to the swimming pool.

Merkaufgabe 13

Probiere es gleich aus. Nimm dir einen englischen Text, den du in letzter Zeit geschrieben hast. Lies ihn dir zweimal durch und wende dabei die Punkte von oben an.

Inhalt

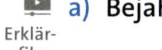
Erklärfilm   Dieses Symbol zeigt dir, dass du einen Erklärfilm zu diesem Thema in der App findest.

Revision 1

Das Verb *be* (The verb 'be')

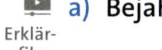
Erklärfilm

a) Bejahte Aussagesätze *(Positive statements)*

Kurzformen	Langformen	Yes
I'm old.	I am old.	
You're old.	You are old.	
He's old.	Grandpa is old.	
She's old.	Ms Lang is old.	
It's old.	The bike is old.	
We're old.	Tom and I are old.	
They're old.	Mum and Dad are old.	

Es gibt Kurz- und Langformen. Bei den Kurzformen fällt ein Buchstabe weg. Dafür steht ein Apostroph (').

Kurzformen werden eher beim Sprechen und in persönlichen E-Mails oder Chats verwendet. Sie stehen nach Pronomen *(I, you, ...)*.

Langformen benutzt du nach Eigennamen *(Zane, Sunita)* oder Nomen *(bike, teachers)*. Man verwendet sie auch bei offiziellen Schreiben.

Revision 1

Das Verb *be* (The verb 'be')

Erklär-film **b)** Verneinte Aussagesätze *(Negative statements)*

Kurzformen	Langformen	No
I'm not old.	(I am not old.)	
You aren't old.	(You are not old.)	
He isn't old.	(Grandpa is not old.)	
She isn't old.	(Ms Lang is not old.)	
It isn't old.	(The bike is not old.)	
We aren't old.	(Tom and I are not old.)	
They aren't old.	(Mum and Dad are not old.)	

Bei der Verneinung benutzt du fast immer die Kurzformen.

I'm not messy, I'm smart!

Erklär-film **c)** Fragen und Kurzantworten *(Questions and short answers)*

Fragen	?	Kurzantworten
		Yes, I am.
		Yes, he / she / it is.
Am I		Yes, you / we / they are.
Are you		
Is he / she / it	late?	No, I'm not.
Are we		No, he / she / it isn't.
Are they		No, you / we / they aren't.

Antworte auf eine Frage im Englischen nicht einfach mit *yes* oder *no*. Das klingt meist unhöflich. Verwende Kurzantworten.

Are you a parrot?

No, I'm not.

Revision 2

Die einfache Gegenwart *(The simple present)*

Erklär-film **a)** Bejahte Aussagesätze *(Positive statements)*

bejahte Sätze	Yes
I	
You	
We	start.
They	
He	
David	
She	starts.
Anna	
It	

He, she, it – ein -s muss mit!

Mit dem *simple present* sagst du, was oft oder täglich oder auch selten oder nie geschieht. Diese Signalwörter findest du oft in Sätzen im *simple present: always, never, often, rarely, sometimes, usually.*

Bei *he, she* und *it* musst du immer ein *-s* ans Verb anhängen.

! Manchmal gibt es Besonderheiten, z. B.:

do – does   have – has   tidy – tidies

klär-film

b) Verneinte Aussagesätze *(Negative statements)*

verneinte Aussagesätze	No
I / You / We / They	**don't** start.
He / She / It	**doesn't** start.

Aussagen im *simple present* musst du mit *don't* oder *doesn't* verneinen. Das Verb steht dann immer im Infinitiv (der Grundform): *He doesn't start.*

klär-film

c) Fragen mit *do/does (Do/Does questions)*

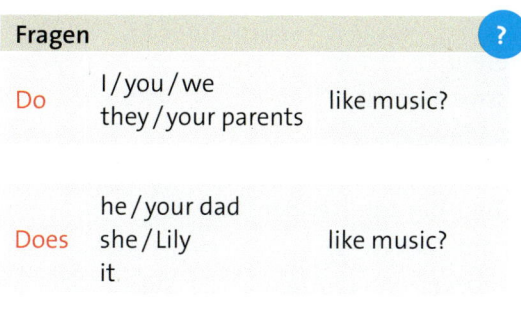

Fragen		?
Do	I / you / we they / your parents	like music?
Does	he / your dad she / Lily it	like music?

Fragen, auf die man mit „Ja" oder „Nein" antworten kann, heißen Entscheidungsfragen. Sie beginnen mit *do* oder *does*.

Mit *I, you, we, they* verwendest du *do*.

Mit *he, she, it* verwendest du *does*.

! Eine Ausnahme bilden Fragen, die mit dem Verb *to be* beginnen.

d) Kurzantworten *(Short answers)*

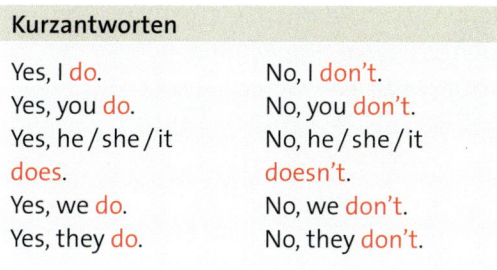

Kurzantworten	
Yes, I **do**.	No, I **don't**.
Yes, you **do**.	No, you **don't**.
Yes, he / she / it **does**.	No, he / she / it **doesn't**.
Yes, we **do**.	No, we **don't**.
Yes, they **do**.	No, they **don't**.

Es wirkt unhöflich, auf Entscheidungsfragen nur mit *yes* oder *no* zu antworten. Besser ist eine Kurzantwort.

Do you live in Brighton too?

Yes, I do.

klär-film

e) Fragen mit Fragewörtern *(Questions with question words)*

How **do** you get home?
Wie kommst du nach Hause?

Who **does** Luca love?
Wen liebt Luca?

Who **loves** Luca?
Wer liebt Luca?

Auch Fragen mit Fragewörtern stellst du mit *do* oder *does*. Das Fragewort steht wie im Deutschen am Anfang.

Wenn mit *Who* oder *What* nach dem Subjekt des Satzes gefragt wird, bildest du die Frage ohne *do* oder *does*.

Revision 3

Erklär-
film

Die Verlaufsform der Gegenwart *(The present progressive)*

I'm read**ing** a comic.
Ich lese gerade einen Comic.

Dad **is** cook**ing** dinner.
Papa macht gerade das Abendessen.

What **are** you do**ing** at the moment?
Was machst du jetzt gerade?

bejahte Aussagesätze	Yes
I'm / You're / He's / She's / It's We're / You're / They're	work**ing**.

verneinte Aussagesätze	No
I'm not You aren't He / She / It isn't We / You / They aren't	work**ing**.

Entscheidungsfragen	?
Am I Are you Is he / she / it Are we / you / they	work**ing**?

Mit dem *present progressive* sagst du, was jemand gerade tut und beschreibst, was auf Bildern passiert.
Signalwörter: *now, at the moment, today*

Im Deutschen sagst du meist
„Ich bin gerade am / beim …"

Das *present progressive* besteht aus zwei Teilen:

am ('m)		
are ('re)	+	Verb + *-ing*
is ('s)		

Bei Verben, die auf *-e* enden, fällt das *-e* bei der *ing*-Form weg:
have – having
make – making
give – giving

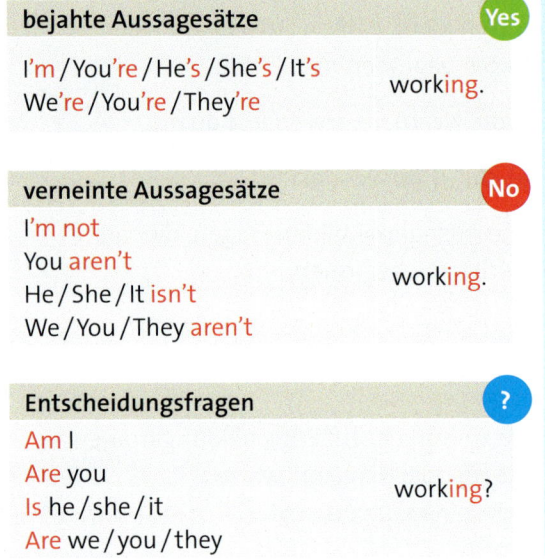

Scout **is** giv**ing** a talk.

Bei einigen Verben wird der letzte Buchstabe verdoppelt, z. B.: *plan — planning, stop — stopping, sit — sitting*

LF 1

Die einfache Vergangenheit *(The simple past)*

I **was** in Berlin last weekend.
Letztes Wochenende war ich in Berlin.

Yesterday Dad and I visit**ed** Grandma.
Gestern haben Papa und ich Oma besucht.

Mit dem *simple past* sprichst du über Dinge, die in der Vergangenheit geschehen sind.
Du verwendest es oft mit Zeitangaben wie *yesterday, last week / year / summer, in 2020*.

Erklär-
film

a) Das Verb *be (The verb 'be')*

▶ Unit 1 | p. 13

bejahte und verneinte Aussagesätze

I / He / She / It Noah / Mum	was wasn't	at home.
We / You / They	were weren't	at home.

Fragen ❓

Was	he / she	at home?
Were	you / they	at home?

Das Verb *be* (sein) hat besondere Vergangenheitsformen: *was* und *were*.

Yesterday Scout *was* at the beach.

LF 2

 Erklär-
film

b) Bejahte Aussagessätze *(Positive statements)*

▶ Unit 1 | p. 14

Yesterday evening I watch*ed* TV.
Gestern Abend habe ich ferngesehen /
sah ich fern.

I arriv*ed* in London last week.
Ich bin letzte Woche in London
angekommen. /
Ich kam letzte Woche in London an.

Bejahte Aussagesätze **Yes**

I / You He / She / It We / They	watch*ed* TV yesterday.

Die Vergangenheitsform der Verben
ist für alle Personen gleich.

Bei regelmäßigen Verben hängst du *-ed*
an das Verb: *walk – walked*
Bei Verben, die auf *-e* enden, wird nur *-d*
angehängt: *arrive – arrived*.

❗ Manchmal gibt es Besonderheiten, z. B.:
plan – planned   try – tried

Unregelmäßige Formen musst du lernen, z. B.:
do – did   go – went   see – saw
Du kannst sie auf S. 312–313 nachschlagen.

LF 3

Die einfache Vergangenheit *(The simple past)*

 Erklär-
film

c) Verneinte Aussagesätze *(Negative statements)*

▶ Unit 1 | p. 20

I *didn't* watch TV yesterday.
Gestern habe ich nicht ferngesehen. /
Gestern sah ich nicht fern.

verneinte Aussagesätze **No**

I / You He / She / It We / They	*didn't* help.

Wenn du sagen willst, dass etwas nicht
geschah, setzt du *didn't* vor das Verb.

Das Verb steht dann immer im Infinitiv
(der Grundform): *He didn't help.*

💡

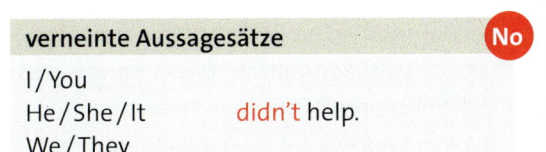

Wenn Di*di* kommt, muss E*de* gehen!

LF 4

Erklär-
film

d) Fragen und Kurzantworten (Questions and short answers) ▶ Unit 2 | p. 52

Did you watch the parade last weekend?
Hast du letztes Wochenende den Umzug gesehen?

Fragen		?
Did	I / you he / she / it we / they	help?

Yes, I / you did.   No, I / you didn't.
Yes, he / she / it did.   No, he / she / it didn't.
Yes, we / they did.   No, we / they didn't.

Fragen im *simple past* bildest du mit *did* und dem Infinitiv des Verbs: *Did he help?*

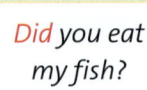

Did you eat my fish?

No, I didn't.

Kurzantworten bildest du mit *did* oder *didn't*.
Eine Ausnahme bilden Fragen, die mit dem Verb *to be* beginnen, und deren Antworten.

LF 5

Erklär-
film

e) Fragen mit Fragewörtern (Questions with question words) ▶ Unit 2 | p. 53

Fragen			?
What	did	she	watch?
When	did	it	finish?
Where	did	they	go?

How did it go? – It went well.

Auch bei Fragen mit Fragewörtern verwendest du *did* bei allen Personen und das Verb im Infinitiv: *How did it go?*

Bei den Antworten wird das Verb in die Vergangenheitsform gesetzt.

LF 6

Indirekte Rede (Reported speech) ▶ Unit 2 | p. 51

The woman says (that) she loves her dog.
Die Frau sagt, dass sie ihren Hund liebt.

The sign says (that) you can't park here.
Auf dem Schild steht, dass man hier nicht parken darf.

Mit der indirekten Rede berichtest du, was jemand sagt / schreibt / denkt. Einleitende Verben sind z. B. *answer, say, tell sb., think*.

❗ Im Englischen steht vor der indirekten Rede kein Komma. *That* („dass") wird oft weggelassen.

Bei der indirekten Rede achte darauf, wer spricht bzw. schreibt. Entsprechend musst du Personen und Pronomen ändern:
"I love my dog." → *... she loves her dog.*

Nebensätze mit Konjunktionen
(Subordinate clauses with conjunctions)

▶ Unit 2 | p. 57

She left because she had a headache.
Sie ging, weil sie Kopfschmerzen hatte.

He was hungry so he had lunch.
Er war hungrig, also aß er Mittag.

I listen to music when I do my homework.
Ich höre Musik, wenn ich meine
Hausaufgaben mache.

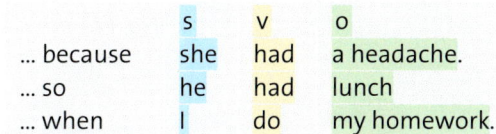

	s	v	o
... because	she	had	a headache.
... so	he	had	lunch
... when	I	do	my homework.

Mit Konjunktionen wie *because*, *so* oder *when*
kannst du Sätze miteinander verknüpfen.

Dabei ist die Wortstellung im Nebensatz nach
der Konjunktion genauso wie im Hauptsatz:
subject – verb – object.

Im Deutschen ist das im Nebensatz anders:

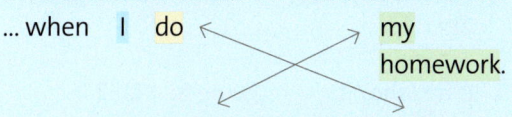

... wenn ich meine Hausaufgaben mache.

Erklär-
film

Die Zukunft mit *going to* (The going to-future)

a) Aussagesätze *(Statements)*

▶ Unit 3 | p. 82

We're going to have a picnic on Sunday.
Wir haben vor, am Sonntag zu picknicken. /
Wir werden am Sonntag picknicken.

Lily isn't going to bring a cake.
Lily wird keinen Kuchen mitbringen.

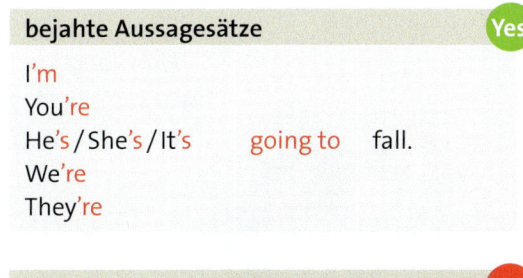

bejahte Aussagesätze   **Yes**

I'm		
You're		
He's / She's / It's	going to	fall.
We're		
They're		

verneinte Aussagesätze   **No**

I'm not		
You aren't		
He / She / It isn't	going to	fall.
We aren't		
They aren't		

Mit *going to ...* sagst du, was du vorhast oder
planst.

Going to hat hier nichts mit dem deutschen
„gehen" zu tun, sondern bedeutet „werden".

Das *going to-future* besteht aus drei Teilen:

am ('m)				
are ('re)	+	going to	+	Verb
is ('s)				

Das Verb bleibt immer im Infinitiv:
I'm going to watch a video.

*I'm going to
make dinner.*

Erklär-film

LF 9

Die Zukunft mit *going to* (The going to-future)

b) Fragen und Kurzantworten (*Questions and short answers*) ▶ Unit 3 | p. 83

Are you **going to** leave soon?
Wirst du bald gehen?

Is Lily **going to** bring a cake?
Wird Lily einen Kuchen mitbringen?

Bei Fragen stehen *am*, *are* oder *is* am Beginn des Fragesatzes (vor dem Subjekt).

Entscheidungsfragen ?

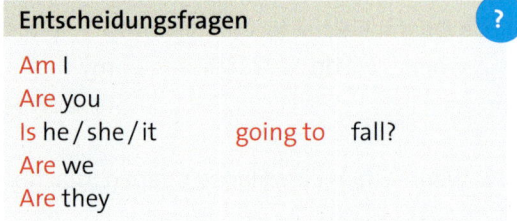

Am I			
Are you			
Is he / she / it	**going to**	fall?	
Are we			
Are they			

Kurzantworten

Yes, I **am**.	No, I'm **not**.
Yes, you **are**.	No, you **aren't**.
Yes, he / she / it **is**.	No, he / she / it **isn't**.
Yes, we **are**.	No, we **aren't**.
Yes, they **are**.	No, they **aren't**.

Are you going to swim?

No, I'm not.

LF 10

c) Fragen mit Fragewörtern (*Questions with question words*) ▶ Unit 3 | p. 83

Who am I **going to** meet?
Wen werde ich treffen?

Why are you **going to** leave so early?
Warum wirst du so früh gehen?

Fragewörter stehen wie im Deutschen am Satzanfang.

Fragen ?

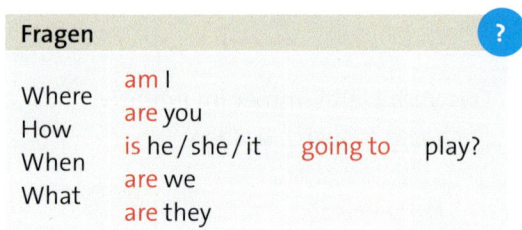

Where	**am** I		
How	**are** you		
When	**is** he / she / it	**going to**	play?
What	**are** we		
	are they		

How long are we going to stay here in the rain?

Erklär-
film

Steigerung und Vergleich *(Comparison)*

a) Der Komparativ *(The comparative)*   ▶ Unit 3 | p. 85

Mum is tall**er** than Dad.
Mama ist größer als Papa.

This shop is more expensive than the market.
Dieses Geschäft ist teurer als der Markt.

| fast | fast**er** |
| loud | loud**er** |

hot	hot**t**er
shy	shy**er**
noisy	nois**ier**
happy	happ**ier**

| famous | more famous |
| expensive | more expensive |

Leon is as old as Malik.
The red bike is as expensive as the blue one.

Personen und Sachen kann man vergleichen, indem man Adjektive steigert.

Bei einsilbigen Adjektiven hängst du *-er* an das Adjektiv. Zweisilbige Adjektive auf *-y* werden mit *-ier* gesteigert.

! Eine Ausnahme von dieser Regel bildet *shy*.

! Diese Ausnahmen musst du lernen:
good – better   *bad – worse*   *little – less*

Bei dreisilbigen Adjektiven und zweisilbigen Adjektiven, die nicht auf *-y* enden, setzt du *more* vor das Adjektiv.

Wenn du sagen willst, dass zwei Personen oder Dinge genau gleich groß, alt, teuer usw. sind, verwendest du *as … as*.
Im Deutschen sagst du so … wie:
Leon ist so alt wie Malik.

Erklär-
film

b) Der Superlativ *(The superlative)*   ▶ Unit 3 | p. 86

Leon is the old**est** student in our class.
Leon ist der älteste Schüler in unserer Klasse.

This game is the most expensive.
Dieses Spiel ist am teuersten.

| fast | the fast**est** |
| loud | the loud**est** |

| big | the big**g**est |
| happy | the happ**iest** |

| famous | the most famous |
| expensive | the most expensive |

Mit dem Superlativ sagst du, dass etwas am größten, ältesten, teuersten, besten usw. ist. Dazu hängst du bei einsilbigen Adjektiven und bei zweisilbigen, die auf *-y* enden, *-est* an das Adjektiv.

! Bei einigen Adjektiven musst du bei der Schreibung aufpassen (z. B. *big* oder *happy*).

! Diese Ausnahmen musst du lernen:
good – best   *bad – worst*   *little – least*

Bei dreisilbigen Adjektiven und zweisilbigen Adjektiven, die nicht auf *-y* enden, setzt du *most* vor das Adjektiv.

LF 13

Erklär-
film

some und *any*

▶ Unit 4 | p. 116

some

I can make some sandwiches.
Can I have some sugar, please?

Would you like some pizza?

any

There isn't any tea.
We don't have any cake today.

Anders als im Deutschen muss man im Englischen *some* oder *any* einsetzen, wenn man über eine Menge oder Anzahl spricht und keine genaue Zahl nennen kann.

Some bedeutet „einige" oder „etwas".
Du verwendest *some*
– in bejahten Aussagen,
– wenn du um etwas bittest,
– wenn du jemandem etwas anbietest.

In verneinten Sätzen verwendest du *not ... any*. Auf Deutsch: kein, keine, keinen.

LF 14

a little und *a few*

▶ Unit 4 | p. 116

nicht zählbar

zählbar

a little

Can I have a little milk in my tea, please?
I take my coffee with a little sugar.

a few

There are only a few sausages left.
There are a few pencils on the table.

Wenn du über Mengen sprichst, ist es wichtig, ob es sich um nicht zählbare oder zählbare Nomen handelt.

Nicht zählbare Nomen kannst du nicht in die Mehrzahl setzen: *cheese, fruit, music, love.*

Zählbare Nomen haben eine Pluralform: *one apple – two apples.*

Für größere Mengen kennst du schon *much* (für nicht zählbare Nomen) und *many* (für zählbare Nomen).

Mit *a little* oder *a few* kannst du über kleine Mengen sprechen.

Bei nicht zählbaren Nomen sagst du *a little* (ein wenig).

Bei zählbaren Nomen verwendest du *a few* (einige).

Erklär-film

Das *present perfect* *(The present perfect)*

a) Aussagesätze *(Statements)* ▶ Unit 4 | p. 119

Ben is happy. He has done his homework.
Ben ist froh. Er hat seine Hausaufgaben gemacht.

My little sister has never been on a plane.
Meine kleine Schwester ist noch nie geflogen.

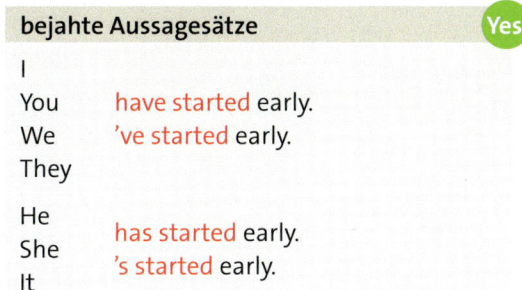

bejahte Aussagesätze	Yes
I You We They	have started early. 've started early.
He She It	has started early. 's started early.

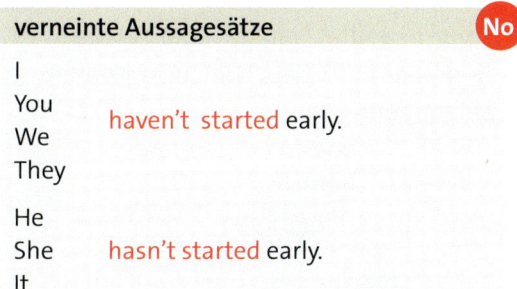

verneinte Aussagesätze	No
I You We They	haven't started early.
He She It	hasn't started early.

Mit dem *present perfect* sagst du,
– dass du etwas schon oder gerade eben gemacht hast. Oft hat die Handlung Auswirkungen auf die Gegenwart. Signalwörter: *already, just, yet*
– dass du etwas schon einmal, öfter oder noch nie gemacht hast. Signalwörter: *ever, never, once, twice, lots of times*

Das *present perfect* besteht aus zwei Teilen:

have ('ve)
has ('s)   +   *past participle*

Wie bildest du das *past participle*?
Bei regelmäßigen Verben hängst du -ed an das Verb: *walk – walked*.
Bei Verben, die auf -e enden, wird nur -d angehängt: *arrive – arrived*.

Unregelmäßige *past participle*-Formen musst du lernen, z. B.:
be – been
do – done
eat – eaten
give – given
go – gone
have – had
see – seen
sing – sung

I've just had lunch.

Du kannst sie in der dritten Spalte der *List of irregular verbs* auf S. 312–313 nachschlagen.

LF 16

Das *present perfect* (The present perfect)

b) Fragen und Kurzantworten *(Questions and short answers)* ▶ Unit 4 | p. 121

Erklär-film

Have you ever been to France?
Bist du schon einmal in Frankreich gewesen? /
Wast du schon einmal in Frankreich?

Fragen und Kurzantworten	?
Have you started?	Yes, I have. No, I haven't.
Has she started?	Yes, she has. No, she hasn't.

Entscheidungsfragen im *present perfect* beginnen mit *have* oder *has*.

Have we met before?

No, we haven't.

LF 17

Zusammensetzungen mit *some* und *any*
(Compounds with some and any)
▶ Unit 4 | p. 123

some

Some of my friends live in America.
Einige meiner Freunde leben in Amerika.

There's somebody in the kitchen.
Da ist jemand in der Küche.

It must be somewhere in my room.
Es muss irgendwo in meinem Zimmer sein.

any

There isn't any tea. Is there any juice?
Es ist kein Tee da. Gibt es Saft?

I don't have anything to wear.
Ich habe nichts anzuziehen.

Can you see Mum anywhere?
Kannst du Mama irgendwo sehen?

Some bedeutet „einige" oder „etwas".
Es gibt das Wort auch in Zusammmen-setzungen:
somebody / someone – jemand
something – etwas
somewhere – irgendwo

Du benutzt *some* und seine Zusammen-setzungen in bejahten Aussagen.

In verneinten Aussagen und Fragen verwendest du *any* und seine Zusammen-setzungen:
not ... anybody / anyone – niemand
not ... anything – nichts
not ... anywhere – nirgendwo
anybody / anyone – jemand
anything – etwas
anywhere – irgendwo

Auch *every* und *no* gibt es in Zusammen-setzungen, z. B. *everyone, nowhere*.

Erklär-
film

Die Zukunft mit *will* (The will-future)

▶ Unit 5 | p. 148

I think you'll have a great party.
Ich glaube, du wirst eine tolle Party haben.

Maybe we'll go swimming tomorrow.
Vielleicht gehen wir morgen schwimmen.

bejahte Aussagesätze		Yes
It	will	be sunny tomorrow.
	'll	

verneinte Aussagesätze		No
It	will not	be sunny tomorrow.
	won't	

Fragen und Kurzantworten		?
Will it be sunny?	Yes, it will.	
	No, it won't.	

Wenn du sagst, was in der Zukunft wahrscheinlich geschehen wird, verwendest du das *will-future*.

Die Sätze beginnen oft mit *I think, maybe, I'm sure*.

Du bildest das *will-future* mit *will* und dem Infinitiv des Verbs.

Die Kurzform von *will* ist *'ll*.

I think we'll be good friends.

Die Kurzform von *will not* ist *won't*.

Adverbien der Art und Weise (Adverbs of manner)

▶ Unit 5 | p. 155

Please speak slowly and clearly.
Bitte sprich langsam und deutlich.

clear	clearly
nervous	nervously
quick	quickly
slow	slowly
sad	sadly

angry	angrily
happy	happily
full	fully

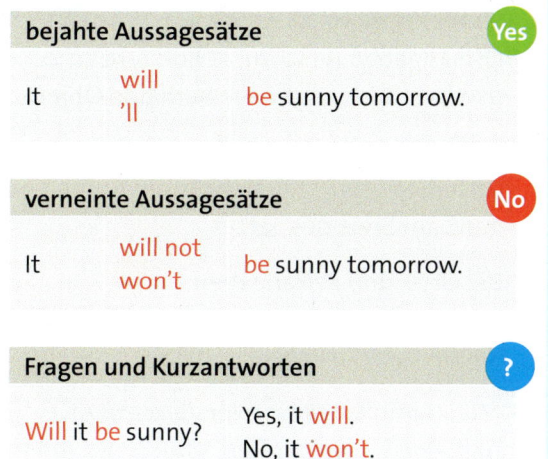

Scout is singing very well.

Adverbien der Art und Weise beschreiben, wie etwas geschieht.
Verwechsle sie nicht mit Adjektiven.
Adjektive beschreiben eine Person oder eine Sache genauer.

Adjektiv   Adverb
a careful driver ⟷ *She drives carefully.*

Die meisten Adverbien bildet man durch Anfügen von *-ly* an ein Adjektiv.

! Manchmal gibt es Unregelmäßigkeiten bei der Schreibung (z.B. *angrily* oder *fully*).

! Diese Ausnahmen musst du lernen:
Das Adverb zu *good* ist *well*: *She did well*.
Bei *hard* sind Adjektiv und Adverb gleich: *He worked hard*.

LF 20

Die Wortstellung *(Word order)*

▶ Unit 5 | p. 155

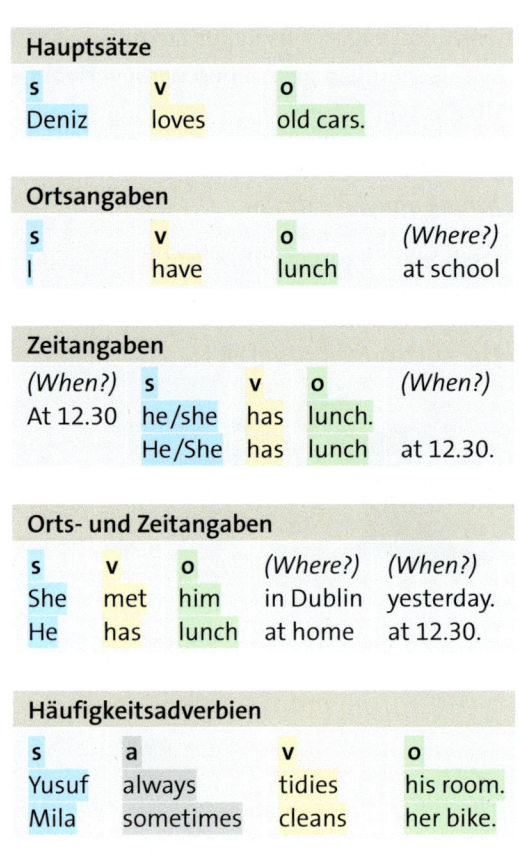

Hauptsätze

s	v	o
Deniz	loves	old cars.

Ortsangaben

s	v	o	(Where?)
I	have	lunch	at school

Zeitangaben

(When?)	s	v	o	(When?)
At 12.30	he/she	has	lunch.	
	He/She	has	lunch	at 12.30.

Orts- und Zeitangaben

s	v	o	(Where?)	(When?)
She	met	him	in Dublin	yesterday.
He	has	lunch	at home	at 12.30.

Häufigkeitsadverbien

s	a	v	o
Yusuf	always	tidies	his room.
Mila	sometimes	cleans	her bike.

In einfachen Aussagesätzen ist die Wortstellung wie im Deutschen:
subject – verb – object.

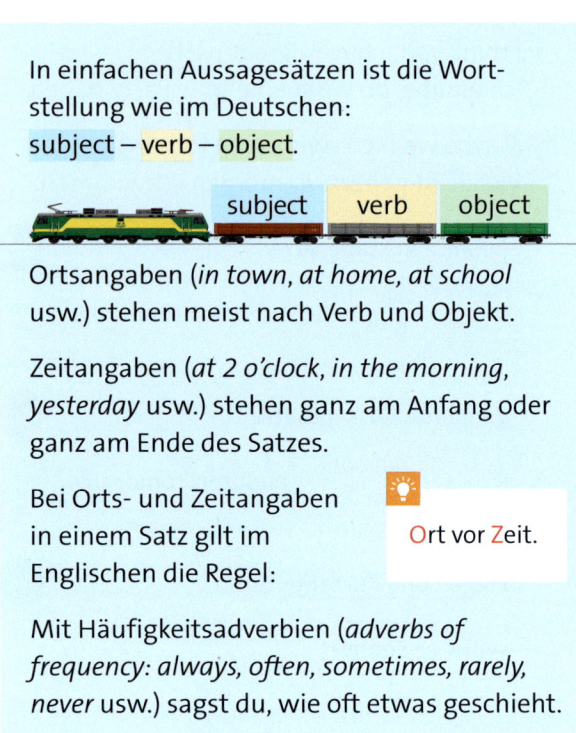

Ortsangaben (*in town, at home, at school* usw.) stehen meist nach Verb und Objekt.

Zeitangaben (*at 2 o'clock, in the morning, yesterday* usw.) stehen ganz am Anfang oder ganz am Ende des Satzes.

Bei Orts- und Zeitangaben in einem Satz gilt im Englischen die Regel:

Ort vor Zeit.

Mit Häufigkeitsadverbien (*adverbs of frequency: always, often, sometimes, rarely, never* usw.) sagst du, wie oft etwas geschieht.

Anders als im Deutschen stehen sie im Englischen meist direkt vor dem Hauptverb.

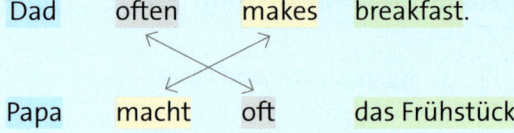

Dad often makes breakfast.

Papa macht oft das Frühstück.

LF 21

Erklär-
film

Bedingungssätze Typ 1 *(Conditional sentences type 1)*

▶ Unit 5 | p. 171

If you send me a message, I'll come.
Wenn du mir eine Nachricht schickst, komme ich.

If it rains tomorrow, we won't play football.
Wenn es morgen regnet, spielen wir nicht Fußball.

We won't play football if it rains tomorrow.

Mit Bedingungssätzen sagst du, was unter bestimmten Bedingungen geschehen wird.

Sie bestehen aus zwei Teilen:
– einem Nebensatz mit *if* im *simple present*
– einem Hauptsatz mit *will*, *'ll* oder *won't*.

Der Nebensatz (*if*-Teil) kann vor oder nach dem Hauptsatz stehen.

Grammatical terms *(Grammatische Fachbegriffe in diesem Buch)*

adjective	das Adjektiv	*good, old, popular*
adverb of frequency	das Häufigkeitsadverb	*often, always, sometimes, rarely, never*
adverb of manner	das Adverb der Art und Weise	*well, carefully, quietly, angrily*
article	der Artikel	***a / the** book, **an / the** apple*
auxiliary verb	das Hilfsverb	*(to) be, (to) do, (to) have*
comparative	der Komparativ	*better, older, more popular*
conditional sentence	der Bedingungssatz	*If it's rainy, I'll stay at home.*
countable nouns	zählbare Nomen	*kid(s), car(s), house(s)*
going to-future	das Futur mit *going to*	*I'm going to eat ...; We're going to watch ...*
infinitive	der Infinitiv (die Grundform eines Verbs)	*(to) do, (to) go, (to) love*
irregular verbs	unregelmäßige Verben	*(to) be, was / were, been; (to) do, did, done*
long form	die Langform	*I **am**, we do **not**, you **are***
negative form	die negative Form	***don't** go, **can't** go, **aren't** going, **hasn't** gone*
object	das Objekt	*I like **cats**.*
past participle	das Partizip Perfekt (die 3. Form des Verbs)	*loved, eaten, seen, done, gone*
personal pronoun	das Personalpronomen	*I, you, he, she, it, we, you, they*
plural	der Plural, die Mehrzahl	*book**s**, child**ren**, potato**es**, stor**ies***
possessive determiner	der Possessivbegleiter	*my, your, his, her, its, our, their*
possessive form	die Possessivform (besitzanzeigende Form)	*the girl's dog*
preposition	die Präposition, das Verhältniswort	*in the house, on the desk, near the river*
present perfect	das Perfekt	*I've gone.; Have you seen?*
present progressive	die Verlaufsform der Gegenwart	*I**'m** speak**ing**.; She**'s** walk**ing**.; We**'re** look**ing**.*
regular verbs	regelmäßige Verben	*(to) move, moved, moved; (to) hug, hugged, hugged; (to) try, tried, tried*
short answer	die Kurzantwort	*Yes, I do.; No, I'm not.; Yes, she does.*
short form	die Kurzform	*I**'m**, we don**'t**, you**'re***
simple past	die einfache Vergangenheit	*It **was**.; I **went**.; He **talked**.*
simple present	die einfache Gegenwart	*I **speak** English.; He **likes** it.*
singular	der Singular, die Einzahl	*book, child, potato, story*
statement	Aussage(satz)	*I like oranges.*
subject	das Subjekt	***They** eat dinner.; **The cat** is cute.*
superlative	der Superlativ	*(the) oldest, (the) best, (the) most popular*
uncountable nouns	nicht zählbare Nomen	*milk, sugar, wind*
wh-question	die Frage mit Fragewort	*What's this? Who are you?*
will-future	das Futur mit *will*	*Noah **will** phone.; You'll see.; He won't buy.*
word order	die Wortstellung	*subject – verb – object: We know them.*
yes/no question	die Entscheidungsfrage	*Are you OK?; Will she go?; Did it go well?*

Wichtige Schreibregeln und Zeichensetzung im Englischen

Groß- und Kleinschreibung

Im Englischen wird fast alles kleingeschrieben. Merke dir nur diese Ausnahmen:
– das Wort *I* (ich);
– Monatsnamen *(January, February, …)*;
– Wochentage *(Monday, Tuesday, …)*;
– Eigennamen und geografische Namen *(Tom, Lisa, Brighton, …)*;
– Länder, deren Bewohnerinnen / Bewohner und Adjektive *(Germany, the Germans, German)*;
– das erste Wort am Satzanfang und in Überschriften.

Stumme Buchstaben

Manche Wörter enthalten Buchstaben, die du zwar schreibst, aber nicht sprichst:
b   lamb
c   science
d   sandwich
g   design
h   technology
i   fruit
k   (to) know, knife
l   (to) walk, (to) talk
u   guitar, building
t   (to) listen
w   (to) answer, two, wrong, (to) write

Verdoppelung der Endkonsonanten

(to) stop – stopping, stopped
(to) win – winning, winner

y wird zu ie

– im Plural: *story – stories, a pony – three ponies;*

– in der 3. Person Singular: *(to) tidy – he tidies;*
– bei der Steigerung von Adjektiven: *busy – busier, easy – easier.*

Buchstabenverbindungen

Manche Buchstabenverbindungen kommen häufiger vor. Wenn du sie dir merkst, können sie dir beim Schreiben helfen:
-ee-   see, deep, meet, street
-ea-   beach, meat, pea
-igh-   sight, fight, right, night
-oo-   book, good, look
-ous   dangerous, nervous, famous
-tion   station, competition

Kommasetzung

Im Englischen kannst du oft entscheiden, ob du ein Komma setzt oder nicht.
Sind zwei Hauptsätze durch *and, but, or* oder *so* miteinander verbunden, können sie – je nach Länge des Satzes – durch ein Komma getrennt werden.
It started to rain, but we decided to stay outside anyway.
Es hat angefangen zu regnen, aber wir sind trotzdem draußen geblieben.
It was raining but I didn't care.
Es regnete, aber das war mir egal.
Kein Komma steht vor einem Nebensatz mit *that, what, where, why* usw. (auch in der indirekten Rede).

Wordbank 1: Holiday activities

► Unit 1 | p. 17

(to) go rafting

(to) go snorkelling

(to) do a treetop walk

(to) ride an alpine slide

water activities

(to) go windsurfing

(to) go to a water park

mountain activities

(to) go hiking

(to) go on a zipline

(to) go on a boat ride

(to) go paddleboarding

holiday activities

(to) go mountain biking

(to) have a sleepover

(to) make videos / a playlist

(to) go sightseeing

(to) watch a parade

(to) paint my room

activities at home

(to) relax with friends

city activities

(to) make a cake / ice cream / pizza

(to) go to the cinema

(to) do origami

(to) visit a castle / museum / market

(to) play crazy golf

(to) have a picnic

(to) have a water fight

Wordbank 2: Describing a person

▶ Unit 2 | p. 4   ▶ Unit 5 | p. 160

He / She has braces / glasses / …
He / She has blond / brown / red / short / long / straight / curly hair.

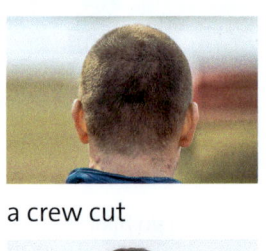
a crew cut

gelled hair

a ponytail

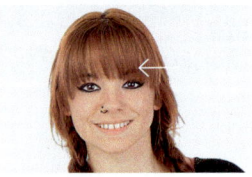
a fringe

plaits

a beard

freckles

nail varnish

airbrushed nails

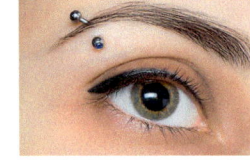
a piercing

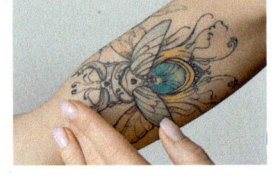
a tattoo

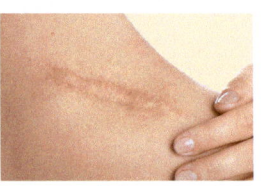
a scar

Skills and activities

He / She is good at drawing / listening / maths / organizing things / solving problems / sports / …
He / She is good with animals / children / computers / …

Personality

ambitious	ehrgeizig	honest	ehrlich
artistic	künstlerisch	imaginative	fantasievoll
brave	mutig	independent	unabhängig, eigenständig
calm	ruhig, gelassen	motivated	motiviert
caring	mitfühlend, fürsorglich	open-minded	aufgeschlossen, offen
cheerful	fröhlich	organized	organisiert
clever, smart	klug, schlau	patient	geduldig
confident	selbstbewusst	practical	praktisch
creative	kreativ	punctual	pünktlich
curious	neugierig	reliable	verlässlich, zuverlässig
dramatic	theatralisch	romantic	romantisch
easy-going	gelassen, locker	sensitive	sensibel, empfindsam
energetic	energisch, tatkräftig	shy	schüchtern
flexible	flexibel	sociable	kontaktfreudig, gesellig
generous	großzügig	strong	stark
hard-working	fleißig	tidy	ordentlich
helpful	hilfsbereit	tolerant	tolerant

clothes

cape
coat
jacket
hoodie
jumper
underwear
swimsuit
T-shirt
tights
shirt
dress
tie
skirt
jeans
socks
trousers
shorts

shoes
trainers
boots
sandals

jewellery
helmet
gloves
sunglasses
accessories
scarf
belt
hat
mask

Wordbank 4: Parts of the body

▶ Unit 2 | pp. 58, 62

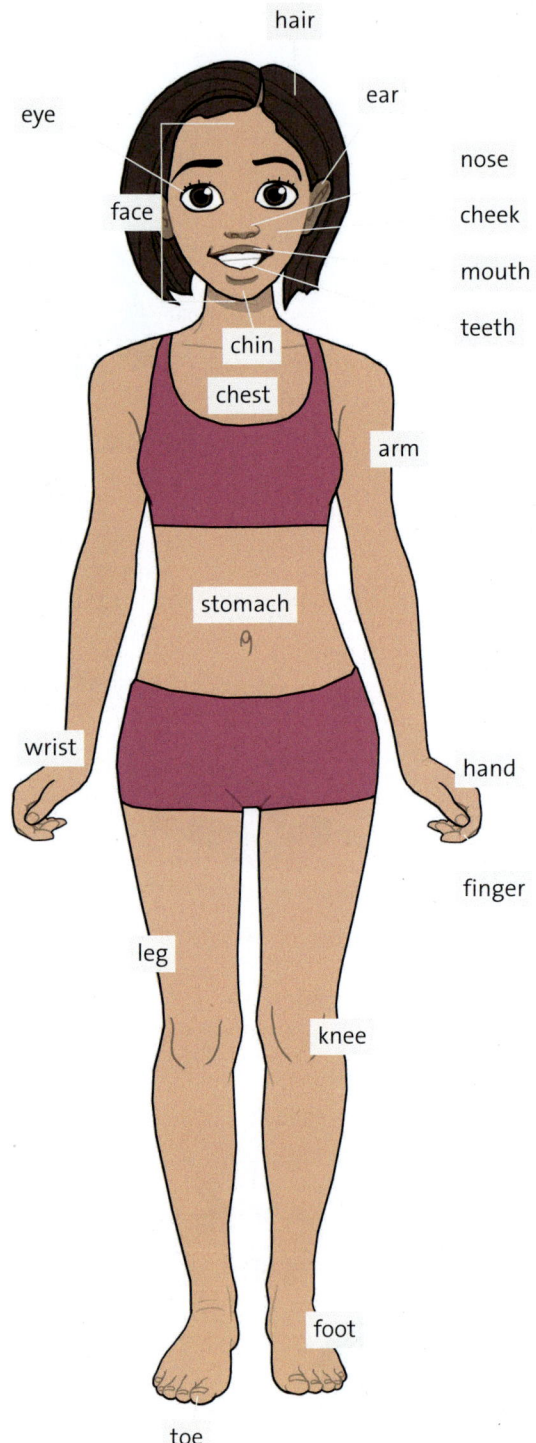

hair

eye

ear

nose

cheek

mouth

teeth

face

chin

chest

arm

stomach

wrist

hand

finger

leg

knee

foot

toe

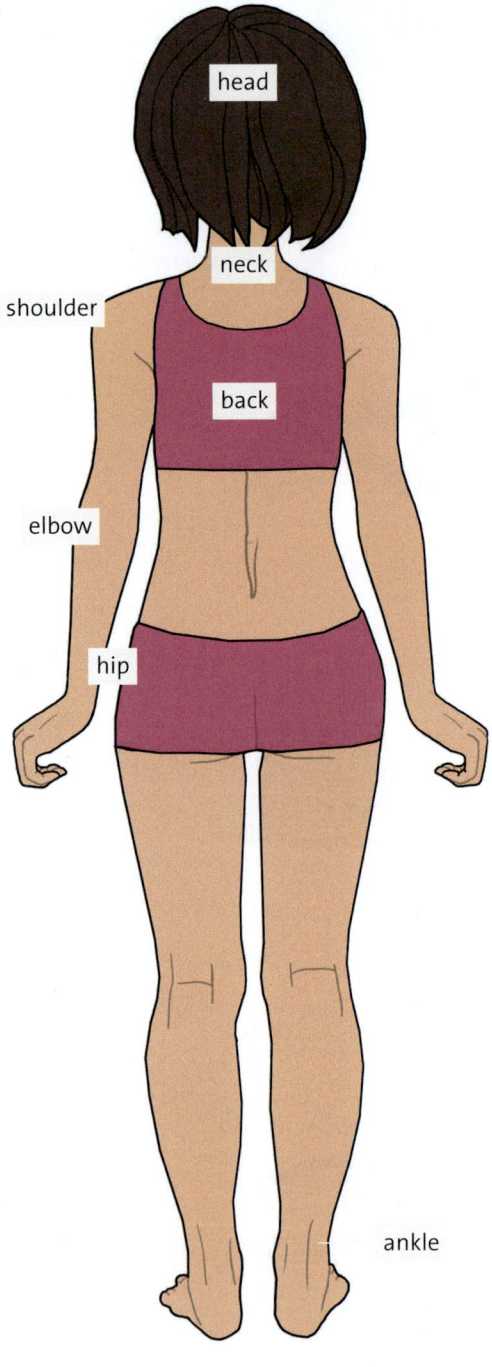

head

neck

shoulder

back

elbow

hip

ankle

Wordbank 5: Films and shows

▶ Unit 3 | p. 87

action film

cartoon

comedy

cooking show

disaster film

documentary

fantasy film

game show

horror film

reality show

romance

science fiction / sci-fi film

soap opera / soap

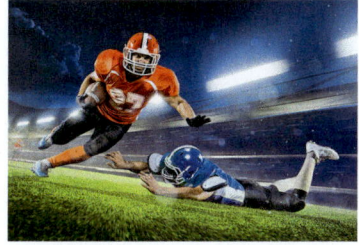

sports show

thriller

Wordbank 6: Online activities

▶ Unit 3 | p. 92

Social media
(to) like photos / posts
(to) post comments
(to) post photos
(to) write on my page / timeline

Soziale Medien
Fotos / Posts liken
Kommentare posten
Fotos posten
auf meine Seite / Chronik schreiben

Video-sharing sites
(to) watch videos for fun
(to) watch fitness videos and
   do workouts
(to) upload videos

Webseiten zum Austausch von Videos
Videos zum Spaß anschauen
Fitness-Videos anschauen und trainieren

Videos hochladen

Messaging services
(to) chat
(to) make new friends
(to) send / (to) read messages

Messaging-Dienste
chatten
neue Freunde gewinnen
Nachrichten senden / lesen

Gaming and puzzle sites
(to) play multiplayer games
(to) play e-sports
(to) do interactive puzzles

Spiel- und Rätselwebseiten
Multiplayer-Spiele spielen
E-Sportarten spielen
interaktive Spiele spielen

Music sites
(to) listen to music
(to) make playlists

Musik-Webseiten
Musik hören
Playlists erstellen

Sites for information and help
(to) find the way
(to) plan routes
(to) look up new words
(to) check facts
(to) find photos
(to) watch online tutorials

Informations- und Hilfewebseiten
den Weg finden
Routen planen
neue Wörter nachschlagen
Fakten überprüfen
Fotos finden
Online-Anleitungen anschauen

Other websites
(to) take a virtual tour
(to) listen to podcasts and
   audio stories
(to) create stories
(to) do slide shows
(to) make short films
(to) create animations

Andere Webseiten
eine virtuelle Tour machen
Podcasts und
   Hörbücher anhören
Geschichten schreiben
Slideshows erstellen
Kurzfilme drehen
Animationen erstellen

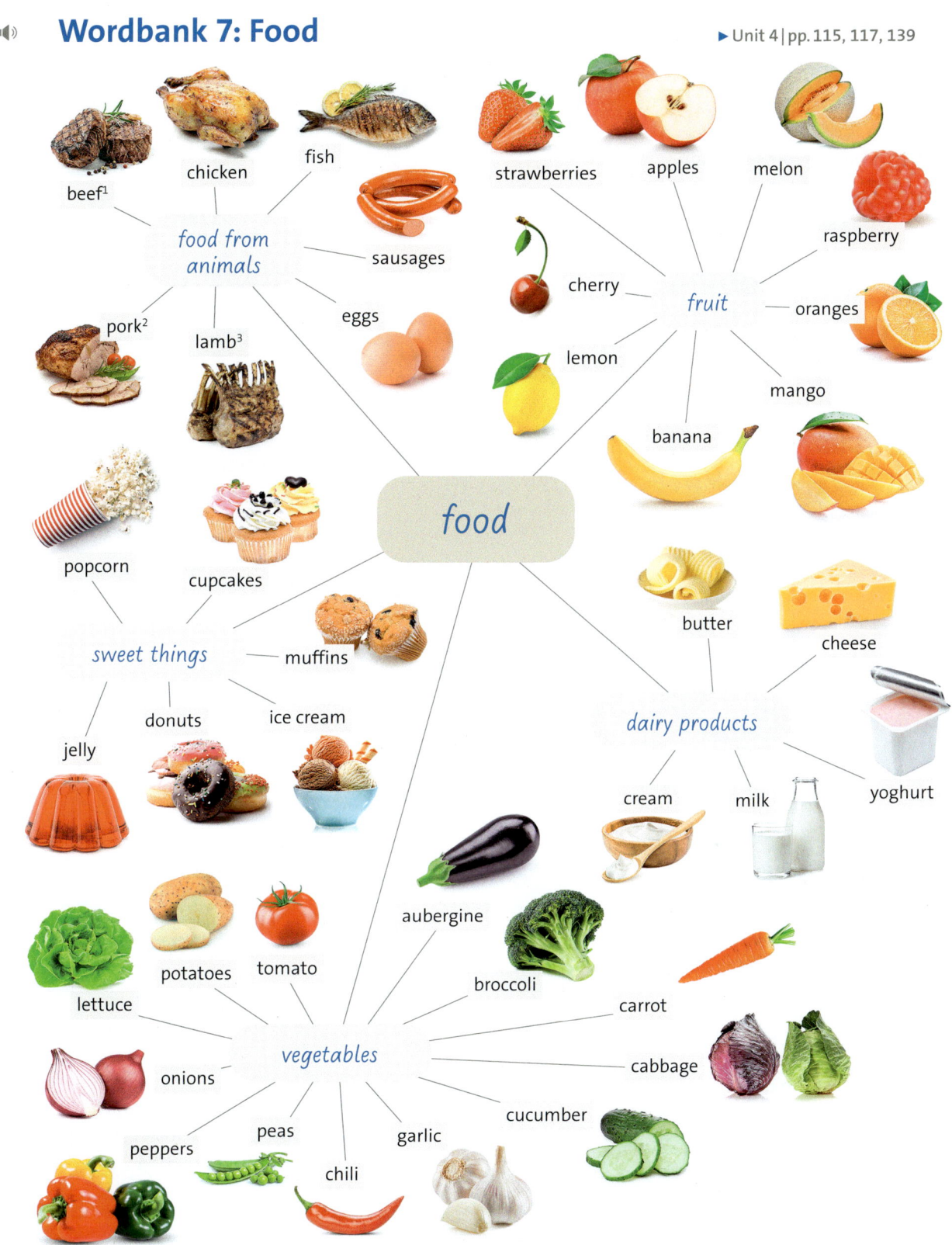

beef[1]

chicken

fish

sausages

food from animals

pork[2]

lamb[3]

eggs

strawberries

apples

melon

raspberry

cherry

fruit

oranges

lemon

mango

banana

food

popcorn

cupcakes

butter

cheese

sweet things

muffins

donuts

ice cream

jelly

dairy products

cream

milk

yoghurt

aubergine

broccoli

carrot

lettuce

potatoes

tomato

cabbage

onions

vegetables

cucumber

peppers

peas

garlic

chili

---

[1] **beef** *das Rindfleisch*   [2] **pork** *das Schweinefleisch*   [3] **lamb** *das Lamm; Lammfleisch*

Wordbank 8: Presentations

▶ Unit 4 | pp. 130, 131

Start the presentation

Good morning.

Hello.

Good afternoon.

My presentation today is about ...

Can everyone hear me?

I'm going to talk about ...

Continue the presentation

First ...

Let me start with ...

Next ...

Then ...

Finally ...

Talk about pictures and videos

Let's look at this picture of ...

In this picture you can see ...

At the top / bottom you can see ...

On the left there is ...

On the right there are ...

Now I'm going to show a short video.

End the presentation

Thank you for listening. Do you have any questions?

Thank you. Any questions?

Answering questions

I'm sorry, I don't understand your question. Could you repeat that, please?

Maybe, but I think ...

Good question, thank you.

Explain and correct yourself

This word means ...

Sorry, that's the wrong word. I mean ...

Sorry, I've forgotten the word. It's when ...

▶ Skills file 11, p. 194

Wordbank 9: Jobs and workplaces

My mum / dad / ... is a/an ...

architect, artist, builder, bus driver, business owner, cook, dancer, firefighter, footballer, gamer, hairdresser, mechanic, nurse, police officer, programmer, teacher, train driver, vet, writer

beautician

call centre agent

care worker

cashier

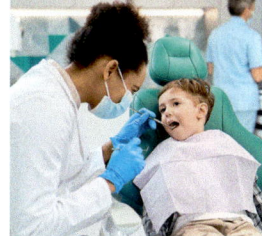

dentist

electrician

engineer

lawyer

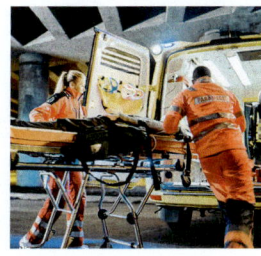

paramedic

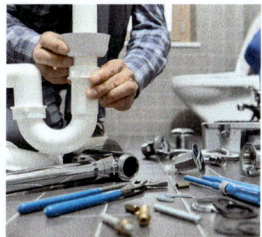

plumber

secretary

shop assistant

My dad / mum / ... works at/on/in a/an ...

cafe, cinema, hospital, library, museum, office, restaurant, school, shop, shopping centre, sports centre, supermarket, train station

in / at a factory

on / at a farm

in / at a garage

in / at a laboratory

My aunt / uncle / ... is unemployed – she / he doesn't have a job.
My dad / mum is a full-time parent.

Wordbank 10: Chores

▶ Unit 5 | p. 152

(to) babysit, (to) clean the bathroom, (to) do the washing, (to) empty the dishwasher, (to) fold the clean clothes, (to) look after the family's pet, (to) make my bed, (to) set the table, (to) take out the rubbish, (to) tidy my room, (to) vacuum the floors

Cleaning

(to) clean out my pet's cage
den Käfig meines Haustiers saubermachen

(to) do the dusting
Staub wischen

(to) take bottles to the bottle bank   *Flaschen zum Container bringen*

(to) take cans / paper / plastic to the recycling containers
Dosen / Papier / Plastik zu den Recyclingcontainern bringen

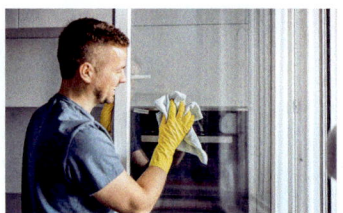

(to) clean the windows
die Fenster putzen

(to) clean my bike
mein Fahrrad putzen

Meals

(to) clear the table
den Tisch abräumen

(to) dry the dishes
abtrocknen

(to) feed the pets
die Haustiere füttern

(to) wash up
abwaschen

(to) load the dishwasher
die Spülmaschine einräumen

Clothes

(to) clean my shoes
meine Schuhe putzen

(to) do the ironing
bügeln

(to) tidy up the wardrobe
den Kleiderschrank aufräumen

(to) hang up the washing
die Wäsche aufhängen

🔊 Hier findest du englische Sätze mit ihrer deutschen Übersetzung. Höre sie dir in der App an. Da jede Sprache anders funktioniert, ist eine wortwörtliche Übersetzung oft nicht möglich: Achte daher auf die kleinen Unterschiede.

1 Sich und andere vorstellen

Sich kennenlernen

(Band 1)	Hello, I'm … / Hi! I'm …	Hallo, ich bin …
	What's your name?	Wie heißt du?
	How old are you?	Wie alt bist du?
	I'm … (years old). What about you?	Ich bin … (Jahre alt). Und du?
	Nice to meet you. – Nice to meet you too.	Freut mich, dich / euch / Sie kennenzulernen. – Freut mich auch.
Unit 1	I'm from (Dresden).	Ich komme aus (Dresden).
Unit 2	I grew up in (China).	Ich bin in (China) aufgewachsen.

Über Hobbys, Vorlieben und Abneigungen sprechen

(Band 1)	My favourite animal is (a fish).	Meine Lieblingstiere sind (Fische).
	What's your favourite animal / hobby / …?	Was ist dein Lieblingstier / -hobby / …?
	My favourite sport is … What about you?	Mein Lieblingssport ist … Und deiner?
	Which places / things / … do you like?	Welche Orte / Dinge / … magst du?
	I (don't) like …	Ich mag … (nicht).
Unit 1	What do you like to do in your free time?	Was machst du gerne in deiner Freizeit?
	Do you have any pets? – We have (a cat).	Hast du Haustiere? – Wir haben (eine Katze).
	I love (cake), but I don't like (chocolate).	Ich liebe (Kuchen), aber (Schokolade) mag ich nicht.
Unit 3	What kind of (music) do you like?	Welche Art von (Musik) magst du?
	I love (photography)!	Ich liebe (Fotografie)!
	I'm not really a fan (of history).	Ich bin eigentlich kein (Geschichts-)Fan.
	I think (Scout's world) is the best (show) ever.	Ich finde, dass (Scout's world) die beste (Show) überhaupt ist.
	I'm sorry, I think it's (boring).	Es tut mir leid, ich finde es (langweilig).

Sich und andere beschreiben
▶ Wordbank 2, p. 214

Unit 2	She has (brown) eyes and (blond) hair.	Sie hat (braune) Augen und (blondes) Haar.
	I have curly / straight hair.	Ich habe lockiges / glattes Haar.
	My mum is (tall) and my dad is (short).	Meine Mutter ist (groß) und mein Vater ist (klein).
	My uncle is (funny) and (kind).	Mein Onkel ist (witzig) und (nett).
	I am very (creative) and (calm).	Ich bin sehr (kreativ) und (gelassen).
	Finn is good with (computers).	Finn kann gut mit (Computern) umgehen.
	Lily is good at (drawing).	Lily kann gut (zeichnen).
	He always helps others.	Er hilft anderen immer gerne.

2 Sich verabreden und etwas planen

Eine Einladung schreiben und auf eine Einladung reagieren

(Band 1)	Please RSVP by text or phone by (10th May).	Um Antwort wird gebeten per Textnachricht oder Telefon.
	Where's the party?	Wo ist die Party?
Unit 4	I'd like to invite you to (my birthday).	Ich möchte dich / euch zu (meinem Geburtstag) einladen.
	I hope you can come!	Ich hoffe, du kannst / ihr könnt kommen!
	Thanks for the invitation to (your party).	Danke für die Einladung zu (deiner / eurer Party).
	Should I / we bring something?	Soll ich / Sollen wir etwas mitbringen?

Sich verabreden: Vorschläge machen und darauf reagieren

(Band 1)	Let's meet in the afternoon.	Lass uns nachmittags / am Nachmittag treffen.
	Let's meet at the weekend.	Lass uns am Wochenende treffen.
	Are you free on (Sunday)?	Hast du am (Sonntag) Zeit?
	What do you do in your free time?	Was machst du in deiner Freizeit?
Unit 3	What are we doing this (weekend)?	Was machen wir am (Wochenende)?
	What are you going to do on (Sunday) morning / afternoon / evening?	Was machst du am (Sonntag-)morgen / -nachmittag / -abend?
	Are you doing anything (today)?	Machst du (heute) irgendetwas?
	Do you want to come round and have (dinner) with (us)?	Möchtest du vorbeikommen und mit (uns) (zu Abend) essen?
	I'm sorry, I'm really busy.	Es tut mir leid, ich bin sehr beschäftigt.
	I'm not going to do anything special then.	Ich mache zu dem Zeitpunkt nichts Besonderes.
	Sorry, I can't. I'm (going to) …	Tut mir leid, da kann ich nicht. Ich (werde) …
	What time is it?	Wie viel Uhr ist es?
	What time is your (dance class)?	Um wie viel Uhr / Wann ist dein (Tanzunterricht)?
	Can we meet?	Können wir uns treffen?
	(Saturday) would be best.	(Samstag) wäre am besten.
	Let's meet at (the station) / in (the park) at (7.30 p.m.).	Lass uns um (19.30 Uhr) am (Bahnhof) / im (Park) treffen.

3 Beim Essen und bei Tisch

► Wordbank 7, p. 219

(Band 1)	Are you hungry?	Hast du Hunger?
	I'm really hungry.	Ich habe großen Hunger. / Ich bin sehr hungrig.
	No, I'm not hungry.	Nein, ich habe keinen Hunger. / Nein, ich bin nicht hungrig.
	My favourite dish is (pizza).	Mein Lieblingsgericht ist (Pizza).
Unit 2	Would you like some more (cake)?	Möchtest du noch mehr (Kuchen)?
	No, thanks; I'm full.	Nein, danke; ich bin satt.

Unit 4	Would you like some (potato curry)?	Möchtest du etwas (Kartoffelcurry)?
	Yes, please! / No, thanks.	Ja, bitte! / Nein, danke.
	May I have some (salad), please?	Könnte ich bitte etwas (Salat) haben?
	Could I have a little (fruit), please?	Kann ich bitte ein bisschen (Obst) haben?
	Enjoy your meal!	Guten Appetit!
	Would you like some more (juice)?	Möchtest du noch etwas mehr (Saft)?
	No, thanks, I still have a little (juice).	Nein danke, ich habe noch etwas (Saft).

4 Über die Ferien und das Wetter sprechen

Über Ferienaktivitäten sprechen

▶ Wordbank 1, p. 213

Unit 1	What did you do on your holiday?	Was hast du im Urlaub gemacht?
	How were your holidays?	Wie waren deine Ferien?
	I was in (Spain) with (my family).	Ich war mit (meiner Familie) in (Spanien).
	We were in a holiday apartment / in a hotel.	Wir waren in einer Ferienwohnung / in einem Hotel.
	I was at home in (Brighton).	Ich bin zuhause in (Brighton) geblieben.
	I went to the (cinema) with (my sister).	Ich war mit (meiner Schwester) im (Kino).
	I went to my (grandparents') house.	Ich war bei meinen (Großeltern).
Unit 3	Where are you going for your holiday?	Wohin fährst du in Urlaub?

Über das Wetter sprechen

Unit 1	How is / was the weather?	Wie ist / war das Wetter?
	What was the weather like (in Spain)?	Wie war das Wetter (in Spanien)?
	The weather is / was (hot) and (sunny).	Das Wetter ist / war (heiß) und (sonnig).
	It is / was (rainy), (windy) and (cold).	Es ist / war (regnerisch), (windig) und (kalt).

Einen Brief schreiben

Unit 5	Dear Finn ...	Lieber Finn, ...
	Hello, everyone!	Hallo an alle!
	How are you?	Wie geht es dir / euch?
	I hope everything is OK (in Dresden).	Ich hoffe, dass alles OK ist (in Dresden).
	I'm sending you (German chocolate).	Ich schicke dir (deutsche Schokolade).
	I'm happy because ...	Ich bin glücklich, weil ...
	What are your (summer) plans?	Was sind deine Pläne (für den Sommer)?
	I hope you have a great holiday!	Ich hoffe, dass du einen großartigen Urlaub hast!
	I miss you. / I'll miss you.	Ich vermisse dich. / Ich werde dich vermissen.
	Please write soon.	Bitte schreibe mir bald.
	Best wishes from (Sunita)	Herzliche / Liebe Grüße von (Sunita)

5 Über Berufe und die Zukunft sprechen

▶ Wordbank 9, p. 221

Unit 5	My dad is a firefighter / an artist.	Mein Vater ist ein Feuerwehrmann / Künstler.
	I want to be a police officer / an architect.	Ich möchte Polizist / Polizistin / Architekt / Architektin werden.
	When I was little, I wanted to be a / an …	Als ich klein war, wollte ich … werden.
	Now I want to be a / an …	Jetzt möchte ich … werden.
	In the future maybe I'll be a / an …	In der Zukunft werde ich vielleicht … sein.
	I'll live in (a big house).	Ich werde in (einem großen Haus) leben.

6 Seine Meinung äußern und diskutieren

(Band 1)	I (don't) think … because …	Ich denke / glaube (nicht) …, weil …
	Let me think.	Lass mich nachdenken.
	I don't know.	Das weiß ich nicht. / Ich weiß (es) nicht.
	Please be polite.	Bitte sei höflich.
	Yes, that's right. / No, that's wrong.	Ja, das stimmt. / Nein, das ist falsch.
	I think you're right / wrong.	Ich glaube, da hast du recht / unrecht.
	I think that's true / false.	Ich glaube, das ist richtig / falsch.
	Do you think it's interesting?	Findest du es interessant?
	Why do you think it's interesting?	Warum findest du es interessant?
	Sorry, can you say that again?	Entschuldigung, kannst du das noch einmal sagen?
Unit 1	I'm sorry, I don't understand.	Es tut mir leid; das verstehe ich nicht.
	What do you mean?	Was meinst du?
Unit 3	That looks really interesting.	Das sieht sehr interessant aus.
	I'd like to do that too.	Das würde ich auch gerne tun.
	I (don't) agree with (Lily).	Ich stimme (Lily) (nicht) zu.
	In my opinion, …	Meiner Meinung nach …
	I'm sorry, I don't agree.	Es tut mir leid, ich stimme nicht zu.
	That's not a good idea.	Das ist keine gute Idee.
	Sorry, but I don't like …	Es tut mir leid, aber ich mag … nicht.
	I'm not really a fan of …	Ich bin nicht wirklich Fan von …
	For me that isn't true.	Für mich ist das nicht so.
	What do you think?	Was meinst du?
Unit 5	That's a great idea!	Das ist eine sehr gute / super Idee!

7 Feedback geben

(Band 1)	I like the photos on your poster.	Ich mag die Bilder auf deinem Poster.
	You can use more words or pictures.	Du kannst mehr Wörter oder Bilder verwenden.
	Your presentation was quite long / short.	Deine Präsentation war ziemlich lang / kurz.
	Please speak more loudly / clearly.	Sprich bitte ein bisschen lauter / deutlicher.
	Don't speak so fast, please.	Sprich bitte nicht so schnell.
	Please look at me / us more.	Schau mich / uns bitte öfter an.
	That was useful information.	Das waren nützliche Informationen.
	Your notes are really helpful.	Deine Notizen sind wirklich nützlich.
	Check your spelling.	Prüfe deine Rechtschreibung.
Unit 1	Your story / presentation needs a better structure.	Deine Geschichte / Präsentation sollte besser strukturiert werden.
Unit 4	You've done a great job!	Das hast du toll gemacht!
	The text on your slides was a bit small.	Der Text auf deinen Folien war etwas zu klein.
	You spoke loudly and clearly.	Du hast laut und deutlich gesprochen.
	I'm sorry, you spoke too quickly / quietly.	Es tut mir leid, du hast zu schnell / leise gesprochen.
	I understood everything that you said.	Ich habe alles verstanden, was du gesagt hast.
	I understood most of / some of what you said.	Ich habe das meiste / einiges verstanden.
	You looked at me / at the audience.	Du hast mich / das Publikum angesehen.
	You looked at your cards.	Du hast auf deine Karten geschaut.
	You smiled / didn't smile.	Du hast gelächelt / nicht gelächelt.
	I've learned about (a new celebration).	Ich habe (ein neues Fest) kennengelernt.

8 Einkaufen und über Preise sprechen

(Band 1)	How much does (a bus ticket) cost?	Wie viel kostet (eine Busfahrkarte)?
	How much is / are the ...?	Wie viel kostet / kosten der / die / das ...?
	The ... costs / is fifty pence / pounds.	Der / Die / Das ... kostet fünfzig Pence / Pfund.
Unit 3	That's too expensive.	Das ist zu teuer.
Unit 5	Can I help you? – I'm just looking.	Kann ich dir / Ihnen helfen? – Ich schaue nur.
	Could you help me, please?	Könnten Sie mir bitte helfen?
	Do you have this / these in size ...?	Haben Sie das / die in Größe ...?
	Do you have this / these in black / in size M?	Haben Sie das / diese in Schwarz / in M?
	Can I try this / these on?	Kann ich das / diese anprobieren?
	I'll take it / them.	Ich nehme es / sie.
	I'd like to pay cash / by card.	Ich würde gerne (in) bar / mit Karte zahlen.
	I'd like a bag, please.	Ich hätte gerne eine Tüte, bitte.
	Can I have a receipt, please?	Kann ich bitte einen Beleg haben?

🔊 Classroom English

You and your teacher	**Du und deine Lehrerin / dein Lehrer**
Good morning, Mr / Mrs / Ms … (bis 12 Uhr)	Guten Morgen, Herr / Frau …
Good afternoon, Mr / Mrs / Ms … (ab 12 Uhr)	Guten Tag, Herr / Frau …
Sorry, I'm late.	Entschuldigung, dass ich zu spät komme.
Can I open / close the window, please?	Kann ich bitte das Fenster öffnen / zumachen?
Can I go to the toilet, please?	Kann ich bitte zur Toilette gehen?

Homework and exercises	**Hausaufgaben und Übungen**
Sorry, I don't have my exercise book.	Es tut mir leid, ich habe mein Heft nicht dabei.
I don't understand this exercise.	Ich verstehe die Übung nicht.
I can't do number 3.	Ich kann Nummer 3 nicht lösen.
Sorry, I haven't finished.	Entschuldigung, ich bin noch nicht fertig.
I have … Is that right too?	Ich habe … Ist das auch richtig?
Sorry, I don't know.	Es tut mir leid, das weiß ich nicht.
What's for homework?	Was haben wir (als Hausaufgabe) auf?

You need help	**Du brauchst Hilfe**
Can you help me, please?	Können Sie / Kannst du mir bitte helfen?
What page is it, please?	Auf welcher Seite sind wir / steht das?
What's … in English / German?	Was heißt … auf Englisch / Deutsch?
Can you write it on the board, please?	Können Sie das bitte an die Tafel schreiben?
Can I say it in German?	Kann ich das auf Deutsch sagen?
Can you speak more loudly, please?	Können Sie / Kannst du bitte lauter sprechen?
Can you say / play that again, please?	Können Sie das bitte noch einmal sagen / abspielen?

Work with a partner	**Partnerarbeit**
Can I work with Julian?	Kann ich mit Julian arbeiten?
Can I use your (pen), please?	Kann ich bitte deinen (Stift) benutzen?
Yes, here you are.	Hier, bitte.
It's my / your turn.	Ich bin dran. / Du bist dran.
Let's make / draw a / an …	Lass uns ein / eine / einen … machen / zeichnen.
Let's act out the story / the dialogue.	Lass uns die Geschichte / den Dialog spielen.

What your teacher says	**Was deine Lehrerin / dein Lehrer sagt**
Let's start.	Lasst uns anfangen. / Los geht's.
Listen, please. / Quiet, please.	Hört bitte zu. / Ruhe bitte.
Open your books at page 24, please.	Schlagt bitte Seite 24 auf.
Do exercise 5 for homework, please.	Macht bitte Übung 5 als Hausaufgabe.
Write the correct words.	Schreibt die richtigen Wörter auf.
Correct the false sentences.	Korrigiert die falschen Sätze.
Where's your book, Dana?	Wo ist dein Buch, Dana?
Try again!	Versuche es noch einmal.
That's all for today. You may go now.	Das ist alles für heute. Ihr dürft jetzt gehen.

🔊 The English alphabet

a	[eɪ]	h	[eɪtʃ]	o	[əʊ]	v	[viː]
b	[biː]	i	[aɪ]	p	[piː]	w	[ˈdʌbljuː]
c	[siː]	j	[dʒeɪ]	q	[kjuː]	x	[eks]
d	[diː]	k	[keɪ]	r	[ɑː]	y	[waɪ]
e	[iː]	l	[el]	s	[es]	z	[zed]
f	[ef]	m	[em]	t	[tiː]		
g	[dʒiː]	n	[en]	u	[juː]		

🔊 English sounds

💡 Die Lautschrift zeigt dir die Aussprache von Wörtern und Lauten *(sounds)*.

❗ Einige dieser Laute kommen im Deutschen nicht vor oder werden anders geschrieben. Sie sind hier mit einem Ausrufezeichen gekennzeichnet. Übe sie mit Hilfe der App.

	[iː]	green, he, sea		[d]	day, window, good
	[ɑː]	ask, class, car, park		[t]	ten, letter, at
❗	[ɔː]	or, ball, door, four, morning		[g]	go, again, bag
	[uː]	ruler, blue, too, two, you		[k]	kitchen, car, back
	[ɜː]	early, her, girl, work, T-shirt		[m]	man, remember, mum
	[ɪ]	in, big, expensive		[n]	no, one, ten
	[e]	yes, bed, again, breakfast	❗	[ŋ]	wrong, young, uncle, thanks
	[æ]	animal, apple, black, cat		[l]	like, old, small
	[ʌ]	mum, bus, colour		[r]	ruler, friend, sorry
	[ɒ]	song, on, dog, what	❗	[w]	we, where, one
	[ʊ]	book, good, put, bully		[j]	yes, you, uniform
	[ə]	again, today, a sister		[f]	family, after, laugh
	[i]	happy, monkey	❗	[v]	very, seven, have
	[eɪ]	name, eight, play, great		[s]	six, poster, yes
	[aɪ]	I, time, right, my	❗	[z]	zoo, quiz, his, music, please
	[ɔɪ]	boy, toilet, noise		[ʃ]	she, station, English
	[əʊ]	old, no, road, yellow	❗	[ʒ]	ususally, revision, garage
	[aʊ]	now, house		[tʃ]	chain, teacher, watch
	[ɪə]	where, pair, share, their	❗	[dʒ]	job, German, project, orange
	[eə]	here, material, really, year	❗	[θ]	thing, three, bathroom, north
	[ʊə]	tour	❗	[ð]	the, weather, with
	[b]	bike, table, verb		[h]	house, who, behind
	[p]	pen, paper, shop			

🔊 English numbers

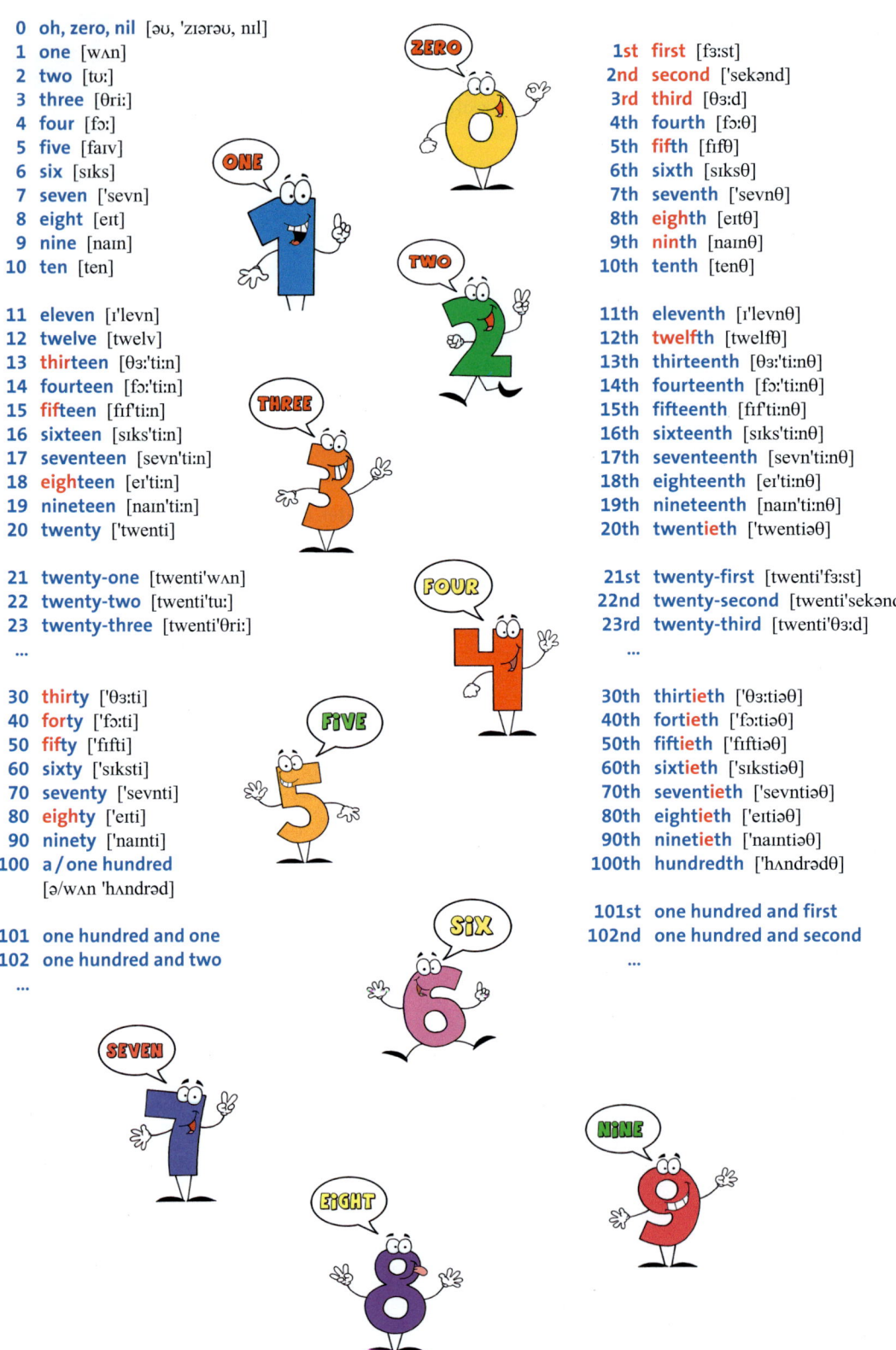

0   oh, zero, nil [əʊ, ˈzɪərəʊ, nɪl]
1   one [wʌn]
2   two [tuː]
3   three [θriː]
4   four [fɔː]
5   five [faɪv]
6   six [sɪks]
7   seven [ˈsevn]
8   eight [eɪt]
9   nine [naɪn]
10 ten [ten]

11 eleven [ɪˈlevn]
12 twelve [twelv]
13 thirteen [θɜːˈtiːn]
14 fourteen [fɔːˈtiːn]
15 fifteen [fɪfˈtiːn]
16 sixteen [sɪksˈtiːn]
17 seventeen [sevnˈtiːn]
18 eighteen [eɪˈtiːn]
19 nineteen [naɪnˈtiːn]
20 twenty [ˈtwenti]

21 twenty-one [twentiˈwʌn]
22 twenty-two [twentiˈtuː]
23 twenty-three [twentiˈθriː]
...

30 thirty [ˈθɜːti]
40 forty [ˈfɔːti]
50 fifty [ˈfɪfti]
60 sixty [ˈsɪksti]
70 seventy [ˈsevnti]
80 eighty [ˈeɪti]
90 ninety [ˈnaɪnti]
100 a / one hundred
       [ə/wʌn ˈhʌndrəd]

101 one hundred and one
102 one hundred and two
...

1st   first [fɜːst]
2nd   second [ˈsekənd]
3rd   third [θɜːd]
4th   fourth [fɔːθ]
5th   fifth [fɪfθ]
6th   sixth [sɪksθ]
7th   seventh [ˈsevnθ]
8th   eighth [eɪtθ]
9th   ninth [naɪnθ]
10th tenth [tenθ]

11th eleventh [ɪˈlevnθ]
12th twelfth [twelfθ]
13th thirteenth [θɜːˈtiːnθ]
14th fourteenth [fɔːˈtiːnθ]
15th fifteenth [fɪfˈtiːnθ]
16th sixteenth [sɪksˈtiːnθ]
17th seventeenth [sevnˈtiːnθ]
18th eighteenth [eɪˈtiːnθ]
19th nineteenth [naɪnˈtiːnθ]
20th twentieth [ˈtwentiəθ]

21st twenty-first [twentiˈfɜːst]
22nd twenty-second [twentiˈsekənd]
23rd twenty-third [twentiˈθɜːd]
...

30th thirtieth [ˈθɜːtiəθ]
40th fortieth [ˈfɔːtiəθ]
50th fiftieth [ˈfɪftiəθ]
60th sixtieth [ˈsɪkstiəθ]
70th seventieth [ˈsevntiəθ]
80th eightieth [ˈeɪtiəθ]
90th ninetieth [ˈnaɪntiəθ]
100th hundredth [ˈhʌndrədθ]

101st one hundred and first
102nd one hundred and second
...

Im *Vocabulary* findest du alle neuen Wörter und Wendungen, die du lernen musst.
Sie stehen in der Reihenfolge, in der sie im Buch zum ersten Mal vorkommen.
Höre dir in der App jedes Wort beim Lernen genau an und sprich es nach.

Inhalt

Seite ... Seite

Symbole und Abkürzungen

▶ p. 14 ▶ pp. 46/47	Die Seitenzahl in der linken Spalte zeigt dir, wo das Wort zum ersten Mal vorkommt.
▶▶ kid(s)	Die doppelten Pfeile weisen auf ein Wort mit gleicher Bedeutung hin, das du bereits kennst.
[kɪd(z)]	Die Lautschrift zeigt dir, wie ein Wort ausgesprochen wird. Eine Übersicht findest du auf S. 229.
first ◀▶ last	Das „Gegenteil"-Zeichen bedeutet: *first* ist das Gegenteil von *last*.
❗ *German:* **lange** schlafen *English:* (to) **sleep late**	Das ❗ bedeutet: Hier keinen Fehler machen!
when 1. wann **When** is your birthday? 2. wenn You can start **when** you're ready. 3. als I started **when** I was ready.	In den Merkboxen findest du wichtige Hinweise zu den neuen Wörtern und Wendungen. Hier ein Beispiel für die Verwendung von „when".

sb. = *somebody* (jemand)   adj = *adjective* (Adjektiv)
sth. = *something* (etwas)   adv = *adverb* (Adverb)
infml. = *informal* (informell, umgangssprachlich)   pl = *plural* (Plural, Mehrzahlform)

Hinweise

Tipps zum Vokabellernen findest du im Skills file auf S. 183–196.
Die Wordbanks (S. 213–222) bieten dir nach wichtigen Themen gesammelte Stichwörter.
Let's talk (S. 223–228) enthält Wendungen für wichtige Situationen, z. B. „Feedback geben".
Eine Liste mit unregelmäßigen Verben findest du auf den Seiten 312–313.
Englische Wörter, die Wörtern im Deutschen ähnlich sind, findest du auf S. 314.
Im Dictionary (S. 277–311) kannst du englische und deutsche Wörter nachschlagen.

Aussprache: die Lautschrift

Wie man englische Wörter ausspricht, zeigt dir die **Lautschrift** hinter dem Wort. Sie steht immer in eckigen Klammern.

Beispiele: **autumn** [ˈɔːtəm]   **window** [ˈwɪndəʊ]

Eine Übersicht über die **Lautschriftzeichen** findest du auf S. 229 *(English sounds)*.

Das Zeichen [ˈ] ist das **Betonungszeichen** – es steht <u>vor</u> der Silbe, die du betonen musst.

Zum Beispiel sieht der Name „Brighton" in der Lautschrift so aus: [ˈbraɪtn].   ▶ English sounds, p. 229

🔊 Hello again!

▶ pp. 10/11	**last** [lɑːst]	letzte(r, s); als letztes	first ◀ ▶ **last** **last** week/month/year = die letzte/vorige Woche, der letzte/vorige Monat, das letzte/vorige Jahr
	tomorrow [təˈmɒrəʊ]	morgen	Today is Friday, so **tomorrow** is Saturday.
	(to) **look for** [ˈlʊk fɔː]	suchen; Ausschau halten nach	I'm **looking for** my red T-shirt. Do you know where it is? (to) **look** + Präposition: Let's **look for** Scout. = suchen **Look after** your sister. = sich kümmern um **Look at** this! = anschauen

	(to) **wait (for)** [ˈweɪt fɔː]	warten (auf)	• **Wait a minute.**
			  = Warte mal. / Einen Moment.
			• **I can't wait!** = Ich kann es kaum erwarten!
			  I can't wait to go to France and see my French friends again!

	(to) **sleep late** [sliːp ˈleɪt], *simple past:* **slept** [slept]	lange schlafen	❗ *German:* **lange** schlafen *English:* (to) **sleep late**

🔊 Unit 1: Travel and holidays

▶ pp. 12/13	**I was ...** [wɒz]	Ich war ...	• **I am** **I was**
			  ich bin ich war
			• **he/she/it is** **he/she/it was**
			  er/sie/es ist er/sie/es war

	trip [trɪp]	der Ausflug; die Reise	**class trip / school trip** = der Klassenausflug/Schulausflug

	We were ... [wɜː]	Wir waren ...	• **we are** **we were**
			  wir sind wir waren
			• **you are** **you were**
			  du bist; ihr seid du warst; ihr wart
			• **they are** **they were**
			  sie sind sie waren

I wasn't [ˈwɒznt] **(= was not) ... /** **We weren't** [wɜːnt] **(= were not) ...**	Ich war nicht ... / Wir waren nicht ...	**YES** **NO** I was I wasn't you were you weren't he/she/it was he/she/it wasn't we were we weren't you were you weren't they were they weren't
capital (city) [ˈkæpɪtl ˈsɪti]	die Hauptstadt	❗ **capital =** **1.** (= capital city) die Hauptstadt **2.** (= capital letter) der Großbuchstabe
mountain [ˈmaʊntən]	der Berg	
campsite [ˈkæmpsaɪt]	der Campingplatz	a **campsite** in the **mountains**
apartment [əˈpɑːtmənt]	die Wohnung	►► flat
a bit [ə bɪt]	ein bisschen, ein wenig	►► a little

Topic 1

► p. 14 **(to) stay** [steɪ]	bleiben; übernachten	Why can't I **stay** in bed? (bleiben) During our holidays we **stay** in a hotel. (übernachten)
(to) sunbathe [ˈsʌnbeɪð]	sonnenbaden	►► (to) lie in the sun
father [ˈfɑːðə]	der Vater	your **mother** (**mum**) and your **father** (**dad**) = your **parents**
foot [fʊt], *pl* **feet** [fiːt]	der Fuß	❗ **foot = 1.** der Fuß *(Körperteil)* **2.** der Fuß *(Längenmaß; ca. 30 cm)*
► p. 15 **grandparents** *(pl)* [ˈɡrænpeərənts]	die Großeltern	►► your parents' parents
ferry [ˈferi]	die Fähre	
plane [pleɪn]	das Flugzeug	First we went by **ferry**, then by **plane**.
hill [hɪl]	der Hügel	hills
river [ˈrɪvə]	der Fluss	a **river**
by the river [baɪ ðə ˈrɪvə]	am Fluss	►► next to the river, near the river

▶ p. 16 | **sort (of)** [sɔːt] | die Art (von) | What **sort of** music do you like?
all **sorts of** things (lauter Dinge, alles Mögliche)
❗ *English:* a **sort** of ... – *German:* eine **Art** (von) ...
English: **art** – *German:* **Kunst**

scary [ˈskeəri] | unheimlich, beängstigend, gruselig |

when [wen] | als *(zeitlich)* |
when
1. **wann**   **When** is your birthday?
2. **wenn**   You can start **when** you're ready.
3. **als**   I started **when** I was ready.

ghost [gəʊst] | der Geist, das Gespenst |

a **scary ghost**

ghost tour = die Geistertour *(Stadtführung mit gruseligen Themen/Elementen)*

dark [dɑːk] | dunkel | adj: **dark** – nouns: **dark** or **darkness**
He saw someone in the **darkness** / in the **dark**.
(in der Dunkelheit oder im Dunkeln)

vampire [ˈvæmpaɪə] | der Vampir | ❗ Betonung auf der 1. Silbe: **vam**pire

costume [ˈkɒstjuːm] | das Kostüm, die Verkleidung | ❗ Betonung auf der 1. Silbe: **cos**tume

underground [ʌndəˈgraʊnd] | unterirdisch, unter der Erde | adj: **underground** –
noun: **underground** (die U-Bahn)
❗ Betonung: under**ground** *(adjective)*
underground *(noun)*

a long time **ago** [əˈgəʊ] | vor langer Zeit | ❗ *German:* **vor** langer Zeit / **vor** fünf Minuten
English: a long time **ago** / five minutes **ago**

(to) scream [skriːm] | schreien | He **screamed** when he saw the mouse.

(to) touch [tʌtʃ] | anfassen, berühren | Please don't **touch** the photos.

out [aʊt] | heraus, hinaus, nach draußen | The weather is nice. Let's go **out** and play football.

▶ p. 17 | **past** [pɑːst] | vergangene(r, s) | adj: **past** – noun: **past** (die Vergangenheit)

blind [blaɪnd] | blind | Kasia is **blind**. She can't see you.

through [θrəʊ] | durch | Let's walk **through** the field.
❗ Beachte Aussprache und Schreibung!
Du schreibst **thr**ough –
du sprichst ein langes **u**.

mask [mɑːsk] | die Maske | Remember to wear a face **mask**.

eye [aɪ] | das Auge |

an **eye**

(to) **put your hands out,** *simple past:* **put** [pʊt]	die Hände ausstrecken	It was dark in the house, so I **put my hands out** to find my way.
experience [ɪkˈspɪəriəns]	die Erfahrung; das Erlebnis	Our trip to India was an amazing **experience**.
transport *(no pl)* [ˈtrænspɔːt]	das Fortbewegungsmittel, das Verkehrsmittel; die Beförderung	noun: **transport** – Which **transport** do you use to go to school? verb: (to) **transport** (transportieren, befördern) – I have a special bike. It can **transport** my kids and lots of shopping! **!** Betonung: **tran**sport *(noun)* (to) tran**sport** *(verb)*
(to) **relax** [rɪˈlæks]	sich entspannen	**!** *German:* Ich **entspanne mich**. *English:* I'm **relaxing**.

▶ p. 18

(to) **hope** [həʊp]	hoffen	I **hope** you like my school uniform.
pride [praɪd]	der Stolz	

pride – proud (of)
- noun: **pride** – She looked at her work with **pride**.
- adj: **proud (of)** (stolz (auf)) – She was **proud** of her work.

Pride (oder **Pride parade**) ist ein jährlich stattfindender Fest-, Gedenk- und Demonstrationstag von Lesben, Schwulen, Bisexuellen und Transgender-Personen. In Deutschland wird er meist Christopher Street Day (CSD) genannt. **parade** = die Parade, der Umzug

LGBTQ
LGBTQ steht für **lesbian, gay, bisexual, transgender, queer** (lesbisch, schwul, bisexuell, transgender, queer) und bezeichnet homo-, bi- und transsexuelle sowie (andere) queere Personen.

event [ɪˈvent]	das Ereignis	The first day at school is a big **event** for most kids.
thousand [ˈθaʊznd]	tausend	ten **thousand** (10,000) = zehntausend (10.000)

Im Englischen steht oft ein **Komma** in Zahlen, die größer als 1 000 sind. Im Deutschen steht dort manchmal ein **Punkt**.	*English:* **10,400** (ten thousand four hundred) *German:* **10.400** (zehntausendvierhundert)	

arrival [əˈraɪvl]	die Ankunft	noun: **arrival** – verb: (to) **arrive** (ankommen)
platform [ˈplætfɔːm]	der Bahnsteig	**!** *German:* Der Zug kommt **auf Gleis 4** an. *English:* The train arrives **at platform 4**.

Topic 2

▶ p. 19

destination [destɪˈneɪʃn]	das Ziel, der Bestimmungsort	the place where you want to go
single [ˈsɪŋgl]	Einzel-, einzelne(r, s)	**single ticket** ▶▶ **one-way ticket** (einfache Fahrkarte) A **single ticket** is a ticket for only **one way**.
return [rɪˈtɜːn] *(kurz für:* **return ticket***)*	die (Hin- und) Rückfahrkarte	**return ticket** ◀▶ **one-way ticket** / **single ticket** noun: **return** (die Rückkehr) – verb: (to) **return** (zurückkehren, -kommen)
cheap [tʃiːp]	billig, preiswert	**cheap** ◀▶ **expensive**

| ▶ p. 20 | they **didn't go …** [ˈdɪdnt gəʊ] **(= did not)** | sie gingen nicht; sie sind nicht gegangen | **I went ◀ ▶ I didn't go** |
| | **flag** [flæg] | die Fahne, die Flagge | the British **flag** |

| | **not … anything** [ˈeniθɪŋ] | nichts | It's so dark – I ca**n't** see **anything**. |
| | **not … at all** [ət ˈɔːl] | überhaupt nicht(s), gar nicht(s); überhaupt kein/e, gar kein/e | He did**n't** say anything **at all**. I do**n't** have any money **at all**. |

not … at all

We did**n't** understand anything **at all**.	Wir haben überhaupt nichts verstanden.
I do**n't** like meat **at all**.	Ich mag Fleisch überhaupt nicht. / Ich mag überhaupt kein Fleisch.
It was dark, but I was**n't** scared **at all**.	Es war dunkel, aber ich hatte überhaupt keine Angst.
The ghost train was**n't** scary **at all**.	Die Geisterbahn war überhaupt nicht gruselig.

| | **rainbow** [ˈreɪnbəʊ] | der Regenbogen | |

	even [ˈiːvn]	sogar, selbst	• **even** (sogar) Everybody helped, **even** the children.
			• **even if** (selbst wenn) **Even if** I'm tired, I must do my homework.
			• **not even** (nicht einmal) He doesn't like sweets, **not even** ice cream.

	girlfriend [ˈgɜːlfrend]	die (feste) Freundin	**girlfriend ◀ ▶ boyfriend** (der (feste) Freund)
	area [ˈeəriə]	die Gegend, der Bereich	I live in an **area** with lots of shops.
	child [tʃaɪld], *pl* **children** [ˈtʃɪldrən]	das Kind	▶ ▶ kid(s) ❗ one **child** – two **children** Das **i** in **child** klingt wie das **y** in **my**. Das **i** in **children** klingt wie das **i** in **skill**.
	concert [ˈkɒnsət]	das Konzert	❗ Betonung auf der 1. Silbe: **con**cert
	musician [mjuˈzɪʃn]	der Musiker, die Musikerin	I'm a **musician**. I play the guitar in a band. **street musician** = der Straßenmusiker, die Straßenmusikerin

| ▶ p. 21 | **wonderful** [ˈwʌndəfl] | wunderbar | ▶ ▶ very good, great |
| | **piano** [piˈænəʊ] | das Klavier | ❗ *German:* **Klavier spielen**
 English: (to) **play the piano** |

Topic 3

| ▶ p. 23 | (to) **make a friend** [meɪk ə ˈfrend]; (to) **make friends** [meɪk ˈfrendz] | einen Freund/eine Freundin finden; Freunde/-innen finden | I **made a lot of new friends** on the campsite. |

sight [saɪt]	die Sehenswürdigkeit	**sight** = **1.** die Sehenswürdigkeit; **2.** der Anblick, die Sicht(weite), die Sehkraft
tower [ˈtaʊə]	der Turm	The Eiffel **Tower** is a famous sight in Paris.
silent [ˈsaɪlənt]	still, lautlos	(to) **fall/go silent** = still werden, verstummen adj: **silent** – noun: **silence** (die Stille; das Schweigen)
plastic [ˈplæstɪk]	das Plastik, der Kunststoff	No **plastic** bags for me, please. I always bring my own shopping bag.
bottle [ˈbɒtl]	die Flasche	**!** *German:* eine **Flasche** Wasser *English:* a **bottle of** water
safe [seɪf]	sicher *(gefahrlos)*	adj: **safe** – noun: **safety** (die Sicherheit)
(to) **borrow** [ˈbɒrəʊ]	(aus)leihen, sich borgen	Can I **borrow** your glue stick, please?
equipment *(no pl)* [ɪˈkwɪpmənt]	die Ausrüstung	walking **equipment**
(to) **pick** [pɪk]	pflücken; (aus)wählen, aussuchen	(to) **pick sth. up** = etwas aufheben *(vom Boden)*, etwas hochheben **picker** = **1.** die Greifzange *(z. B. für Müll)*; **2.** *(person)* der Pflücker, die Pflückerin
glove [glʌv]	der Handschuh	a **pair of gloves** = ein Paar Handschuhe **pair** = das Paar
▶ p. 24 **yesterday** [ˈjestədeɪ]	gestern	**Yesterday** was Monday, so today is Tuesday.

Background file

▶ p. 25 **sign** [saɪn]	das Schild; das Zeichen	
stage [steɪdʒ]	die Bühne	The **sign** shows you the way to the **stage**.
hair [heə]	das Haar, die Haare	**!** *German:* Deine **Haare sind** schwarz. *English:* Your **hair is** black.
instrument [ˈɪnstrəmənt]	das Instrument	**!** Betonung auf der 1. Silbe: **in**strument
front [frʌnt]	der vordere Teil, die Vorderseite	What's that sign at the **front** of the building?

Story

▶ p. 26 **adventure** [ədˈventʃə]	das Abenteuer	A bike trip to Italy? What an **adventure**!
out of ... [ˈaʊt əv]	aus ... (heraus/hinaus)	He opened the door and walked **out of** the room. **into** the room ◀ ▶ **out of** the room

▶ p. 26   **time** [taɪm]   das Mal   Today I travelled alone for the first **time**.

time
1. die Zeit   We had a great **time**. / Do you have **time**? / It's **time** for lunch.
2. das Mal   **for the first time** (zum ersten Mal) / **this time** (dieses Mal) / **three times** (dreimal) /
                lots of times (viele Male, oft) / **the last time** (letztes Mal) / **(the) next time** (nächstes Mal)

once [wʌns]   einmal   ! **once** =   1. einmal –
                                                                    I was in York only **once** in 2013.
                                                                 2. einst –
                                                                    This city was **once** a small town.

once a month [ə]   einmal pro Monat   I go to my yoga class once **a** week –
                                                  every Tuesday.

easy [ˈiːzi]   einfach, leicht   **easy** ◄ ► **difficult/hard**

(to) **get (to)** [get]   gelangen, (hin)kommen (nach)

(to) get, *simple past:* **got**
1. bekommen   She **got** a job in London.   Sie bekam eine Stelle in London.
2. holen, besorgen   Can you go and **get** some fruit?   Kannst du etwas Obst holen gehen?
3. gelangen, (hin)kommen   How do we **get** to the museum? Wie kommen wir zum Museum?

(to) **try** [traɪ]   versuchen, (aus)probieren   **Try** to answer my question. (versuchen)
                                                         I'd like to **try** parkour. (ausprobieren)

excited [ɪkˈsaɪtɪd]   aufgeregt, gespannt   **excited** = aufgeregt, gespannt
                                                    exciting = aufregend
                                                    ! Beachte die Schreibweise: **exc̲ited**

this morning/afternoon/ heute Morgen/Nachmittag/   ! *German* **heute** = **today**
evening [ðɪs ˈmɔːnɪŋ/   Abend   *German* **heute Morgen/Nachmittag/Abend**
ɑːftəˈnuːn/ˈiːvnɪŋ]   = **this morning/afternoon/evening**

(to) **get on** [get ˈɒn]   einsteigen (in einen Zug/Bus)
(a train/bus), (to) **get off**   aussteigen (aus einem Zug/Bus)
[get ˈɒf] **(a train/bus)**
                                                            Get on...   Get off...

nearly [ˈnɪəli]   fast   It's **nearly** 8 o'clock! We're late!

(to) **change (trains)** [tʃeɪndʒ]   umsteigen

(to) change
1. ändern   They needed to **change** their plans.   Sie mussten ihre Pläne ändern.
2. sich verändern This town is **changing** fast.   Diese Stadt verändert sich schnell.
3. sich umziehen   Give me five minutes. I'd like to **change** first.   ... Ich möchte mich erst umziehen.
4. wechseln   Do you **change** rooms for your different lessons?   Wechselt ihr das Klassenzimmer ...?
                   Can you **change** your clothes before we go?   Kannst du deine Kleidung wechseln ...?
5. umsteigen   Do I need to **change** (trains)?   Muss ich umsteigen?

you [juː]   man   **You** get great pizza at Angelo's.
                                                 No, **you** don't do it like that.
                                                 ! **you** = 1. du; ihr; Sie; 2. man

onto the platform [ˈɒntə]   auf den Bahnsteig
                                                 He's trying to get
                                                 onto the stage.

	announcement [əˈnaʊnsmənt]	die Durchsage, die Ansage; die Bekanntgabe, die Ankündigung	What was that? I didn't understand that **announcement**! noun: **announcement** – verb: (to) **announce** (verkünden, bekanntgeben; durchsagen)
▶ p. 27	**the wrong way** [rɒŋ ˈweɪ]	(in) die falsche Richtung	Come back! You're walking **the wrong way**! **this way** = hier entlang, in diese(r) Richtung **that way** = da entlang, in jene(r) Richtung
	(to) be glad [glæd]	froh sein	❗ You use **glad** with a form of 'be', but not in front of nouns: **I'm glad / She's glad / We're glad that …**
	calm [kɑːm]	ruhig, besonnen	Please stay **calm**. It's only a little mouse!
	(to) hug (sb.) [hʌg]	(jn.) umarmen; einander umarmen	Beth is **hugging** Jill. = They're **hugging**.
	support [səˈpɔːt]	die Unterstützung	• nouns: **support** – My parents are a great **support**. (person) **supporter** – I'm a Manchester United **supporter**. (der Anhänger, die Anhängerin; der Fan) • verb: (to) **support** (unterstützen) – My parents always **support** me.
	(to) be grateful (to sb. **for** doing sth.**)** [ˈgreɪtfl]	(jm. für etwas) dankbar sein	I phoned Sunita when I was on the wrong train. **I'm** so **grateful to** my friend **for** helping me.
	feeling [ˈfiːlɪŋ]	das Gefühl	noun: **feeling** – verb: (to) **feel** (fühlen; sich fühlen)
▶ p. 28	**awesome** (infml) [ˈɔːsəm]	klasse, stark, großartig	▶▶ super, great
	(to) walk around [wɔːk əˈraʊnd]	umhergehen (in)	❗ **around** = **1.** in … umher – Let's walk **around** the old town. **2.** um … herum – Why are you running **around** the tree?
	(to) agree (with sb./sth.**)** [əˈgriː]	jm. zustimmen; mit etwas einverstanden sein	❗ German: Ich **stimme dir zu**. English: I **agree with you**. (to) **agree** ◀ ▶ (to) **disagree** (nicht zustimmen, widersprechen) (to) **agree on** sth. = sich auf etwas einigen

Study skills

▶ p. 30	**structure** [ˈstrʌktʃə]	die Struktur	Your presentation needs a better **structure**.
	everything [ˈevriθɪŋ]	alles	Do you have all your school things? – Yes, **everything** is in my bag.
	beginning [bɪˈgɪnɪŋ]	der Anfang	**beginning** ◀ ▶ **end** ❗ German: **am Anfang** English: **in the beginning** noun: **beginning** – verb: (to) **begin**, simple past: **began** (anfangen, beginnen)

middle [ˈmɪdl]	die Mitte	**in the middle (of)** = in der Mitte (von)
(to) **link (to/with)** [lɪŋk]	verbinden (mit)	**Link** your sentences with *but, or* or *and*.

Verbs and nouns with the same form

(to) **experience**	erfahren; erleben	**experience**	die Erfahrung; das Erlebnis
(to) **hope**	hoffen	**hope**	die Hoffnung
(to) **hug**	umarmen	**hug**	die Umarmung
(to) **link**	verbinden	**link**	die Verbindung; der Link
(to) **scream**	schreien	**scream**	der Schrei
(to) **stay**	bleiben; übernachten	**stay**	der Aufenthalt
(to) **structure**	strukturieren, aufbauen	**structure**	die Struktur
(to) **support**	unterstützen	**support**	die Unterstützung
(to) **transport**	transportieren, befördern	**transport**	das Fortbewegungsmittel; das Verkehrsmittel; die Beförderung
(to) **try**	versuchen, (aus)probieren	**try**	der Versuch

(to) **think hard** [θɪŋk ˈhɑːd]	scharf nachdenken	**!** adj: **hard** = hart, schwer: It's **hard** work. adv: **hard** = hart: We work **hard**.
alternative [ɔːlˈtɜːnətɪv]	die Alternative; alternativ	• noun: The bus journey takes four hours. The train is an **alternative**, and it only takes one hour. • adj: Our village has no train station. There is only the bus – no **alternative** transport.

Unit task

▶ p. 31

object [ˈɒbdʒɪkt]	das Objekt, der Gegenstand	**!** Betonung auf der 1. Silbe: **ob**ject
mistake [mɪˈsteɪk]	der Fehler	There are some **mistakes** in your text. Please correct them. Is this your pen? I'm sorry, I took it **by mistake**. (aus Versehen; versehentlich)
recording [rɪˈkɔːdɪŋ]	die Aufnahme *(Ton-, Bild-)*	noun: **recording** – verb: (to) **record**
(to) **include** [ɪnˈkluːd]	(mit) einschließen	£80 – does that **include** breakfast?

Irregular verbs

Infinitive	Simple past		Infinitive	Simple past	
(to) **be**	was/were	sein	(to) **hang (out)**	hung (out)	(rum)hängen, (ab)hängen
(to) **begin**	began	beginnen	(to) **make**	made	machen, herstellen
(to) **buy**	bought	kaufen	(to) **put**	put	legen, stellen
(to) **cost**	cost	kosten	(to) **say**	said	sagen
(to) **cut**	cut	schneiden	(to) **see**	saw	sehen
(to) **do**	did	machen, tun	(to) **sleep**	slept	schlafen
(to) **eat**	ate	essen	(to) **swim**	swam	schwimmen
(to) **get**	got	bekommen; holen; gelangen	(to) **take**	took	(mit)nehmen
			(to) **tell**	told	erzählen
(to) **go**	went	gehen, fahren	(to) **think**	thought	denken
(to) **have**	had	haben	(to) **wear**	wore	tragen, anhaben
(to) **hear**	heard	hören			

🔊 Unit 2: Friends and heroes

▶ pp. 46/47

hero [ˈhɪərəʊ], *pl* **heroes** [ˈhɪərəʊz]	der Held, die Heldin	She always helps others even if it's hard work. She's a **hero**!
head student [ˈhed stjuːdnt]	der Vertrauensschüler, die Vertrauensschülerin; der Schulsprecher, die Schulsprecherin	
braces *(pl)* [ˈbreɪsɪz]	die Zahnspange, die Zahnklammer	**braces** **glasses**
glasses *(pl)* [ˈɡlɑːsɪz]	die Brille	❗ Die Wörter **glasses, sunglasses** (die Sonnenbrille) und **braces** sind Pluralwörter: I need my **glasses**. Where **are they**? (... Wo **ist sie**?) A lot of kids wear **braces**. (... tragen **eine Zahnspange**.)
curly [ˈkɜːli]	lockig	He has **curly** hair. = He has **curls**. **curl** = die Locke
straight [streɪt]	gerade; *(Haare)* glatt	**curly** **straight** — They have **blonde** hair.

Topic 1

▶ p. 48

hard-working [hɑːd ˈwɜːkɪŋ]	fleißig	working a lot and trying to do your job well
confident [ˈkɒnfɪdənt]	(selbst)sicher; zuversichtlich	

confident – confidence
- adj: **confident** — (selbst)sicher, zuversichtlich — You're a great person. Why aren't you more **confident**? I have a good feeling – I'm **confident** that my test went well.
- noun: **confidence** — das Vertrauen, das Selbstvertrauen, die Zuversicht — Do all the players in your team have **confidence** in your trainer? He thinks he's a very good student – he has a lot of **confidence**. I have **confidence** that they can be friends again.

(to) **make** sb. **do** sth. [meɪk]	jn. dazu bringen, etwas zu tun	You can give people good tips, but you can't **make them do** what you want. Listening to music always **makes me feel** good.
(to) **laugh (at)** [lɑːf]	lachen (über)	He's a bit slow sometimes, but it's not fair to **laugh at** him. (to) **laugh at sb.** = jn. auslachen
strong [strɒŋ]	stark	
tall [tɔːl]	groß *(Person)*; hoch *(Gebäude)*	**tall** ◀ ▶ **short** *(Person:* klein) ❗ Wenn man einen Menschen **big** nennt, dann meint man „schwer" oder „dick".

reliable [rɪˈlaɪəbl]	verlässlich, zuverlässig	My best friend is very **reliable**. She's always there for me.
patient [ˈpeɪʃnt]	geduldig	adj: **patient** ◄ ► **impatient** (ungeduldig) nouns: **patience** (die Geduld) ◄ ► **impatience** (die Ungeduld)
shy [ʃaɪ]	scheu, schüchtern	**shy** ◄ ► **confident**
personality [pɜːsəˈnæləti]	die Persönlichkeit; der Charakter	Ann has the perfect **personality** for a head student. nouns: **person**; **personality** – adj: **personal** (persönlich)
height [haɪt]	die Höhe; die Größe *(bei Menschen)*	adj: **high** (hoch); *(person)* **tall** noun: **height**
▶ p. 49 **yourself** [jɔːˈself]	du/dir/dich (selbst)	Write a short text about **yourself**. This isn't easy. Be patient with **yourself**.

honest [ˈɒnɪst]	ehrlich	• adj: To be **honest**, I don't know the answer.
		  (Um ehrlich zu sein, ...)
		  I like you because you're **honest**.
		• noun: **honesty** (die Ehrlichkeit) –
		  I like your **honesty**.
		❗ Wie bei **hour** wird das „h" von **honest** und **honesty** nicht gesprochen!

▶ p. 50 **no one** [ˈnəʊ wʌn]/ **nobody** [ˈnəʊbədi]	niemand	**No one/Nobody** is at home. The house is very quiet.
no one else [nəʊ wʌn ˈels]	niemand anders, niemand sonst	**No one else** wanted to go to the beach, so we stayed at home.

... else

Why can't I have a pet? **Everybody else** has a pet.	alle anderen; jede/r andere; sonst jede/r
I'm so tired. **Somebody else** must make dinner today.	jemand anders
Thank you. I don't need **anything else**.	nichts anderes; sonst nichts
What else do you want to know?	was (sonst) noch

(to) **think of** sb./sth. [ˈθɪŋk əv]	an jn./etwas denken	❗ (to) **think of sb./sth.** = an jn./etwas denken; (to) **think of sth.** = sich etwas überlegen, sich etwas ausdenken
right [raɪt]	rechts; nach rechts	❗ **right** = **1.** (nach) rechts; **2.** richtig
left [left]	links; nach links	

left – right

Do you write with your **left** hand or your **right** hand? I looked **left** and **right**, but there was no one there.

on the left = links, auf der linken Seite ◄ ► **on the right** = rechts, auf der rechten Seite
to the left of sb./sth. = links von jm./etwas ◄ ► **to the right of** sb./sth. = rechts von jm./etwas

moon [muːn]	der Mond	 the **moon** over the sea (to) **be over the moon** *(infml)* = ganz aus dem Häuschen sein (= hocherfreut sein)

▶ p. 51 | (to) **report (on)** [rɪˈpɔːt] | berichten (über) | Ava often travels to really cool places and **reports on** them in our school magazine.

Topic 2

▶ p. 52 | (to) **save** [seɪv] | retten; sparen; sichern *(Daten)*
- There's a cat in the water! Can we **save** it? (retten)
- I need to **save** money. (sparen)
- When you write your presentation, remember to **save** your files. (sichern)

life [laɪf], *pl* **lives** [laɪvz] | das Leben | ❗ one **life** – nine **lives**

who [huː] | wen; wem

who
1. **wer?** **Who** helps you with your homework?
2. **wen?** **Who** did you meet?
3. **wem?** **Who** did you send a message to?
Who did you get the book from?

underwater [ʌndəˈwɔːtə] | unter Wasser, Unterwasser- | We stayed **underwater** for some time and took lots of **underwater** photos with our **underwater** cameras.

(to) **hurt** [hɜːt], *simple past:* **hurt** [hɜːt] | verletzen; wehtun
- I **hurt** my hand on a knife. (Ich habe mir die Hand an einem Messer verletzt.)
- And now my hand **hurts**. (tut weh)
(to) **be hurt** = verletzt sein
(to) **get hurt** = sich verletzen; verletzt werden

(to) **leave** [liːv], *simple past:* **left** [left] | lassen; verlassen; zurücklassen

(to) leave, *simple past:* left
1. **lassen** Don't **leave** the windows open when you go. / Please **leave** your pets at home.
2. **verlassen** I don't want to **leave** my country. / Many people **left** the village.
3. **zurücklassen** Don't **leave** your bag on the bus. / Where did you **leave** your bike?
❗ (to) **leave sb. alone** = 1. jn. allein lassen – We can't **leave** our dog **alone** at home.
2. jn. in Ruhe lassen – Just go away and **leave** me **alone**!

▶ p. 53 | (to) **grow up** [grəʊ ˈʌp], *simple past:* **grew up** [gruː ˈʌp] | aufwachsen; erwachsen werden | My grandfather **grew up** on a small farm. Jo wants to be a teacher when she **grows up**. (to) **grow**, *simple past:* **grew** = wachsen

off [ɒf] | weg von; hinunter von

off
(to) come off	The chain **came off** (my bike).	abgehen, sich lösen
(to) fall off	My friend **fell off** his bike / a wall.	herunterfallen
(to) get off	He hurt his leg when he **got off** his horse / his bike.	absteigen
	Be careful when you **get off** the train / the bus.	aussteigen

▶ p. 54 | **activist** [ˈæktɪvɪst] | der Aktivist, die Aktivistin | **activism** = der Aktivismus
❗ Betonung auf der 1. Silbe: **ac**tivist, **ac**tivism

artist [ˈɑːtɪst] | der Künstler, die Künstlerin | nouns: **art**; *(person)* **artist** – adj: **artistic** (kunstvoll, künstlerisch)
❗ Betonung: **ar**tist, *but:* ar**ti**stic

opposite [ˈɒpəzɪt]	das Gegenteil	

opposite
• noun: The **opposite** of 'shy' is 'confident'.	Das Gegenteil von „schüchtern" ist „selbstsicher".	
• adj: the **opposite** meaning	die entgegengesetzte / gegensätzliche Bedeutung	
• prep: I sat **opposite** Zoe, not next to her.	Zoe gegenüber, gegenüber von Zoe	
The museum is **opposite** the bank.	gegenüber der Bank	

stupid [ˈstjuːpɪd]	dumm, blöd; albern	Don't do that. It's a **stupid** idea. (= not a good/clever idea)
lazy [ˈleɪzi]	faul	My brother is **lazy** – he often sleeps late. **lazy** ◄ ► hard-working

▶ p. 55

(to) **spend** [spend] **time/ money (on)**, *simple past:* **spen** [spent]	Zeit verbringen (mit) / Geld ausgeben (für)	I **spend** a lot of **time** with my friends. My brother **spends** a lot of **money** on sweets.
positive [ˈpɒzətɪv]	positiv	**positive** ◄ ► negative
doctor (Dr) [ˈdɒktə]	der Arzt, die Ärztin	**!** *German:* **beim Arzt / zur Ärztin** *English:* **at the doctor's / to the doctor's**
nurse [nɜːs]	der Krankenpfleger, die Krankenpflegerin	

nurses

accident [ˈæksɪdənt]	der Unfall; der Zufall	**!** **accident** = **1.** Unfall – Finn had an **accident**. He was hurt. **2.** Zufall – It's no **accident** that her test went well. I met her **by accident** at the station. (zufällig, versehentlich, unabsichtlich)

Topic 3

▶ p. 56

he was **born** [bɔːn]	er wurde geboren	**!** *German:* Wann **bist** du **geboren**? – Ich **bin** 2012 **geboren**. *English:* When **were** you **born**? – I **was born** in 2012.
earth [ɜːθ]	die Erde	life **on earth** = das Leben **auf der Erde** **!** *German* "Erde": **1.** *(der Planet)* earth **2.** *(der Erdboden)* ground
(to) **become** [bɪˈkʌm], *simple past:* **became** [bɪˈkeɪm]	werden	My cousin **became** a superhero, and now he's always tired. Too much work!

German 'werden'

Die häufigsten englischen Entsprechungen von „werden" sind (to) **become** und (to) **get**. In der Umgangssprache wird eher (to) **get** verwendet.	(to) **become** / (to) **get** angry, tired, ill, … cold, warm, windy, dark, … exciting, boring, interesting, …
❗ Vor <u>Nomen</u> kann nur (to) **become** stehen:	She **became** a <u>teacher</u> / a <u>singer</u> / …
Das Verb (to) **go** wird verwendet – für Farbveränderungen: – wenn es um Verschlechterungen geht:	(to) **go** red, brown, green, … (to) **go** hard *(bread)*, (to) **go** bad *(fish, cheese, eggs)*

power [ˈpaʊə]	die Kraft, die Macht, die Energie; der (elektrische) Strom	Do we have the **power** to change all the bad things on earth? **super** = super – **superpower** = die Superkraft
▶ p. 57 **planet** [ˈplænɪt]	der Planet	our **planet** ❗ Betonung auf der 1. Silbe: **pla**net
far [fɑː]	weit (entfernt)	You want to go to Peru? But that's **far** away! far ◀ ▶ near
any [ˈeni]	jede(r/s) (beliebige), jegliche(r/s)	

any
• in **Fragen** und **verneinten Sätzen**: • in **bejahten Sätzen**:	Did you learn **any** new skills? I do**n't** have **any** money. You can use this ticket on **any** train. You can call me **(at) any time**.	… (irgendwelche) neuen Fertigkeiten …? … kein Geld … in jedem (beliebigen) Zug … zu jeder Zeit, jederzeit

(to) **fight (for)** [faɪt], *simple past:* **fought** [fɔːt]	kämpfen (für); bekämpfen	verb: (to) **fight** – nouns: **fight** (der Kampf); *(person)* **fighter** (der Kämpfer, die Kämpferin)
metal [ˈmetl]	das Metall; Metall-, aus Metall	❗ Betonung auf der 1. Silbe: **me**tal
body [ˈbɒdi]	der Körper	You already know the English words for some parts of the **body**: head, hand, arm, foot …
helmet [ˈhelmɪt]	der Helm	**helmets**
dare [deə]	die Mutprobe	• noun: **dare** – Would you do this **for a dare**? (als Mutprobe) • verb: (to) **dare** (wagen; sich trauen) – Would you **dare** to say this in front of the class?
leg [leg]	das Bein	We have two arms and two **legs**.
nose [nəʊz]	die Nase	
(to) **know** sb./sth. **by …** [nəʊ], *simple past:* **knew** [njuː]	jn./etwas erkennen an …	This is my favourite band! I always **know** them **by** their special sound.

dolphin [ˈdɒlfɪn]	der Delfin	

a **dolphin**

guy [gaɪ]	der Typ, der Kerl	Philip is a really nice **guy**.
chemical [ˈkemɪkl]	die Chemikalie; chemisch	Be careful when you work with this **chemical**. (die Chemikalie) Please draw the **chemical** structure of water. (chemisch)
land [lænd]	das Land *(Grund und Boden)*	❗ *German "Land":* **1.** *(Staat)* **country** **2.** *(Grund und Boden)* **land**
normal [ˈnɔːml]	normal	❗ Betonung auf der 1. Silbe: **nor**mal
police *(pl)* [pəˈliːs]	die Polizei	❗ **police** ist ein <u>Pluralwort</u>: Where **are** the **police**? Did you call **them**? (Wo **ist** die **Polizei**? Hast du **sie** gerufen?)
villain [ˈvɪlən]	der Verbrecher, die Verbrecherin; der Schurke, die Schurkin	a mean person; a bad character in a story
ear [ɪə]	das Ohr	

← hair
← eye
face
↖ nose
ear

swimsuit [ˈswɪmsuːt]	der Badeanzug	**Swimsuits** or bikinis are clothes that you wear for swimming.
(to) **climb** [klaɪm]	klettern (auf)	verb: (to) **climb** – nouns: **climb** (der Aufstieg, die Klettertour; der Anstieg); **climber** (der Kletterer, die Kletterin) ❗ *German:* **auf** einen Hügel/Baum klettern *English:* (to) **climb a hill/tree**
(to) **kill** [kɪl]	töten	verb: (to) **kill** – noun: *(person)* **killer** (der Mörder, die Mörderin)
dress [dres]	das Kleid	

a nice red **dress**

invisible [ɪnˈvɪzəbl]	unsichtbar	I felt as if I was **invisible**. I had the feeling nobody saw me.
▶ p. 58 (to) **protect (from/against)** [prəˈtekt]	(be)schützen (vor)	I cycle every day. In the winter, warm clothes **protect** me **from** the cold and the rain.

Background file

▶ p. 59 (to) **die (of)** [daɪ] sterben (an)

! (to) **die:**
simple past: **died** – She **died** last year.

-ing form: **dying** –
This tree is **dying**.

verb: (to) **die** –
adj: **dead**

---

creative [kriˈeɪtɪv] kreativ

adj: **creative** – verb: (to) **create** ((er)schaffen, erstellen) – noun: **creativity** (die Kreativität)
! Betonung: cre**a**tive, cre**a**te
but: crea**ti**vity

---

right [raɪt] das Recht

Nobody has the **right** to read my emails.
(das Recht, ... zu lesen)

---

head teacher [hed ˈtiːtʃə] der Schulleiter, die Schulleiterin; der Direktor, die Direktorin

Ms Jones is our maths teacher, and she's also our school's **head teacher**.

---

interested (in) [ˈɪntrəstɪd] interessiert (an)

interested – interesting – ...

• adj:	**interested (in)**	interessiert (an)	Are you **interested in learning** more about whales?
			Are you **interested in** science? Then join the science club.
	interesting	interessant	Science can be very **interesting**.
• verb:	(to) **interest sb. (in)**	jn. interessieren (für)	How can we **interest** more people **in** science?
• noun:	**interest (in)**	das Interesse (an)	Many of my friends take/show an **interest in** science.

---

against [əˈɡenst] gegen

against ◀ ▶ **for**

---

disease [dɪˈziːz] die Krankheit

They say that wearing a mask can protect you against some **diseases**.

---

award [əˈwɔːd] der Preis (die Auszeichnung)

award-winning = preisgekrönt
award-winner = der Preisträger, die Preisträgerin

---

philosophy [fəˈlɒsəfi] die Philosophie

My **philosophy** of life is not to worry too much and have fun.
! Betonung auf der 2. Silbe: phi**lo**sophy

---

world war [wɜːld ˈwɔː] der Weltkrieg

• **the First World War** (or: **World War I**)
  = der Erste Weltkrieg
• **the Second World War** (or: **World War II**)
  = der Zweite Weltkrieg
• **world** = die Welt
! German: der beste Ort **der Welt /**
                auf der Welt
English: the best place **in the world**

---

during [ˈdjʊərɪŋ] während (Präposition)

German 'während'

• vor <u>Nomen</u> (Präposition):	**during**	– I slept **during** <u>the film</u>.
• vor <u>Nebensatz</u> (Konjunktion):	**while**	– I slept **while** <u>my friends watched the film</u>.

---

peace [piːs] der Frieden

Why can't we have **peace** in the world?
peace ◀ ▶ **war**

famous (for) [ˈfeɪməs]	berühmt (für, wegen)	This town is **famous for** its museum. adj: **famous** – noun: **fame** (der Ruhm)
machine [məˈʃiːn]	der Automat, die Maschine	**ticket machines**

(to) program [ˈprəʊɡræm]	programmieren	verb: **(to) program** –
		nouns: **program** (das (Computer-)Programm);
		    (person) **programmer**
		        (der Programmierer,
		        die Programmiererin)
		! **program** = das (Computer-)Programm
		    programme = das (Fernseh-)Programm,
		        die Sendung

whose [huːz]	wessen	This isn't your bike? **Whose** is it? – It's Joe's.

Story

▶ p. 60 **ambulance** [ˈæmbjələns]	der Krankenwagen	**an ambulance** **!** Betonung auf der 1. Silbe: **am**bulance
(to) fall [fɔːl], *simple past:* **fell** [fel]	fallen; hinfallen	Finn **fell** off a wall.
(to) jump [dʒʌmp]	springen	They're **jumping** into the water.

side [saɪd]	die Seite *(z. B. Straßenseite)*	How can I get to the other **side** of the river?
		! *German "Seite":*
		    1. *(Buchseite u. Ä.)* **page**
		    2. *(Straßenseite u. Ä.)* **side**

▶ p. 61 **dangerous** [ˈdeɪndʒərəs]	gefährlich	a **dangerous** fish adj: **dangerous** – noun: **danger** (die Gefahr)
shocked [ʃɒkt]	schockiert	adj: **shocked** (schockiert) / **shocking** (schockierend) – verb: **(to) shock sb.** (jn. schockieren) – noun: **shock** (der Schock)
ankle [ˈæŋkl]	der Knöchel, das Fußgelenk	My **ankle** hurts.

(to) **hit** [hɪt], *simple past:* **hit** [hɪt]	treffen auf, schlagen, prallen, stoßen gegen/auf	**(to) hit** **treffen** **schlagen** **prallen/** **stoßen** — The ball **hit** a window. Don't **hit** your little sister. They nearly **hit** a tree with their car.

! *German:* Ich **habe** <u>mir den Kopf</u> **gestoßen**.
English: I **hit** <u>my head</u>.

back [bæk]	der Rücken; die Rückseite, der hintere Teil	• **at the back of the hall/bus/cinema** = hinten im Saal / im Bus / im Kino • **at the back of your book** = hinten in deinem Buch • **on the back of the card** = auf der Rückseite der Karte **back, at the back ◄ ► front, at the front**

(to) **keep** [kiːp], *simple past:* **kept** [kept]	halten; behalten; aufbewahren	

(to) keep, *simple past:* kept
1. halten — Here's some hot tea to **keep** you warm. Don't tell the others about our plan. Let's **keep** it secret.

2. behalten — Can I **keep** your pen or do you want it back?
3. aufbewahren — Where do you **keep** fruit and vegetables?

(to) **fall asleep** [fɔːl əˈsliːp]	einschlafen	I was so tired that I **fell asleep** on the sofa.

(to) **breathe (in/out)** [briːð]	(ein-/aus-)atmen	You can't **breathe** when you're underwater.

blanket [ˈblæŋkɪt]	die Decke *(zum Zudecken u. Ä.)*	a **blanket**

joke [dʒəʊk]	der Witz, der Scherz	• nouns: **joke**; *(person)* **joker** (der Witzbold, der Joker) – • verb: (to) **joke** (Witze machen, scherzen) You're **joking**! = Du machst wohl Witze!

neck [nek]	der Hals, der Nacken	It was horrible – the elephant had a chain around its **neck**.

upset [ʌpˈset]	bestürzt; aufgebracht, verärgert	I was very **upset** when my sister had an accident. adj: **upset** = aufgebracht, verärgert – verb: (to) **upset sb.**, *simple past:* **upset** (jn. erschüttern; jn. aufregen, ärgern)

(to) **drive** [draɪv], *simple past:* **drove** [drəʊv]	*(mit dem Auto)* fahren	I usually take the bus. I don't like to **drive**. (= I don't like to take the car.) verb: (to) **drive** – noun: **driver** (der Fahrer, die Fahrerin)

fire engine [ˈfaɪər endʒɪn]	das Feuerwehrauto	a **fire engine** **fire** = das Feuer

▶ p. 62   **broken** [ˈbrəʊkən]   kaputt; zerbrochen

broken windows

promise [ˈprɒmɪs]   das Versprechen   He's very reliable – he always keeps his **promises**.
(to) **keep a promise** = ein Versprechen halten

Verbs and nouns with the same form

(to) **climb**	klettern (auf)	**climb**	der Aufstieg, die Klettertour; der Anstieg
(to) **dare**	wagen, sich trauen	**dare**	die Mutprobe
(to) **dress**	sich kleiden, sich anziehen	**dress**	das Kleid
(to) **fight**	kämpfen; bekämpfen	**fight**	der Kampf
(to) **interest**	interessieren	**interest**	das Interesse
(to) **joke**	Witze machen, scherzen	**joke**	der Witz, der Scherz
(to) **jump**	springen	**jump**	der Sprung, das Hindernis
(to) **land**	landen	**land**	das Land *(Grund und Boden)*
(to) **laugh**	lachen	**laugh**	das Lachen
(to) **promise**	versprechen	**promise**	das Versprechen
(to) **report**	berichten	**report**	der Bericht
(to) **shock**	schockieren	**shock**	der Schock

Study skills

▶ p. 64   (to) **work** sth. **out** [wɜːk ˈaʊt]   etwas herausfinden, etwas erarbeiten, etwas verstehen   Try and **work out** the answers to the questions.

bravery [ˈbreɪvəri]   der Mut, die Tapferkeit   noun: **bravery** – adj: **brave**

happiness [ˈhæpinəs]   das Glück, die Zufriedenheit   adj: **happy** ◄ ► **unhappy** (unglücklich, unzufrieden) –
nouns: **happiness** ◄ ► **unhappiness** (die Unzufriedenheit, die Traurigkeit)

false friend [fɔːls ˈfrend]   der „falsche Freund" *(die Übersetzungsfalle)*   **false** = falsch, unrichtig
The English word 'become' is a **false friend**: It looks like the German word 'bekommen', but it means 'werden'.

Unit task

▶ p. 65   **scientist** [ˈsaɪəntɪst]   der (Natur-)Wissenschaftler, die (Natur-)Wissenschaftlerin   I love science. I want to become a **scientist**.

presenter [prɪˈzentə]   der Moderator, die Moderatorin

a radio **presenter** talking to a guest

sportsperson [ˈspɔːtspɜːsn], *pl* **sportspeople** [ˈspɔːtspiːpl]   der Sportler, die Sportlerin

fact [fækt]	die Tatsache	This isn't a new building. The **fact** is, it's very old. **In fact**, it's over 500 years old. **in fact** = tatsächlich, in Wirklichkeit, genau genommen
(to) **discover** [dɪˈskʌvə]	entdecken	Did you know that a woman **discovered** this chemical? • verb: (to) **discover** – • nouns: **discovery** (die Entdeckung); *(person)* **discoverer** (der Entdecker, die Entdeckerin)
correct [kəˈrekt]	korrekt	adj: **correct** – verb: (to) **correct** (korrigieren)
at least [æt ˈliːst]	wenigstens, zumindest	A good bike costs **at least** £600. (= £600 or more)
I think so. [aɪ ˈθɪŋk səʊ]	Ich glaube/denke ja.	

I think so. / I hope so. / ...
- Are they at home? – **I think so. / I hope so.**   Ich glaube/denke ja. / Das hoffe ich.
- Is that correct? – **I don't think so.**   Ich glaube nicht. / Das glaube/denke ich nicht.
- Is she going to be at home? – **She said so.**   Das hat sie (jedenfalls) gesagt.
- Do you like the story? **If so,** say why.   Wenn ja, ...

Irregular verbs

Infinitive	Simple past		Infinitive	Simple past	
(to) **become**	**became**	werden	(to) **keep**	**kept**	(be)halten; aufbewahren
(to) **come**	**came**	(mit)kommen	(to) **know**	**knew**	wissen; (er)kennen
(to) **draw**	**drew**	zeichnen	(to) **leave**	**left**	(ver)lassen, zurücklassen
(to) **drive**	**drove**	(Auto) fahren	(to) **meet**	**met**	(sich) treffen
(to) **fall**	**fell**	(hin)fallen	(to) **read**	**read**	lesen
(to) **feel**	**felt**	fühlen; sich fühlen	(to) **run**	**ran**	rennen
(to) **fight**	**fought**	kämpfen; bekämpfen	(to) **spend**	**spent**	*(Zeit)* verbringen; *(Geld)* ausgeben
(to) **find**	**found**	finden			
(to) **give**	**gave**	geben	(to) **upset**	**upset**	erschüttern; aufregen, ärgern
(to) **grow**	**grew**	wachsen	(to) **win**	**won**	gewinnen
(to) **hit**	**hit**	treffen, schlagen, stoßen	(to) **write**	**wrote**	schreiben
(to) **hurt**	**hurt**	verletzen; wehtun			

🔊 Unit 3: Activities and games

▶ pp. 78/79	**beauty** [ˈbjuːti]	die Schönheit	noun: **beauty** – Your horse is a **beauty**! – adj: **beautiful** – Your horse is very **beautiful**! (wunderschön)
	beast [biːst]	das Tier; die Bestie; das Biest	▶▶ an animal (often very big or dangerous)
	full (of ...) [fʊl]	voll; voller ...	Help! Our house is **full of** mice! More sandwiches? – No thanks, I'm **full**. (... ich bin satt.)
	zip wire [ˈzɪp waɪə] *(kurz auch:* **zip**)	die Seilrutsche	a girl on a **zip wire**
	challenge [ˈtʃælɪndʒ]	die Herausforderung	

challenge – challenging – (to) challenge
- noun: **challenge** – It is a **challenge** to learn a new language.
     (to) **take on a challenge** = eine Herausforderung annehmen, sich einer Herausforderung stellen
- adj: **challenging** – Learning a new language can be quite **challenging**.   anspruchsvoll, (heraus)fordernd
- verb: (to) **challenge sb. (to sth.)** – They **challenged** us to a football match.   jn. (zu etwas) herausfordern

a **two-hour** class [ˈtuː aʊə klɑːs]	ein zweistündiger Kurs	

a two-hour class / a three-week holiday / …

a **two-hour** class	ein zweistündiger Kurs	**!** Im Englischen steht das
a **24-hour** supermarket	ein Supermarkt, der 24 Stunden geöffnet ist	Nomen im <u>Singular</u>:
a **three-week** holiday	ein dreiwöchiger Urlaub	a **two-<u>hour</u>** class
a **ten-kilometre** walk	eine Zehn-Kilometer-Wanderung	(*nicht:* a **two-hours** class)
a **55-year-old** teacher	ein 55-jähriger Lehrer / eine 55-jährige Lehrerin	

insect [ˈɪnsekt]	das Insekt	**Insects** are small. They have six legs and their bodies have three parts. **!** Betonung auf der 1. Silbe: **in**sect
(to) **book** [bʊk]	buchen; reservieren	verb: (to) **book** – noun: **booking** (die Buchung, die Reservierung)
(to) **be on** [biː ˈɒn]	gezeigt werden, „laufen" (*Kino, Fernsehen*), stattfinden; an sein (*eingeschaltet sein*)	What**'s on** at the theatre this evening? All the lights **are on**. They must be at home. (to) **be on** ◄ ► (to) **be off** (aus sein (*ausgeschaltet sein*))
musical [ˈmjuːzɪkl]	musikalisch, Musik-	adj: **musical** – noun: **musical** (das Musical)
actor [ˈæktə]	der Schauspieler, die Schauspielerin	Which **actor** played the killer in this film?
seat [siːt]	der (Sitz-)Platz	(to) **take a seat** = Platz nehmen noun: **seat** – verbs: (to) **sit** / (to) **sit down**

Topic 1

► p. 80	**dungeon** [ˈdʌndʒən]	der Kerker, das Verlies (*in einer Burg*)	a **dungeon**
	dragon [ˈdrægən]	der Drache	dragons
	(to) **role-play** sth. [ˈrəʊlpleɪ]	etwas in einem Rollenspiel darstellen	**role** = die Rolle (*Film, Theater*)
	(to) **train** sb. [treɪn]	jn. trainieren; ausbilden	(to) **train sb.** = jn. trainieren; ausbilden verb: (to) **train** – nouns: (*what you do*) **training**; (*person*) **trainer**

professional [prəˈfeʃənl]	professionell, Profi-	adj: **professional** – noun: **professional,** *infml auch:* **pro** (der Fachmann, die Fachfrau, der Profi)
castle [ˈkɑːsl]	die Burg	a Scottish **castle**
(to) **knit** [nɪt]	stricken	**!** Wie bei **knife** und **know** wird der erste Buchstabe von **knit** nicht gesprochen – die Aussprache beginnt mit dem Laut „n".
course [ˈkɔːs]	der Kurs	**!** **course** = **1.** der Kurs; **2.** das Gericht *(Gang beim Essen),* z. B. **main course**
(to) **prepare (for)** [prɪˈpeə]	vorbereiten, zubereiten; sich vorbereiten (auf)	Let's **prepare** food for the party. (vorbereiten, zubereiten) I must **prepare for** the maths test tomorrow. (mich vorbereiten auf) verb: (to) **prepare** – noun: **preparation** (die Vorbereitung; die Zubereitung)
(to) **act** [ækt]	Theater spielen, schauspielern	

(to) act – act – actor – action
- verb: (to) **act** = **1.** Theater spielen, schauspielern — I'd like to **act** in a play.
  2. handeln; sich verhalten — She **acted** very fast. / They **acted** like little kids.
  (to) **act sth. out** = etwas aufführen, vorspielen — Read the dialogue and **act it out** in front of the class.
- nouns: **act** (die Tat, die Handlung); **actor** (der Schauspieler, die Schauspielerin);
  action (die Action *(z. B. Film)*; die Aktion, die Handlung)

photography [fəˈtɒgrəfi]	die Fotografie *(Hobby),* das Fotografieren	**!** Betonung: • **photo(graph)** das Foto • (to) **photograph** fotografieren • **photography** die Fotografie *(Hobby)* • **photographer** der Fotograf, die Fotografin
sporty [ˈspɔːti]	sportlich	She's a **sporty** person. = She likes sport and is good at it.
(to) **take place** [teɪk ˈpleɪs]	stattfinden	The festival **takes place** every year. **!** (to) **take a seat** = Platz nehmen (to) **take place** = stattfinden
▶ p. 81 **I'm going to** choose … [ˈgəʊɪŋ]	Ich werde … (aus)wählen. / Ich habe vor, … zu wählen/auszuwählen.	What **are** you **going to** do on Saturday? – **I'm going to** go to the cinema.
camera [ˈkæmrə]	die Kamera	a **camera**
▶ p. 83 **tonight** [təˈnaɪt]	heute Nacht, heute Abend	It's too hot now, but we can sit in the garden **tonight** when it gets cooler.

| date | die Verabredung, das Date (auch die Person, mit der man ausgeht) | **date** = **1.** das Datum;
        2. die Verabredung, das Date |
| **somewhere** ['sʌmweə] | irgendwo(hin) | **everywhere** – **somewhere** –
nowhere (nirgendwo, nirgendwohin) |

Topic 2

▶ p. 84	**classical** ['klæsɪkl]	klassisch	**classical music** = die klassische Musik
	acoustic [əˈkuːstɪk]	akustisch	I like **acoustic** music because it's not so loud.
▶ p. 85	louder/older **than** … [ðən]	lauter/älter als …	**!** *German:* älter **als ich/er/wir/**… *English:* older **than me/him/us/**…
	the last one [ðə ˈlɑːst wʌn]	der/die/das Letzte	Their new CD is better than **the last one**.

one / ones

Wenn du ein schon einmal genanntes **Nomen** nicht wiederholen willst,
verwendest du **one** (Singular) bzw. **ones** (Plural):

I have three **cats**, two black **ones** and a white **one**.   Ich habe drei Katzen, zwei schwarze und eine weiße.
Can you give me a **pen**? – Which **one**? This **one**?   Kannst du mir einen Stift geben? – Welchen? Diesen?
– No, the blue **one**, please.   – Nein, den blauen, bitte.

lyrics *(pl)* ['lɪrɪks]	der Liedtext	**!** *German:* Der **Liedtext ist** sehr schön. *English:* The **lyrics are** very nice.
energetic [enəˈdʒetɪk]	aktiv, tatkräftig, energiegeladen	adj: **energetic** – noun: **energy** (die Energie) **!** Betonung auf der 1. Silbe: **en**ergy
worse [wɜːs]	schlechter, schlimmer	**!** good – **better** ◀ ▶ bad – **worse** Your text isn't **better** or **worse** than Sam's, it's just different!
as good **as** … [æz]	so gut wie …	My new bike is better than my old one, but still not **as good as** my mum's. **as … as** = genauso … wie **not as … as** = nicht so … wie
(to) **compare** sth. (**to** sth. / **with** sth.) [kəmˈpeə]	etwas vergleichen (mit etwas)	Work with a partner and **compare** your texts. **Compare** your text **with/to** your partner's.
▶ p. 86 **science fiction** [saɪəns ˈfɪkʃn] *(infml auch:* **sci-fi** ['saɪ faɪ])	die Science-Fiction	In this **science fiction** film, horrible monsters from another planet land on earth.
(to) **rate** sth. [reɪt]	etwas bewerten, beurteilen	verb: (to) **rate** – noun: **rating** (die Bewertung, die Beurteilung)
effect (on) [ɪˈfekt]	die (Aus-)Wirkung (auf), der Einfluss (auf); der Effekt	noun: **effect** – adj: **effective** (effektiv, wirksam) **!** Betonung auf der 2. Silbe: ef**fec**tive **special effects** *(pl)* = die Special Effects
worst [wɜːst]	der/die/das Schlechteste, Schlimmste; am schlechtesten, am schlimmsten	**!** good – **better** – best ◀ ▶ bad – **worse** – worst

space [speɪs]	der Raum, der Platz;
	der Weltraum
		• My flat is too small. I need more **space**.
		  (der Platz)
		• Would you like to fly through **space**?
		  (der Weltraum)

▶ p. 87 | **alien** [ˈeɪliən] | der/die Außerirdische; außerirdisch | adj: **alien** – noun: **alien**

magazine [mægəˈziːn] (*infml auch:* **mag** [mæg]) | die Zeitschrift

magazines

Topic 3

▶ p. 88 | **real** [rɪəl] | echt, wirklich
- adj: **real** – That's a plastic tree, not a **real** tree.
- adv: **really** – Our maths teacher is **really** nice.

forest [ˈfɒrɪst] | der Wald

bridge [brɪdʒ] | die Brücke

a **bridge** over a river in a **forest**

stairs *(pl)* [steəz] | die Treppe; die (Treppen-)Stufen

! **stairs** ist ein Pluralwort: **Those stairs are** dangerous. (**Die Treppe** dort **ist** gefährlich.)

key [kiː] | der Schlüssel; Schlüssel-

an old **key**

(to) **keep doing** sth. [kiːp ˈduːɪŋ] | etwas dauernd / immer wieder tun | (to) **keep going** = (immer) weiter gehen

(to) **turn right/left** [tɜːn] | (nach) rechts/links abbiegen

straight on [streɪt ˈɒn] | geradeaus (weiter)

Turn left.   **Turn right.**   **Go straight on.**

past [pɑːst] | vorbei an, vorüber an | It's not far to the library. Walk **past** the station, then turn left.

across a bridge / a street /… [əˈkrɒs] | über eine Brücke/Straße/… | A rabbit ran **across** the street in front of us.

▶ p. 89 | **trophy** [ˈtrəʊfi] | die Trophäe; der Pokal

trophies

above [əˈbʌv] | über, oberhalb (von); oben

above ◄ ► **below**
1. *(prep)* **über** ◄ ► **unter** The title of the story is **above** the text. | Write your name **below** the other names.
2. *(adv)* **oben** ◄ ► **unten** Find the new words in the text **above**. | Look at the pictures **below**.

bird [bɜːd] | der Vogel

Birds can fly across the sea.

square [skweə]	rechteckig	• adj: a **square** table/room (rechteckig) • noun: a statue in the middle of the **square** (der Platz *(in der Stadt)*)
score [skɔː]	der Spiel-/Punktestand; *(im Spiel/Sport erzielter)* Punkt	The match finished with a **score** of 5–0.
bottom [ˈbɒtəm]	das untere Ende	**(at the) top ◄ ► (at the) bottom**
level [ˈlevl]	der Grad, die Stufe; das Niveau, die Ebene	It's often not easy to get to the next **level** in a computer game. **sea level** = der Meeresspiegel
row [rəʊ]	die Reihe, die (Häuser-)Zeile	a **row** of houses

► p.90

until [ənˈtɪl]/**till** [tɪl]	bis *(zeitlich)*	We can play **until/till** 2 o'clock.
		❗ **not until / not till** = erst, wenn
		   German: Wir können **erst** essen, **wenn**
		       Mama heimkommt.
		   English: We ca**n't** eat **until/till** Mum comes
		       home.

(to) suggest sth. **(to** sb.**)**
[səˈdʒest]
	(jm.) etwas vorschlagen	*German:* Tom **schlug vor**, ins Kino **zu gehen**.
		English: Tom **suggested (that) we go** to the
		       cinema. *or*
		       Tom **suggested going** to the cinema.
		       ❗ *never:* Tom **suggested** to go …
		verb: (to) **suggest** –
		noun: **suggestion** (der Vorschlag)

quarter to 7 [ˈkwɔːtə]	viertel vor 7	quarter to 7
quarter past 7 [pɑːst]	viertel nach 7	quarter past 7
half past 6 [hɑːf]	halb 7	half past 6

half
• *German:* **halb sieben**
  English: **half past six**
	• *German:* **eine** halbe Stunde / **eine** halbe Orange / **eine** halbe Zitrone
	  English: **half an** hour / **half an** orange / **half a** lemon	

(to) match [mætʃ]	(passend) zusammenfügen	Look at the pairs of words and pictures …
		   … and **match** them.
		   … and **match** the words to the pictures.
		       (ordne die Wörter den Bildern zu)

expert [ˈekspɜːt]	der Experte, die Expertin	❗ Betonung auf der 1. Silbe: **ex**pert

directions (pl) [dəˈrekʃnz]	die Wegbeschreibung(en)	❗ (to) **ask for directions** / (to) **give directions** = nach dem Weg fragen / den Weg beschreiben **direction** = die Richtung

Background file

▶ p. 91	**international** [ɪntəˈnæʃnəl]	international	**national** ◀ ▶ **international**
	probably [ˈprɒbəbli]	wahrscheinlich	I'm sure you know … = You **probably** know …
	web [web]	das Netz; das Internet	(to) **surf the web** = im Internet surfen
	social media (pl) [səʊʃl ˈmiːdiə]	die sozialen Medien	*German:* **in** den sozialen Medien *English:* **on** social media **social** = sozial • **media** (pl) = die Medien
	all over the world [ˈɔːl əʊvə ðə wɜːld]	überall auf der Welt, auf der ganzen Welt	**all over** the world / the country = **everywhere** in the world / the country = **(all) around** the world / the country
	screen [skriːn]	der Bildschirm; die Leinwand (Kino)	a computer **screen**
	lingua franca [lɪŋgwə ˈfræŋkə]	die Lingua Franca (Verkehrssprache)	English is a **lingua franca** in many parts of the world.
	situation [sɪtʃuˈeɪʃn]	die Situation	❗ Betonung auf der 3. Silbe: situation

Story

▶ p. 92	**too much of a good thing** [tuː mʌtʃ ɒv ə ˈgʊd θɪŋ]	zu viel des Guten	
	(to) chat (with) [tʃæt]	chatten (mit); sich unterhalten (mit)	• verb: (to) **chat** – Let's make tea, sit down and **chat**. • noun: **chat** (die Unterhaltung; der Chat) – Let's make tea, sit down and **have a chat**. • adj: **chatty** (gesprächig; geschwätzig)
	bored [bɔːd]	gelangweilt	(to) **be bored** / **get bored** = sich langweilen ❗ The film was **boring**. (langweilig) I was really **bored**. (Mir war langweilig.) I **got bored** after ten minutes. (Mir wurde … langweilig.)
	cough [kɒf]	der Husten	Zane has a bad **cough**. ❗ Beachte Aussprache und Schreibung! Du schreibst **cough** – aber du sprichst es wie c**off**ee.
	(to) have a headache [hæv ə ˈhedeɪk]	Kopfschmerzen haben	❗ Mit Artikel: I **have a headache**. (Ich habe Kopfschmerzen.) I **have a cough**. (Ich habe Husten.)

Get better/well soon! [get ˈbetə suːn], [get ˈwel suːn]	Gute Besserung! / Werde bald gesund!	**!** **well** = 1. *(adj)* gesund; 2. *(adv)* gut
(to) **click (on)** [klɪk]	klicken (auf), anklicken	Don't **click on** the link in this email!
a while [ə ˈwaɪl]	eine Weile, einige Zeit	**!** **while** = 1. *(conj)* während – **While** we were waiting ... 2. *(noun)* die Weile – I'd like to lie down **for a while**.
rule [ruːl]	die Regel	This game is fun because its **rules** are so easy.
▶ p. 93 **What's wrong?** [wɒts ˈrɒŋ]	Was ist los? / Was/Wo ist das Problem?	• Something **is wrong**. = Irgendetwas ist nicht in Ordnung / stimmt nicht. • Nothing **is wrong**. = Everything is OK.
calendar [ˈkælɪndə]	der Kalender	**!** Betonung auf der 1. Silbe: **ca**lendar
(to) **study** [ˈstʌdi]	lernen; studieren *(z. B. für Prüfungen)*	I must stay at home this afternoon and **study** for tomorrow's test. She wants to **study** history.
(to) **come round (to** sb.) [kʌm ˈraʊnd]	vorbeikommen, vorbeischauen (bei jm.)	▶▶ (to) visit sb.
puzzled [ˈpʌzld]	verwundert	▶▶ surprised
mark [mɑːk]	die (Schul-)Note, die Zensur; die Markierung; das Zeichen	I love art. I always get good **marks** in art. The **mark** on the map shows you where I live.

Verbs and nouns with the same form

(to) **challenge**	herausfordern	**challenge**	die Herausforderung
(to) **chat**	chatten; sich unterhalten	**chat**	die Unterhaltung; der Chat
(to) **click**	klicken, anklicken	**click**	der Klick, das Klicken
(to) **cough**	husten	**cough**	der Husten
(to) **mark**	kennzeichnen, markieren	**mark**	die (Schul-)Note, die Zensur; die Markierung; das Zeichen
(to) **match** sth.	(etwas passend) zusammenfügen	**match**	das (passende) Gegenstück
(to) **photograph**	fotografieren	**photograph**	das Foto
(to) **role-play** sth.	etwas in einem Rollenspiel darstellen	**role-play**	das Rollenspiel
(to) **score**	erzielen *(Punkt/Tor/Treffer)*	**score**	der Spiel-/Punktestand; *(im Spiel/Sport erzielter)* Punkt

▶ p. 94 **ending** [ˈendɪŋ]	die Endung; das Ende *(Text, Geschichte)*	**!** *German:* **Happy End** *English:* **happy ending**
not (...) any more [nɒt eni ˈmɔː]	nicht mehr	This bag is very old. I do**n't** use it **any more**.

Study skills

▶ p. 96 **especially** [ɪˈspeʃəli]	insbesondere	I love team sports, **especially** football.

Unit task

▶ p. 97 (to) **discuss** sth. [dɪˈskʌs]	über etwas diskutieren; etwas besprechen	**!** *German:* **über** etwas diskutieren *English:* (to) **discuss sth.** verb: (to) **discuss** – noun: **discussion** (die Diskussion)

it **should ...** [ʃʊd]	es sollte ...	What **should** I do? – I think you **should** talk to your parents.
attention [əˈtenʃn]	die Aufmerksamkeit	

| **attention**
 • (to) **pay attention (to)**
   (*simple past:* **paid**)
 • (to) **get sb.'s attention**

 • (to) **keep sb.'s attention** | Stop talking now and **pay attention**, please.
 You never **pay attention to** what I'm saying.
 He called her name to **get her attention**.

 The story was boring and didn't **keep my attention**. | aufpassen, aufmerksam sein
 Beachtung schenken, zuhören <br> js. Aufmerksamkeit erregen, gewinnen <br> js. Aufmerksamkeit aufrecht erhalten |

🔊 Unit 4: Celebrate!

pp. 112/113	(to) **celebrate** [ˈselɪbreɪt]	feiern	My grandma **celebrated** her 70th birthday last week. verb: (to) **celebrate** – noun: **celebration** (die Feier, das Fest)
	(to) **break the fast** [breɪk ðə ˈfɑːst], **broke** [brəʊk], **broken** [ˈbrəʊkən]	das Fasten brechen	noun: **fast** (das Fasten, die Fastenzeit) – verb: (to) **fast** (fasten)
	carnival [ˈkɑːnɪvl]	der Karneval	This is my **carnival** costume: I'm a green monster!
	bonfire [ˈbɒnfaɪə]	das *(große Freuden-)*Feuer	**❗ Bonfire Night** oder **Guy Fawkes Night** ist der Abend des 5. November, an dem zum Gedenken an den missglückten Anschlag auf das Parlamentsgebäude im Jahre 1605 Freudenfeuer und Feuerwerke stattfinden.

a **bonfire**

	candle [ˈkændl]	die Kerze	

a **candle**

	firework [ˈfaɪəwɜːk]	der Feuerwerkskörper	

fireworks *(pl)* (das Feuerwerk) a **firework**

Topic 1

▶ p. 114	**Muslim** [ˈmʊzlɪm]	der Muslim, die Muslima; muslimisch	I'm a **Muslim**. My religion is Islam.
	a **practising** Muslim [ˈpræktɪsɪŋ]	ein praktizierender Muslim, eine praktizierende Muslima	a **practising doctor** = ein praktizierender Arzt, eine praktizierende Ärztin *(seinen/ihren Beruf ausübend)*
	(to) **be thirsty** [ˈθɜːsti]	durstig sein, Durst haben	(to) **be hungry** ◀ ▶ (to) **be thirsty**
	sunrise [ˈsʌnraɪz]	der Sonnenaufgang	**sunrise** ◀ ▶ **sunset** (der Sonnenuntergang)

(to) **pray** [preɪ]	beten	verb: (to) **pray** – noun: **prayer** (das Gebet)
(to) **thank** sb. [θæŋk]	sich bei jm. bedanken	I'd like to **thank** everybody for their help. (= say thank you to everybody)
charity [ˈtʃærəti]	die wohltätige Organisation	**animal charity** = die wohltätige Organisation, die Tiere unterstützt **charity shop** = das Geschäft, das gespendete Waren für wohltätige Zwecke verkauft
flower [ˈflaʊə]	die Blume; die Blüte	**flowers** in **flowerpots** **flowerpot** = der Blumentopf
god [gɒd]	der Gott	People pray to many different **gods**.
▶ p. 115 **biscuit** [ˈbɪskɪt]	der Keks, das Plätzchen	**!** *German* **Keks** – *English* **biscuit** *German* **Kuchen** – *English* **cake**
chocolate [ˈtʃɒklət]	die Praline	**!** **chocolate** = **1.** die Schokolade; **2.** die Praline
baked beans *(pl)* [beɪkt ˈbiːnz]	die weißen Bohnen in Tomatensoße	**bean** = die Bohne **coffee beans**
juice [dʒuːs]	der Saft	**orange juice**
yoghurt [ˈjɒgət]	der Joghurt	
pot [pɒt]	der Topf; die Kanne (z. B. Tee-, Kaffeekanne)	a **pot** a **teapot** a **pot of yoghurt**
carton [ˈkɑːtn]	der (Papp-)Karton; die Packung	**!** Betonung auf der 1. Silbe: **car**ton
jar [dʒɑː]	das Glas(gefäß)	
tin [tɪn]	die Dose, die Büchse	**tins, jars and bottles**
mosque [mɒsk]	die Moschee	a **mosque**
(to) **wish** [wɪʃ]	(sich) wünschen	(to) **make a wish** = sich etwas wünschen **Best wishes** = Viele Grüße *(Briefschluss)*
each other [iːtʃ ˈʌðə]	einander, sich (gegenseitig)	Work together – you can learn a lot **from each other**! (voneinander) They talked **to each other**. (miteinander)

bath [bɑːθ]	das (Wannen-)Bad; die Badewanne	❗ *German:* **baden, ein Bad nehmen** *(in der Badewanne)* *English:* (to) **have a bath** or (to) **take a bath**
▶ p. 116 **beef** [biːf]	das Rindfleisch	**Beef** is meat from cows. **cow** = die Kuh
lamb [læm]	das Lamm(fleisch)	▶▶ a young sheep; meat from a young sheep
sheep [ʃiːp], *pl* **sheep**	das Schaf	❗ one **sheep** – two **sheep**
pork [pɔːk]	das Schweinefleisch	**Pork** is meat from pigs. **pig** = das Schwein
respect (for) [rɪˈspekt]	der Respekt (vor)	They have a lot of **respect for** each other.
a few [ə ˈfjuː]	ein paar, einige	Are you hungry? I still have **a few** sandwiches. **in the last few weeks** = in den letzten paar Wochen
▶ p. 117 **collection** [kəˈlekʃn]	die Sammlung	noun: **collection** – verb: (to) **collect**
May I ...? [meɪ]	Darf ich ...?	**May I** use your pen? – Sure! Here you are.
soup [suːp]	die Suppe	**tomato soup**
pancake [ˈpænkeɪk]	der Pfannkuchen	You need eggs, milk and flour to make **pancakes**. You fry them in oil.
strange [streɪndʒ]	seltsam, sonderbar	adj: **strange** – What a **strange** question! I don't know what to say. noun: **stranger** (der/die Fremde) – I don't like to talk to **strangers**.

Topic 2

▶ p. 118 **romantic** [rəʊˈmæntɪk]	romantisch	I like **romantic** stories – stories about love.
surprise [səˈpraɪz]	die Überraschung	noun: **surprise** – verb: (to) **surprise** (überraschen) Don't tell her! It's a **surprise** party! (= We want to **surprise** her with the party!)
▶ p. 119 **just** [dʒʌst]	gerade (eben)	I've **just** baked biscuits. Do you want to try one? ❗ **just** = 1. gerade (eben); 2. nur, bloß; einfach
so far [ˈsəʊ fɑː]	bis jetzt, bis hierher	**So far** my holiday has been great. ▶▶ till/until now

	(to) **finish** [ˈfɪnɪʃ]	enden; beenden, zu Ende machen	School **finishes** at 15.05. = We **finish** school at 15.05. (Wir haben um 15.05 Schulschluss.) ▶▶ (to) end
	not ... yet [nɒt ˈjet]	noch nicht ...	**yet** **1.** *in verneinten Sätzen:* **noch nicht** – I'm hungry. I have**n't** had dinner **yet**.
	... yet? [jet]	... schon ...?	**2.** *in Fragen:* **schon** – Have you had dinner **yet**?
	(to) **lose** [luːz], **lost** [lɒst], **lost** [lɒst]	verlieren	**!** win ◀ ▶ lose: We **lost** the match. find ◀ ▶ lose: I think I've **lost** my ticket!
	(to) **blow** [bləʊ], **blew** [bluː], **blown** [bləʊn]	pusten, blasen; wehen	A cold wind was **blowing**. (wehen) **Blow** on your tea if it's too hot! (pusten) Can you **blow up** the balloons? (aufblasen)
▶ p. 120	**poor** [pɔː], [pʊə]	arm	**Poor** George! = Der arme George! / Armer George!
	(to) **feed** [fiːd], **fed** [fed], **fed** [fed]	füttern; ernähren	Can I **feed** the rabbits? (füttern) It's hard to **feed** a family of six. (ernähren)
	both [bəʊθ]	beide	Do you want to buy **both** T-shirts? = Do you want to buy **both** the red **and** the green T-shirt? (... sowohl das rote als auch das grüne T-Shirt ...) **both ... and ...** = sowohl ... als auch ...
▶ p. 121	**ever** [ˈevə]	jemals	ever ◀ ▶ never Have you **ever** ...? = Bist/Hast du schon einmal ... **!** ever = **1.** jemals, schon einmal; **2.** the best son ever = der beste Sohn überhaupt / der beste Sohn, den man sich wünschen kann

Topic 3

▶ p. 122	**cheesy** [ˈtʃiːzɪ]	kitschig	I don't like **cheesy** love stories.
	member [ˈmembə]	das Mitglied	I've been a **member** of the drama club for two years.
▶ p. 123	**anybody** [ˈenibɒdi] / **anyone** [ˈeniwʌn]	irgendjemand	Do you know **anybody/anyone** from Spain?

any – anybody/anyone – anything – anywhere

- Das Wort **any** und die Zusammensetzungen **anybody/anyone**, **anything** und **anywhere** stehen vor allem in **verneinten Aussagesätzen (1)** und in **Fragen (2)**:

1) I **don't** have **any** money.	*kein Geld*	I **didn't** know **anybody/anyone**.	*niemand*
I **can't** see **anything**.	*nichts*	I **can't** find my keys **anywhere**.	*nirgends*
2) Do you have **any** questions?	*(irgendwelche) Fragen*	**Can** you see **anybody/anyone**?	*(irgend)jemand*
Can you see **anything**?	*(irgend)etwas*	**Did** you go **anywhere** nice?	*irgendwo(hin)*

- **any, anybody/anyone, anything** oder **anywhere** können auch in **bejahten Aussagesätzen** stehen:

You can call me **any** time.	*jederzeit*	You can ask **anybody/anyone**.	*jeder (beliebige)*
You can ask her **anything**.	*alles*	Accidents happen **anywhere**.	*überall*

	nothing [ˈnʌθɪŋ]	nichts	**nothing** ◀ ▶ everything

colourful [ˈkʌləfl]	farbig, bunt	a **colourful** toy train
(to) **hold** [həʊld], **held** [held], **held** [held]	halten	Can you **hold** my bag for a minute, please?
▶ p.124 **christening** [ˈkrɪsnɪŋ]	die Taufe	a **christening**
house-warming (party) [ˈhaʊs wɔːmɪŋ]	die Einzugsfeier	We've moved into our new house. Come to our **house-warming party** next Saturday!
(to) **scare** sb. [skeə]	jn. erschrecken, jm. Angst machen	Mice **scare** me. = I find them **scary**. = I'm **scared** of them.
embarrassing [ɪmˈbærəsɪŋ]	peinlich	• adj: **embarrassing** (peinlich) – Sometimes you do **embarrassing** things. **embarrassed** (verlegen, peinlich berührt) – Aren't you **embarrassed**? / Don't you feel **embarrassed**? • verb: (to) **embarrass sb.** (jn. in Verlegenheit bringen, jm. peinlich sein) – Her questions **embarrassed** me.

Background file

▶ p.125 **bride** [braɪd]	die Braut	the **(bride)groom** the **bride**
bridegroom [ˈbraɪdgruːm] (*kurz auch:* **groom**)	der Bräutigam	
suit [suːt]	der (Herren-)Anzug; das (Damen-)Kostüm	**suits**
niece [niːs]	die Nichte	**niece** (your brother's or sister's daughter) ◀ ▶ **nephew** (your brother's or sister's son)
bridesmaid [ˈbraɪdzmeɪd]	die Brautjungfer	A **bridesmaid** helps the bride before and during the wedding.
groomsman [ˈgruːmzmən], *pl* **groomsmen**	der Trauzeuge (*des Bräutigams*)	Who did your brother choose as his **groomsmen** for his wedding?
afterwards [ˈɑːftəwədz]	nachher, danach	We had fish and chips, and **afterwards** we went to the cinema and watched a film.

Story

| ▶ p.126 **on time** [taɪm] | pünktlich | Our train arrived **on time**. |

(to) **put** sth. **on** [pʊt], **put** [pʊt], **put** [pʊt]	etwas anziehen *(Kleidung)*, aufsetzen *(Hut, Brille)*	(to) put sth. on ◄ ► (to) **take** sth. **off, took, taken** (etwas ausziehen *(Kleidung)*, ablegen *(Hut, Brille)*) He **took off** his glasses and **put on** a pullover.
(to) **organize** [ˈɔːgənaɪz]	organisieren	verb: (to) **organize** – noun: **organization** (die Organisation) adj: **organized** ((gut) organisiert); **disorganized** (schlecht organisiert, chaotisch) Jill is **(well-)organized.** = Jill ist gut organisiert / hat alles voll im Griff.
awake [əˈweɪk]	wach	**asleep** ◄ ► **awake** Hey, are you still asleep? – Very funny! Now I'm **awake**!
for hours [fɔːr ˈaʊəz]	seit Stunden, stundenlang	**for a long time** = seit langem; lange *(für eine lange Zeit)*
(to) **set** [set], **set** [set], **set** [set]	stellen, legen, setzen	(to) **set the table** = den Tisch decken (to) **set the alarm** = (sich) den/einen Wecker stellen **alarm** = der Wecker; der Alarm; die Alarmanlage
he looked at **himself** [hɪmˈself]	er sah sich (selbst) an	When Finn fell off the wall, he hurt **himself**. Maybe Jeff can tell us a bit about **himself**.
► p.127 **suddenly** [ˈsʌdənli]	plötzlich, auf einmal	**Suddenly** the music stopped and it was very quiet.
(to) **steal** [stiːl], **stole** [stəʊl], **stolen** [ˈstəʊlən]	stehlen, rauben	I didn't lose my phone. I'm sure someone **stole** it **from me**. (... hat es **mir** gestohlen.)
downstairs [daʊnˈsteəz]	(nach) unten *(die Treppe hinunter)*	**downstairs** ◄ ► **upstairs** (nach) oben *(die Treppe hinauf)*
(to) **believe (in** sth.) [bɪˈliːv]	(an etwas) glauben	**!** *German:* **Glaubst** du **an** Geister? *English:* Do you **believe in** ghosts?
(to) **lock** [lɒk]	abschließen *(z. B. Tür)*	(to) **be locked out** = ausgesperrt sein (to) **lock** ◄ ► (to) **unlock** (aufschließen, entsperren)

Verbs and nouns with the same form

(to) **fast**	fasten	**fast**	das Fasten, die Fastenzeit
(to) **finish**	enden; beenden, zu Ende machen	**finish**	das Ende, das Ziel *(beim Sport)*
(to) **lock**	abschließen	**lock**	das (Tür-)Schloss
(to) **respect**	respektieren, achten	**respect**	der Respekt
(to) **surprise**	überraschen	**surprise**	die Überraschung
(to) **wish**	(sich) wünschen	**wish**	der Wunsch

pocket [ˈpɒkɪt]	die Tasche *(an Kleidungsstücken)*	This hoodie has big **pockets** for my phone, my keys and my money. **pocket money** = das Taschengeld
slippers *(pl)* [slɪpə]	die Hausschuhe	a pair of **slippers**

| **as** [æz], [əz] | als, während | My dog watched me **as** I ate my sandwich. |

as
1. *(Konjunktion)* **wie** — As I was saying, it's not easy.
2. *(Konjunktion)* **als, während** — As I walked home, I heard someone playing a guitar.
3. *(Präposition)* **als** — Did you have a pet **as** a kid?
4. *(Adverb)* **so ... wie** — My bike is **as** good **as** new.

| **disappointed (in/with)** [dɪsəˈpɔɪntɪd] | enttäuscht (von) | |

disappointed – disappointing – disappointment – (to) disappoint

- adj: **disappointed** — enttäuscht — The zoo was closed! I was very **disappointed**.
  disappointing — enttäuschend — The show was boring – very **disappointing**.
- noun: **disappointment** — die Enttäuschung — He didn't show his **disappointment**.
- verb: (to) **disappoint sb.** — jn. enttäuschen — The show **disappointed** the fans.

| **for better** [betə] **or (for) worse** [wɜːs] | was auch immer geschieht, in guten wie in schlechten Zeiten *(beim Ehegelöbnis)* | I'll always be there for you, **for better or for worse**. (= in good and in bad times) |

| **sickness** [ˈsɪknəs] | die Krankheit | **in sickness or in health** = wenn man krank oder gesund ist noun: **sickness** – adj: **sick** |

ill – sick

- Nach <u>Verben</u> kann **ill** oder **sick** stehen: (to) **be**/**look ill**, (to) **be**/**look sick** — krank sein/aussehen
- Vor <u>Nomen</u> kann nur **sick** stehen: a **sick child** — ein krankes Kind
- Das Wort **sick** bedeutet auch „schlecht, übel": I feel **sick**. — Mir ist schlecht/übel.
- (to) **be sick** heißt „sich übergeben": I'm going to **be sick**. — Ich muss mich übergeben.

▶ p. 128 | **jacket** [ˈdʒækɪt] | die Jacke; das Jackett |

a **jacket**   a **rain jacket**

| **multicultural** [mʌltiˈkʌltʃərəl] | multikulturell | |

| **scarf** [skɑːf], *pl* **scarves** [skɑːvz] | der Schal | |

two **scarves**

| **global** [ˈgləʊbl] | global, weltweit | ❗ Betonung auf der 1. Silbe: **glo**bal adj: **global** – noun: **globe** (der Globus; die Kugel) **across the globe** = **all (a)round the globe** = all over the world |

| **citizen** [ˈsɪtɪzn] | der (Staats-)Bürger, die (Staats-)Bürgerin | Her family came to Britain many years ago, but they're all British **citizens** now. |

Study skills

▶ p. 130	**slide** [slaɪd]	das Dia; die Folie (Präsentationssoftware)	I've prepared my presentation and found some funny pictures for my **slides**.
	keyword [ˈkiːwɜːd]	das Stichwort, das Schlagwort	What do you think about when you hear the **keyword** "game"?

Unit task

▶ p. 131	**ceremony** [ˈserəməni]	die Feier, die Zeremonie	**prize ceremony** = die Preisverleihung ❗ Betonung auf der 1. Silbe: **ce**remony
	order [ˈɔːdə]	die Reihenfolge	Put these pictures **in order**. = Bring sie in eine Reihenfolge. Put them **in the right order**. = ... in die richtige Reihenfolge.
	audio [ˈɔːdiəʊ]	Audio-, Ton-	Do we need a video? Or is an **audio** recording enough? (= a recording only of sound/music)
	visual [ˈvɪʒuəl]	visuell, optisch	**audio** effects = effects that you can hear **visual** effects = effects that you can see

Irregular verbs

Infinitive	Simple past	Past participle		Infinitive	Simple past	Past participle	
(to) **be**	was/were	**been**	sein	(to) **lose**	lost	**lost**	verlieren
(to) **blow**	blew	**blown**	blasen; wehen	(to) **make**	made	**made**	machen, herstellen
(to) **break**	broke	**broken**	(zer)brechen	(to) **meet**	met	**met**	(sich) treffen
(to) **buy**	bought	**bought**	kaufen	(to) **put**	put	**put**	legen, stellen
(to) **come**	came	**come**	(mit)kommen	(to) **ride**	rode	**ridden**	(Rad) fahren; reiten
(to) **do**	did	**done**	machen, tun	(to) **see**	saw	**seen**	sehen
(to) **eat**	ate	**eaten**	essen	(to) **send**	sent	**sent**	senden, schicken
(to) **feed**	fed	**fed**	füttern	(to) **set**	set	**set**	stellen, setzen
(to) **find**	found	**found**	finden	(to) **sing**	sang	**sung**	singen
(to) **forget**	forgot	**forgotten**	vergessen	(to) **sleep**	slept	**slept**	schlafen
(to) **get**	got	**got**	bekommen; holen; gelangen	(to) **steal**	stole	**stolen**	stehlen
				(to) **swim**	swam	**swum**	schwimmen
(to) **give**	gave	**given**	geben	(to) **take**	took	**taken**	(mit)nehmen
(to) **hear**	heard	**heard**	hören	(to) **think**	thought	**thought**	denken
(to) **hold**	held	**held**	halten	(to) **wear**	wore	**worn**	tragen, anhaben
(to) **leave**	left	**left**	verlassen, weggehen	(to) **win**	won	**won**	gewinnen

◀)) Unit 5: Getting ready for the future

▶ pp. 144/145	**future** [ˈfjuːtʃə]	die Zukunft; zukünftige(r, s)	❗ Betonung auf der 1. Silbe: **fu**ture noun: **future** – I'll be more careful in the **future**. adj: **future** – What are your **future** plans?
	builder [ˈbɪldə]	der Bauarbeiter, die Bauarbeiterin; der Bauunternehmer, die Bauunternehmerin	nouns: **building**; (person) **builder** – verb: (to) **build, built, built** (bauen)

firefighter [ˈfaɪəfaɪtə]	der Feuerwehrmann, die Feuerwehrfrau	a **firefighter** trying to stop a **fire** 
hairdresser [ˈheədresə]	der Friseur, die Friseurin	

> ❗ Wenn man das Geschäft oder den Laden meint, wird **'s** an die Berufsbezeichnung angehängt.
> Vergleiche: **hairdresser** = der Friseur/die Friseurin *(die Person)*
> **hairdresser's** = der Friseursalon — Jake is **at the hairdresser's**.

mechanic [mɪˈkænɪk]	der Mechaniker, die Mechanikerin	Our car has a problem. A car **mechanic** needs to check it.

Topic 1

▶ p. 146	**I want to be a nurse.** [nɜːs]	Ich möchte Krankenpflegerin/ Krankenpfleger werden.	❗ Wenn es um Berufswünsche geht („was man einmal werden möchte"), wird meist **be** benutzt, nicht **become**.
	police officer [pəˈliːs ɒfɪsə]	der Polizeibeamte, die Polizeibeamtin	**officer** = der Beamte, die Beamtin
	architect [ˈɑːkɪtekt]	der Architekt, die Architektin	❗ Betonung auf der 1. Silbe: <u>ar</u>chitect
▶ p. 148	**I'll** [aɪl] **(= I will** [wɪl]**)** be ...	ich werde ... sein	❗ Nicht verwechseln: I **will** have fun. = Ich **werde** Spaß haben. I **want to** have fun. = Ich **möchte** Spaß haben.
	they **won't (= will not)** believe ... [wəʊnt]	sie werden ... nicht glauben	
	manager [ˈmænɪdʒə]	der Manager, die Managerin	noun: **manager** – verb: (to) **manage sth.** (etwas verwalten, regeln, leiten)

People's jobs: verb + -er

(to) **bake** – **baker**	(to) **drive** – **driver**	(to) **sing** – **singer**
(to) **build** – **builder**	(to) **manage** – **manager**	(to) **swim** – **swimmer**
(to) **clean** – **cleaner**	(to) **photograph** – **photographer**	(to) **teach** – **teacher**
(to) **dance** – **dancer**	(to) **play** – **player**	(to) **train** – **trainer**
(to) **design** – **designer**	(to) **program** – **programmer**	(to) **write** – **writer**

crazy [ˈkreɪzi]	verrückt	You want to walk home in this weather? You must be **crazy**. (to) **be crazy about sth.** = wild auf etwas sein, versessen auf etwas sein
prediction [prɪˈdɪkʃn]	die Vorhersage, die Voraussage	Can you make a **prediction** about how much this will cost?
(to) **earn** [ɜːn]	verdienen *(Geld)*	❗ *German* "Geld verdienen": **1.** *(Gehalt bekommen)* (to) **earn money** **2.** *(Profit machen)* (to) **make money**

▶ p. 149 (to) **imagine** sth. [ɪˈmædʒɪn]	sich etwas vorstellen	**Imagine** your dream house. What's it like? Can you **imagine** being a famous film star? (to) **imagine being/doing sth.** = sich vorstellen, etwas zu sein / etwas zu tun
successful [səkˈsesfl]	erfolgreich	adj: **successful** – Mo had a good business idea – it was very **successful**. noun: **success** – His business was a big **success**.
(to) **come true** [kʌm ˈtruː]	wahr werden	I hope all your dreams will **come true**.

Topic 2

▶ p. 150 **conversation** [kɒnvəˈseɪʃn]	das Gespräch	▶▶ a talk between people; a chat
explanation [ekspləˈneɪʃn]	die Erklärung	noun: **explanation** – verb: (to) **explain sth. to sb.**
chore [tʃɔː]	die (Haus-)Arbeit, die *(lästige)* Pflicht	(to) **do chores** = (Haus-)Arbeiten erledigen
(to) **fold** [fəʊld]	falten	You can save space if you **fold** your clothes when you put them into your wardrobe.
(to) **wash** [wɒʃ]	(sich) waschen	**washing** = die Wäsche (to) **do the washing** = die Wäsche erledigen, Wäsche waschen
(to) **babysit** [ˈbeɪbisɪt], **babysat** [ˈbeɪbisæt], **babysat** [ˈbeɪbisæt]	babysitten	(to) **babysit a baby / a child** verb: (to) **babysit** – nouns: *(what you do)* **babysitting**; *(person)* **babysitter**
(to) **empty** [ˈempti]	leeren	adj: **empty** – verb: (to) **empty** (leeren)
dishwasher [ˈdɪʃwɒʃə]	die Geschirrspülmaschine	The **dishwasher** is finished! Can you **empty** it, please?
(to) **vacuum** [ˈvækjuəm]	Staub saugen	verb: (to) **vacuum** – noun: **vacuum cleaner** (der Staubsauger)
▶ p. 151 (to) **have to do** sth. [hæv], **had** [hæd], **had** [hæd]	etwas tun müssen	Look, it's late. We **have to go** now. ❗ German "müssen" = 1. (to) **have to**; 2. **must** (**have to** wird häufiger verwendet als **must**.)
bar chart [ˈbɑː tʃɑːt]	das Säulendiagramm	a **bar chart** **pie charts** (Tortendiagramme) **bar** = die Säule, die Stange *(z. B. Eisen-)*, **chart** = das Diagramm; die Tabelle

horizontal [ˌhɒrɪˈzɒntl]	waagerecht, horizontal	the **vertical axis** (or **Y-axis**)
axis [ˈæksɪs], *pl* **axes** [ˈæksiːz]	die Achse	
vertical [ˈvɜːtɪkl]	senkrecht, vertikal	the **horizontal axis** (or **X-axis**)

large [lɑːdʒ]	groß	Eight brothers and sisters? What a **large** family! ❗ You don't use **large** to describe people. People are **tall** (groß), **big** (dick, schwer) or **great** (bedeutend, angesehen).
▶ p.152 **I don't mind ...** [maɪnd]	Es macht mir nichts aus ...	**I don't mind** helping you. (Ich helfe dir gern.) **I don't mind** the rain, but I hate the cold.

Background file

▶ p.153 **typical (of)** [ˈtɪpɪkl]	typisch (für)	❗ That's **typical of** him. = Das ist **typisch für** ihn.
corner shop [ˈkɔːnə ʃɒp]	der Eckladen, der Tante-Emma-Laden	**corner** = die Ecke
That's when they're useful. [ˈðæts wen]	Dann / Genau dann sind sie nützlich.	

That's/This is + when/why/what/how/...

- **That's when ...**   The door closed, and **that's when** they noticed their keys were still inside.
     (... und genau dann / in dem Moment bemerkten sie ...)
- **That's why ...**   I'm allergic to strawberries. **That's why** I can't eat your cake.
     (Deswegen ... / Darum ...)
- **That's what ...**   A hot bath – **that's what** I really need now.
     (... genau das brauche ich jetzt / ... das ist genau das, was ich jetzt brauche)
- **This is how ...**   Look here. **This is how** you do it.
     (... (genau) so macht man das)

(to) **sell** [sel], **sold** [səʊld], **sold** [səʊld]	verkaufen	I need money. I'll **sell** some clothes that I never wear. (to) **buy** ◀ ▶ (to) **sell**
early [ˈɜːli]	früh	I always try to be on time – not too late, and not too **early**. **early** ◀ ▶ **late**

size [saɪz]	die Größe	❗ *German:* Welche **Größe hast** du?
		    English: What **size** do you **take**? *or*
		              What **size are** you?

(shop) assistant [ˈʃɒp əsɪstənt]	der Verkäufer, die Verkäuferin	❗ **assistant** = **1.** der Verkäufer, die Verkäuferin; **2.** der Assistent, die Assistentin

Topic 3

▶ p.154 **treat** [triːt]	der Hochgenuss, das besondere Vergnügen; die (besondere) Leckerei	I'll **treat** you **to** a meal in your favourite restaurant. – Oh wow, thanks, that's a wonderful **treat**!

(to) **shop (for** sth.**)** [ʃɒp]	(ein)kaufen, „shoppen"; etwas kaufen (gehen)	I need to **shop for** (= go and buy) new shoes. verb: (to) **shop** – nouns: **shop**; (person) **shopper** (der Kunde, die Kundin; der Einkäufer, die Einkäuferin)
per cent (%) [pə ˈsent]	das Prozent	There are eight kids: four are girls. That's 50 **per cent**.
spotlight [ˈspɒtlaɪt]	das Spotlight, der Scheinwerfer; die Aufmerksamkeit	(to) **turn the spotlight on sb./sth.** = den Scheinwerfer / die Aufmerksamkeit auf jn./ etwas richten **in/under the spotlight** = im Rampenlicht, im Blickpunkt des Interesses
cash [kæʃ]	das Cash, das Bargeld	You can only **pay (in) cash** in this shop. (bar bezahlen) (to) **pay cash** / (to) **pay in cash** ◄ ► (to) **pay by card** (mit Karte bezahlen)
cash machine [ˈkæʃ məʃiːn]	der Geldautomat	I need some cash. Is there a **cash machine** near here?
(to) **walk the dog** [wɔːk ðə ˈdɒg]	mit dem Hund rausgehen, mit dem Hund Gassi gehen	► ► (to) take the dog for a walk
I **mustn't** buy … [ˈmʌsnt]	ich darf nicht … kaufen	**!** **you mustn't** = du darfst nicht **you don't have to** = du musst nicht, du brauchst nicht

must – mustn't – don't have to

Mit **must** sagst du, dass jemand etwas tun muss:	Mit **mustn't** sagst du, dass jemand etwas nicht tun darf:	Wenn du sagen willst, dass jemand etwas nicht tun muss, verwendest du **don't have to** bzw. **doesn't have to**:
I **must** feed the rabbits. They're hungry. *Ich muss … füttern.*	I **mustn't** forget to feed the rabbits. *Ich darf nicht vergessen, …*	You **don't have to** feed the rabbits. I've already fed them. *Du musst … nicht füttern.*

savings account [ˈseɪvɪŋz əkaʊnt]	das Sparkonto	**savings** (pl) = die Ersparnisse **account** = das (Bank-)Konto; der Account
coin [kɔɪn]	die Münze	Only a few **coins** – that's not a lot of cash!
piggy bank [ˈpɪgi bæŋk]	das Sparschwein	I need some cash … I can empty my **piggy bank**. coins →
► p. 155 (to) **paint** [peɪnt]	(an)malen; lackieren, (an)streichen	Can we **paint** this wardrobe blue?
bakery [ˈbeɪkəri]	die Bäckerei	shop: the **bakery** person: **baker** (der Bäcker, die Bäckerin)

electronics *(pl)*
[ɪlekˈtrɒnɪks]

die Elektronik;
die elektronischen Geräte

noun: **electronics** –
adj: **electronic** (elektronisch)

---

gift [gɪft]

das Geschenk, die Gabe;
das Talent

▶▶ present
gift shop = der Geschenk(artikel)laden,
der Souvenirladen

---

newsagent [ˈnjuːzeɪdʒənt]

der Zeitungshändler,
die Zeitungshändlerin

❗ **newsagent** = der Zeitungshändler,
die Zeitungshändlerin *(die Person)*
newsagent's = der Zeitschriftenladen,
der Zeitungskiosk: I work **at a newsagent's**.

---

comfortable [ˈkʌmftəbl]

bequem, gemütlich

Please wear **comfortable** clothes for your
yoga class.
comfortable ◀ ▶
uncomfortable (unbequem, ungemütlich)

▶ p. 156 **How much is …?** [haʊ ˈmʌtʃ]
How much are …?

Was (Wie viel) kostet …?
Was (Wie viel) kosten …?

Excuse me, please, **how much is** the football?
And **how much are** the books? –
The football **is** £3. The books **are** £2.

---

brand [brænd]

die (Produkt-)Marke

This shop doesn't sell expensive **brands**,
but their bikes are very good.
What **brand** is your new bike?

Could you …? [kʊd ˈju]

Könntest du …? / Könnten Sie …?

could = **1. konnte** – I looked everywhere,
but I **couldn't** find my keys.
2. könnte – **Could** you say that again,
please?

(to) try sth. **on** [traɪ ˈɒn]

etwas anprobieren *(Kleidung)*

Excuse me, where can I **try on** these trousers?

---

changing room
[ˈtʃeɪndʒɪŋ ruːm]

der Umkleideraum;
die Anprobe *(im Geschäft)*

(to) change = sich umziehen *(andere/frische
Kleidung anziehen)*
a change of clothes = (frische) Kleidung zum
Wechseln

---

change [tʃeɪndʒ]

das Wechselgeld

change *(noun)* =
1. die Veränderung, der Wechsel,
die Verwandlung; **2.** das Wechselgeld

Verbs and nouns with the same form

(to) **change**	(sich) (ver)ändern, verwandeln; wechseln; umsteigen; sich umziehen	**change**	die Veränderung, die Verwandlung, der Wechsel; das Wechselgeld
(to) **paint**	(an)malen; lackieren, (an)streichen	**paint**	die Farbe, der Lack
(to) **shop**	(ein)kaufen, „shoppen"	**shop**	das Geschäft, der Laden
(to) **treat** sb. **(to** sth.**)**	jn. (zu etwas) einladen	**treat**	der Hochgenuss, das besondere Vergnügen; die (besondere) Leckerei

receipt [rɪˈsiːt]	der (Kauf-)Beleg, die Quittung, der Kassenzettel	❗ False friends: **receipt** = **Beleg, Quittung, Kassenzettel** **recipe** = **(Koch-)Rezept**

▶ p. 157 **price** [praɪs]	der (Kauf-)Preis	❗ German "Preis" = **1. price** – £150 is a good **price** for this bike. *(der Kaufpreis)* **2. prize** – She's the winner of a special **prize** in the show for clever kids. *(der Gewinn)*
postcard [ˈpəʊstkɑːd]	die Postkarte	Do you write **postcards** to your friends when you're on holiday?
shorts *(pl)* [ʃɔːts]	die kurze Hose, die Shorts	

Pluralwörter
Einige englische Wörter sind immer **Plural** – sie haben keine Singularform.

braces	die Zahnspange, die Zahnklammer	❗ Zugehörige Begleiter *(these, those)*, Pronomen *(they, them)* und Verben stehen im Plural: Look at **those clothes**! I'd love to buy **them**, but **they are** so expensive. Be careful, **those stairs are** dangerous. **Vegetables are** good for me. I love **them**.
clothes	die Kleidung(sstücke)	
electronics	die Elektronik	
fireworks	das Feuerwerk	
lyrics	der Liedtext	
stairs	die Treppe; die Stufen	
vegetables	das Gemüse	
trousers / jeans / shorts	die Hose / die Jeans / die kurze Hose, die Shorts	❗ Mit **a pair of**, **two pairs of** usw. kannst du eine genaue Anzahl von Hosen, Brillen usw. nennen: I need **a new pair of trousers/jeans/shorts**. Why do you have **two pairs of glasses**?
glasses, sunglasses	die Brille, die Sonnenbrille	
headphones	der Kopfhörer	
customer [ˈkʌstəmə]	der Kunde, die Kundin	'Do you need any help?' the shop assistant asked the **customer**.

Story

▶ p. 158 **(to) go** [gəʊ]: he **has gone** [gɒn]	er ist gegangen/gefahren	Jonathan **has** already **gone** home. (… ist schon nach Hause gegangen.) ❗ **(to) be gone** = weg sein Where's the dog? He was here two minutes ago and now he **is gone**.
(to) miss [mɪs]	vermissen; verpassen; versäumen, auslassen	❗ **(to) miss** = **1.** vermissen – I enjoyed my trip to France, but I **missed** my friends. **2.** verpassen – I'm late! I'll **miss** the bus. **3.** versäumen, auslassen – I was so late that I **missed** the first lesson.
▶ p. 159 **(to) move (to)** [muːv]	(um)ziehen (nach)	They **moved to** York, to a nice flat in town.
such (a) [sʌtʃ]	so (ein/e), solch (ein/e)	**such a** thing/person = a thing/person **like this** / **like that**

such a + noun		so + adjective	
Olivia is **such a** nice **person**.	... so ein netter Mensch	Olivia is **so nice**.	... so nett
It was **such a** good **film** that I watched it again.	... so ein guter Film	The film was **so good** that I watched it again.	... so gut

(to) **follow** [ˈfɒləʊ]	(be)folgen; verfolgen	• Always **follow** the rules, please. (befolgen) • My dog **follows** me everywhere. (folgen, verfolgen)
(to) **annoy** sb. [əˈnɔɪ]	jn. ärgern	• It **annoys** me that the bus is always late. • I find it very **annoying** that ... (ärgerlich) • I'm really **annoyed about** the bus. (verärgert über)
independent (of/from) [ˌɪndɪˈpendənt]	unabhängig (von)	**independent (of/from)** ◄ ► **dependent (on)** (abhängig (von), angewiesen (auf))
bowl [bəʊl]	die Schüssel, die Schale	a salad **bowl**
business [ˈbɪznəs]	das Geschäft, der Betrieb	(to) **start a business** = ein Geschäft aufmachen, einen Betrieb gründen/eröffnen **business card** = die Visitenkarte, die Geschäftskarte
► p. 160 **connection** [kəˈnekʃn]	die Verbindung; der Anschluss	• noun: **connection** – Something is wrong with our internet **connection** this morning. The train **connections** to the city centre are good. • verb: (to) **connect** ((sich) verbinden (mit)) – Now **connect** the printer to the computer.
(to) **repeat** [rɪˈpiːt]	wiederholen	Can you **repeat** that, please? (= Can you say/do that again, please?)
strength [streŋθ]	die Stärke, die Kraft	One of my **strengths** is that I speak three languages. noun: **strength** – adj: **strong**
(to) **solve** [sɒlv]	lösen (Rätsel, Problem), lüften (Geheimnis)	verb: (to) **solve (a problem)** – noun: **solution (to a problem)** (die Lösung (eines Problems))

Study skills

► p. 162 (to) **look forward to** sth. [lʊk ˈfɔːwəd tu], (to) **look forward to doing** sth.	sich auf etwas freuen sich darauf freuen, etwas zu tun	**!** *German:* Wir **freuen uns darauf**, von Ihnen **zu hören**. *English:* We **look forward to hearing** from you.
luckily [ˈlʌkɪli]	glücklicherweise	We were a bit late, but **luckily** the train was late too.

Unit task

▶ p.163	**horoscope** [ˈhɒrəskəʊp]	das Horoskop	❗ Betonung auf der 1. Silbe: **hor**oscope
	star sign [ˈstɑː saɪn]	das Sternzeichen	❗ **star** = 1. der Stern; 2. der (Film-/Pop-)Star **sign** = das Zeichen; das Schild
	pronunciation [prənʌnsiˈeɪʃn]	die Aussprache	noun: **pronunciation** – verb: (to) **pronounce** (aussprechen)
	dictionary [ˈdɪkʃənri]	das Wörterbuch, das (alphabetische) Wörterverzeichnis	Can you look up these French words in the **dictionary**, please?
	imaginative [ɪˈmædʒɪnətɪv]	fantasievoll, einfallsreich, kreativ	adj: **imaginative** – verb: (to) **imagine sth.**
	curious (about) [ˈkjʊəriəs]	neugierig (auf)	My little sister is **curious about** everything. She always asks questions.
	tolerant (of) [ˈtɒlərənt]	tolerant (gegenüber)	**tolerant (of)** ◄ ► **intolerant (of)** ❗ Betonung: **tol**erant, in**tol**erant
	dramatic [drəˈmætɪk]	dramatisch	I saw a **dramatic** film about a woman who fought monsters from other planets.
	practical [ˈpræktɪkl]	praktisch	Work in my bakery for a few days and get some **practical** experience! (to) **play a practical joke on sb.** = jm. einen Streich spielen
	sociable [ˈsəʊʃəbl]	kontaktfreudig, gesellig	When you're **sociable**, you like being with people and meeting new people.
	generous [ˈdʒenərəs]	großzügig	Grandma gave me £150 for my birthday. That was really a **generous** present!

Irregular verbs

Infinitive	Simple past	Past participle		Infinitive	Simple past	Past participle	
(to) **babysit**	**babysat**	**babysat**	babysitten	(to) **keep**	**kept**	**kept**	halten; behalten; aufbewahren
(to) **build**	**built**	**built**	bauen	(to) **pay**	**paid**	**paid**	(be)zahlen
(to) **feel**	**felt**	**felt**	(sich) fühlen	(to) **say**	**said**	**said**	sagen
(to) **fight**	**fought**	**fought**	(be)kämpfen	(to) **sell**	**sold**	**sold**	verkaufen
(to) **go**	**went**	**gone**	gehen, fahren	(to) **spend**	**spent**	**spent**	(Zeit) verbringen; (Geld) ausgeben
(to) **have**	**had**	**had**	haben				
(to) **hit**	**hit**	**hit**	treffen, schlagen, stoßen	(to) **tell**	**told**	**told**	erzählen

🔊 °Unit 6: The treasure hunt!

> Die Unit 6 ist keine Pflicht-Unit, deshalb sind die neuen Wörter alle mit einem Kringel (°) markiert. Wenn du die Story liest, kannst du die neuen Wörter lernen, aber sie werden nicht in Band 3 vorausgesetzt.

▶ p.176	°**treasure hunt** [ˈtreʒə hʌnt]	die Schatzsuche	**treasure** = der Schatz • **hunt** = die Jagd
	°**nature reserve** [ˈneɪtʃə rɪzɜːv]	das Naturschutzgebiet	**nature** = die Natur **reserve** = das Schutzgebiet
	°**pretty** [ˈprɪti]	hübsch	a **pretty** picture/village/flower/garden/...
	°**(to) shout** [ʃaʊt]	rufen	"Look!" he **shouted**. "Someone is taking your bike!"

°**trail** [treɪl]	der Weg, die Route	There are lots of good **trails** for hiking in the hills behind our house.
▶ p. 177 °**(to) divide (up) (into)** [dɪˈvaɪd]	auf-/einteilen (in)	The teacher **divided** the class **into** groups of four.
°**(to) hide** [haɪd], **hid** [hɪd], **hidden** [ˈhɪdn]	verstecken; sich verstecken	I **hid** some money in an old book. Let's **hide** in the wardrobe.
°**clue** [kluː]	der (Lösungs-)Hinweis; der Anhaltspunkt	• Nobody knows who killed the man. The police are still looking for **clues** in his flat. • I don't have a **clue**. / I have no **clue**. (infml) = Ich habe keine Ahnung. / Keine Ahnung.
°**along the trail** [əlɒŋ ðə ˈtreɪl]	den Weg entlang	❗ German: Geh **die Straße entlang**. English: Walk **along** the street.
°**(to) hand** sth. **out (to** sb.**)** [hænd ˈaʊt]	(jm.) etwas aushändigen, etwas (an jn.) verteilen	I will now **hand out** pictures **to** all of you. Look at them and write a short text.
°**Good luck.** [lʌk]	Viel Glück!	If you're lucky, you'll win. So – **good luck**! noun: **luck** (das Glück (die glückliche Fügung)) adj: **lucky** (Glücks-, glücklich)
°**counting-out rhyme** [ˈkaʊntɪŋ aʊt raɪm]	der Abzählreim	
°**hers** [hɜːz]	ihrer, ihre, ihres (zu „she")	My bike was broken, so I asked my sister if I could use **hers**.
°**(to) chant** [tʃɑːnt]	singen (Sprechgesänge)	**Chanting** is not really singing a song – it's singing, saying or shouting the same words or phrases many times.
°**duck** [dʌk]	die Ente	**ducks**
°**(to) decide (to do** sth.**)** [dɪˈsaɪd]	sich entscheiden, beschließen (etwas zu tun)	There are so many nice things on the menu, I just can't **decide**! I felt ill, so I **decided** not **to** go to the party.
°**without** [wɪˈðaʊt]	ohne	**Without** clouds, there can't be rain. with ◀ ▶ without
▶ p. 178 °**(to) point (at/to)** [pɔɪnt]	zeigen, deuten (auf)	Look at this map of Ireland. Can you **point to** Dublin?
°**pond** [pɒnd]	der Teich	We have a little **pond** in our garden with some fish in it.
°**(to) lead** [liːd], **led, led** [led]	führen, leiten	verb: (to) **lead, led, led** – noun: (person) **leader**
°**bush** [bʊʃ]	der Busch	**bushes** ❗ Das **u** in b**u**sh klingt wie das **u** in p**u**t.

°**bell** [bel]	die Glocke; die Klingel	bells
°**grass** [grɑːs]	das Gras; der Rasen	grass
°(to) **look up** [lʊk ˈʌp]	nach oben schauen	**!** (to) **look up** = nach oben schauen (to) **look sth. up** = etwas nachschlagen
▶ p. 179 °**dandelion** [ˈdændɪlaɪən]	der Löwenzahn	
°**bench** [bentʃ]	die Bank (*zum Sitzen*)	**!** bench bank
°(to) **catch** [kætʃ], **caught** [kɔːt], **caught** [kɔːt]	(ein)fangen; erwischen; nehmen (*z. B. einen Zug, einen Bus*)	• Our cat sometimes **catches** mice. (fangen) • I want to **catch** the train at 2:55. (nehmen)
▶ p. 180 °**factory** [ˈfæktri]	die Fabrik	a **factory**
▶ p. 181 °**Congratulations (on …)!** [kəngrætʃəˈleɪʃnz]	Herzlichen Glückwunsch (zu …)!	**Congratulations on** your good maths test!
°**result** [rɪˈzʌlt]	das Ergebnis	He was too lazy at school. And the **result**? Bad marks!
°(to) **clap (your hands)** [klæp]	(in die Hände) klatschen	It was a great concert. At the end everyone **clapped**.
°**We did it!** [dɪd]	Wir haben es geschafft!	Congratulations! **You did it!** You won!
°**teammate** [ˈtiːmmeɪt]	der Mannschaftskamerad, die Mannschaftskameradin	Are you and Dave **teammates**? = Is Dave in the same team as you?
°(to) **cheat** [tʃiːt]	betrügen, mogeln, schummeln (*z. B. beim Spiel*)	My friend is clever and honest – she would never **cheat** in tests!

Im *English-German Dictionary* kannst du nachschlagen, was ein Wort bedeutet oder wie es ausgesprochen wird.

Es werden folgende **Abkürzungen und Symbole** verwendet:

infml = informal (umgangssprachlich)   *pl = plural* (Mehrzahl)
sb. = somebody (jemand)   *sth. = something* (etwas)
jd. = jemand   jm. = jemandem   jn. = jemanden

°Mit diesem Kringel sind Wörter markiert, die nicht zum Lernwortschatz gehören.

Die **Fundstellenangaben** zeigen, wo ein Wort zum ersten Mal vorkommt.   1 = Lighthouse Advanced 1
Die Ziffern in Klammern bezeichnen Seitenzahlen.   2: 1 (26) = Lighthouse Advanced 2, Unit 1, Seite 26

A

a [ə] ein, eine 1 **once a month** einmal pro Monat 2: 1 (26)
about [əˈbaʊt]**: about me/you/...** über mich/dich/... 1 **How about ...?** Wie wäre es mit ...? 2: 5 (157) **What about a ...?** Wie wäre es mit einer/einem ...? 1 **What about you?** Und du? / Was ist mit dir? 1
above [əˈbʌv] über, oberhalb (von); oben 2: 3 (89)
accident [ˈæksɪdənt]:
1. der Unfall 2: 2 (55)
2. der Zufall 2: 2 (55)
by accident zufällig 2: 2 (55)
account [əˈkaʊnt] das (Bank-)Konto; der Account 2: 5 (154)
acoustic [əˈkuːstɪk] akustisch 2: 3 (84)
across [əˈkrɒs] über *(quer über)* 2: 3 (88)
act [ækt]:
1. die Tat, die Handlung 2: 3 (80)
2. handeln, sich verhalten 2: 3 (80)
3. Theater spielen, schauspielern 2: 3 (80)
4. aufführen, spielen 1
act sth. out etwas vorspielen, aufführen 1
acting [ˈæktɪŋ] die Schauspielerei 1
action [ˈækʃn] die Action *(z. B. Film)*; die Aktion, die Handlung 2: 3 (80)
active [ˈæktɪv] aktiv 1
activism [ˈæktɪvɪzəm] der Aktivismus 2: 2 (54)
activist [ˈæktɪvɪst] der Aktivist, die Aktivistin 2: 2 (54)
activity [ækˈtɪvəti] die Aktivität, die Tätigkeit 1
actor [ˈæktə] der Schauspieler, Schauspielerin 2: 3 (78/79)
add [æd] hinzufügen, addieren 1
address [əˈdres] die Adresse 1
adventure [ədˈventʃə] das Abenteuer 2: 1 (26)
after [ˈɑːftə]:
1. **after (school)** nach (der Schule) 1
2. **after (you read)** nachdem (du liest) 1
afternoon [ɑːftəˈnuːn] der Nachmittag 1 **in the afternoon** nachmittags, am Nachmittag 1

afternoon tea [ɑːftənuːn ˈtiː] der Nachmittagstee, der Fünfuhrtee 1
afterwards [ˈɑːftəwədz] nachher, danach 2: 4 (125)
again [əˈgen] wieder, noch einmal 1
against [əˈgenst] gegen 2: 2 (59)
agent [ˈeɪdʒənt] der Agent, die Agentin 2: 3 (86)
ago [əˈgəʊ]: **a long time ago** vor langer Zeit 2: 1 (16)
agree [əˈgriː]: **agree (with sb./sth.)** jm. zustimmen; mit etwas einverstanden sein 2: 1 (28) **agree on** sich einigen auf 2: 1 (28)
airport [ˈeəpɔːt] der Flughafen 2: 1 (15)
alarm [əˈlɑːm] der Wecker; der Alarm; die Alarmanlage 2: 4 (126)
alien [ˈeɪliən]:
1. außerirdisch 2: 3 (87)
2. der/die Außerirdische 2: 3 (87)
all [ɔːl] alle(s) 1 **all over the world** überall auf der Welt, auf der ganzen Welt 2: 3 (91) **all the family** die ganze Familie 1 **all the time** die ganze Zeit, ständig 1 **all weekend** das ganze Wochenende 1 **not ... at all** überhaupt nicht(s), gar nicht(s); überhaupt kein/e, gar kein/e 2: 1 (20)
Allah [ˈælə] Allah 2: 4 (114)
allergic (to) [əˈlɜːdʒɪk] allergisch (gegen) 1
alone [əˈləʊn] allein 1
°**along the trail** [əˈlɒŋ] den Weg entlang
alphabet [ˈælfəbet] das Alphabet 1
already [ɔːlˈredi] schon 1
also [ˈɔːlsəʊ] auch 1
alternative [ɔːlˈtɜːnətɪv]:
1. die Alternative 2: 1 (30)
2. alternativ 2: 1 (30)
always [ˈɔːlweɪz] immer 1
am [æm]: **I'm (= I am)** ich bin 1
a.m. [eɪˈem]: **4 a.m.** 4 Uhr (früh)morgens 1 **9 a.m.** 9 Uhr vormittags 1
amazing [əˈmeɪzɪŋ] erstaunlich; großartig 1
ambulance [ˈæmbjələns] der Krankenwagen 2: 2 (60)
an [ən] ein/e *(vor Vokalen)* 1
and [ænd], [ənd] und 1
angry [ˈæŋgri] wütend 1 **angry at sb.** wütend auf jn. 2: 1 (16)
animal [ˈænɪml] das Tier 1

animal charity [ˈænɪml tʃærəti] die wohltätige Organisation, die Tiere unterstützt 2: 4 (114)
ankle [ˈæŋkl] der Knöchel, das Fußgelenk 2: 2 (61)
announce [əˈnaʊns] verkünden, bekanntgeben; durchsagen 2: 1 (26)
announcement [əˈnaʊnsmənt]:
1. die Durchsage, die Ansage 2: 1 (26)
2. die Bekanntgabe, die Ankündigung 2: 1 (26)
annoy sb. [əˈnɔɪ] jn. ärgern 2: 5 (159)
annoyed (about) [əˈnɔɪd] verärgert (über) 2: 5 (159)
annoying [əˈnɔɪɪŋ] ärgerlich 2: 5 (159)
another [əˈnʌðə] ein/e andere/r/s; noch ein/e 1
answer [ˈɑːnsə]:
1. die Antwort 1
2. (be)antworten 1
any [ˈeni] jegliche/r/s, jede/r/s beliebige 2: 2 (57) **(at) any time** zu jeder Zeit, jederzeit 2: 2 (57) **Do you have any questions?** Habt ihr / Hast du (irgendwelche) Fragen? 1 **not (...) any more** nicht mehr 2: 3 (94) **there aren't any ...** es gibt keine ... 1
anybody [ˈenibɒdi] irgendjemand; jede/r (beliebige) 2: 4 (123) **Can you see anybody?** Kannst du (irgend)jemanden sehen? 2: 4 (123) **not ... anybody** niemand 2: 4 (123)
anyone [ˈeniwʌn] irgendjemand; jede/r (beliebige) 2: 4 (123) **Can you see anyone?** Kannst du (irgend)jemanden sehen? 2: 4 (123) **not ... anyone** niemand 2: 4 (123)
anything [ˈeniθɪŋ] (irgend)etwas; alles; egal, was 2: 4 (123) **Can you see anything?** Kannst du (irgend)etwas sehen? 2: 4 (123) **not ... anything** nichts 2: 1 (20)
anywhere [ˈeniweə] irgendwo(hin); überall 2: 4 (123)
apartment [əˈpɑːtmənt] die Wohnung 2: 1 (12/13)
app [æp] die App 1
apple [ˈæpl] der Apfel 1
April [ˈeɪprəl] der April 1
°**Aquarius** [əˈkweəriəs] der Wassermann *(Sternzeichen)*
architect [ˈɑːkɪtekt] der Architekt, die Architektin 2: 5 (146)

are [ɑː]: **The books are £2.** Die Bücher kosten 2 Pfund. 2: 5 (156) **we/they are** wir/sie sind 1 **you are** du bist / ihr seid 1

area [ˈeəriə] die Gegend, der Bereich 2: 1 (20)

°**Aries** [ˈeəriːz] der Widder *(Sternzeichen)*

arm [ɑːm] der Arm 2: 1 (16)

around … [əˈraʊnd] um (… herum), in … umher 2: 1 (28) **(all) around the globe** auf der ganzen Welt 2: 4 (128) **(all) around the world** überall auf der Welt, auf der ganzen Welt 2: 3 (91)

arrival [əˈraɪvl] die Ankunft 2: 1 (18)

arrive [əˈraɪv] ankommen 2: 1 (18)

art [ɑːt] die Kunst 1

article [ˈɑːtɪkl] der Artikel 1

artist [ˈɑːtɪst] der Künstler, die Künstlerin 2: 2 (54)

artistic [ɑːˈtɪstɪk] kunstvoll, künstlerisch 2: 2 (54)

as [æz], [əz]:
1. als, während *(Konjunktion)* 2: 4 (127)
2. als *(Präposition)* 1 **as the winner** als Gewinner/in 1
3. wie *(Präposition)* 2: 3 (85) **(not) as good as** (nicht) so gut wie 2: 3 (85)

as if [əz ˈɪf] als ob, als wenn 2: 1 (21)

ask [ɑːsk]:
1. fragen 1 **ask a question** eine Frage stellen 1
2. **ask sb. for sth.** jn. um etwas bitten 1
ask sb. to do sth. jn. bitten, etwas zu tun 1

asleep [əˈsliːp]: **be asleep** schlafen 1 **fall asleep** einschlafen 2: 2 (61)

assembly [əˈsembli] die Schulversammlung 1

assistant [əˈsɪstənt] der Assistent, die Assistentin 2: 5 (153) *(shop assistant)* der Verkäufer, die Verkäuferin 2: 5 (153)

at [æt], [ət] an; in; bei; auf 1 **at 8 o'clock** um 8 Uhr 1 **at a place** an einem Ort 2: 3 (80) **at least** wenigstens, zumindest 2: 2 (65) **at night** nachts, in der Nacht 1 **at the cinema** im Kino 1 **at work** bei der Arbeit, am Arbeitsplatz 1 **be good at sth. / at doing sth.** etwas gut können; gut in etwas sein 1 **Open your books at page 10.** Schlagt eure Bücher auf Seite 10 auf. 1

ate [eɪt], [et] *siehe* eat

attention [əˈtenʃn] die Aufmerksamkeit 2: 3 (97) **get sb.'s attention** js. Aufmerksamkeit erregen, gewinnen 2: 3 (97) **keep sb.'s attention** js. Aufmerksamkeit aufrecht erhalten 2: 3 (97) **pay attention (to)** aufpassen (auf), aufmerksam sein; Beachtung schenken, zuhören 2: 3 (97)

audience [ˈɔːdiəns] das Publikum; die Zuschauer/-innen, die Zuhörer/-innen 1

audio [ˈɔːdiəʊ] Audio-, Ton- 2: 4 (131)

August [ˈɔːgəst] der August 1

aunt [ɑːnt] die Tante 1

autumn [ˈɔːtəm] der Herbst 1

awake [əˈweɪk] wach 2: 4 (126)

award [əˈwɔːd] der Preis *(die Auszeichnung)* 2: 2 (59)

award-winner [əˈwɔːd wɪnə] der Preisträger, die Preisträgerin 2: 2 (59)

award-winning [əˈwɔːd wɪnɪŋ] preisgekrönt 2: 2 (59)

away [əˈweɪ] weg, fort 1

awesome [ˈɔːsəm] *(infml)* klasse, stark, großartig 2: 1 (28)

axes [ˈæksiːz] *Plural von* axis

axis [ˈæksɪs], *pl* **axes** die Achse 2: 5 (151)

B

baby [ˈbeɪbi] das Baby 2: 5 (150)

babysat [ˈbeɪbisæt] *siehe* babysit

babysit [ˈbeɪbisɪt], **babysat, babysat** babysitten 2: 5 (150)

babysitter [ˈbeɪbisɪtə] der Babysitter, die Babysitterin 2: 5 (150)

babysitting [ˈbeɪbisɪtɪŋ] das Babysitten 2: 5 (150)

back [bæk]:
1. zurück 1 **back at home** wieder zu Hause 1
2. der Rücken; die Rückseite, der hintere Teil 2: 2 (61) **at the back (of your book)** hinten (in deinem Buch) 2: 2 (61) **on the back of the card** auf der Rückseite der Karte 2: 2 (61)

°**background** [ˈbækgraʊnd] der Hintergrund

°**background file** [ˈbækgraʊnd faɪl] die Hintergrundinformation(en)

bad [bæd] schlecht; schlimm 1

badminton [ˈbædmɪntən] das Badminton, der Federball *(Spiel)* 1

bag [bæg] die Tasche 1

bake [beɪk] backen 1

baked beans *(pl)* [beɪkt ˈbiːnz] die weißen Bohnen in Tomatensoße 2: 4 (115)

baker [ˈbeɪkə] der Bäcker, die Bäckerin 2: 5 (148)

bakery [ˈbeɪkəri] die Bäckerei 2: 5 (155)

baking powder [ˈbeɪkɪŋ paʊdə] das Backpulver 1

balcony [ˈbælkəni] der Balkon 1

ball [bɔːl] der Ball 1

balloon [bəˈluːn] der Ballon 1

banana [bəˈnɑːnə] die Banane 1

band [bænd] die Band, die Musikgruppe 1

°**bandstand** [ˈbændstænd] der Musikpavillon

bank [bæŋk] die Bank *(Geldinstitut)* 1

bar [bɑː] die Säule, die Stange *(z. B. Eisen-)* 2: 5 (151)

bar chart [ˈbɑː tʃɑːt] das Säulendiagramm 2: 5 (151)

barbecue [ˈbɑːbɪkjuː] das Grillfest, das Grillen 1

bark [bɑːk]:
1. das Bellen 1
2. **bark (at sb.)** (jn. an)bellen 1

basketball [ˈbɑːskɪtbɔːl] der Basketball 1

bat [bæt] der Schläger *(Sport)* 1

bath [bɑːθ] das (Wannen-)Bad; die Badewanne 2: 4 (115)

bathroom [ˈbɑːθruːm] das Bad(ezimmer) 1

°**Bavaria** [bəˈveəriə] Bayern

be [biː], **was/were, been** sein 1 **I want to be a nurse.** Ich möchte Krankenschwester/Krankenpfleger werden. 2: 5 (146)

beach [biːtʃ] der Strand 1 **on the beach** am Strand 1 **to the beach** zum Strand, an den Strand 1

bean [biːn] die Bohne 2: 4 (115) **baked beans** *(pl)* die weißen Bohnen in Tomatensoße 2: 4 (115)

beast [biːst] das Tier; die Bestie; das Biest 2: 3 (78/79)

beautiful [ˈbjuːtɪfl] wunderschön 1

beauty [ˈbjuːti] die Schönheit 2: 3 (78/79)

became [bɪˈkeɪm] *siehe* become

because [bɪˈkɒz] weil 1

become [bɪˈkʌm], **became, become** werden 2: 2 (56)

bed [bed] das Bett 1 **go to bed** ins Bett gehen 1

bedroom [ˈbedruːm] das Schlafzimmer 1

beef [biːf] das Rindfleisch 2: 4 (116)

been [biːn] *siehe* be

before [bɪˈfɔː]:
1. before (the lesson) vor (der Unterrichtsstunde) 1
2. before (you take a photo) bevor (du ein Foto machst) 1

began [bɪˈgæn] *siehe* begin

begin [bɪˈgɪn], **began, begun** anfangen, beginnen 2: 1 (30)

beginning [bɪˈgɪnɪŋ] der Anfang 2: 1 (30)

behind [bɪˈhaɪnd]:
1. hinter 1
2. dahinter 2: 2 (50)

belief [bɪˈliːf] der Glaube, die Überzeugung 2: 4 (127)

believe (in) [bɪˈliːv] glauben (an) 2: 4 (127)

°**bell** [bel] die Glocke; die Klingel

below [bɪˈləʊ] unter(halb von); unten 2: 3 (89)

°**bench** [bentʃ] die Bank *(zum Sitzen)*

best [best] beste(r, s); am besten 1 **Best wishes** Viele Grüße *(Briefschluss)* 2: 4 (115) **like sth. best** etwas lieber / am liebsten mögen 1

better [ˈbetə] besser 1 **for better or (for) worse** was auch immer geschieht, in guten wie in schlechten Zeiten *(beim Ehegelöbnis)* 2: 4 (127) **Get better soon!** Gute Besserung! 2: 3 (92) **like sth. better** etwas lieber mögen 1

between [bɪˈtwiːn] zwischen 1

big [bɪɡ]:
1. groß 1
2. schwer, dick *(Person)* 2: 2 (48)

biggest [ˈbɪɡɪst] der/die/das größte; am größten 1

bike [baɪk] das Fahrrad 1

bin [bɪn] der (Müll-)Eimer 1

biology [baɪˈɒlədʒi] die Biologie 1

bird [bɜːd] der Vogel 2: 3 (89)

birthday [ˈbɜːθdeɪ] der Geburtstag 1 **Happy birthday!** Herzlichen Glückwunsch zum Geburtstag! 1 **My birthday is in April.** Ich habe im April Geburtstag. 1 **on my birthday** an meinem Geburtstag 1 **When's your birthday?** Wann hast du Geburtstag? 1

biscuit [ˈbɪskɪt] der Keks, das Plätzchen 2: 4 (115)

bisexual [baɪˈsekʃuəl]:
1. bisexuell 2: 1 (18)
2. der/die Bisexuelle 2: 1 (18)

bit [ə ˈbɪt]: **a bit** ein bisschen, ein wenig 2: 1 (12/13)

black [blæk] schwarz 1

blanket [ˈblæŋkɪt] die Decke *(zum Zudecken u. Ä.)* 2: 2 (61)

blazer [ˈbleɪzə] der Blazer *(Jackett, oft Teil der Schuluniform)* 1

blew [bluː] *siehe* **blow**

blind [blaɪnd] blind 2: 1 (17)

block [blɒk] der (Wohn-)Block 1

block of flats [blɒk əv ˈflæts] das Mehrfamilienhaus 1

blonde [blɒnd] blond 2: 2 (46/47)

blow [bləʊ], **blew, blown** pusten, blasen; wehen 2: 4 (119) **blow sth. up** etwas aufblasen *(z. B. Ballon)* 2: 4 (119)

blown [bləʊn] *siehe* **blow**

blue [bluː] blau 1

board [bɔːd] die Tafel 1

body [ˈbɒdi] der Körper 2: 2 (57)

boil [bɔɪl] kochen *(in Wasser)*; sieden 1

bonfire [ˈbɒnfaɪə] das *(große Freuden-)* Feuer 2: 4 (112/113)

Bonfire Night [ˈbɒnfaɪə naɪt] der Abend des 5. November *(GB)* 2: 4 (112/113)

book [bʊk]:
1. das Buch 1
2. buchen; reservieren 2: 3 (78/79)

booking [ˈbʊkɪŋ] die Buchung, die Reservierung 2: 3 (78/79)

bookshop [ˈbʊkʃɒp] der Buchladen 2: 5 (155)

boot [buːt] der Boot, der Stiefel 2: 2 (57)

bored [bɔːd] gelangweilt 2: 3 (92) **be bored / get bored** sich langweilen 2: 3 (92) **I'm bored** mir ist langweilig 2: 3 (92)

boring [ˈbɔːrɪŋ] langweilig 1

born [bɔːn]: **he was born** er wurde geboren 2: 2 (56)

borrow [ˈbɒrəʊ] (aus)leihen, sich borgen 2: 1 (23) **borrowed** (aus)geliehen, geborgt 2: 4 (125)

boss [bɒs] der Boss, der Chef, die Chefin 2: 5 (148)

both [bəʊθ] beide 2: 4 (120) **both ... and ...** sowohl ... als auch ... 2: 4 (120)

bottle [ˈbɒtl] die Flasche 2: 1 (23) **°message in a bottle** die Flaschenpost

bottom [ˈbɒtəm] das untere Ende 2: 3 (89)

bought [bɔːt] *siehe* **buy**

bowl [bəʊl] die Schüssel, die Schale 2: 5 (159)

bowling [ˈbəʊlɪŋ] das Bowling, das Kegeln 1

box [bɒks] die Box, der Kasten 2: 4 (115)

box [bɒks] boxen 1

boxing [ˈbɒksɪŋ] das Boxen 1

boy [bɔɪ] der Junge 1

boyfriend [ˈbɔɪfrend] der (feste) Freund 2: 1 (20)

braces *(pl)* [ˈbreɪsɪz] die Zahnspange, die Zahnklammer 2: 4 (46/47)

°brainstorm [ˈbreɪnstɔːm] Ideen (ungeordnet) sammeln

brand [brænd] die (Produkt-)Marke 2: 5 (156)

brave [breɪv] mutig 1

bravery [ˈbreɪvəri] der Mut, die Tapferkeit 2: 2 (64)

bread [bred] das Brot 1

break [breɪk] die Pause 1 **at break** in der Pause 1

break [breɪk], **broke, broken: break sth.** etwas zerbrechen 1 **break the fast** das Fasten brechen 2: 4 (112/113)

breakfast [ˈbrekfəst] das Frühstück 1

breathe (in/out) [briːð] (ein-/aus-) atmen 2: 2 (61)

bride [braɪd] die Braut 2: 4 (125)

bridegroom [ˈbraɪdgruːm] der Bräutigam 2: 4 (125)

bridesmaid [ˈbraɪdzmeɪd] die Brautjungfer 2: 4 (125)

bridge [brɪdʒ] die Brücke 2: 3 (88)

bring [brɪŋ], **brought, brought** bringen, mitbringen 1

Britain [ˈbrɪtn] Großbritannien 1

British [ˈbrɪtɪʃ] britisch 1

broke [brəʊk] *siehe* **break**

broken [ˈbrəʊkən] *siehe* **break** **be broken** kaputt, sein; zerbrochen sein 2: 2 (62)

brother [ˈbrʌðə] der Bruder 1

brown [braʊn] braun 1

browser [ˈbraʊzə] der Browser *(Computerprogramm zum Finden und Lesen von Websites)* 1

brunch [brʌntʃ] das Brunch 2: 3 (93)

brush [brʌʃ]:
1. die Bürste 1
2. bürsten 1
brush your teeth (sich) die Zähne putzen 1

build [bɪld], **built, built** bauen 2: 5 (144)

builder [ˈbɪldə] der Bauarbeiter, die Bauarbeiterin; der Bauunternehmer, die Bauunternehmerin 2: 5 (144)

building [ˈbɪldɪŋ] das Gebäude 1

built [bɪlt] *siehe* **build**

bully [ˈbʊli]:
1. der Mobber, die Mobberin / der Tyrann, die Tyrannin 1
2. tyrannisieren, mobben 1

burger [ˈbɜːɡə] der Hamburger *(Frikadelle)* 1

bus [bʌs] der Bus 1 **by bus** mit dem Bus 1 **on the bus** im Bus 1

bus stop [ˈbʌs stɒp] die Bushaltestelle 1

°bush [bʊʃ] der Busch

business [ˈbɪznəs] das Geschäft, der Betrieb 2: 5 (159) **start a business** ein Geschäft aufmachen, einen Betrieb gründen/eröffnen 2: 5 (159)

business card [ˈbɪznəs kɑːd] die Visitenkarte, die Geschäftskarte 2: 5 (159)

°business owner [ˈbɪznəs əʊnə] der Geschäftsinhaber, die Geschäftsinhaberin

busy [ˈbɪzi]:
1. hektisch, belebt 1
2. (viel)beschäftigt 1
be busy (viel)beschäftigt sein, (viel) zu tun haben 1

but [bʌt], [bət] aber 1

butter [ˈbʌtə] die Butter 1

°button [ˈbʌtn] der Button; die Schaltfläche; der Knopf

buy [baɪ], **bought, bought** kaufen 1

°buyer [ˈbaɪə] der (Ein-)Käufer, die (Ein-)Käuferin

by [baɪ]: **by bus** mit dem Bus 1 **by phone** per Telefon / telefonisch 1 **by the river** am Fluss 2: 1 (15) **by the sea** am Meer, an der See 1 **pay by card** mit Karte (be)zahlen *(z. B. Bankkarte)* 2: 5 (154)

Bye. [baɪ] Tschüs. / Auf Wiedersehen. 1

C

cafe [ˈkæfeɪ] das Café 1

cake [keɪk] der Kuchen, die Torte 1

calendar [ˈkælɪndə] der Kalender 2: 3 (93)

call [kɔːl]:
1. nennen; rufen; anrufen 1
called ... mit Namen ..., der/die ... heißt 1 **be called** heißen 1
2. der Ruf 1
3. *(kurz für: phone call)* der (Telefon-) Anruf 1

calm [kɑːm] ruhig, besonnen 2: 1 (27)

came [keɪm] *siehe* **come**

camera [ˈkæmərə] die Kamera 2: 3 (81)

campsite [ˈkæmpsaɪt] der Campingplatz 2: 1 (12/13)

can [kæn], [kən] können 1

°Cancer [ˈkænsə] der Krebs *(Sternzeichen)*

candle [ˈkændl] die Kerze 2: 4 (112/113)

can't [kɑːnt]: **I can't (= cannot) see ....** Ich kann ... nicht sehen. 1

canteen [kænˈtiːn] die Kantine, die (Schul-)Mensa 1

cap [kæp] die (Schirm-)Mütze, die Kappe 1

cape [keɪp] das Cape (Umhang) 2: 2 (56)

capital [ˈkæpɪtl]:
1. capital (city) die Hauptstadt 2: 1 (12/13)
2. capital (letter) der Großbuchstabe 2: 1 (12/13)

°Capricorn [ˈkæprɪkɔːn] der Steinbock (Sternzeichen)

°caption [ˈkæpʃn] die Bildunterschrift

car [kɑː] das Auto 1

car light [ˈkɑː laɪt] der Autoscheinwerfer 1

card [kɑːd]:
1. die Karte 1
playing card die Spielkarte 1
2. die (Bank-/Kredit-)Karte 2: 5 (154)
pay by card mit Karte (be)zahlen (z. B. Bankkarte) 2: 5 (154)

careful [ˈkeəfl] vorsichtig 1

carnival [ˈkɑːnɪvl] der Karneval 2: 4 (112/113)

carrot [ˈkærət] die Möhre, die Karotte 1

carton [ˈkɑːtn] der (Papp-)Karton; die Packung 2: 4 (115)

cartoon [kɑːˈtuːn] der Zeichentrickfilm; der/das Comic; der Cartoon 2: 3 (86)

case [keɪs] das Etui, der Behälter, der Kasten 1

cash [kæʃ] das Cash, das Bargeld 2: 5 (154) pay (in) cash bar bezahlen 2: 5 (154)

cash machine [ˈkæʃ məʃiːn] der Geldautomat 2: 5 (154)

castle [ˈkɑːsl] die Burg 2: 3 (80)

cat [kæt] die Katze 1 rain cats and dogs stark regnen 1

°catch [kætʃ], caught, caught (ein)fangen; erwischen; nehmen (z. B. Zug, Bus)

°caught [kɔːt] siehe catch

°'cause [kɔːz] (infml) weil (= because)

celebrate [ˈselɪbreɪt] feiern 2: 4 (112/113)

celebration [selɪˈbreɪʃn] die Feier, das Fest 2: 4 (112/113)

cent [sent] der Cent 1

centre [ˈsentə] das Zentrum; die Mitte 1

ceremony [ˈserəməni] die Feier, die Zeremonie 2: 4 (131)

chain [tʃeɪn] die Kette 1

chair [tʃeə] der Stuhl 1

challenge [ˈtʃælɪndʒ]:
1. die Herausforderung 2: 3 (78/79) take on a challenge eine Herausforderung annehmen, sich einer Herausforderung stellen 2: 3 (78/79)
2. challenge sb. (to sth.) jn. (zu etwas) herausfordern 2: 3 (78/79)

challenging [ˈtʃælɪndʒɪŋ] anspruchsvoll, (heraus)fordernd 2: 3 (78/79)

change [tʃeɪndʒ]:
1. sich umziehen (die Kleidung wechseln) 2: 1 (26) change (into) (sich) (ver)ändern (zu/in); wechseln; (sich) verwandeln (in), werden (zu) 2: 1 (26) change (trains) umsteigen 2: 1 (26)
2. die Veränderung, der Wechsel, die Verwandlung 1
change of clothes die (frische) Kleidung zum Wechseln 2: 5 (156)
3. das Wechselgeld 2: 5 (156)

changing room [ˈtʃeɪndʒɪŋ ruːm] der Umkleideraum; die Anprobe (im Geschäft) 2: 5 (156)

°chant [tʃɑːnt] singen (Sprechgesänge)

character [ˈkærəktə] der Charakter; die Figur (aus einer Geschichte) 1

charity [ˈtʃærəti] die wohltätige Organisation 2: 4 (114) animal charity die wohltätige Organisation, die Tiere unterstützt 2: 4 (114)

charity shop [ˈtʃærəti ʃɒp] das Geschäft, das gespendete Waren für wohltätige Zwecke verkauft 2: 4 (114)

chart [tʃɑːt] das Diagramm; die Tabelle 2: 5 (151) pie chart das Tortendiagramm 2: 5 (151)

chat [tʃæt]:
1. chat (with) chatten (mit); sich unterhalten (mit) 2: 3 (92)
2. die Unterhaltung; der Chat 2: 3 (92)
have a chat eine Unterhaltung führen, sich unterhalten 2: 3 (92)

chatty [ˈtʃæti] gesprächig 2: 3 (92)

cheap [tʃiːp] billig, preiswert 2: 1 (19)

°cheat [tʃiːt] betrügen, mogeln, schummeln (z. B. beim Spiel)

check [tʃek]:
1. die (Über-)Prüfung, die Kontrolle 1
2. (über)prüfen, kontrollieren 1
check sb./sth. out (infml) sich jn./ etwas anschauen, anhören; etwas ausprobieren 2: 2 (61)

checklist [ˈtʃeklɪst] die Checkliste 2: 5 (162)

°checkpoint [ˈtʃekpɔɪnt] der Kontrollpunkt

cheese [tʃiːz] der Käse 1

cheesy [ˈtʃiːzi] kitschig 2: 4 (122)

chemical [ˈkemɪkl]:
1. Chemikalie 2: 2 (57)
2. chemisch 2: 2 (57)

chicken [ˈtʃɪkɪn] das Huhn; das (Brat-)Hähnchen 1

child [tʃaɪld], pl children das Kind 2: 1 (20)

children [ˈtʃɪldrən] Plural von child

China [ˈtʃaɪnə] China 1

Chinese [tʃaɪˈniːz]:
1. chinesisch; Chinesisch 1
2. the Chinese die Chinesen 1

chips (pl) [tʃɪps] die Pommes frites 1 fish and chips der Fisch mit Pommes Frites 1

chocolate [ˈtʃɒklət]:
1. die Praline 2: 4 (115)
2. die Schokolade 1
hot chocolate der Kakao, die heiße (Trink-)Schokolade 1

choose [tʃuːz], chose, chosen (aus)wählen 1

chore [tʃɔː] die (Haus-)Arbeit, die (lästige) Pflicht 2: 5 (150) do chores (Haus-)Arbeiten erledigen 2: 5 (150)

christening [ˈkrɪsnɪŋ] die Taufe 2: 4 (124)

Christmas [ˈkrɪsməs] (das) Weihnachten 1

Christmas Day [krɪsməs ˈdeɪ] der 1. Weihnachtstag (25. 12.) 1

°churros (pl) [ˈtʃuːrəʊz] die Churros (längliches Gebäck aus Spanien/ Portugal)

cinema [ˈsɪnəmə] das Kino 1 at the cinema im Kino 1

circle [ˈsɜːkl] der Kreis 1

circus [ˈsɜːkəs] der Zirkus 1

citizen [ˈsɪtɪzn] der (Staats-)Bürger, die (Staats-)Bürgerin 2: 4 (128)

city [ˈsɪti] die City, die (Groß-)Stadt 1

°clap (your hands) [klæp] (in die Hände) klatschen

class [klɑːs] die Klasse; der Unterricht; der Kurs 1 in class im Unterricht 1

class teacher [ˈklɑːs tiːtʃə] der Klassenlehrer, die Klassenlehrerin 1

classical [ˈklæsɪkl] klassisch 2: 3 (84)

classical music [klæsɪkl ˈmjuːzɪk] klassische Musik 2: 3 (84)

°classmate [ˈklɑːsmeɪt] der Mitschüler, die Mitschülerin

classroom [ˈklɑːsruːm] das Klassenzimmer 1

clean [kliːn]:
1. sauber 1
2. sauber machen, putzen 1
clean sth. up etwas aufräumen, sauber machen 1

clean-up [ˈkliːn ʌp] das Säubern, das Saubermachen 1

clean-up day [ˈkliːn ʌp deɪ] der Dreck-weg-Tag (Aktionstag zum Müllsammeln) 1

cleaner [ˈkliːnə] die Reinigungskraft 1

clear [klɪə] klar, deutlich 1

clearly [ˈklɪəli]: speak clearly deutlich sprechen 1

clever [ˈklevə] schlau, klug 1

click [klɪk]:
1. der Klick, das Klicken 2: 3 (92)
2. click (on) klicken (auf), anklicken 2: 3 (92)

climb [klaɪm]:
1. der Aufstieg, die Klettertour; der Anstieg 2: 2 (57)
2. klettern (auf) 2: 2 (57)

climber [ˈklaɪmə] der Kletterer, die Kletterin 2: 2 (57)

clock [klɒk] die (Wand-, Stand-, Turm-)Uhr 1

close [kləʊz] schließen, zumachen 1

closed [kləʊzd] geschlossen 1

clothes (pl) [kləʊðz] die Kleidung, die Kleidungsstücke 1

clothes swap [ˈkləʊðz swɒp] der Kleidertausch, die Kleidertauschparty 1

clotted cream [klɒtɪd ˈkriːm] die besonders dicke Sahne, der Streichrahm 1 cloud [klaʊd] die Wolke 1 **have your head in the clouds** in Gedanken verloren oder unrealistisch sein 1

cloudy [ˈklaʊdi] wolkig, bewölkt 1

club [klʌb] der Klub, der Verein 1 **join a club** bei einer AG mitmachen, in einen Klub eintreten 1 **school club** die AG *(in der Schule)* 1

°clue [kluː] der (Lösungs-)Hinweis; der Anhaltspunkt **I don't have a clue. / I have no clue.** *(infml)* Ich habe keine Ahnung. / Keine Ahnung.

cocoa [ˈkəʊkəʊ] der Kakao 1

code [kəʊd]:
1. programmieren *(Computer)*; kodieren 1
2. der Code 1
3. die Vorwahl(nummer) 1

coding [ˈkəʊdɪŋ] das Programmieren 1

coffee [ˈkɒfi] der Kaffee 1

coin [kɔɪn] die Münze 2: 5 (154)

cola [ˈkəʊlə] die Cola 1

cold [kəʊld]:
1. kalt 1
be cold frieren 1
2. die Kälte 1
3. die Erkältung 1
have a cold erkältet sein 1

collect [kəˈlekt] (ein)sammeln 1

collection [kəˈlekʃn] die Sammlung 2: 4 (117)

colour [ˈkʌlə] die Farbe 1 **What colour is ...?** Welche Farbe hat ...? 1

colourful [ˈkʌləfl] farbig, bunt 2: 4 (123)

come [kʌm], came, come:
1. (mit)kommen 1
come off (sth.) abgehen (von etwas), (herunter)fallen (von etwas), sich lösen (von etwas) 2: 2 (53) **come rain or shine** bei jedem Wetter; was auch (immer) geschieht 1 **come round (to)** vorbeikommen, vorbeischauen (bei) 2: 3 (93) **come up** (Sonne) aufgehen 2: 4 (114) °**Come on!** Komm(t) (schon)! Na los! °**come over** hinüberkommen, rüberkommen
2. **come true** wahr werden 2: 5 (149)

comfortable [ˈkʌmftəbl] bequem, gemütlich 2: 5 (155)

comic [ˈkɒmɪk] der Comic 1

°comment (about/on sth.) [ˈkɒment] der Kommentar (über/zu etwas)

compare sth. (to sth. / with sth.) [kəmˈpeə] etwas vergleichen (mit etwas) 2: 3 (85)

competition [kɒmpəˈtɪʃn] der Wettbewerb 1

°complete [kəmˈpliːt]:
1. vervollständigen
2. vollständig, komplett

computer [kəmˈpjuːtə] der Computer 1

computing [kəmˈpjuːtɪŋ] die Informatik 1

concert [ˈkɒnsət] das Konzert 2: 1 (20)

confidence [ˈkɒnfɪdəns] das (Selbst-)Vertrauen, die Zuversicht 2: 2 (48)

confident [ˈkɒnfɪdənt] (selbst)sicher; zuversichtlich 2: 2 (48)

°Congratulations (on ...)! [kənɡrætʃəˈleɪʃnz] Herzlichen Glückwunsch (zu ...)!

connect (with/to) [kəˈnekt] (sich) verbinden (mit) 2: 5 (160)

connection [kəˈnekʃn] die Verbindung; der Anschluss 2: 5 (160)

console [kənˈsəʊl] die Konsole 1

continue [kənˈtɪnjuː] fortfahren, weitermachen; (sich) fortsetzen,-weitergehen 1 **continue to do sth.** etwas weiterhin tun, (mit) etwas weitermachen, fortfahren 1

conversation [kɒnvəˈseɪʃn] das Gespräch 2: 5 (150)

cook [kʊk]:
1. der Koch, die Köchin 1
2. kochen 1

cooking [ˈkʊkɪŋ]:
1. das Kochen 1
2. das *(gekochte)* Essen 1

cool [kuːl] cool 1

°copy [ˈkɒpi] kopieren, abschreiben

corner [ˈkɔːnə] die Ecke 2: 5 (153)

corner shop [ˈkɔːnə ʃɒp] der Eckladen, der Tante-Emma-Laden 2: 5 (153)

cornflake crumbs (pl) [ˈkɔːnfleɪk krʌmz] die zerbröselten Cornflakes 1

cornflakes (pl) [ˈkɔːnfleɪks] die Cornflakes 1

correct [kəˈrekt]:
1. korrekt 2: 2 (65)
2. korrigieren 2: 2 (65)

°correction [kəˈrekʃn] die Berichtigung, die Korrektur

corridor [ˈkɒrɪdɔː] der Korridor 1

cost [kɒst]:
1. die Kosten; der Preis 1
2. cost, cost, cost kosten 1

costume [ˈkɒstjuːm] das Kostüm, die Verkleidung 2: 1 (16)

cottage [ˈkɒtɪdʒ] das Häuschen, das Cottage *(kleines Haus, meist auf dem Land)* 1

cough [kɒf]:
1. der Husten 2: 3 (92)
2. husten 2: 3 (92)

could [kʊd]:
1. **I could** ich konnte 2: 5 (156)
2. **Could you ...?** Könntest du ...? / Könnten Sie ...? 2: 5 (156)

°count [kaʊnt] zählen

°counting-out rhyme [kaʊntɪŋ aʊt ˈraɪm] der Abzählreim

country [ˈkʌntri] das Land, *(auch:)* die ländliche Gegend 1

course [kɔːs]:
1. der Kurs 2: 3 (80)
2. **main course** das Hauptgericht 1

cousin [ˈkʌzn] der Cousin, die Cousine 1

cow [kaʊ] die Kuh 2: 4 (116)

crack [kræk] lösen *(z. B. Problem)*, knacken *(z. B. Code)* 1

crafts (pl) [krɑːfts] das Kunsthandwerk, das Basteln 1

crazy [ˈkreɪzi] verrückt 2: 5 (148) **crazy about sth.** wild auf etwas, versessen auf etwas 2: 5 (148)

cream [kriːm] die Sahne 1

create [kriˈeɪt] (er)schaffen 2: 2 (59)

creative [kriˈeɪtɪv] kreativ 2: 2 (59)

creativity [kriːeɪˈtɪvəti] die Kreativität 2: 2 (59)

cricket [ˈkrɪkɪt]:
1. das Kricket *(Mannschaftssportart)* 1
2. die Grille *(Insekt)* 1

°cross [krɒs]:
1. mit einem Kreuz versehen
2. das Kreuz(chen)

crumb [krʌm] die Flocke, der Krümel 1 **cornflake crumbs (pl)** die zerbröselten Cornflakes 1

culture [ˈkʌltʃə] die Kultur 1

cupcake [ˈkʌpkeɪk] der Cupcake *(kleiner Muffin-ähnlicher Kuchen)* 2: 5 (158)

curious (about) [ˈkjʊəriəs] neugierig (auf) 2: 5 (163)

curl [kɜːl] die Locke 2: 2 (46/47)

curly [ˈkɜːli] lockig 2: 2 (46/47)

curry [ˈkʌri] das Curry *(Gewürz und auch Gericht)* 1

cushion [ˈkʊʃn] das Kissen 1

custard [ˈkʌstəd] der Custard *(Vanillesoße)* 1

customer [ˈkʌstəmə] der Kunde, die Kundin 2: 5 (157)

cut [kʌt]:
1. der Schnitt 1
2. cut, cut, cut schneiden 1
cut sth. out etwas ausschneiden 1

cute [kjuːt] niedlich, süß 1

cycle [ˈsaɪkl] Rad fahren 1

°cycle lane [ˈsaɪkl leɪn] der Radweg 1

cycling [ˈsaɪklɪŋ] das Radfahren 1

D

dad [dæd] der Papa, der Vati 1

dance [dɑːns]:
1. tanzen 1
2. der Tanz 1
do a dance einen Tanz tanzen 1

dancer [ˈdɑːnsə] der Tänzer, die Tänzerin 1

dancing [ˈdɑːnsɪŋ] das Tanzen 1

°dandelion [ˈdændɪlaɪən] der Löwenzahn

danger [ˈdeɪndʒə] die Gefahr 2: 2 (61)

dangerous [ˈdeɪndʒərəs] gefährlich 2: 2 (61)

dare [deə]:
1. wagen, sich trauen 2: 2 (57)
2. die Mutprobe 2: 2 (57)
for a dare als Mutprobe 2: 2 (57)

dark [dɑːk]:
1. dunkel 2: 1 (16)
2. das Dunkel, die Dunkelheit 2: 1 (16)

darkness [ˈdɑːknəs] die Dunkelheit 2: 1 (16)

date [deɪt]
1. das Datum 1
date of birth das Geburtsdatum 1
2. die Verabredung, das Date *(auch die Person, mit der man ausgeht)*
2: 3 (83)
3. **date sb.** mit jm. gehen, eine Beziehung haben 1
daughter [ˈdɔːtə] die Tochter 1
day [deɪ] der Tag 1 **work long days** lange arbeiten, lange Arbeitstage haben 1
dead [ded] tot 1
Dear … [dɪə] Liebe/r … 1
December [dɪˈsembə] der Dezember 1
°**decide (to do sth.)** [dɪˈsaɪd] sich entscheiden, beschließen (etwas zu tun)
decorate [ˈdekəreɪt] dekorieren, schmücken 1
decoration [dekəˈreɪʃn] die Dekoration, der Schmuck, die Verzierung 1
°**definition** [defɪˈnɪʃn] die Definition
degree (°) [dɪˈgriː] das/der Grad 1
delicious [dɪˈlɪʃəs] köstlich, lecker 1
dependent (on) [dɪˈpendənt] abhängig (von), angewiesen (auf) 2: 5 (159)
describe [dɪˈskraɪb] beschreiben 1
description [dɪˈskrɪpʃn] die Beschreibung 1
design [dɪˈzaɪn]:
1. die Gestaltung, das Design 1
2. entwerfen, gestalten 1
design and technology [dɪzaɪn ən tekˈnɒlədʒi] das Werken, der Werkunterricht 1
designer [dɪˈzaɪnə] der Designer, die Designerin 2: 3 (90)
desk [desk] der Schreibtisch 1
dessert [dɪˈzɜːt] die Nachspeise, das Dessert 1 **for dessert** zum/als Nachtisch 1
destination [destɪˈneɪʃn] das Ziel, der Bestimmungsort 2: 1 (19)
detached home/house [dɪˈtætʃt] das frei stehende Haus 1
°**detail** [ˈdiːteɪl] Detail, Einzelheit
°**detective** [dɪˈtektɪv] der Detektiv, die Detektivin
°**dialogue** [ˈdaɪəlɒg] der Dialog
dictionary [ˈdɪkʃənri] das Wörterbuch, das *(alphabetische)* Wörterverzeichnis 2: 5 (163)
did [dɪd] *siehe* do **they didn't go …** (= did not) sie gingen nicht / sie sind nicht gegangen 2: 1 (20) °**We did it!** Wir haben es geschafft!
die (of) [daɪ] sterben (an) 2: 2 (59)
difference [ˈdɪfrəns] der Unterschied 1
different (to) [ˈdɪfrənt] verschieden; anders (als) 1
difficult [ˈdɪfɪkəlt] schwierig, schwer 1
dig [dɪg], **dug, dug** graben 1
°**digital** [ˈdɪdʒɪtl] digital
dining room [ˈdaɪnɪŋ ruːm] das Esszimmer 1
dinner [ˈdɪnə] das Abendessen 1 **for dinner** zum Abendessen 1
°**direct** [dəˈrekt] direkt, unmittelbar

°**direct train** [dərekt ˈtreɪn] die Direktverbindung, der durchgehende Zug *(ohne Umsteigen)*
direction [dəˈrekʃn] die Richtung 2: 3 (90)
directions *(pl)* [dəˈrekʃnz] die Wegbeschreibung(en) 2: 3 (90) **ask for directions** nach dem Weg fragen 2: 3 (90) **give directions** den Weg beschreiben 2: 3 (90)
dirty [ˈdɜːti] schmutzig 1
disagree [dɪsəˈgriː] nicht zustimmen, widersprechen 2: 1 (28)
disappoint sb. [dɪsəˈpɔɪnt] jn. enttäuschen 2: 4 (127)
disappointed (in/with) [dɪsəˈpɔɪntɪd] enttäuscht (von) 2: 4 (127)
disappointing [dɪsəˈpɔɪntɪŋ] enttäuschend 2: 4 (127)
disappointment [dɪsəˈpɔɪntmənt] die Enttäuschung 2: 4 (127)
disco [ˈdɪskəʊ] die Disco 2: 3 (97)
discover [dɪˈskʌvə] entdecken 2: 2 (65)
discoverer [dɪsˈkʌvərə] der Entdecker, die Entdeckerin 2: 2 (65)
discovery [dɪˈskʌvəri] die Entdeckung 2: 2 (65)
discuss [dɪˈskʌs] diskutieren 2: 3 (97)
discussion [dɪˈskʌʃn] die Diskussion 2: 3 (97)
disease [dɪˈziːz] die Krankheit 2: 2 (59)
dish [dɪʃ]:
1. die Schüssel, die Schale 1
2. das Gericht *(Mahlzeit)* 1
main dish das Hauptgericht 1
dishwasher [ˈdɪʃwɒʃə] die Geschirrspülmaschine 2: 5 (150)
disorganized [dɪsˈɔːgənaɪzd] schlecht organisiert, chaotisch 2: 4 (126)
°**divide (up) (into)** [dɪˈvaɪd] auf-/einteilen (in)
do [duː], **did, done** machen, tun 1
do your homework Hausaufgaben machen 1
doctor (Dr) [ˈdɒktə] der Arzt, die Ärztin 2: 2 (55)
dog [dɒg] der Hund 1 **rain cats and dogs** stark regnen 1 **walk the dog** mit dem Hund rausgehen, mit dem Hund Gassi gehen 2: 5 (154)
dog walker [ˈdɒg wɔːkə] der Hundeausführer, die Hundeausführerin 2: 5 (154)
dog walking [ˈdɒg wɔːkɪŋ] Hunde ausführen 2: 5 (154)
dolphin [ˈdɒlfɪn] der Delfin 2: 2 (57)
done [dʌn] *siehe* do **Well done.** Gut gemacht! 1
donut [ˈdəʊnʌt] der Donut *(ringförmiges Gebäck aus Hefeteig)* 2: 5 (156)
door [dɔː] die Tür 1
°**double** [ˈdʌbl] doppelt, Doppel-
dough [dəʊ] der Teig 1
down [daʊn] hinunter, herunter 1 **down a hill** einen Hügel hinunter, herunter 2: 3 (88)
downstairs [daʊnˈsteəz] (nach) unten *(die Treppe hinunter)* 2: 4 (127)
dragon [ˈdrægən] der Drache 2: 3 (80)

drama [ˈdrɑːmə] das Schauspiel, die darstellende Kunst 1
dramatic [drəˈmætɪk] dramatisch 2: 5 (163)
draw [drɔː], **drew, drawn** zeichnen 1
drawing [ˈdrɔːɪŋ]:
1. die Zeichnung 1
2. das Zeichnen 1
dream [driːm]:
1. der Traum 1
2. **dream (of/about sth.)** träumen (von etwas) 1
dress [dres]:
1. das Kleid 2: 2 (57)
2. sich kleiden, sich anziehen 2: 2 (57) **get dressed** sich anziehen 1
drew [druː] *siehe* draw
drink [drɪŋk]:
1. das Getränk 1
2. **drink, drank, drunk** trinken 1
drive [draɪv], **drove, driven** *(mit dem Auto)* fahren 2: 2 (61)
driver [ˈdraɪvə] der Fahrer, die Fahrerin 2: 5 (146)
drone [drəʊn] die Drohne 1
drove [drəʊv] *siehe* drive
°**duck** [dʌk] die Ente
duke [djuːk] der Herzog 1
dungeon [ˈdʌndʒən] der Kerker, das Verlies *(in einer Burg)* 2: 3 (80)
during [ˈdjʊərɪŋ] während *(Präposition)* 2: 2 (59)

E

each [iːtʃ] jede(r, s) (einzelne), jeweils 1
each other [iːtʃ ˈʌðə] einander, sich (gegenseitig) 2: 4 (115)
ear [ɪə] das Ohr 2: 2 (57)
early [ˈɜːli] früh 2: 5 (153)
earn [ɜːn] verdienen *(Geld)* 2: 5 (148)
earth [ɜːθ] die Erde 2: 2 (56)
easy [ˈiːzi] einfach, leicht 2: 1 (26)
eat [iːt], **ate, eaten** essen; fressen 1
eaten [ˈiːtn] *siehe* eat
effect (on) [ɪˈfekt] die (Aus-)Wirkung (auf), der Einfluss (auf); der Effekt 2: 3 (86)
effective [ɪˈfektɪv] effektiv, wirksam 2: 3 (86)
egg [eg] das Ei 1
°**Eid al-Fitr** [iːd ɔːl ˈfitrə] das Zuckerfest *(im Islam)*
°**Eid Mubarak!** [iːd mʊˈbɑːrək] Eid Mubarak! *(Frohes (Zucker-)Fest!)*
eight [eɪt] acht 1
eighteen [eɪˈtiːn] achtzehn 1
eighty [ˈeɪti] achtzig 1
electric [ɪˈlektrɪk] elektrisch, Elektro- 1
electro [ɪˈlektrəʊ] der Electro, die Elektromusik 2: 3 (84)
electronic [ɪlekˈtrɒnɪk] elektronisch 2: 5 (155)
electronics *(pl)* [ɪlekˈtrɒnɪks] die Elektronik; die elektronischen Geräte 2: 5 (155)
elephant [ˈelɪfənt] der Elefant 1
eleven [ɪˈlevən] elf 1

else [els]: **everybody/everyone else** alle anderen; jede/r andere 2: 2 (50) **no one else** niemand anders, niemand sonst 2: 2 (50) **somebody/ someone else** jemand anders 2: 2 (50) **What else?** Was sonst noch? 1

embarrass sb. [ɪmˈbærəs] jn. in Verlegenheit bringen, jn. bloßstellen, jm. peinlich sein 2: 4 (124)

embarrassed [ɪmˈbærəst] verlegen, peinlich berührt 2: 4 (124)

embarrassing [ɪmˈbærəsɪŋ] peinlich 2: 4 (124)

empty [ˈempti]:
1. leer 2: 5 (150)
2. leeren 2: 5 (150)

end [end]:
1. enden; beenden 1
2. das Ende, der Schluss 1
at the end (of) am Ende (von) 1 **in the end** schließlich; zum Schluss 1

ending [ˈendɪŋ] die Endung; das Ende *(Text, Geschichte)* 2: 3 (94)

energetic [enəˈdʒetɪk] aktiv, tatkräftig, energiegeladen 2: 3 (85)

energy [ˈenədʒi] die Energie 2: 3 (85)

England [ˈɪŋglənd] England 1

English [ˈɪŋglɪʃ] das Englisch; englisch 1

enjoy [ɪnˈdʒɔɪ] genießen 1 **enjoy doing sth.** es genießen, etwas zu tun 1 **Enjoy!** Viel Vergnügen! / Guten Appetit! 1

enough [ɪˈnʌf] genug 1

°**envelope** [ˈenvələʊp] der (Brief-) Umschlag

equipment *(no pl)* [ɪˈkwɪpmənt] die Ausrüstung 2: 1 (23)

°**erm** [ɜːm] äh *(Verlegenheitslaut)*

especially [ɪˈspeʃəli] insbesondere 2: 3 (96)

estate [ɪˈsteɪt] die Wohnsiedlung; das Gewerbegebiet 1

°**etc.** [etˈsetərə] *(aus dem Lateinischen)* usw. (und so weiter)

euro [ˈjʊərəʊ], *pl* euros der Euro 1

even [ˈiːvn] sogar, selbst 2: 1 (20) **even if** selbst wenn, sogar wenn 2: 1 (20) **not even** nicht einmal 2: 1 (20)

evening [ˈiːvnɪŋ] der Abend 1 **in the evening** abends, am Abend 1

event [ɪˈvent] das Ereignis 2: 1 (18)

ever [ˈevə] jemals, schon einmal 2: 4 (121) **the best son ever** der beste Sohn überhaupt / der beste Sohn, den man sich wünschen kann 1

every [ˈevri] jede(r, s) 1 **every 30 minutes** alle 30 Minuten 1

everybody [ˈevribɒdi] jeder; alle 1 **Hello everybody!** Hallo allerseits! 1

everyone [ˈevriwʌn] jeder, alle 1

everything [ˈevriθɪŋ] alles 2: 1 (30)

everywhere [ˈevriweə] überall 1

example [ɪgˈzɑːmpl] das Beispiel 1 **for example** zum Beispiel 1

°**exchange student** [ɪksˈtʃeɪndʒ stjuːdnt] der Austauschschüler, die Austauschschülerin

excited [ɪkˈsaɪtɪd] aufgeregt, gespannt 2: 1 (26)

exciting [ɪkˈsaɪtɪŋ] aufregend 1

Excuse me, ... [ɪkˈskjuːz miː] Entschuldigung, ... / Entschuldigen Sie, ... 1

exercise [ˈeksəsaɪz] die Übung, die Aufgabe 1

exercise book [ˈeksəsaɪz bʊk] das Schulheft, das Übungsheft 1

expensive [ɪkˈspensɪv] teuer 1

experience [ɪkˈspɪəriəns]:
1. die Erfahrung; das Erlebnis 2: 1 (17)
2. **experience sth.** etwas erfahren; erleben 2: 1 (17)

expert [ˈekspɜːt] der Experte, die Expertin 2: 3 (90)

explain sth. to sb. [ɪkˈspleɪn] jm. etwas erklären 1

explanation [ekspləˈneɪʃn] die Erklärung 2: 5 (150)

extra [ˈekstrə] Extra-, zusätzliche(r, s) 2: 4 (131)

eye [aɪ] das Auge 2: 1 (17)

F

face [feɪs] das Gesicht 1

fact [fækt] die Tatsache 2: 2 (65) **in fact** tatsächlich, in Wirklichkeit, genau genommen 2: 2 (65)

°**factory** [ˈfæktri] die Fabrik

fair [feə] fair 2: 2 (48)

fall [fɔːl], **fell, fallen** fallen; hinfallen 2: 2 (60) **fall asleep** einschlafen 2: 2 (61) **fall off** herunterfallen 2: 2 (53)

false [fɔːls] falsch, unrichtig 1

false friend [fɔːls ˈfrend] der „falsche Freund" *(die Übersetzungsfalle)* 2: 2 (64)

fame [feɪm] der Ruhm 2: 2 (59)

family [ˈfæməli] die Familie 1

family name [ˈfæməli neɪm] der Familienname, der Nachname 1

famous (for) [ˈfeɪməs] berühmt (für, wegen) 2: 2 (59)

fan [fæn] der Fan 1

far [fɑː] weit (entfernt) 2: 2 (57) **so far** bis jetzt, bis hierher 2: 4 (119) °**go far** es weit bringen

farm [fɑːm] der Bauernhof, die Farm 2: 3 (80)

fast [fɑːst] schnell 1

fast [fɑːst]:
1. fasten 2: 4 (112/113)
2. das Fasten, die Fastenzeit 2: 4 (112/113)
break the fast das Fasten brechen 2: 4 (112/113)

father [ˈfɑːðə] der Vater 2: 1 (14)

favourite [ˈfeɪvərɪt]:
1. Lieblings- 1
2. der Liebling, der Favorit, die Favoritin 1

°**feather** [ˈfeðə] die Feder *(eines Vogels)*

February [ˈfebruəri] der Februar 1

fed [fed] *siehe* feed

feed [fiːd], **fed, fed** füttern; ernähren 2: 2 (120)

feedback *(no pl)* [ˈfiːdbæk] das Feedback *(Rückmeldung)* 1

feel [fiːl], **felt, felt** sich fühlen; fühlen 1 **be/feel sorry for sb.** Mitleid haben mit jm. 1

feeling [ˈfiːlɪŋ] das Gefühl 2: 1 (27)

feet [fiːt] *Plural von* foot

fell [fel] *siehe* fall

felt [felt] *siehe* feel

ferry [ˈferi] die Fähre 2: 1 (15)

festival [ˈfestɪvl] das Fest(ival) 2: 1 (21)

few [fjuː]: **a few** ein paar, einige 2: 4 (116) **in the last few weeks** in den letzten paar Wochen 2: 4 (116)

°**fictional** [ˈfɪkʃənl] erfunden, fiktional *(auf Fiktion beruhend)*

field [fiːld]:
1. das Feld; die Weide; die Wiese 1 **in the field** auf der Weide 1
2. das Spielfeld, der Platz *(im Sport, z. B. Fußballplatz)* 1 **on the field** auf dem Spielfeld, auf dem Platz 1

fifteen [fɪfˈtiːn] fünfzehn 1

fifty [ˈfɪfti] fünfzig 1

fight [faɪt]:
1. der Kampf 2: 2 (57) **have a fight** sich prügeln; sich streiten 2: 4 (119)
2. **fight, fought, fought** kämpfen, bekämpfen 2: 2 (57)

fighter [ˈfaɪtə] der Kämpfer die Kämpferin 2: 2 (57)

file [faɪl] die Datei; der Ordner, die Liste 1

°**fill in** [fɪl ˈɪn] einsetzen; ausfüllen

film [fɪlm]:
1. der Film 1
°2. filmen

finally [ˈfaɪnəli] schließlich, endlich 1

find [faɪnd], **found, found** finden 1 **find out (about)** herausfinden; sich informieren (über) 1

fine [faɪn]: **I'm fine.** Mir geht es gut. 1

finger [ˈfɪŋgə] der Finger 1

finish [ˈfɪnɪʃ]:
1. das Ende, das Ziel ((z. B. beim Sport)) 2: 4 (119)
2. enden; beenden, zu Ende machen 2: 4 (119)

fire [ˈfaɪə] das Feuer 2: 2 (61) **stop a fire** ein Feuer löschen 2: 5 (144)

fire engine [ˈfaɪər endʒɪn] das Feuerwehrauto 2: 2 (61)

firefighter [ˈfaɪəfaɪtə] der Feuerwehrmann, die Feuerwehrfrau 2: 5 (144)

firework [ˈfaɪəwɜːk] der Feuerwerkskörper 2: 4 (112/113) **fireworks** *(pl)* das Feuerwerk 2: 4 (112/113)

first [fɜːst]:
1. erste(r, s) 1
2. zuerst, als Erstes 1
at first zuerst, am Anfang 1

first name [ˈfɜːst neɪm] der Vorname 1

fish [fɪʃ], *pl* **fish** der Fisch 1
fish and chip shop [fɪʃ ən ˈtʃɪp ʃɒp] *die Imbissstube, die Fisch mit Pommes Frites verkauft* 1
fit [fɪt] fit 2: 3 (80)
fitness [ˈfɪtnəs] die Fitness 2: 3 (80)
five [faɪv] fünf 1
°**fix sth.** [fɪks] *(infml)* etwas in Ordnung bringen; reparieren
flag [flæg] die Fahne, die Flagge 2: 1 (20)
flamenco [fləˈmeŋkəʊ] der Flamenco *(Tanz)* 2: 1 (14)
flat [flæt] die Wohnung 1
floor [flɔː]:
　1. der Fußboden 1
　2. die Etage, der Stock, das Stockwerk 1
flour [ˈflaʊə] das Mehl 1
flower [ˈflaʊə] die Blume; die Blüte 2: 4 (114)
flowerpot [ˈflaʊəpɒt] der Blumentopf 2: 4 (114)
fly [flaɪ] fliegen 1
fold [fəʊld] falten 2: 5 (150)
°**flyer** [ˈflaɪə] der Handzettel, der Flyer
folder [ˈfəʊldə] die Mappe, der Ordner 1
follow [ˈfɒləʊ] (be)folgen; verfolgen 2: 5 (159)
food [fuːd] das Essen, das Lebensmittel; das Futter 1
foot [fʊt], *pl* **feet**:
　1. der Fuß *(Körperteil)* 2: 1 (14)
　2. der Fuß *(Längenmaß; ca. 30 cm)* 2: 1 (14)
football [ˈfʊtbɔːl] der Fußball 1
footballer [ˈfʊtbɔːlə] der Fußballspieler, die Fußballspielerin 2: 5 (146)
for [fɔː] für 1 **for 30 seconds** für 30 Sekunden, 30 Sekunden lang 1 **for a dare** als Mutprobe 2: 2 (57) **for a long time** seit langem; lange *(für eine lange Zeit)* 2: 4 (126) **for hours** seit Stunden, stundenlang 2: 4 (126) **for the first time** zum ersten Mal 2: 1 (26) **What's for homework?** Was haben wir als Hausaufgabe(n) auf? 1
forest [ˈfɒrɪst] der Wald 2: 3 (88)
forget [fəˈget], **forgot**, **forgotten** vergessen 1 **Don't forget.** Vergiss (es) nicht. / Denk dran! 1
forgot [fəˈgɒt] *siehe* **forget**
forgotten [fəˈgɒtn] *siehe* **forget**
fork [fɔːk] die Gabel 1
°**form** [fɔːm] formen, bilden
°**fort** [fɔːt] das Fort *(Befestigungsanlage)*
forty [ˈfɔːti] vierzig 1
forward [ˈfɔːwəd]: **look forward to doing sth.** sich darauf freuen, etwas zu tun 2: 5 (162) **look forward to sth.** sich auf etwas freuen 2: 5 (162)
fought [fɔːt] *siehe* **fight**
found [faʊnd] *siehe* **find**
four [fɔː] vier 1
fourteen [fɔːˈtiːn] vierzehn 1

free [friː]:
　1. kostenlos 1
　for free kostenlos 2: 1 (19)
　2. frei 1
　free time die Freizeit, die freie Zeit 1 **Are you free after school?** Hast du nach der Schule Zeit? 1
freeze [friːz] (ge)frieren; erstarren 1
freeze-frame [ˈfriːz freɪm] das Standbild *(Film)* 1
French [frentʃ] Französisch; französisch 1
Friday [ˈfraɪdeɪ], [ˈfraɪdi] der Freitag 1
fried [fraɪd] frittiert, gebraten 1
friend [frend] der Freund, die Freundin 1 **make friends** Freunde/-innen finden 2: 1 (23)
friendly [ˈfrendli] freundlich, nett 1
from [frɒm] von, aus 1 **Where are you from?** Wo kommst du her? 1
front [frʌnt] der vordere Teil, die Vorderseite 2: 1 (25) **at the front** vorne 2: 1 (25) **in front of** vor 1
fruit [fruːt] das Obst 1
fry [fraɪ] braten; frittieren 1
full [fʊl]:
　1. voll 2: 3 (78/79)
　full of ... voller ... 2: 3 (78/79)
　2. satt 2: 3 (78/79)
fun [fʌn] der Spaß 1 **be fun** Spaß machen; lustig sein 1 **have fun** Spaß haben 1
fun run [ˈfʌn rʌn] der Volkslauf *(z. B. zum Geldsammeln für wohltätige Zwecke)* 2: 3 (97)
funny [ˈfʌni]:
　1. seltsam 1
　2. witzig, lustig 1
　What's funny about ...? Was ist lustig an ...? 1
furniture [ˈfɜːnɪtʃə] die Möbel(stücke) 1
°**further** [ˈfɜːðə] weiter (entfernt)
future [ˈfjuːtʃə]:
　1. die Zukunft 2: 5 (144)
　2. zukünftige(r, s) 2: 5 (144)

G

°**gallery** [ˈgæləri] die Galerie
game [geɪm]:
　1. das Spiel 1
　2. Computerspiele spielen 2: 5 (146)
gamer [ˈgeɪmə] der Gamer, die Gamerin *(Computerspieler/in)* 2: 5 (146)
gaming [ˈgeɪmɪŋ] das Gaming *(Spielen am Computer)* 1
°**gap** [gæp] die Lücke
garage [ˈgærɑːʒ] die Garage 1
garden [ˈgɑːdn] der Garten 1
garlic [ˈgɑːlɪk] der Knoblauch 1
gate [geɪt] das Tor, das Gatter 1
gave [geɪv] *siehe* **give**
gay [geɪ]:
　1. der Schwule 2: 1 (18)
　2. schwul 2: 1 (18)
°**Gemini** [ˈdʒemɪnaɪ] die Zwillinge *(Sternzeichen)*

generous [ˈdʒenərəs] großzügig 2: 5 (163)
geography [dʒiˈɒgrəfi] die Geografie, die Erdkunde 1
German [ˈdʒɜːmən] deutsch; Deutsch; der/die Deutsche 1
Germany [ˈdʒɜːməni] Deutschland 1
get [get], **got**, **got**:
　1. bekommen 1
　get sth. *(sich etwas)* holen/besorgen 1
　°**get to know** kennenlernen
　2. werden 1
　Get better/well soon! Gute Besserung! / Werde bald gesund! 2: 3 (92)
　get dressed sich anziehen 1 **get ready (for)** sich fertig machen (für), sich vorbereiten (auf) 2: 4 (120) **get warm** warm werden 1
　3. **get (to)** gelangen, (hin)kommen (nach) 2: 1 (26)
　get off your bike/your horse vom Fahrrad / vom Pferd absteigen 2: 2 (53) **get on a train/bus** in einen Zug/Bus einsteigen 2: 1 (26) **get off a train/bus** aus einem Zug/Bus aussteigen 2: 1 (26) **get up** aufstehen 1
ghost [gəʊst] der Geist, das Gespenst 2: 1 (16)
ghost tour [ˈgəʊst tʊə] die Geistertour *(Stadtführung mit gruseligen Themen/Elementen)* 2: 1 (16)
gift [gɪft] das Geschenk, die Gabe; das Talent 2: 5 (155)
gift shop [ˈgɪft ʃɒp] der Geschenk(artikel)laden, der Souvenirladen 2: 5 (155)
girl [gɜːl] das Mädchen 1
girlfriend [ˈgɜːlfrend] die (feste) Freundin 2: 1 (20)
give [gɪv], **gave**, **given** geben 1
given [ˈgɪvn] *siehe* **give**
glad [glæd]: **be glad** froh sein 2: 1 (27)
glass [glɑːs] das Glas 1 **a glass of milk** ein Glas Milch 1
glasses *(pl)* [ˈglɑːsɪz] die Brille 2: 2 (46/47)
global [ˈgləʊbl] global, weltweit 2: 4 (128)
globe [gləʊb] der Globus; die Kugel 2: 4 (128) **across the globe** auf der ganzen Welt 2: 4 (128) **all (a)round the globe** auf der ganzen Welt 2: 4 (128)
glove [glʌv] der Handschuh 2: 1 (23)
glue [gluː] der Kleber, der Klebstoff 1
glue stick [ˈgluː stɪk] der Klebestift 1
go [gəʊ], **went**, **gone**:
　1. gehen, fahren 1
　go down (Sonne) untergehen 2: 4 (114) **go up** aufgehen (Sonne); hochgehen; (an)steigen 1 **How's it going?** *(infml)* Wie geht's? / Wie läuft's? 2: 5 (146) **I must go.** Ich muss Schluss machen. *(am Telefon/Briefschluss)* 1
　2. werden 1
　go green grün/umweltfreundlich werden 1 °**go wrong** schiefgehen

3. I'm going to ... ich werde ... *(Plan, Vorhaben)* 2: 3 (81)

goat [gəʊt] die Ziege 1

god [gɒd] der Gott 2: 4 (114)

gold [gəʊld]:
1. das Gold 1
2. goldfarben 1

gone [gɒn] *siehe* **go**
be gone weg sein 2: 5 (158)

°**gonna** [ˈgɒnə] *infml für* **going to**

good [gʊd]:
1. brav 1
2. gut 1
be good with ... gut umgehen können mit ... 1 too much of a good thing zu viel des Guten 2: 3 (92)

Goodbye. [gʊdˈbaɪ] Auf Wiedersehen! 1

got [gɒt] *siehe* **get**

gram (g) [græm] das Gramm 1

grandma [ˈgrænmɑː] die Oma 1

grandpa [ˈgrænpɑː] der Opa 1

grandparents *(pl)* [ˈgrænpeərənts] die Großeltern 2: 1 (15)

°**grass** [grɑːs] das Gras; der Rasen

grateful [ˈgreɪtfl]: be grateful (to sb. for sth.) (jm. für etwas) dankbar sein 2: 1 (27)

great [greɪt]:
1. großartig, toll 1
2. groß *(bedeutend, angesehen)* 2: 5 (151)

Great Britain [greɪt ˈbrɪtn] Großbritannien 1

green [griːn]:
1. grün 1
2. umweltbewusst 1
go green grün/umweltfreundlich werden 1

greet [griːt] begrüßen 1

greeting [ˈgriːtɪŋ] die Begrüßung; der Gruß 1

grew [gruː] *siehe* **grow**

grey [greɪ] grau 1

groom [gruːm] der Bräutigam 2: 4 (125)

groomsman [ˈgruːmzmən], *pl* groomsmen der Trauzeuge *(des Bräutigams)* 2: 4 (125)

groomsmen [ˈgruːmzmən] *Plural von* groomsman

ground [graʊnd] der (Erd-)Boden 1

ground floor [graʊnd ˈflɔː] das Erdgeschoss 1

group [gruːp]:
1. die Gruppe 1
2. gruppieren 1

grow [grəʊ], **grew, grown** wachsen 2: 2 (53) grow up aufwachsen; erwachsen werden 2: 2 (53)

grown [grəʊn] *siehe* **grow**

guess [ges]:
1. die Vermutung 1
Make/Have/Take a guess! Rate mal! 1
2. (er)raten 1
Guess what! Stell dir / Stellt euch (mal) vor! 1 I guess ich glaube, ich nehme an 1

°**guest** [gest] der Gast

guide [gaɪd]:
1. führen, leiten 1
2. (tour) guide der Reiseleiter, die Reiseleiterin / der Fremdenführer, die Fremdenführerin 1

guide dog [ˈgaɪd dɒg] der Blindenhund 1

guitar [gɪˈtɑː] die Gitarre 1

guy [gaɪ] der Typ, der Kerl 2: 2 (57)

guys *(pl)* [gaɪz] Leute *(Anrede)* 1

°**gymnastics** [dʒɪmˈnæstɪks] das Turnen, die Gymnastik do gymnastics Gymnastik machen

H

had [hæd] *siehe* **have**

hair [heə] das Haar, die Haare 2: 1 (25)

hairdresser [ˈheədresə] der Friseur, die Friseurin 2: 5 (144)

hairdresser's [ˈheədresəz] der Friseursalon 2: 5 (144)

half [hɑːf]: half a lemon / an orange / an hour eine halbe Zitrone/Orange/ Stunde 2: 3 (90) half past 6 halb 7 2: 3 (90)

hall [hɔːl]:
1. der Flur, die Diele 1
2. die Halle, der Saal 1
sports hall die Sporthalle 1

Halloween [hæləʊˈiːn] (das) Halloween *(der Abend des 31. Oktober)* 2: 4 (118)

ham [hæm] der Schinken 1

hamster [ˈhæmstə] der Hamster 1

hand [hænd]:
1. die Hand 1
put your hand up / put up your hand sich melden, aufzeigen 1
°**2. hand sth. out (to sb.)** (jm.) etwas aushändigen, etwas (an jn.) verteilen

hang [hæŋ], **hung, hung: hang out** rumhängen, abhängen 1 °hang sth. on the wall etwas an die Wand hängen

Hanukkah [ˈhænʊkə] die Chanukka *(jüdisches Lichterfest)* 2: 4 (131)

happen (to sb.) [ˈhæpən] (jm.) geschehen, passieren 1

happiness [ˈhæpinəs] das Glück, die Zufriedenheit 2: 2 (64)

happy [ˈhæpi] glücklich, froh 1 Happy birthday! Herzlichen Glückwunsch zum Geburtstag! 1

hard [hɑːd] schwer, schwierig; hart 1 think hard scharf nachdenken 2: 1 (30)

hard-working [hɑːd ˈwɜːkɪŋ] fleißig 2: 2 (48)

has [hæz], [həz]: he/she/it has er/sie/es hat 1

hat [hæt] der Hut, die Mütze 1

hate [heɪt]:
1. hassen 1
2. der Hass 1

have [hæv], **had, had** haben 1 have (food) (Nahrung/etwas) essen; *(im Restaurant:)* nehmen 2: 1 (15) have to do sth. etwas tun müssen

2: 5 (151) I have to go. Ich muss Schluss machen. *(am Telefon/Briefschluss)* 2: 5 (151)

he [hiː] er 1 he's (= he is) er ist 1

head [hed] der Kopf 1 have your head in the clouds in Gedanken verloren oder unrealistisch sein 1

head student [hed ˈstjuːdnt] der Vertrauensschüler, die Vertrauensschülerin; der Schulsprecher, die Schulsprecherin 2: 2 (46/47)

head teacher [ˈhed tiːtʃə] der Schulleiter, die Schulleiterin; der Direktor, die Direktorin 2: 2 (59)

headache [ˈhedeɪk] die Kopfschmerzen 2: 3 (92) have a headache Kopfschmerzen haben 2: 3 (92)

heading [ˈhedɪŋ] die Überschrift 1

headphones *(pl)* [ˈhedfəʊnz] der Kopfhörer 1

health [helθ] die Gesundheit 1 in sickness or in health wenn man krank oder gesund ist 2: 4 (127)

healthy [ˈhelθi] gesund 1

hear [hɪə], **heard, heard** hören 1

heard [hɜːd] *siehe* **hear**

heat [hiːt]:
1. die Hitze, die Wärme 1
2. erwärmen, erhitzen 1

height [haɪt] die Höhe, die Größe *(bei Menschen)* 2: 2 (48)

held [held] *siehe* **hold**

Hello. [həˈləʊ] Hallo. 1 Hello everybody! Hallo allerseits! 1

helmet [ˈhelmɪt] der Helm 2: 2 (57)

help [help]:
1. helfen 1
2. die Hilfe 1

helpful [ˈhelpfl] hilfsbereit; hilfreich, nützlich 1

her [hɜː], [hə]:
1. sie; ihr 1
like her wie sie 2: 2 (48)
2. her friends ihre Freunde/ Freundinnen 1

here [hɪə] hier; hierher 1 Here you are. Bitte schön. / Hier, bitte. 1

hero [ˈhɪərəʊ], *pl* heroes der Held, die Heldin 2: 2 (46/47)

°**hers** [hɜːz] ihrer, ihre, ihres *(zu „she")*

Hi. [haɪ] Hallo. 1

°**hid** [hɪd] *siehe* **hide**

°**hidden** [ˈhɪdn] *siehe* **hide**

°**hide** [haɪd], **hid, hidden** verstecken; sich verstecken

high [haɪ] hoch 2: 2 (48)

highlight [ˈhaɪlaɪt]:
1. das Highlight *(Höhepunkt)* 1
2. hervorheben, markieren, unterstreichen 1

hike [haɪk] wandern 1

hiking [ˈhaɪkɪŋ] das Wandern 1

hill [hɪl] der Hügel 2: 1 (15)

him [hɪm] ihm, ihn 1

himself [hɪmˈself]: he looked at himself er sah sich (selbst) an 2: 4 (126)

his friends [hɪz] seine Freunde/ Freundinnen 1

history [ˈhɪstri] die Geschichte
(vergangene Zeiten) 1
hit [hɪt], hit, hit stoßen gegen, zusammenstoßen mit; treffen auf 2: 2 (61)
hobby [ˈhɒbi] das Hobby 1
hockey [ˈhɒki] das Hockey 1
hold [həʊld], held, held halten
2: 4 (123)
°Holi [ˈhəʊli] das Holi-Fest (hinduistisches Frühlingsfest)
holiday [ˈhɒlədeɪ] der Urlaub 1
holidays die Ferien 1 on holiday
im/in den Urlaub 1
home [həʊm]:
1. das Heim, das Zuhause 1
at home zu Hause 1
2. nach Hause 1
go home nach Hause gehen 1
homework [ˈhəʊmwɜːk] die Hausaufgabe(n) 1 do your homework
Hausaufgaben machen 1 What's for
homework? Was haben wir als
Hausaufgabe(n) auf? 1
honest [ˈɒnɪst] ehrlich 2: 2 (49)
honesty [ˈɒnəsti] die Ehrlichkeit
2: 2 (49)
honey [ˈhʌni] der Honig 1
hope [həʊp]:
1. die Hoffnung 2: 1 (18)
2. hoffen 2: 1 (18)
horizontal [hɒrɪˈzɒntl] waagerecht,
horizontal 2: 5 (151)
horoscope [ˈhɒrəskəʊp] das Horoskop
2: 5 (163)
horrible [ˈhɒrəbl] schrecklich 1
horse [hɔːs] das Pferd 1
hospital [ˈhɒspɪtl] das Krankenhaus 1
hostel [ˈhɒstl] das Hostel (die günstige
Unterkunft für Reisende) 2: 1 (12/13)
hot [hɒt] heiß, warm 1
hot chocolate [hɒt ˈtʃɒklət] der Kakao,
die heiße (Trink-)Schokolade 1
hot meal [hɒt ˈmiːl] die warme Mahlzeit 1
hotel [həʊˈtel] das Hotel 2: 1 (12/13)
hour [ˈaʊə] die Stunde 1 a two-hour
class ein zweistündiger Kurs
2: 3 (78/79) per hour pro Stunde 1
house [haʊs] das Haus 1
house-warming (party) [ˈhaʊs wɔːmɪŋ]
die Einzugsfeier 2: 4 (124)
how [haʊ] wie 1 How about ...? Wie
wäre es mit ...? 2: 5 (157) How are
you? Wie geht's? / Wie geht es dir/
euch/Ihnen? 1 How much is/are ...?
Was (Wie viel) kostet/kosten ...?
2: 5 (156) how to do sth. wie man
etwas tut/tun kann/tun soll 1
hug [hʌg]:
1. die Umarmung 2: 1 (27)
2. hug (sb.) (jn.) umarmen; einander
umarmen 2: 1 (27)
hundred [ˈhʌndrəd]: a/one hundred
(ein)hundert 1
hung [hʌŋ] siehe hang
hungry [ˈhʌŋgri] hungrig 1 I'm
hungry. Ich habe Hunger. 1
°hunt [hʌnt] die Jagd

°hurry [ˈhʌri] sich beeilen; eilen
hurt [hɜːt], hurt, hurt verletzen;
wehtun 2: 2 (52) be hurt verletzt
sein 2: 2 (52) get hurt sich verletzen
2: 2 (52)
husband [ˈhʌzbənd] der (Ehe-)Mann 1

I

I [aɪ] ich 1 I'm (= I am) ich bin 1
ice cream [ˈaɪs kriːm] das (Speise-)
Eis 1
ice rink [ˈaɪs rɪŋk] die Schlittschuhbahn 1
icing [ˈaɪsɪŋ] die Glasur, der Zuckerguss 1
icing sugar [ˈaɪsɪŋ ʃʊgə] der Puderzucker 1
idea [aɪˈdɪə] die Idee 1
if [ɪf]:
1. ob 1
2. wenn, falls 1
even if selbst wenn, sogar
wenn 2: 1 (20) What if? Was wäre,
wenn? 1
ill [ɪl] krank 1
illness [ˈɪlnəs] die Krankheit 1
imaginative [ɪˈmædʒɪnətɪv] fantasievoll, einfallsreich, kreativ 2: 5 (163)
imagine sth. [ɪˈmædʒɪn] sich etwas
vorstellen 2: 5 (149) imagine being/
doing sth. sich vorstellen, etwas zu
sein/etwas zu tun 2: 5 (149)
impatience [ɪmˈpeɪʃns] die Ungeduld
2: 2 (48)
impatient [ɪmˈpeɪʃnt] ungeduldig
2: 2 (48)
important [ɪmˈpɔːtnt] wichtig 1
What's important to you in a friend?
Was ist dir an/bei einem Freund /
einer Freundin wichtig? 2: 2 (49)
in [ɪn] in; auf 1 in a place an einem
Ort 2: 3 (80) in English auf Englisch 1
in the afternoon nachmittags, am
Nachmittag 1 in the country auf
dem Land 1 in the evening abends,
am Abend 1 in the field auf der
Weide 1 in the morning morgens,
am Morgen 1 in the photo auf dem
Foto 1 in the picture auf dem Bild 1
in town in der Stadt 1 What's
important to you in a friend? Was
ist dir an/bei einem Freund / einer
Freundin wichtig? 2: 2 (49) °in the
sky am Himmel
include [ɪnˈkluːd] (mit) einschließen
2: 1 (31)
including [ɪnˈkluːdɪŋ] einschließlich,
inklusive 2: 1 (31)
independent (of/from) [ɪndɪˈpendənt]
unabhängig (von) 2: 5 (159)
India [ˈɪndɪə] Indien 1
Indian [ˈɪndɪən]:
1. indisch 1
2. der Inder, die Inderin 1
influencer [ˈɪnfluənsə] der Influencer,
die Influencerin 2: 2 (54)
information [ɪnfəˈmeɪʃn] die
Information(en) 1

insect [ˈɪnsekt] das Insekt 2: 3 (78/79)
inside [ɪnˈsaɪd]:
1. (dr)innen; nach (dr)innen 1
2. innerhalb (von) 1
instruction [ɪnˈstrʌkʃn] die Anweisung 1
instrument [ˈɪnstrəmənt] das Instrument 2: 1 (25)
interest [ˈɪntrəst]:
1. interest sb. (in) jn. interessieren
(für) 2: 2 (59)
2. interest (in) das Interesse (an)
2: 2 (59) take/show an interest (in)
Interesse zeigen (an) 2: 2 (59)
interested (in) [ˈɪntrəstɪd] interessiert
(an) 2: 2 (59)
interesting [ˈɪntrəstɪŋ] interessant 1
international [ɪntəˈnæʃnəl] international 2: 3 (91)
internet [ˈɪntənet] das Internet 1
°interview [ˈɪntəvjuː] befragen,
interviewen
into [ˈɪntu], [ˈɪntə] in (... hinein) 1
intolerant (of) [ɪnˈtɒlərənt] intolerant
(gegenüber) 2: 5 (163)
introduction [ɪntrəˈdʌkʃn] die Einführung, die Einleitung 1
invisible [ɪnˈvɪzəbl] unsichtbar 2: 2 (57)
invitation (to) [ɪnvɪˈteɪʃn] die Einladung (zu, nach) 1
invite (to) [ɪnˈvaɪt] einladen (zu,
nach) 1
is [ɪz] (er/sie/es) ist 1 he isn't (= is
not) er ist nicht 1 The football is £3.
Der Fußball kostet 3 Pfund. 2: 5 (156)
island [ˈaɪlənd] die Insel 1
it [ɪt] es (bei Sachen und Tieren auch:
er; sie) 1 it's (= it is) es ist 1
its [ɪts] sein/seine, ihr/ihre (besitzanzeigend: Dinge und Tiere) 1

J

jacket [ˈdʒækɪt] die Jacke; das Jackett
2: 4 (128) rain jacket die Regenjacke
2: 4 (128)
jam [dʒæm] die Marmelade 1
January [ˈdʒænjuəri] der Januar 1
jar [dʒɑː] das Glas(gefäß) 2: 4 (115)
jeans (pl) [dʒiːnz] die
Jeans(hose) 2: 5 (150)
jelly [ˈdʒeli] das Gelee; der Wackelpudding 1
jigsaw (puzzle) [ˈdʒɪgsɔː] das Puzzle 1
job [dʒɒb] der Job, die (Arbeits-)Stelle;
die Aufgabe 2: 2 (53)
join sb./sth. [dʒɔɪn] sich jm. anschließen; bei etwas mitmachen 1 join a
club bei einer AG mitmachen, in
einen Klub eintreten 1
joke [dʒəʊk]:
1. der Witz, der Scherz 2: 2 (61)
2. Witze machen, scherzen 2: 2 (61)
You're joking! Du machst wohl
Witze! 2: 2 (61)
°journal [ˈdʒɜːnl] das Tagebuch; das
Journal (Zeitschrift)
journey [ˈdʒɜːni] die Reise, die Fahrt;
der Weg 1

juggle [ˈdʒʌgl] jonglieren 1
juice [dʒuːs] der Saft 2: 4 (115)
July [dʒuˈlaɪ] der Juli 1
°**jumbled** [ˈdʒʌmbld] durcheinander(geworfen)
jump [dʒʌmp]:
　1. springen 2: 2 (60)
　2. der Sprung, das Hindernis 2: 2 (60)
June [dʒuːn] der Juni 1
just [dʒʌst]:
　1. nur, bloß; einfach 1
　2. gerade (eben) 2: 4 (119)

K

karaoke [kæriˈəʊki] das Karaoke 1
karate [kəˈrɑːti] das Karate 2: 3 (80)
kebab [kɪˈbæb] der Kebab 1
keep [kiːp], **kept, kept:**
　1. halten; behalten; aufbewahren 2: 2 (61)
　°**keep a journal** Tagebuch führen
　2. keep doing sth. etwas dauernd/immer wieder tun 2: 3 (88)
　keep going (immer) weiter gehen 2: 3 (88)
kept [kept] *siehe* **keep**
key [kiː] der Schlüssel; Schlüssel- 2: 3 (88)
keyword [ˈkiːwɜːd] das Stichwort, das Schlagwort 2: 4 (130)
kid [kɪd] das Kind, der/die Jugendliche 1
kill [kɪl] töten 2: 2 (57)
killer [ˈkɪlə] der Mörder, die Mörderin 2: 2 (57)
kilometre (km) [ˈkɪləmiːtə] der Kilometer 1
kind [kaɪnd] freundlich, nett 1
kind (of) [kaɪnd] die Art (von), die Sorte (von) 1
°**kindness** [ˈkaɪndnəs] die Güte, die Freundlichkeit
Kingdom [ˈkɪŋdəm]: **the United Kingdom (the UK)** das Vereinigte Königreich 1
kiosk [ˈkiːɒsk] der Kiosk, die Verkaufsbude, der Verkaufsstand 1
kitchen [ˈkɪtʃɪn] die Küche 1
knew [njuː] *siehe* **know**
knife [naɪf], *pl* **knives** das Messer 1
knit [nɪt] stricken 2: 3 (80)
knives [naɪvz] *Plural von* **knife**
know [nəʊ], **knew, known** wissen; kennen 1 **know sb./sth. by ...** jn./etwas erkennen an ... 2: 2 (57)

L

lab [læb] *siehe* **laboratory**
laboratory [ləˈbɒrətri], *infml auch* **lab** das Labor 1
°**lady** [ˈleɪdi] die Dame 1
lamb [læm] das Lamm(fleisch) 2: 4 (116)
lamp [læmp] die Lampe 1
land [lænd]:
　1. das Land (*Grund und Boden*) 2: 2 (57)
　2. landen 2: 2 (57)

language [ˈlæŋgwɪdʒ] die Sprache 1
large [lɑːdʒ] groß 2: 5 (151)
last [lɑːst] letzte(r, s); als letztes 2: (10/11) **last week** letzte/vorige Woche 2: (10/11) **last week/year/month** letzte/vorige Woche, letztes/voriges Jahr, letzten/vorigen Monat 2: (10/11)
late [leɪt] (zu) spät 1 **I'm late.** Ich habe mich verspätet. 1
later [ˈleɪtə] später 1 **Speak later.** Tschüs./Bis später. 1
laugh [lɑːf]:
　1. das Lachen 2: 2 (48)
　2. laugh (at) lachen (über) 2: 2 (48) **laugh out loud** laut auf-/loslachen 2: 3 (92)
lazy [ˈleɪzi] faul 2: 2 (54)
°**lead** [liːd] führen, leiten
learn [lɜːn] lernen 1
least [liːst]: **at least** wenigstens, zumindest 2: 2 (65) °**your least favourite music** die Musik, die du am wenigsten magst
leave [liːv], **left, left** lassen; zurücklassen 2: 2 (52) **leave sb. alone** jn. allein lassen; jn. in Ruhe lassen 2: 2 (52)
left [left] *siehe* **leave**
left [left] links; nach links 2: 2 (50) **on the left** auf der linken Seite 2: 2 (50) **to the left of ...** links von ... 2: 2 (50)
leg [leg] das Bein 2: 2 (57)
lemon [ˈlemən] die Zitrone 1
lemonade [leməˈneɪd] die Limonade 1
°**Leo** [ˈliːəʊ] der Löwe (*Sternzeichen*)
lesbian [ˈlezbiən]:
　1. lesbisch 2: 1 (18)
　2. die Lesbe 2: 1 (18)
lesson [ˈlesn] die (Unterrichts-)Stunde 1
let's (= let us) [lets] lass(t) uns 1
letter [ˈletə]:
　1. der Brief 1
　2. der Buchstabe 1
level [ˈlevl] der Grad, die Stufe; das Niveau, die Ebene 2: 3 (89)
LGBTQ [el dʒi bi tiː ˈkjuː] LGBTQ 2: 1 (18)
°**Libra** [ˈliːbrə] die Waage (*Sternzeichen*)
library [ˈlaɪbrəri] die Bücherei, die Bibliothek 1
lie [laɪ] liegen 1 **lie down** sich hinlegen 2: 3 (92)
life [laɪf], *pl* **lives** das Leben 2: 2 (52)
°**life skills (pl)** [ˈlaɪf skɪlz] die Alltagskompetenzen, die lebenswichtigen Fertigkeiten
°**lifeguard** [ˈlaɪfgɑːd] der Rettungsschwimmer, die Rettungsschwimmerin; der Bademeister, die Bademeisterin
light [laɪt] das Licht; die Lampe 1 **car light** der Autoscheinwerfer 1
like [laɪk] mögen 1 **I'd (= I would) like ...** Ich hätte gern .../Ich möchte ... 1 **I'd (= I would) like to meet ...** Ich

würde mich gerne mit ... treffen. 1 **Would you like ...?** Möchtest du ...? 1
like [laɪk] wie; wie zum Beispiel 1 **like this** so, auf diese Art 1 **a story like this** so/solch eine Geschichte 1 **It looks like rain.** Es sieht nach Regen aus. 1 **something like that** so etwas 2: 5 (159) **What does it look like?** Wie sieht es aus? 1 **What's ... like?** Wie ist ...?/Wie sieht ... aus? 1
line [laɪn]:
　1. die Reihe 1
　2. die Zeile 1
lingua franca [lɪŋgwə ˈfræŋkə] die Lingua Franca (*Verkehrssprache*) 2: 3 (91)
link [lɪŋk]:
　1. die Verbindung; der Link 2: 1 (30)
　2. link (to/with) verbinden (mit) 2: 1 (30)
lion [ˈlaɪən] der Löwe 1
list [lɪst]:
　1. die Liste 1
　2. (auf)listen 1
listen (to) [ˈlɪsn] zuhören; (sich etwas) anhören 1
little [ˈlɪtl]:
　1. klein 1
　2. a little ein wenig, ein bisschen 1
live [lɪv] leben, wohnen 1
lives [laɪvz] *Plural von* **life**
living room [ˈlɪvɪŋ ruːm] das Wohnzimmer 1
lizard [ˈlɪzəd] die Eidechse 1
lock [lɒk]:
　1. das Schloss (*Türschloss*) 2: 4 (127)
　2. abschließen (*z. B. Tür*) 2: 4 (127) **be locked out** ausgesperrt sein 2: 4 (127)
long [lɒŋ] lang 1 **(for) a long time** lange 1 **work long days** lange arbeiten, lange Arbeitstage haben 1
°**long-legged** [lɒŋ ˈlegɪd] langbeinig, mit langen Beinen
look [lʊk]:
　1. aussehen 1 **It looks like rain.** Es sieht nach Regen aus. 1
　2. sehen, schauen 1 **look after** sich kümmern um; aufpassen auf 1 **look at sth.** sich etwas anschauen 1 **look for** suchen; Ausschau halten nach 2: (10/11) **look forward to doing sth.** sich darauf freuen, etwas zu tun 2: 5 (162) **look forward to sth.** sich auf etwas freuen 2: 5 (162) **look sth. up** etwas nachschlagen, nachschauen 1 °**look out for** Ausschau halten nach, achten auf °**look up** nach oben schauen
　3. der Look, das Aussehen 2: 2 (48) **looks (pl)** das Aussehen 2: 2 (48)
lose [luːz], **lost, lost** verlieren 2: 4 (119)
lost [lɒst] *siehe* **lose Are you lost?** Hast du dich verlaufen/verirrt? 1 **be lost** sich verlaufen/verirrt haben 1 **get lost** sich verlaufen, sich verirren 1

lot [lɒt]:
1. a lot (of) / lots (of) viel/e 1
2. a lot sehr 1

loud [laʊd] laut 1 **laugh out loud** laut auf-/loslachen 2: 3 (92)

loudly [ˈlaʊdli]: **speak loudly** laut sprechen 1

love [lʌv]:
1. der Liebling 1
2. die Liebe 1
3. lieben, sehr mögen 1
I'd (= I would) love … Ich hätte liebend gern … / Ich möchte liebend gern … 1 **I'd (= I would) love to meet …** Ich würde mich liebend gerne mit … treffen. 1

°**luck** [lʌk] das Glück *(glückliche Fügung)* **do sth. for luck** etwas tun, damit es Glück bringt **Good luck.** Viel Glück! 1

luckily [ˈlʌkɪli] glücklicherweise 2: 5 (162)

lucky [ˈlʌki] Glücks-, glücklich 1 **lucky number** die Glückszahl 1 **be lucky** Glück haben 1

lunch [lʌntʃ] das Mittagessen 1 **at lunch** beim Mittagessen 1 **What's for lunch?** Was gibt es zum Mittagessen? 1

lunchtime [ˈlʌntʃtaɪm] die Mittagszeit 1 **at lunchtime** zur Mittagszeit 1

lyrics *(pl)* [ˈlɪrɪks] der Liedtext 2: 3 (85)

M

machine [məˈʃiːn] der Automat, die Maschine 2: 2 (59) **cash machine** der Geldautomat 2: 5 (154) **ticket machine** der Fahrkartenautomat 2: 2 (59)

made [meɪd] *siehe* **make**

mag [mæg] *siehe* **magazine**

magazine [mægəˈziːn], *infml auch* **mag** die Zeitschrift 2: 3 (87)

magic [ˈmædʒɪk]:
1. magisch 1
2. die Zauberei 1
do magic zaubern 1

magic set [ˈmædʒɪk set] der Zauberkasten 1

magic trick [ˈmædʒɪk trɪk] der Zaubertrick 1

main [meɪn] Haupt-, wichtigste(r, s) 1 **main course/dish** das Hauptgericht 1

make [meɪk], **made, made** machen, herstellen 1 **make (money)** (Geld) verdienen 2: 5 (148) **make friends** Freunde/-innen finden 2: 1 (23) **make notes** sich Notizen machen 1 **make sb. do sth.** jn. dazu bringen, etwas zu tun 2: 2 (48) °**I'll make a great …** Ich werde ein/e großartige/r …, / Aus mir wird ein/e großartige/r …

make-up [ˈmeɪk ʌp] das Make-up 2: 1 (18)

man [mæn], *pl* **men** der Mann 1

manage sth. [ˈmænɪdʒ] etwas verwalten, regeln, leiten 2: 5 (148)

manager [ˈmænɪdʒə] der Manager, die Managerin 2: 5 (148)

many [ˈmeni] viele 1 **how many?** wie viele? 1

map [mæp] die Landkarte, der Stadtplan 1

March [mɑːtʃ] der März 1

marina [məˈriːnə] der Jachthafen 1

mark [mɑːk]:
1. die (Schul-)Note, die Zensur 2: 3 (93)
2. die Markierung; das Zeichen 2: 3 (93)
3. kennzeichnen, markieren 2: 3 (93)

market [ˈmɑːkɪt] der Markt 1

married (to) [ˈmærid] verheiratet (mit) 1 **get married (to sb.)** jn. heiraten 2: 2 (53)

marry [ˈmæri] heiraten 1

mask [mɑːsk] die Maske 2: 1 (17)

match [mætʃ]:
1. (passend) zusammenfügen 2: 3 (90)
2. **match to** zuordnen 2: 3 (90)

match [mætʃ] das Spiel, der Wettkampf 1

maths [mæθs] die Mathe(matik) 1

May [meɪ] der Mai 1

may [meɪ] dürfen 2: 4 (117) **May I …?** Darf ich …? 2: 4 (117)

maybe [ˈmeɪbi] vielleicht 1

me [miː] mich; mir 1 **Me, too.** Ich auch. 1 **It's me.** Ich bin's. 1 **Not me!** Ich nicht! (= Ich bin/war/habe/… es/das nicht!) 1

meal [miːl] die Mahlzeit, das Essen 1 **hot meal** die warme Mahlzeit 1

mean [miːn] gemein, fies 1

mean [miːn], **meant, meant** bedeuten; sagen wollen 1

meaning [ˈmiːnɪŋ] die Bedeutung 1

meat [miːt] das Fleisch 1

mechanic [mɪˈkænɪk] der Mechaniker, die Mechanikerin 2: 5 (144)

media *(pl)* [ˈmiːdiə] die Medien 2: 3 (91) **social media** soziale Medien 2: 3 (91)

°**mediation** [miːdiˈeɪʃn] die Vermittlung, die Sprachmittlung

medium [ˈmiːdiəm] medium *(Kleidergröße: mittelgroß/M)* 2: 5 (157)

meet [miːt], **met, met** kennenlernen; (sich) treffen 1 **Nice to meet you.** Freut mich, dich/euch/Sie kennenzulernen. 1

meeting [ˈmiːtɪŋ] das Meeting *(Treffen, Zusammenkunft)* 2: 3 (92)

melon [ˈmelən] die Melone 1

member [ˈmembə] das Mitglied 2: 4 (122)

men [men] *Plural von* **man**

menu [ˈmenjuː] die Speisekarte 1

°**meow** [miˈaʊ] miau

mess [mes] das Chaos, die Unordnung 1

message [ˈmesɪdʒ]:
1. die Botschaft, die Aussage 1
2. die Nachricht, die Mitteilung 1
°**message in a bottle** die Flaschenpost
3. **message (sb.)** (sb.) (jm.) Nachrichten schicken, Nachrichten austauschen (mit jm.) 1

messy [ˈmesi] unordentlich 1

met [met] *siehe* **meet**

metal [ˈmetl]:
1. das Metall 2: 2 (57)
2. Metall-, aus Metall 2: 2 (57)

metre [ˈmiːtə] der Meter 1

mice [maɪs] *Plural von* **mouse**

middle [ˈmɪdl] die Mitte 2: 1 (30) **in the middle (of)** in der Mitte (von) 2: 1 (30)

midnight [ˈmɪdnaɪt] die Mitternacht 1

mile [maɪl] die Meile *(ca. 1,6 km)* 1

miles per hour (mph) [maɪlz pər ˈaʊə] Meilen pro Stunde 1 **at 30 miles per hour** mit 30 Meilen pro Stunde 1

milk [mɪlk] die Milch 1

millilitre (ml) [ˈmɪlilitə] der Milliliter 1

°**mime** [maɪm] vorspielen, pantomimisch darstellen

mind [maɪnd]: **I don't mind doing sth.** Es macht mir nichts aus, etwas zu tun. 2: 5 (152)

°**mind** [maɪnd]: **make your mind up** sich entscheiden, sich entschließen

mind map [ˈmaɪnd mæp] die Gedankenkarte, das Wörternetz, die Mindmap 1

mini [ˈmɪni] Mini- 1

mini-drone [mɪni ˈdrəʊn] die Minidrohne 1

minute [ˈmɪnɪt] die Minute 1 **Wait a minute.** Warte mal. / Einen Moment. 2: (10/11)

mirror [ˈmɪrə] der Spiegel 1

miss [mɪs]:
1. vermissen 2: 5 (158)
2. verpassen 2: 5 (158)
3. versäumen, auslassen 2: 5 (158)

missing [ˈmɪsɪŋ] vermisst 1

mistake [mɪˈsteɪk] der Fehler 2: 1 (31) **by mistake** aus Versehen 2: 1 (31)

mix [mɪks] (ver)mischen 1

mixture [ˈmɪkstʃə] die Mischung 1

mobile phone [məʊbaɪl ˈfəʊn] das Handy, das Telefon 1

modern [ˈmɒdn] modern 1

moment [ˈməʊmənt] der Moment 1 **at the moment** im Moment, zurzeit 1 **have a moment in the sun** kurz im Mittelpunkt stehen 1

Monday [ˈmʌndeɪ], [ˈmʌndi] der Montag 1

money [ˈmʌni] das Geld 1 **pocket money** das Taschengeld 2: 4 (127)

monkey [ˈmʌŋki] der Affe 1

month [mʌnθ] der Monat 1

moon [muːn] der Mond 2: 2 (50) **be over the moon** *(infml)* ganz aus dem Häuschen sein (= hocherfreut sein) 2: 2 (50)

more [mɔː] mehr, weitere 1 **three more** noch drei, drei weitere 1

morning [ˈmɔːnɪŋ] der Morgen 1 **in the morning** morgens, am Morgen 1

mosque [mɒsk] die Moschee 2: 4 (115)

most [məʊst] die meisten, am meisten 1 **most schools** die meisten Schulen 1

mother [ˈmʌðə] die Mutter 2: 1 (14)

motto [ˈmɒtəʊ] das Motto 2: 1 (25)

mountain [ˈmaʊntən] der Berg 2: 1 (12/13)

mouse [maʊs], *pl* **mice** die Maus 1

move [muːv]:
1. (sich) bewegen 1
2. **move (to)** (um)ziehen (nach) 2: 5 (159)

Mr Lee [ˈmɪstə] Herr Lee 1

Mrs Lee [ˈmɪsɪz] Frau Lee *(Anrede für verheiratete Frauen)* 1

Ms Lee [mɪz] Frau Lee 1

much [mʌtʃ] viel; sehr 1 **How much is/are …?** Was (Wie viel) kostet/kosten …? 2: 5 (156) **Thank you very much.** Vielen Dank. / Danke vielmals. 1 **too much of a good thing** zu viel des Guten 2: 3 (92)

multicultural [mʌltiˈkʌltʃərəl] multikulturell 2: 4 (128)

mum [mʌm] die Mama, die Mutti 1

museum [mjuˈziːəm] das Museum 1

music [ˈmjuːzɪk] die Musik 1 **classical music** klassische Musik 2: 3 (84)

musical [ˈmjuːzɪkl]:
1. das Musical 2: 3 (78/79)
2. musikalisch, Musik- 2: 3 (78/79)

musician [mjuˈzɪʃn] der Musiker, die Musikerin 2: 1 (20)

Muslim [ˈmʊzlɪm]:
1. muslimisch 2: 4 (114)
2. Muslim/Muslima 2: 4 (114) **a practising Muslim** ein/e praktizierende/r Muslim/a *(gläubig)* 2: 4 (114)

must [mʌst] müssen 1 **I must go.** Ich muss Schluss machen. *(am Telefon/Briefschluss)* 1

mustn't do [ˈmʌsnt] nicht tun dürfen 2: 5 (154)

my [maɪ] mein/e 1

N

name [neɪm] der Name 1 **first name** der Vorname 1 **What's your name?** Wie heißt du? 1

name day [ˈneɪm deɪ] der Namenstag 2: 4 (124)

national [ˈnæʃnəl] national 2: 3 (91)

°**nature** [ˈneɪtʃə] die Natur 1

°**nature reserve** [ˈneɪtʃə rɪzɜːv] das Naturschutzgebiet 1

near [nɪə] nahe (bei), in der Nähe von 1

nearly [ˈnɪəli] fast 2: 1 (26)

neck [nek] der Hals, der Nacken 2: 2 (61)

need [niːd] brauchen 1 **need to do sth.** etwas tun müssen 1

negative [ˈnegətɪv] negativ 2: 2 (55)

neighbour [ˈneɪbə] der Nachbar, die Nachbarin 1

neighbourhood [ˈneɪbəhʊd] die Nachbarschaft, die Gegend, das Viertel 1

nephew [ˈnefjuː] der Neffe 2: 4 (125)

nest [nest] das Nest 2: 5 (152)

never [ˈnevə] nie, niemals 1

new [njuː] neu 1

news [njuːz] die Nachrichten 1

newsagent [ˈnjuːzeɪdʒənt] der Zeitungshändler, die Zeitungshändlerin 2: 5 (155)

newsagent's [ˈnjuːzeɪdʒənts] der Zeitschriftenladen, der Zeitungskiosk 2: 5 (155)

newspaper [ˈnjuːspeɪpə] die (Tages-)Zeitung 1

next [nekst]:
1. nächste(r, s) 1
the next day am nächsten Tag 1
2. **Next …** Als Nächstes … 1

next to [ˈnekst tə] neben 1

nice [naɪs] nett, schön 1 **Nice to meet you.** Freut mich, dich/euch/Sie kennenzulernen. 1

niece [niːs] die Nichte 2: 4 (125)

Nigeria [naɪˈdʒɪəriə] Nigeria 1

Nigerian [naɪˈdʒɪəriən]:
1. nigerianisch 1
2. der Nigerianer, die Nigerianerin 1

night [naɪt] die Nacht 1 **at night** nachts, in der Nacht 1

nine [naɪn] neun 1

nineteen [naɪnˈtiːn] neunzehn 1

ninety [ˈnaɪnti] neunzig 1

no [nəʊ]:
1. nein 1
2. kein, keine; verboten 1

no one [ˈnəʊ wʌn] niemand 2: 2 (50)

nobody [ˈnəʊbədi] niemand 2: 2 (50)

noise [nɔɪz] das Geräusch; der Lärm 1

noodles *(pl)* [ˈnuːdlz] die Nudeln 1

noon [nuːn] der Mittag; 12 Uhr mittags 1

normal [ˈnɔːml] normal 2: 2 (57)

north [nɔːθ] der Norden; nördlich; Nord- 1

nose [nəʊz] die Nase 2: 2 (57)

not [nɒt] nicht 1 **I'm not a boy.** Ich bin kein Junge. 1

note [nəʊt] die Notiz; der kurze Brief 1 **make notes** (sich) Notizen machen *(zur Vorbereitung)* 1 **take notes** (sich) Notizen machen *(beim Lesen oder Zuhören)* 2: 2 (55)

nothing [ˈnʌθɪŋ] nichts 2: 4 (123)

notice [ˈnəʊtɪs]:
1. (be)merken 1
2. der Anschlag, die Bekanntmachung *(an einem Schwarzen Brett)* 1

November [nəʊˈvembə] der November 1

now [naʊ] nun, jetzt 1

nowhere [ˈnəʊweə] nirgendwo(hin) 2: 3 (83)

number [ˈnʌmbə]:
1. die Anzahl 2: 5 (151)
2. die Zahl, die Ziffer, die Nummer 1

nurse [nɜːs] der Krankenpfleger, die Krankenpflegerin 2: 2 (55)

O

object [ˈɒbdʒɪkt] das Objekt, der Gegenstand 2: 1 (31)

o'clock [əˈklɒk]: **at 8 o'clock** um 8 Uhr 1

October [ɒkˈtəʊbə] der Oktober 1

°**odd word (out)** [ɒd wɜːd ˈaʊt] das Wort, das nicht zu den anderen passt 1

of [ɒv], [əv] von 1 **a glass of milk** ein Glas Milch 1 **bags of rubbish** Tüten/Säcke (mit/voller) Müll 1 **the first of April (1st April)** der erste April 1

of course [əv ˈkɔːs] natürlich, selbstverständlich 1

off [ɒf]:
1. weg von; hinunter von 2: 2 (53) **come off (sth.)** abgehen (von etwas), (herunter)fallen (von etwas), sich lösen (von etwas) 2: 2 (53) **fall off** herunterfallen 2: 2 (53) **get off (a train/bus)** aussteigen (aus einem Zug/Bus) 2: 1 (26) **get off your bike/your horse** vom Fahrrad / vom Pferd absteigen 2: 2 (53)
2. **be off** aus sein *(ausgeschaltet sein)* 2: 3 (78/79)

office [ˈɒfɪs] das Büro 1

officer [ˈɒfɪsə] der Beamte, die Beamtin 2: 5 (146)

often [ˈɒfn], [ˈɒftən] oft 1

oh [əʊ] Null *(im gesprochenen Englisch)* 1

oil [ɔɪl] das Öl 1

OK [əʊˈkeɪ]: **I'm OK.** Es geht mir gut. 1 **That's OK.** Schon gut. / Kein Problem. 1

old [əʊld] alt 1 **How old are you?** Wie alt bist du? 1

on [ɒn]:
1. auf 1
on holiday im/in den Urlaub 1 **on Monday** am Montag 1 **on Mondays** an jedem Montag, montags 1 **on my birthday** an meinem Geburtstag 1 **on the beach** am Strand 1 **on the bus** im Bus 1 **on the field** auf dem Spielfeld, auf dem Platz 1 **on the phone** am Telefon 1 **get on (a train/bus)** einsteigen (in einen Zug/Bus) 2: 1 (26)
2. **be on** gezeigt werden, „laufen" *(Kino, Fernsehen)*, stattfinden; an sein (eingeschaltet sein) 2: 3 (78/79) **What's on?** Was läuft? / Was findet statt? *(Kino, Theater)* 2: 3 (78/79)

once [wʌns] einmal; einst 2: 1 (26)

one [wʌn]:
1. eins 1
one way eine Strecke (= ohne Rückfahrt/Rückflug) 2: 1 (19) **one-way ticket** die einfache Fahrkarte (= ohne Rückfahrt) 2: 1 (19)
2. **the last one** der/die/das Letzte 2: 3 (85)

onion [ˈʌnjən] die Zwiebel 1

online [ɒnˈlaɪn] online, Online- 1

only [ˈəʊnli]:
1. nur, bloß 1
2. erst 1

onto the platform [ˈɒntu], [ˈɒntə] auf den Bahnsteig 2: 1 (26)

open [ˈəʊpən]:
1. öffnen; aufschlagen *(Buch)* 1
2. offen, geöffnet 1

opinion (of) [əˈpɪnjən] die Meinung (zu/bezüglich) 1 **in my opinion** meiner Meinung nach 1

opposite [ˈɒpəzɪt]:
1. das Gegenteil 2: 2 (54)
2. gegensätzlich, entgegengesetzt 2: 2 (54)
3. gegenüber (von) 2: 2 (54)

or [ɔː] oder; sonst 1

orange [ˈɒrɪndʒ]:
1. orange(farben) 1
2. die Orange 1

order [ˈɔːdə] die Reihenfolge 2: 4 (131) **in order** in eine(r) Reihenfolge 2: 4 (131) **put in the right order** in die richtige Reihenfolge bringen 2: 4 (131)

organization [ɔːɡənaɪˈzeɪʃn] die Organisation 2: 4 (126)

organize [ˈɔːɡənaɪz] organisieren · 2: 4 (127) **(well) organized** (gut) organisiert 2: 4 (127)

other [ˈʌðə] andere(r, s) 1 **each other** einander, sich (gegenseitig) 2: 4 (115) **the others** die anderen 1

our [ˈaʊə] unser/e 1

out (of ...) [aʊt]: **out** heraus, hinaus, nach draußen 2: 1 (16) **out of ...** aus ... (heraus/hinaus) 2: 1 (26) **put your hands out** die Hände ausstrecken 2: 1 (17)

outside [aʊtˈsaɪd]:
1. draußen; nach draußen 1
2. außerhalb (von) 1

oven [ˈʌvn] der Backofen 1

over [ˈəʊvə]:
1. über; mehr als 1 **over here** hier herüber; hier drüben 1 **over there** da drüben, dort drüben 1 **all over the world** überall auf der Welt, auf der ganzen Welt 2: 3 (91)
°**be over** vorbei sein, zu Ende sein
°**2.** hinüber, herüber
°**come / walk over** hinüberkommen/ -gehen, rüberkommen/-gehen

own [əʊn]: **your own room** dein/ein eigenes Zimmer 1

P

packet [ˈpækɪt] die Packung, das Päckchen 1

page (= p.) [peɪdʒ] die (Buch-/Heft-) Seite 1

paid [peɪd] *siehe* pay

paint [peɪnt]:
1. die Farbe, der Lack 2: 5 (155)
2. (an)malen; lackieren, (an)streichen 2: 5 (155)

pair [peə] das Paar 2: 1 (23)

palace [ˈpæləs] der Palast, das Schloss 1

pancake [ˈpænkeɪk] der Pfannkuchen 2: 4 (117)

°**panic** [ˈpænɪk] in Panik geraten **Don't panic.** Keine Panik. / Immer mit der Ruhe.

°**pantomime** [ˈpæntəmaɪm], *kurz auch* **panto** [ˈpæntəʊ] *das lustige, traditionelle, meist zu Weihnachten aufgeführte Theaterstück, besonders für Kinder* 2: 3 (78)

paper [ˈpeɪpə]:
1. die (Tages-)Zeitung 1
2. das Papier 1
piece of paper das Stück Papier, der Zettel 1

parade [pəˈreɪd] die Parade, der Umzug 2: 1 (18)

°**paragraph** [ˈpærəɡrɑːf] der (Text-) Abschnitt

parents *(pl)* [ˈpeərənts] die Eltern 1

park [pɑːk] der Park 1

parkour [pɑːˈkʊə] der Parkour *(akrobatischer Hindernislauf in der Stadt)* 1

parrot [ˈpærət] der Papagei 1

part (of) [pɑːt] der Teil (von) 1

partner [ˈpɑːtnə] der Partner, die Partnerin 1

party [ˈpɑːti] die Party 1

passive [ˈpæsɪv] passiv 1

°**passport** [ˈpɑːspɔːt] der (Reise-)Pass

past [pɑːst]:
1. die Vergangenheit 2: 1 (17)
2. vergangene(r, s) 2: 1 (17)

past [pɑːst]:
1. nach *(bei Uhrzeitangaben)* 2: 3 (90) **half past 6** halb 7 2: 3 (90)
2. vorbei an, vorüber an 2: 3 (88)

pasta [ˈpæstə] die Pasta *(italienische Bezeichnung für Teigwaren)* 1

patience [ˈpeɪʃns] die Geduld 2: 2 (48)

patient [ˈpeɪʃnt] geduldig 2: 2 (48)

pay (for sth.) [peɪ], **paid, paid** zahlen; (etwas) bezahlen 1 **pay (in) cash** bar bezahlen 2: 5 (154) **pay attention (to)** aufpassen (auf), aufmerksam sein; Beachtung schenken, zuhören 2: 3 (97) **pay by card** mit Karte (be) zahlen *(z. B. Bankkarte)* 2: 5 (154)

PE (= physical education) [piː ˈiː] der (Schul-)Sport 1

pea [piː] die Erbse 1

peace [piːs] der Frieden 2: 2 (59)

pen [pen] der Kugelschreiber, der Stift; der Füller 1

pence [pens] *Plural von* **penny**

pencil [ˈpensl] der Bleistift 1

pencil case [ˈpensl keɪs] das Federmäppchen 1

pencil sharpener [ˈpensl ʃɑːpnə] der Bleistift(an)spitzer 1

penny (p) [ˈpeni], *pl* **pence** der Penny *(kleinste britische Münze)* 1

people *(pl)* [ˈpiːpl] die Leute, die Menschen 1

pepper [ˈpepə]:
1. der Pfeffer 1
2. die Paprika, die Peperoni 1

per [pɜː], [pə] pro 1 **miles per hour (mph)** Meilen pro Stunde 1

per cent (%) [pə ˈsent] das Prozent 2: 5 (154)

perfect [ˈpɜːfɪkt] perfekt 1

perfectly (still) [ˈpɜːfɪktli] ganz/völlig (still) 1

person [ˈpɜːsn] die Person 1

personal [ˈpɜːsənl] persönlich 2: 2 (48)

personality [pɜːsəˈnæləti] die Persönlichkeit; der Charakter 2: 2 (48)

pet [pet] das (Haus-)Tier 1

philosophy [fəˈlɒsəfi] die Philosophie 2: 2 (59)

phone [fəʊn]:
1. anrufen; telefonieren 1
2. das Handy, das Telefon 1
by phone per Telefon / telefonisch 1 **on the phone** am Telefon 1

phone call [ˈfəʊn kɔːl] der (Telefon-) Anruf 1

phone number [ˈfəʊn nʌmbə] die Telefonnummer 1

photo [ˈfəʊtəʊ] das Foto 1 **in the photo** auf dem Foto 1 **take photos** Fotos machen 1

photograph [ˈfəʊtəɡrɑːf]:
1. das Foto 2: 3 (80)
2. fotografieren 2: 3 (80)

photographer [fəˈtɒɡrəfə] der Fotograf, die Fotografin 1

photography [fəˈtɒɡrəfi] die Fotografie *(Hobby)*, das Fotografieren 2: 3 (80)

phrase [freɪz] der Ausdruck, die (Rede-)Wendung 1

physical education (PE) [fɪzɪkl edʒuˈkeɪʃn] der (Schul-)Sport 1

piano [piˈænəʊ] das Klavier 2: 1 (21) **play the piano** Klavier spielen 2: 1 (21)

pick [pɪk] pflücken; (aus)wählen, aussuchen 2: 1 (23) **pick sth. up** etwas aufheben *(vom Boden)*, etwas hochheben 2: 1 (23)

picker [ˈpɪkə] die Greifzange *(z. B. für Müll)*; der Pflücker, die Pflückerin 2: 1 (23)

picnic [ˈpɪknɪk] das Picknick 1 **have a picnic** ein Picknick machen 1

picture [ˈpɪktʃə] das Bild 1

pie chart [ˈpaɪ tʃɑːt] das Tortendiagramm 2: 5 (151)

piece [piːs] das Stück, der/das Teil 1 **piece of paper** das Stück Papier 1

pier [pɪə] der Pier, die Seebrücke 1

pig [pɪɡ] das Schwein 2: 4 (116)

piggy bank [ˈpɪɡi bæŋk] das Sparschwein 2: 5 (154)

pink [pɪŋk] rosa 1

°**Pisces** [ˈpaɪsiːz] die Fische *(Sternzeichen)*

pizza [ˈpiːtsə] die Pizza 2: 1 (15)

place [pleɪs] der Ort, der Platz 1 **at/in a place** an einem Ort 2: 3 (80) **in this place** an diesem Ort 1 **take place** stattfinden 2: 3 (80)

plan [plæn]:
1. der Plan 1
2. planen 1
plan to do sth. planen, etwas zu tun 1

plane [pleɪn] das Flugzeug 2: 1 (15)

planet [ˈplænɪt] der Planet 2: 2 (57)

plastic [ˈplæstɪk] das Plastik, der Kunststoff 2: 1 (23)

platform [ˈplætfɔːm] der Bahnsteig 2: 1 (18) **at platform 4** auf Gleis 4 2: 1 (18)

play [pleɪ] spielen 1 **play the piano** Klavier spielen 2: 1 (21)

player [ˈpleɪə] der Spieler, die Spielerin 1

playground [ˈpleɪɡraʊnd] der Schulhof; der Spielplatz 1

playing card [ˈpleɪɪŋ kɑːd] die Spielkarte 1

playlist [ˈpleɪlɪst] die Playlist 1

please [pliːz] bitte 1

p.m. [piːˈem]: **4 p.m.** 4 Uhr nachmittags, 16 Uhr 1 **9 p.m.** 9 Uhr abends, 21 Uhr 1

pocket [ˈpɒkɪt] die Tasche *(an Kleidungsstücken)* 2: 4 (127)

pocket money [ˈpɒkɪt mʌni] das Taschengeld 2: 4 (127)

podcast [ˈpɒdkɑːst] der Podcast *(Audiodatei zum Herunterladen aus dem Internet)* 2: 1 (15)

°**poem** [ˈpəʊɪm] das Gedicht 1

point [pɔɪnt]:
1. der Punkt 1
2. das Komma *(Dezimalzeichen)* 1
1.6 (one point six) 1,6 (eins Komma sechs) 1

°**point (at/to)** [pɔɪnt] zeigen, deuten (auf)

police *(pl)* [pəˈliːs] die Polizei 2: 2 (57)

police officer [pəˈliːs ɒfɪsə] der Polizeibeamte, die Polizeibeamtin 2: 5 (146)

polite [pəˈlaɪt] höflich 1

°**pond** [pɒnd] der Teich 1

pool [puːl] das Pool(billiard) 1

poor [pɔː], [pʊə] arm 2: 4 (120) **Poor George!** Der arme George! / Armer George! 2: 4 (120)

pop (music) [ˈpɒp mjuːzɪk] der Pop, die Popmusik 1

popcorn [ˈpɒpkɔːn] das Popcorn 1

popular [ˈpɒpjələ] beliebt, populär 1

pork [pɔːk] das Schweinefleisch 2: 4 (116)

positive [ˈpɒzətɪv] positiv 2: 2 (55)

°**possible** [ˈpɒsəbl] möglich 1

post [pəʊst]:
1. der Post *(Teil eines Blogs)* 1
2. posten *(im Internet veröffentlichen)* 1

postcard [ˈpəʊstkɑːd] die Postkarte 2: 5 (157)

poster [ˈpəʊstə] das Poster 1

pot [pɒt] der Topf; die Kanne *(z. B. Tee-, Kaffeekanne)* 2: 4 (115)

potato [pəˈteɪtəʊ], *pl* **potatoes** die Kartoffel 1

pound (£) [paʊnd] das Pfund *(britische Währung)* 1

powder [ˈpaʊdə] das Pulver 1

power [ˈpaʊə] die Kraft, die Macht, die Energie; der (elektrische) Strom 2: 2 (56)

practical [ˈpræktɪkl] praktisch 2: 5 (163) **play a practical joke on sb.** jm. einen Streich spielen 2: 5 (163)

practice [ˈpræktɪs] die Übung(en) 1

practise [ˈpræktɪs] üben 1 **a practising doctor** ein/e praktizierende/r Arzt/Ärztin *(seinen/ihren Beruf ausübend)* 2: 4 (114) **a practising Muslim** ein/e praktizierende/r Muslim/a *(gläubig)* 2: 4 (114)

pray [preɪ] beten 2: 4 (114)

prayer [preə] das Gebet 2: 4 (114)

prediction [prɪˈdɪkʃn] die Vorhersage, die Voraussage 2: 5 (148)

preheat (the oven to …) [priːˈhiːt] (den Backofen) vorheizen (auf) 1

preparation [prepəˈreɪʃn] die Vorbereitung; die Zubereitung 2: 3 (80)

prepare (for) [prɪˈpeə] vorbereiten, zubereiten; sich vorbereiten (auf) 2: 3 (80)

present [ˈpreznt] das Geschenk 1

°**present** [ˈpreznt] die Gegenwart 1

present sth. (to sb.) [prɪˈzent] (jm.) etwas präsentieren, vorstellen 1

presentation [preznˈteɪʃn] das Referat, die Präsentation 1 **give a presentation** ein Referat halten 1

presenter [prɪˈzentə] der Moderator, die Moderatorin 2: 2 (65)

°**pretty** [ˈprɪti] hübsch

price [praɪs] der (Kauf-)Preis 2: 5 (157)

pride [praɪd] der Stolz 2: 1 (18)

prize [praɪz] der Preis, der Gewinn 1

prize ceremony [ˈpraɪz serəməni] die Preisverleihung 2: 4 (131)

probably [ˈprɒbəbli] wahrscheinlich 2: 3 (91)

problem [ˈprɒbləm] das Problem 1

professional [prəˈfeʃnl]:
1. professionell, Profi- 2: 3 (80)
2. *infml auch* **pro** der Fachmann, die Fachfrau, der Profi 2: 3 (80)

program [ˈprəʊɡræm]:
1. das (Computer-)Programm 2: 2 (59)
2. programmieren 2: 2 (59)

programme [ˈprəʊɡræm] das (Fernseh-)Programm, die Sendung 2: 2 (59)

programmer [ˈprəʊɡræmə] der Programmierer, die Programmiererin 2: 2 (59)

project [ˈprɒdʒekt] das Projekt 1

promise [ˈprɒmɪs]:
1. versprechen 2: 2 (62)
2. das Versprechen 2: 2 (62)
keep a promise ein Versprechen halten 2: 2 (62)

pronounce [prəˈnaʊns] aussprechen 2: 5 (163)

pronunciation [prənʌnsiˈeɪʃn] die Aussprache 2: 5 (163)

°**prop** [prɒp] die Requisite 1

protect (from/against) [prəˈtekt] (be)schützen (vor) 2: 2 (58)

proud (of) [praʊd] stolz (auf) 2: 1 (18)

purple [ˈpɜːpl] violett, lila 1

put [pʊt], **put, put** *(etwas wohin)* tun, legen, stellen, stecken 1 **put in the right order** in die richtige Reihenfolge bringen 2: 4 (131) **put sth. on** etwas anziehen *(Kleidung)*, aufsetzen *(z. B. Hut, Brille)* 2: 4 (126) **put sth. up** etwas aufhängen *(an der Wand)* 1 **put your hand up / put up your hand** sich melden, aufzeigen 1 **put your hands out** die Hände ausstrecken 2: 1 (17)

puzzle [ˈpʌzl] das Rätsel 1

puzzled [ˈpʌzld] verwundert 2: 3 (93)

Q

quarter [ˈkwɔːtə] das Viertel 2: 3 (90) **quarter to 3** viertel vor 3 2: 3 (90)

queen [kwiːn] die Königin 2: 2 (59)

queer [kwɪə] queer *(= durch den Ausdruck der sexuellen Orientierung oder geschlechtlichen Identität von der gesellschaftlichen Norm abweichend)* 2: 1 (18)

question [ˈkwestʃən] die Frage 1 **ask a question** eine Frage stellen 1

quiet [ˈkwaɪət] ruhig, still, leise 1

quite [kwaɪt] ziemlich, ganz 1

quiz [kwɪz], *pl* **quizzes** das Quiz, das Ratespiel; der Test 1 **do a quiz** ein Quiz / ein Ratespiel / einen Test machen 1

quizzes [ˈkwɪzɪz] *Plural von* quiz

R

rabbit [ˈræbɪt] das Kaninchen 1

rain [reɪn]:
1. der Regen 1
come rain or shine bei jedem Wetter; was auch (immer) geschieht 1
2. regnen 1
rain cats and dogs stark regnen 1

rain jacket [ˈreɪn dʒækɪt] die Regenjacke 2: 4 (128)

rainbow [ˈreɪnbəʊ] der Regenbogen 2: 1 (20)

rainy [ˈreɪni] regnerisch 1

Ramadan [ˈræmədæn] der Ramadan *(Fastenmonat im Islam)* 2: 4 (114)

ran [ræn] *siehe* run

rap [ræp]:
1. der Rap 2: 3 (84)
2. rappen 2: 3 (84)

rare [reə] selten *(Adj.)* 1

rarely [ˈreəli] selten *(Adv.)* 1

rate sth. [reɪt] bewerten, beurteilen, einstufen 2: 3 (86)

rating [ˈreɪtɪŋ] die Bewertung, die Beurteilung 2: 3 (86)

ravioli [ræviˈəʊli] die Ravioli 2: 4 (117)

°**reaction (to)** [riˈækʃn] die Reaktion (auf)

read [red] *siehe* read

read [riːd], **read, read** lesen 1

reader [ˈriːdə] der Leser, die Leserin 1

ready [ˈredi] fertig, bereit 1 **get ready (for)** sich fertig machen (für), sich vorbereiten (auf) 2: 4 (120)

real [rɪəl] echt, wirklich 2: 3 (88)

really [ˈriːəli], [ˈrɪəli] wirklich 1

reason [ˈriːzn] der Grund, die Begründung 1 **for this reason** aus diesem Grund 1

receipt [rɪˈsiːt] der (Kauf-)Beleg, die Quittung, der Kassenzettel 2: 5 (156)

recipe [ˈresəpi] das (Koch-)Rezept 1

recipe book [ˈresəpi bʊk] das Kochbuch 1

record [rɪˈkɔːd] aufnehmen, aufzeichnen 1

recording [rɪˈkɔːdɪŋ] die Aufnahme (Ton-, Bild-) 2: 1 (31)

red [red] rot 1

registration [redʒɪˈstreɪʃn] die Anwesenheitskontrolle und Ankündigung aktueller Ereignisse vor dem Unterricht 1

relax [rɪˈlæks] sich entspannen 2: 1 (17)

reliable [rɪˈlaɪəbl] verlässlich, zuverlässig 2: 2 (48)

religion [rɪˈlɪdʒən] die Religion 1

religious [rɪˈlɪdʒəs] religiös 1

remember [rɪˈmembə]:
1. daran denken, nicht vergessen 1
remember to do sth. daran denken, etwas zu tun 1
2. sich erinnern an 1
remember doing sth. sich daran erinnern, etwas getan zu haben 1

repeat [rɪˈpiːt] wiederholen 2: 5 (160)

report [rɪˈpɔːt]:
1. der Bericht 2: 2 (51)
2. **report (on)** berichten (über) 2: 2 (51)

research [rɪˈsɜːtʃ]:
1. erforschen, untersuchen, recherchieren 1
2. die Forschung(en), die Recherche(n) 1
do research recherchieren 1

°**reserve** [rɪˈzɜːv] das Schutzgebiet

respect [rɪˈspekt]:
1. respektieren, achten 2: 4 (116)
2. **respect (for)** der Respekt (vor) 2: 4 (116)

rest [rest]:
1. ruhen; sich ausruhen 1
2. die Ruhe, die Pause, die Erholung 1
take a rest Pause machen 1
3. der Rest 2: 1 (18)

restaurant [ˈrestrɒnt] das Restaurant 1

°**result** [rɪˈzʌlt] das Ergebnis

return [rɪˈtɜːn]:
1. zurückkehren, zurückkommen 2: 1 (19)
2. die Rückkehr 2: 1 (19)
3. **return ticket** (kurz auch: return) (Hin- und) Rückfahrkarte 2: 1 (19)

°**review** [rɪˈvjuː] der Bericht, die Rezension (kritische Besprechung)

°**revision** [rɪˈvɪʒn] die Wiederholung (von Lernstoff)

°**rewrite** [riːˈraɪt], **rewrote, rewritten** neu schreiben, umschreiben

°**rhyme** [raɪm] (sich) reimen

°**rhythm** [ˈrɪðəm] der Rhythmus

rice [raɪs] der Reis 1

ridden [ˈrɪdn] siehe **ride**

ride [raɪd], **rode, ridden: ride (a horse)** reiten 1 **ride a bike** mit dem Fahrrad fahren 1

right [raɪt]:
1. richtig 1
be right Recht haben 1
2. Recht 2: 2 (59)

right [raɪt] rechts; nach rechts 2: 2 (50) **on the right** rechts, auf der rechten Seite 2: 2 (50) **to the right of ...** rechts von ... 2: 2 (50)

°**right here** [raɪt ˈhɪə] genau hier

ring [rɪŋ] der Ring 1 **wedding ring** der Ehering 1

river [ˈrɪvə] der Fluss 2: 1 (15)

robot [ˈrəʊbɒt] der Roboter 1

rock [rɒk] der Rock (die Rockmusik) 2: 1 (21)

rode [rəʊd] siehe **ride**

role [rəʊl] die Rolle (Film, Theater) 2: 3 (80)

role-play [ˈrəʊlpleɪ]:
1. das Rollenspiel 2: 3 (80)
2. **role-play sth.** etwas in einem Rollenspiel darstellen 2: 3 (80)

roll (out) [rəʊl] rollen; ausrollen (Teig) 1

romantic [rəʊˈmæntɪk] romantisch 2: 4 (118)

room [ruːm] der Raum, das Zimmer 1

round [raʊnd]:
1. rund 1
2. die Runde 1
3. **round ...** um (... herum), in ... umher 1
all round the globe auf der ganzen Welt 2: 4 (128) **come round (to)** vorbeikommen, vorbeischauen (bei) 2: 3 (93)

row [rəʊ] die Reihe, die (Häuser-)Zeile 2: 3 (89)

°**RSVP** [ɑːr es viː ˈpi] u.A.w.g. (um Antwort wird gebeten)

rubber [ˈrʌbə] das Radiergummi 1

rubbish [ˈrʌbɪʃ] der (Haus-)Müll, der Abfall 1

rucksack [ˈrʌksæk] der Rucksack 1

°**rude** [ruːd] unhöflich, frech 1

°**rule** [ruːl] herrschen (über)

rule [ruːl] die Regel 2: 3 (92)

ruler [ˈruːlə] das Lineal 1

run [rʌn]:
1. der Lauf, das Rennen 2: 3 (97)
fun run der Volkslauf (z. B. zum Geldsammeln für wohltätige Zwecke) 2: 3 (97)
2. **run, ran, run** rennen, laufen 1

running [ˈrʌnɪŋ] das Laufen (Sport) 1

Russia [ˈrʌʃə] Russland 1

Russian [ˈrʌʃn]:
1. russisch, Russisch 1
2. der Russe, die Russin 1

S

sad [sæd] traurig 1

safe [seɪf] sicher (gefahrlos) 2: 1 (23)

safety [ˈseɪfti] die Sicherheit 2: 1 (23)

°**Sagittarius** [sædʒɪˈteəriəs] der Schütze (Sternzeichen)

said [sed] siehe **say**

°**sailor** [ˈseɪlə] der Seemann, die Seemännin / der Matrose, die Matrosin

salad [ˈsæləd] der Salat (als Gericht oder Beilage) 1

salt [sɔːlt] das Salz 1

same [seɪm]: **the same** gleich; derselbe/dieselbe/dasselbe; dieselben 1

sandwich [ˈsænwɪtʃ], [ˈsænwɪdʒ] das Sandwich 1

sang [sæŋ] siehe **sing**

°**sangeet** [sʌnˈgiːt] das Sangeet (eine traditionelle vorhochzeitliche Zeremonie in Indien)

sari [ˈsɑːri] der Sari (Kleid/Gewand indischer Frauen) 2: 4 (126)

Saturday [ˈsætədeɪ], [ˈsætədi] der Samstag 1

sauce [sɔːs] die Soße 1

sausage [ˈsɒsɪdʒ] das (Brat-, Bock-)Würstchen, die Wurst 1

save [seɪv]:
1. retten 2: 2 (52)
2. sparen 2: 2 (52)
3. sichern (Daten) 2: 2 (52)

savings (pl) [ˈseɪvɪŋz] die Ersparnisse 2: 5 (154)

savings account [ˈseɪvɪŋz əkaʊnt] das Sparkonto 2: 5 (154)

savoury [ˈseɪvəri] herzhaft, salzig 1

saw [sɔː] siehe **see**

say [seɪ], **said, said** sagen 1

scare sb. [skeə] jn. erschrecken, jm. Angst machen 2: 4 (124)

scared [skeəd]: **be scared (of)** Angst haben (vor) 1

scarf [skɑːf], pl **scarves** Schal 2: 4 (128)

scarves [skɑːvz] Plural von **scarf**

scary [ˈskeəri] unheimlich, beängstigend, gruselig 2: 1 (16)

scene [siːn] die Szene 1

school [skuːl] die Schule 1 **at school** in der Schule 1

school club [ˈskuːl klʌb] die AG (in der Schule) 1

school uniform [skuːl ˈjuːnɪfɔːm] die Schuluniform 1

sci-fi [ˈsaɪ faɪ] siehe **science fiction**

science [ˈsaɪəns] die Naturwissenschaft 1

science fiction [saɪəns ˈfɪkʃn] infml auch **sci-fi** die Science-Fiction 2: 3 (86)

scientist [ˈsaɪəntɪst] der (Natur-)Wissenschaftler, die (Natur-)Wissenschaftlerin 2: 2 (65)

scone [skɒn] das kleine runde Milchbrötchen, leicht süß, oft mit Rosinen 1

scooter [ˈskuːtə] der (Tret-)Roller 1

score [skɔː]:
1. der Spiel-/Punktestand; der (im Spiel/Sport erzielte) Punkt 2: 3 (89)
2. (einen Punkt / ein Tor / einen Treffer) erzielen 2: 3 (89)

°**Scorpio** [ˈskɔːpiəʊ] der Skorpion (Sternzeichen)

scream [skriːm]:
1. der Schrei 2: 1 (16)
2. schreien 2: 1 (16)

screen [skriːn] der Bildschirm; die Leinwand *(Kino)* 2: 3 (91)

sea [siː] das Meer, die See 1 **by the sea** am Meer, an der See 1

sea level [ˈsiː levl] der Meeresspiegel 2: 3 (89)

seagull [ˈsiːgʌl] die Möwe 1

season [ˈsiːzn] die Jahreszeit; die Saison 1

seat [siːt] der (Sitz-)Platz 2: 3 (78/79) **take a seat** Platz nehmen 2: 3 (78/79)

second [ˈsekənd]:
1. die Sekunde 1
2. (2nd) zweite(r, s) 1

second-hand [sekənd ˈhænd] second-hand *(gebraucht, aus zweiter Hand)* 2: 5 (153)

second-hand shop [sekənd hænd ˈʃɒp] der Secondhandladen 2: 5 (153)

secondary school [ˈsekəndri skuːl] die weiterführende Schule 1

secret [ˈsiːkrət]:
1. geheim 1
2. das Geheimnis 1

see [siː], **saw, seen** sehen 1 **see sb.** zu jm. gehen, jn. aufsuchen 2: 1 (26) **See you soon. Bis bald!** 1 **See you. Bis dann. / Tschüs.** 1 **go and see sb. / go to see sb. (about sth.)** jn. besuchen (gehen/fahren); jn. (wegen etwas) aufsuchen 2: 1 (26)

seen [siːn] *siehe* see

sell [sel], **sold, sold** verkaufen 2: 5 (153)

°**seller** [ˈselə] der Verkäufer, die Verkäuferin

semi-detached home/house [semi dɪˈtætʃt] die Doppelhaushälfte 1

send [send], **sent, sent** senden, schicken 1

sent [sent] *siehe* send

sentence [ˈsentəns] der Satz 1

September [sepˈtembə] der September 1

set [set], **set, set** stellen, legen, setzen 2: 4 (126) **set the alarm** (sich) den/einen Wecker stellen 2: 4 (126) **set the table** den Tisch decken 2: 4 (126)

seven [ˈsevn] sieben 1

seventeen [sevnˈtiːn] siebzehn 1

seventy [ˈsevnti] siebzig 1

shame [ʃeɪm]: **a shame** schade; eine Schande 1

share [ʃeə]:
1. der (An-)Teil 1
2. teilen 1

sharpener [ˈʃɑːpnə] der Anspitzer 1

she [ʃiː] sie *(weibliche Person)* 1 **she's (= she is)** sie ist 1

sheep [ʃiːp], *pl* **sheep** das Schaf 2: 4 (116)

shelf [ʃelf], *pl* **shelves** das Regal-(brett) 1

shelves [ʃelvz] *Plural von* shelf

shine [ʃaɪn]:
1. scheinen *(Sonne)*; strahlen, glänzen 1
2. der (Sonnen-)Schein; der Glanz 1

come rain or shine bei jedem Wetter; was auch (immer) geschieht 1

shirt [ʃɜːt] das Hemd 1

shock [ʃɒk]:
1. der Schock 2: 2 (61)
2. **shock sb.** jn. schockieren 2: 2 (61)

shocked [ʃɒkt] schockiert 2: 2 (61)

shocking [ˈʃɒkɪŋ] schockierend 2: 2 (61)

shoe [ʃuː] der Schuh 1

shop [ʃɒp]:
1. der Laden, das Geschäft 1
2. (ein)kaufen, „shoppen" 2: 5 (154) **shop for sth.** etwas kaufen (gehen) 2: 5 (154)

shop assistant [ˈʃɒp əsɪstənt] der Verkäufer, die Verkäuferin 2: 5 (153)

shopper [ˈʃɒpə] der Kunde, die Kundin; der Einkäufer, die Einkäuferin 2: 5 (154)

shopping [ˈʃɒpɪŋ] das Einkaufen; die Einkäufe 1 **do the shopping** die Einkäufe erledigen, einkaufen gehen 1 **go shopping** einkaufen gehen 1

shopping centre [ˈʃɒpɪŋ sentə] das Einkaufszentrum 1

shopping list [ˈʃɒpɪŋ lɪst] die Einkaufsliste 1

short [ʃɔːt] kurz; klein *(Person; Körpergröße)* 1

shorts *(pl)* [ʃɔːts] die kurze Hose, die Shorts 2: 5 (157)

should [ʃʊd] **it should …** es sollte … 2: 3 (97)

°**shout** [ʃaʊt] rufen

show [ʃəʊ]:
1. die Show, die Aufführung; die Ausstellung 1
2. **show, showed, shown** zeigen 1
°**show sb. around (a place)** jn. herumführen; jm. einen Ort zeigen

shower [ˈʃaʊə] die Dusche 1 **have a shower** (sich) duschen 1

shy [ʃaɪ] scheu, schüchtern 2: 2 (48)

sick [sɪk] krank 2: 4 (127) **be sick** sich übergeben 2: 4 (127) **I feel sick.** Mir ist schlecht 2: 4 (127)

sickness [ˈsɪknəs] die Krankheit 2: 4 (127) **in sickness or in health** wenn man krank oder gesund ist 2: 4 (127)

side [saɪd] die Seite *(z. B. Straßenseite)* 2: 2 (60)

sight [saɪt]:
1. der Anblick, die Sicht(weite), die Sehkraft 2: 1 (23)
2. die Sehenswürdigkeit 2: 1 (23)

sign [saɪn] das Schild; das Zeichen 2: 1 (25)

silence [ˈsaɪləns] die Stille; das Schweigen 2: 1 (23)

silent [ˈsaɪlənt] still, lautlos 2: 1 (23) **fall/go silent** still werden, verstummen 2: 1 (23)

silver [ˈsɪlvə]:
1. das Silber 1
2. silberfarben 1

°**similar (to sb./sth.)** [ˈsɪmələ] *(jm./einer Sache)* ähnlich

simulation [sɪmjuˈleɪʃn] die Simulation 2: 3 (91)

sing [sɪŋ], **sang, sung** singen 1

singer [ˈsɪŋə] der Sänger, die Sängerin 1

singing [ˈsɪŋɪŋ] das Singen 1

single [ˈsɪŋgl] Einzel-, einzelne(r, s) 2: 1 (19)

single ticket [sɪŋgl ˈtɪkɪt] die einfache Fahrkarte *(= ohne Rückfahrt)* 2: 1 (19)

sister [ˈsɪstə] die Schwester 1

sit [sɪt], **sat, sat** sitzen; sich setzen 1 **sit down** sich hinsetzen 1

situation [sɪtʃuˈeɪʃn] die Situation 2: 3 (91)

six [sɪks] sechs 1

sixteen [sɪksˈtiːn] sechzehn 1

sixty [ˈsɪksti] sechzig 1

size [saɪz] die Größe 2: 5 (153) **What size are you / do you take?** Welche Größe hast du? 2: 5 (153)

skateboard [ˈskeɪtbɔːd]:
1. das Skateboard 1
2. Skateboard fahren 1

skateboarding [ˈskeɪtbɔːdɪŋ] das Skateboardfahren 1

skatepark [ˈskeɪtpɑːk] der Skatepark 1

°**skiing** [ˈskiːɪŋ]: **go skiing** Skilaufen gehen

skill [skɪl] die Fähigkeit, die Fertigkeit 1 °**life skills** *(pl)* die Alltagskompetenzen, die lebenswichtigen Fertigkeiten °**study skills** *(pl)* die Lerntechniken

skirt [skɜːt] der Rock 1

°**sky** [skaɪ] der Himmel **in the sky** am Himmel

sleep [sliːp]:
1. der Schlaf 1
2. **sleep, slept, slept** schlafen 1 **sleep late** lange schlafen 2: (10/11)

slept [slept] *siehe* sleep

slide [slaɪd] das Dia; die Folie *(Präsentationssoftware)* 1

slide show [ˈslaɪd ʃəʊ] die Slideshow, die Bildschirmpräsentation 1

slippers *(pl)* [slɪpə] die Hausschuhe 2: 4 (127)

slow [sləʊ] langsam 1

small [smɔːl] klein 1

small talk [smɔːl tɔːk] der/das Small Talk *(oberflächliche, leichte Konversation)* 1

smart [smɑːt]:
1. schick 1
2. intelligent, clever 1

smell [smel]:
1. der Geruch; der Gestank 1
2. riechen; schlecht riechen 1

smile [smaɪl]:
1. das Lächeln 1
2. lächeln 1
smile at sb. jn. anlächeln 1

smiley [ˈsmaɪli] das Smiley 2: 3 (89)

snack [snæk] der Snack, die kleine Mahlzeit 1

snake [sneɪk] die Schlange 1
snow [snəʊ]:
1. der Schnee 1
2. schneien 1
snowy [ˈsnəʊi] schneebedeckt; verschneit 1
so [səʊ]:
1. so 1
so good so gut 1
2. also, daher 1
3. so (that) sodass 1
4. He said so. Das hat er gesagt. 2: 2 (65)
I don't think so. Das glaube/denke ich nicht. 2: 2 (65) I hope so. Das hoffe ich. 2: 2 (65) I think so. Ich glaube/denke ja. 2: 2 (65) If so, ... Wenn ja, ... 2: 2 (65)
so far [səʊ ˈfɑː] bis jetzt, bis hierher 2: 4 (119)
sociable [ˈsəʊʃəbl] kontaktfreudig, gesellig 2: 5 (163)
social [ˈsəʊʃl] sozial 2: 3 (91)
social media (pl) [səʊʃl ˈmiːdiə] die sozialen Medien 2: 3 (91)
sock [sɒk] die Socke 1
sofa [ˈsəʊfə] das Sofa 1
°soft [sɒft] weich
software [ˈsɒftweə] die Software 1
sold [səʊld] siehe sell
solution (to a problem) [səˈluːʃn] die Lösung (eines Problems) 1
solve [sɒlv] lösen (Rätsel, Problem), lüften (Geheimnis) 2: 5 (160)
some [sʌm], [səm] einige, ein paar; etwas, ein wenig 1
somebody [ˈsʌmbədi] jemand 1
someone [ˈsʌmwʌn] jemand 1
something [ˈsʌmθɪŋ] etwas 1
sometimes [ˈsʌmtaɪmz] manchmal 1
somewhere [ˈsʌmweə] irgendwo(hin) 2: 3 (83)
son [sʌn] der Sohn 1
song [sɒŋ] das Lied 1
soon [suːn] bald 1
sorry [ˈsɒri]: Sorry. / I'm sorry. Tut mir leid. / Entschuldigung. 1 be/feel sorry for sb. Mitleid haben mit jm. 1 I'm / I feel sorry for him. Er tut mir leid. 1
sort (of) [sɔːt] die Art (von) 2: 1 (16)
sound [saʊnd]:
1. das Geräusch; der Klang, der Laut 1
2. klingen (sich ... anhören) 1
soup [suːp] die Suppe 2: 4 (117)
°source [sɔːs] die Quelle (z. B. Website, Text)
space [speɪs] der Raum, der Platz; der Weltraum 2: 3 (86)
spaghetti [spəˈgeti] die Spaghetti 1
speak (to) [spiːk] sprechen (mit) 1 Speak later. Tschüs. / Bis später. 1
speaking [ˈspiːkɪŋ] das Sprechen 1
special [ˈspeʃl] besondere(r, s) 1
special effects (pl) [speʃl ɪˈfekts] die Special Effects (in Filmen) 2: 3 (86)
speech bubble [ˈspiːtʃ bʌbl] die Sprechblase 1

spell [spel] buchstabieren 1
spelling [ˈspelɪŋ] die Schreibweise, die Rechtschreibung 1
spend [spend], spent, spent: spend money (on ...) Geld ausgeben (für ...) 2: 2 (55) spend time Zeit verbringen 2: 2 (55)
spent [spent] siehe spend
spice [spaɪs] das Gewürz 1
spicy [ˈspaɪsi] würzig 1
spoon [spuːn] der Löffel 1
sport [spɔːt] der Sport; die Sportart 1
sports hall [ˈspɔːts hɔːl] die Sporthalle 1
sportsperson [ˈspɔːtspɜːsn], pl sportspeople der Sportler, die Sportlerin 2: 2 (65)
sporty [ˈspɔːti] sportlich 2: 3 (80)
spotlight [ˈspɒtlaɪt] das Spotlight, der Scheinwerfer; die Aufmerksamkeit 2: 5 (154) in/under the spotlight im Rampenlicht, im Blickpunkt des Interesses 2: 5 (154) turn the spotlight on sb./sth. den Scheinwerfer / die Aufmerksamkeit auf jn./etwas richten 2: 5 (154)
spring [sprɪŋ] der Frühling 1
square [skweə]:
1. der Platz (in der Stadt) 2: 3 (89)
2. rechteckig 2: 3 (89)
stadium [ˈsteɪdiəm] das Stadion 1
stage [steɪdʒ] die Bühne 2: 1 (25)
stairs (pl) [steəz] die Treppe; die (Treppen-)Stufen 2: 3 (88)
stand [stænd], stood, stood stehen; sich (hin)stellen 1 stand up aufstehen 1
star [stɑː]:
1. der (Film-/Pop-)Star 1
2. der Stern 2: 5 (163)
star sign [ˈstɑː saɪn] das Sternzeichen 2: 5 (163)
stare [steə]:
1. das Starren, der starre Blick 1
2. stare (at) (an)starren 1
start [stɑːt]:
1. der Anfang, der Start 1
2. beginnen, anfangen (mit) 1
start a business ein Geschäft aufmachen, einen Betrieb gründen/ eröffnen 2: 5 (159)
°statement [ˈsteɪtmənt] der Aussage(satz)
station [ˈsteɪʃn] der Bahnhof 1
stay [steɪ]:
1. der Aufenthalt 2: 1 (14)
2. bleiben; übernachten 2: 1 (14)
stay up aufbleiben (nicht ins Bett gehen) 2: 5 (154)
steal [stiːl], stole, stolen stehlen, rauben 2: 4 (127)
step [step] die Stufe; der Schritt 1
stepbrother [ˈstepbrʌðə] der Stiefbruder 1
stepdad [ˈstepdæd] der Stiefvater 1
stepdaughter [ˈstepdɔːtə] die Stieftochter 1
stepfather [ˈstepfɑːθə] der Stiefvater 1

stepmother [ˈstepmʌθə] die Stiefmutter 1
stepmum [ˈstepmʌm] die Stiemutter 1
stepsister [ˈstepsɪstə] die Stiefschwester 1
stepson [ˈstepsʌn] der Stiefsohn 1
still [stɪl] (immer) noch; trotzdem 1
stir [stɜː] (um)rühren 1
stir-fry [ˈstɜː fraɪ]:
1. das Gericht aus kurz angebratenen Zutaten, z. B. kleinen Stücken Fleisch, Fisch und/oder Gemüse 1
2. (Gemüse- oder Fleischstücke) unter Rühren scharf anbraten 1
stole [stəʊl] siehe steal
stolen [ˈstəʊlən] siehe steal
stop [stɒp]:
1. (an)halten; stoppen; aufhören (mit) 1
stop a fire ein Feuer löschen 2: 5 (144)
2. der Halt, der Haltepunkt; die Unterbrechung 1
bus stop die Bushaltestelle 1
story [ˈstɔːri] die Geschichte (Erzählung) 1
storyteller [ˈstɔːri telə] der (Geschichten-)Erzähler, die (Geschichten-)Erzählerin 2: 1 (16)
straight [streɪt]:
1. gerade; (Haare) glatt 2: 2 (46/47)
2. straight on geradeaus (weiter) 2: 3 (88)
strange [streɪndʒ] seltsam, sonderbar 2: 4 (117)
stranger [ˈstreɪndʒə] der/die Fremde 2: 4 (117)
strawberry [ˈstrɔːbəri] die Erdbeere 1
stream [striːm] streamen 2: 3 (91)
streamer [ˈstriːmə] der Streamer, die Streamerin (Personen, die etwas streamen) 2: 3 (91)
street [striːt] die Straße (in Ortschaften) 1 in the street auf der Straße 1 on a quiet street an einer ruhigen Straße 1
street dance [ˈstriːt dɑːns] der Streetdance (Tanzstil) 1
street music [ˈstriːt mjuːzɪk] die Straßenmusik 1
street musician [ˈstriːt mjuzɪʃn] der Straßenmusiker, die Straßenmusikerin 2: 1 (20)
strength [streŋθ] die Stärke, die Kraft 2: 5 (160)
stressed [strest] gestresst 1
strong [strɒŋ] stark 2: 2 (48)
structure [ˈstrʌktʃə]:
1. die Struktur 2: 1 (30)
2. strukturieren, aufbauen 2: 1 (30)
student [ˈstjuːdnt] der Schüler, die Schülerin; der Student, die Studentin 1
studio [ˈstjuːdiəʊ] das Studio 2: 3 (87)
study [ˈstʌdi] studieren; lernen (z. B. für Prüfungen) 2: 3 (93)
°study skills (pl) [ˈstʌdi skɪlz] die Lerntechniken
stupid [ˈstjuːpɪd] dumm, blöd; albern 2: 2 (54)

subject [ˈsʌbdʒɪkt] das (Schul-)Fach 1
success [səkˈses] der Erfolg 2: 5 (149)
successful [səkˈsesfl] erfolgreich 2: 5 (149)
such (a) [sʌtʃ] so(lch) (ein/e) 2: 5 (159)
suddenly [ˈsʌdənli] plötzlich, auf einmal 2: 4 (127)
sugar [ˈʃʊɡə] der Zucker 1
suggest sth. (to sb.) [səˈdʒest] (jm.) etwas vorschlagen 2: 3 (90)
suggestion [səˈdʒestʃən] der Vorschlag 2: 3 (90)
suit [suːt] der (Herren-)Anzug; das (Damen-)Kostüm 2: 4 (125)
°summary [ˈsʌməri] die Zusammenfassung
summer [ˈsʌmə] der Sommer 1
sun [sʌn] die Sonne **have a moment in the sun** kurz im Mittelpunkt stehen 1
sunbathe [ˈsʌnbeɪð] sonnenbaden 2: 1 (14)
Sunday [ˈsʌndeɪ], [ˈsʌndi] der Sonntag 1
sung [sʌŋ] *siehe* **sing**
sunglasses *(pl)* [ˈsʌnglɑːsɪz] die Sonnenbrille 2: 2 (46/47)
sunny [ˈsʌni] sonnig 1 **It's sunny.** Die Sonne scheint. 1
sunrise [ˈsʌnraɪz] der Sonnenaufgang 2: 4 (114)
sunset [ˈsʌnset] der Sonnenuntergang 2: 4 (114)
super [ˈsuːpə] super 1
superhero [ˈsuːpəhɪərəʊ], *pl* superheroes der Superheld, die Superheldin 1
supermarket [ˈsuːpəmɑːkɪt] der Supermarkt 1
superpower [ˈsuːpəpaʊə] die Superkraft 2: 2 (56)
support [səˈpɔːt]:
  1. die Unterstützung 2: 1 (27)
  2. unterstützen 2: 1 (27)
supporter [səˈpɔːtə] der Anhänger, die Anhängerin, der Fan 2: 1 (27)
sure [ʃʊə], [ʃɔː] sicher 1
surf [sɜːf] surfen 2: 3 (91) **surf the web** im Internet surfen 2: 3 (91)
surfing [ˈsɜːfɪŋ] das Surfing 2: 3 (91)
surprise [səˈpraɪz]:
  1. die Überraschung 2: 4 (118)
  2. überraschen 2: 4 (118)
surprised [səˈpraɪzd] überrascht 1
swam [swæm] *siehe* **swim**
swap [swɒp]:
  1. tauschen 1
  2. der Tausch 1
  clothes swap der Kleidertausch, die Kleidertauschparty 1
sweatshirt [ˈswetʃɜːt] das Sweatshirt 1
sweet [swiːt]:
  1. süß 1
  2. das Bonbon 1
  sweets *(pl)* die Süßigkeiten 1
sweet shop [ˈswiːt ʃɒp] das Süßwarengeschäft 2: 5 (153)
swim [swɪm], **swam, swum** schwimmen 1

swimmer [ˈswɪmə] der Schwimmer, die Schwimmerin 1
swimming [ˈswɪmɪŋ] das Schwimmen 1
swimsuit [ˈswɪmsuːt] der Badeanzug 2: 2 (57)
swum [swʌm] *siehe* **swim**
°symbol [ˈsɪmbl] das Symbol

T

T-shirt [ˈtiː ʃɜːt] das T-Shirt 1
table [ˈteɪbl]:
  1. der Tisch 1
  set the table den Tisch decken 2: 4 (126)
  °2. die Tabelle
table tennis [ˈteɪbl tenɪs] das Tischtennis 1
tablespoon [ˈteɪblspuːn] der Esslöffel 1
take [teɪk], **took, taken:**
  1. dauern, *(Zeit)* brauchen, in Anspruch nehmen 1
  2. (mit)nehmen; bringen 1
  take notes sich Notizen machen 2: 2 (55) **take out the rubbish** den Müll rausbringen 2: 5 (150) **take photos** Fotos machen 1 **take place** stattfinden 2: 3 (80) **take sth. off** etwas ausziehen *(Kleidung),* ablegen *(Hut, Brille)* 2: 4 (126)
taken [ˈteɪkn] *siehe* **take**
talk [tɔːk]:
  1. das Gespräch; die Rede, der Vortrag 1
  2. **talk (to)** sprechen, reden (mit) 1
  talk about sprechen, reden über 1
tall [tɔːl] groß *(Person)*; hoch *(Gebäude)* 2: 2 (48)
°tapas *(pl)* [ˈtæpæs] die Tapas *(Gericht; spanische Appetithäppchen)*
task [tɑːsk] die Aufgabe 1 **do a task** eine Aufgabe machen/erledigen 1
taste [teɪst]:
  1. schmecken; kosten, probieren 1
  2. der Geschmack 1
tasty [ˈteɪsti] schmackhaft, lecker 1
°Taurus [ˈtɔːrəs] der Stier *(Sternzeichen)*
taxi [ˈtæksi] das Taxi 2: 1 (15)
tea [tiː] der Tee 1
teach [tiːtʃ], **taught, taught** lehren, unterrichten 1 **teach sb. to do sth.** jm. beibringen, etwas zu tun 1
teacher [ˈtiːtʃə] der Lehrer, die Lehrerin 1
team [tiːm] das Team, die Mannschaft 1
°teammate [ˈtiːmmeɪt] der Mannschaftskamerad, die Mannschaftskameradin
teamwork [ˈtiːmwɜːk] das Teamwork, die Zusammenarbeit 2: 2 (62)
teapot [ˈpɒt] die Teekanne 2: 4 (115)
teaspoon [ˈtiːspuːn] der Teelöffel 1
tech [tek] *siehe* **technology**
technology [tekˈnɒlədʒi], *infml auch* **tech** die Technik, der Technikunterricht; die Technologie 1

teen [tiːn] der Teenager 2: 2 (59)
teeth [tiːθ] *Plural von* **tooth brush your teeth** (sich) die Zähne putzen 1
tell [tel], **told, told** erzählen, sagen 1
ten [ten] zehn 1
ten thousand [ten ˈθaʊznd] zehntausend (10000) 2: 1 (18)
tennis [ˈtenɪs] das Tennis 1
terraced home/house [ˈterəst] das Reihenhaus 1
terrarium [teˈreəriəm] das Terrarium 1
terrible [ˈterəbl] schrecklich, fürchterlich 1
test [test]:
  1. der Test; die Klassenarbeit 1
  2. testen 1
text [tekst]:
  1. der Text 1
  2. **text (message)** die SMS 1
  3. **text sb.** jm. eine SMS schicken 1
than [ðən]: **louder/older than ...** lauter/älter als ... 2: 3 (85)
thank sb. [θæŋk] sich bei jm. bedanken 2: 4 (114)
thank you [ˈθæŋk juː] danke (schön) 1 **Thank you very much.** Vielen Dank./ Danke vielmals. 1
thanks [θæŋks] danke (schön) 1
that [ðæt]:
  1. das (dort) 1
  that's (= that is) das (da) ist 1 **That's when they're useful.** Dann/Genau dann sind sie nützlich. 2: 5 (153)
  2. dass 1
  I'm happy that ... Ich bin froh, dass ... 1 **so that** sodass 1
  3. der, die, das *(Relativpronomen)* 1
the [ðə] der, die, das 1
theatre [ˈθɪətə] das Theater 1
their [ðeə] ihr/e *(Plural)* 1
them [ðem], [ðəm] sie, ihnen 1
then [ðen] dann, danach 1
there [ðeə] da, dort; dahin, dorthin 1 **there are** es sind .../es gibt ... 1 **there's** (= there is) es ist .../es gibt ... 1
these [ðiːz] diese (hier) 1 **These are my friends.** Das hier sind meine Freunde/Freundinnen. 1
they [ðeɪ] sie *(Plural)* 1 **they're** (= they are) sie sind 1
thing [θɪŋ] das Ding, die Sache 1
think [θɪŋk], **thought, thought** denken, meinen, glauben 1 **think about** nachdenken über 1 **think of sb./sth.** an jn./etwas denken 2: 2 (50) **think of sth.** sich etwas überlegen, ausdenken 2: 2 (50) **I think ...** Ich denke/meine/glaube/finde, ... 1
third (3rd) [θɜːd] dritte(r, s) 1
thirsty [ˈθɜːsti]: **be thirsty** durstig sein, Durst haben 2: 4 (114)
thirteen [θɜːˈtiːn] dreizehn 1
thirty [ˈθɜːti] dreißig 1
this [ðɪs] dies; diese(r, s) 1 **this morning/afternoon/evening** heute Morgen/Nachmittag/Abend 2: 1 (26)
those [ðəʊz] die dort, jene (dort) 1
thought [θɔːt] *siehe* **think**

thousand [ˈθaʊznd] tausend 2 : 1 (18)
three [θriː] drei 1
through [θruː] durch 2 : 1 (17)
°**throw** [θrəʊ], **threw, thrown** werfen
Thursday [ˈθɜːzdeɪ], [ˈθɜːzdi] der
Donnerstag 1
°**thx** [θæŋks] *(infml for* thanks, *in
writing)* danke (schön)
°**tick** [tɪk]:
  1. ankreuzen, abhaken
  2. das Häkchen
ticket [ˈtɪkɪt] die Eintrittskarte, die
Fahrkarte, das Ticket 1 **one-way-
ticket** die einfache Fahrkarte *(= ohne
Rückfahrt)* 2 : 1 (19) **single ticket** die
einfache Fahrkarte *(= ohne Rückfahrt)* 2 : 1 (19)
ticket machine [ˈtɪkɪt məʃiːn] der Fahrkartenautomat 2 : 2 (59)
tidy [ˈtaɪdi]:
  1. ordentlich 1
  2. aufräumen 1
tie [taɪ] die Krawatte 1
till [tɪl] bis 2 : 3 (90) **not ... till** erst,
wenn ... 2 : 3 (90)
time [taɪm]:
  1. die Zeit; die Uhrzeit 1
  have a great/good time (viel) Spaß
haben, sich vergnügen 2 : 1 (20) **on
time** pünktlich 2 : 4 (126) **What time
is it?** Wie spät ist es? 1 **What time?**
Um wie viel Uhr? 1 **What's the time?**
Wie spät ist es? 1
  2. das Mal 2 : 1 (26)
  for the first time zum ersten Mal
2 : 1 (26) **lots of times** viele Male, oft
2 : 1 (26) **three times** dreimal 2 : 1 (26)
°**timeline** [ˈtaɪmlaɪn] die Zeitachse, die
Chronik
timer [taɪmə] der Timer *(elektronischer
Zeitmesser)* 2 : 3 (94)
timetable [ˈtaɪmteɪbl] der Stundenplan 1
tin [tɪn] die Dose, die Büchse 2 : 4 (115)
tip [tɪp] der Tipp 1
tired [ˈtaɪəd] müde 1
title [ˈtaɪtl] der Titel, die Überschrift 1
to [tu], [tə]:
  1. bis 1
  (from) A to Z (von) A bis Z 1
  2. (um) zu 1
  how to do sth. wie man etwas tut /
tun kann / tun soll 1 **things to eat**
Dinge zum Essen 1
  3. vor *(bei Uhrzeitangaben)* 2 : 3 (90)
  quarter to 7 viertel vor 7 2 : 3 (90)
  4. zu, nach 1
  different to you anders als du 1 **the
answer to the question** die Antwort
auf die Frage 1
today [təˈdeɪ] heute 1 **today's letter**
der Brief von heute 1
together [təˈgeðə] zusammen 1
toilet [ˈtɔɪlət] die Toilette 1
told [təʊld] *siehe* tell
tolerant (of) [ˈtɒlərənt] tolerant
(gegenüber) 2 : 5 (163)
tomato [təˈmɑːtəʊ], *pl* tomatoes
  die Tomate 1

tomato sauce [təˈmɑːtəʊ sɔːs]
  die Tomatensoße 1
tomorrow [təˈmɒrəʊ] morgen
  2 : (10/11)
tonight [təˈnaɪt] heute Nacht, heute
Abend 2 : 3 (83)
too [tuː]:
  1. auch 1
  from York too auch aus York 1
  2. **too slow** zu langsam 1
took [tʊk] *siehe* take
tooth [tuːθ], *pl* teeth der Zahn 1
top [tɒp]:
  1. die Spitze, das obere Ende 1
  2. oberste(r, s), höchste(r, s) 2 : 5 (153)
the top shelf das oberste/höchste
Regal 2 : 5 (153) **the top six films** die
sechs besten Filme 1
top floor [tɒp ˈflɔː] das Dach-/Ober-
geschoss, das oberste Stockwerk,
die oberste Etage 1
topic [ˈtɒpɪk] das Thema 1
touch [tʌtʃ]:
  1. anfassen, berühren 2 : 1 (16)
  2. die Berührung 2 : 1 (16)
tour (of) [tʊə] die Tour, die Reise, der
Rundgang / die Rundfahrt 1
tour guide [ˈtʊə gaɪd] der Reiseleiter,
die Reiseleiterin / der Fremdenführer,
die Fremdenführerin 1
tourist [ˈtʊərɪst] der Tourist, die
Touristin 1
tower [ˈtaʊə] der Turm 2 : 1 (23)
town [taʊn] die Stadt 1
town centre [taʊn ˈsentə] das Stadtzentrum 1
toy [tɔɪ] das Spielzeug 1
tradition [trəˈdɪʃn] die Tradition 1
traditional [trəˈdɪʃənl] traditionell 1
°**trail** [treɪl] der Weg, die Route 1
trailer [ˈtreɪlə] der Trailer *(Film-
vorschau)* 2 : 3 (87)
train [treɪn] der Zug, die Eisenbahn 1
train driver [ˈtreɪn draɪvə] der Loko-
motivführer, die Lokomotivführerin
2 : 5 (146)
train sb. [treɪn] jn. trainieren; aus-
bilden 2 : 3 (80)
train station [ˈtreɪn steɪʃn]
  der Bahnhof 1
trainer [ˈtreɪnə] der Trainer, die
Trainerin 1
training [ˈtreɪnɪŋ] das Training 1
trampoline [ˈtræmpəliːn]
  das Trampolin 1
trampolining [ˈtræmpəliːnɪŋ] das
Trampolinspringen/-turnen 1
transgender [trænzˈdʒendə]:
  1. der/die Transgender 2 : 1 (18)
  2. transgender 2 : 1 (18)
transport [trænˈspɔːt] transportieren,
befördern 2 : 1 (17)
transport *(no pl)* [ˈtrænspɔːt]
  das Fortbewegungsmittel, das Ver-
kehrsmittel; die Beförderung 2 : 1 (17)
travel [ˈtrævl]:
  1. das Reisen 1
  2. reisen, fahren 1
°**treasure** [ˈtreʒə] der Schatz

°**treasure hunt** [ˈtreʒə hʌnt]
  die Schatzsuche
treat [ˈtriːt]:
  1. der Hochgenuss, das besondere
Vergnügen; die (besondere) Leckerei
2 : 5 (154)
  2. **treat sb. (to sth.)** jn. (zu etwas) einladen 2 : 5 (154)
tree [triː] der Baum 1
trick [trɪk] der Trick, das Kunststück 1
trifle [ˈtraɪfl] das Trifle *(britischer Nachtisch)* 1
trip [trɪp] der Ausflug; die Reise
2 : 1 (12/13) **class trip** der Klassenaus-
flug 2 : 1 (12/13) **school trip** der
Schulausflug 2 : 1 (12/13)
trophy [ˈtrəʊfi] die Trophäe; der
Pokal 2 : 5 (89)
trouble [ˈtrʌbl] der Ärger, die Schwierigkeiten 1 **be in trouble** Ärger
haben, in Schwierigkeiten sein 1
trousers *(pl)* [ˈtraʊzəz] die Hose 1
true [truː] wahr, richtig 1 **come true**
wahr werden 2 : 5 (149)
try [traɪ]:
  1. versuchen, (aus)probieren 2 : 1 (26)
try sth. on etwas anprobieren *(Kleidung)* 2 : 5 (156) **try to do sth.** versuchen, etwas zu tun 2 : 1 (26)
  2. der Versuch 2 : 1 (26)
  Have a try! / Give it a try! Versuch's/
Probier's doch mal! 2 : 1 (26)
Tuesday [ˈtjuːzdeɪ], [ˈtjuːzdi]
  der Dienstag 1
turn [tɜːn]:
  1. (sich) (um)drehen 1
  Turn it upside down. Dreh/Stell es
auf den Kopf. 1 **turn right/left**
(nach) rechts/links abbiegen 2 : 3 (88)
turn sth. (over) etwas umdrehen 1
  2. **it is sb.'s turn (to do sth.)** jd. ist
dran / an der Reihe (etwas zu tun) 1
take turns / take it in turns (to do sth)
sich abwechseln; sich dabei abwechseln, etwas zu tun 1 **When is (it) my
turn (to do sth.)?** Wann bin ich dran /
an der Reihe (etwas zu tun)? 1
TV [tiːˈviː] der Fernseher; das Fernsehen 1
twelfth (12th) [twelfθ] zwölfte(r, s) 1
twelve [twelv] zwölf 1
twenty [ˈtwenti] zwanzig 1
two [tuː] zwei 1
°**type (of)** [taɪp] die Art (von), die Sorte
(von)
typical (of) [ˈtɪpɪkl] typisch (für)
2 : 5 (153)

U

UK (= United Kingdom) [juː ˈkeɪ] das
Vereinigte Königreich 1
umbrella [ʌmˈbrelə] der (Regen-)
Schirm 1
°**umbrella word** [ʌmˈbrelə wɜːd] der
Oberbegriff, der Sammelbegriff
uncle [ˈʌŋkl] der Onkel 1
uncomfortable [ʌnˈkʌmftəbl]
unbequem, ungemütlich 2 : 5 (155)

uncool [ʌnˈkuːl] uncool 2: 2 (54)

under [ˈʌndə] unter 1

underground [ˈʌndəɡraʊnd] die U-Bahn 2: 1 (16)

underground [ʌndəˈɡraʊnd] unterirdisch, unter der Erde 2: 1 (16)

°**underlined** [ʌndəˈlaɪnd] unterstrichen

understand [ʌndəˈstænd], **understood, understood** verstehen 1

underwater [ʌndəˈwɔːtə] unter Wasser, Unterwasser- 2: 2 (52)

unfair [ʌnˈfeə] unfair 2: 2 (48)

unfriendly [ʌnˈfrendli] unfreundlich 1

unhappiness [ʌnˈhæpinəs] die Unzufriedenheit, die Traurigkeit 2: 2 (64)

unhappy [ʌnˈhæpi] unglücklich, unzufrieden 2: 2 (54)

unhealthy [ʌnˈhelθi] ungesund 2: 2 (64)

unhelpful [ʌnˈhelpfl] wenig hilfreich 2: 2 (54)

uniform [ˈjuːnifɔːm] die Uniform 1

unit [ˈjuːnɪt] die Unit (Lerneinheit) 1

United Kingdom (UK) [juːnaɪtɪd ˈkɪŋdəm] das Vereinigte Königreich 1

unkind [ʌnˈkaɪnd] unfreundlich, herzlos 2: 2 (54)

unlock [ʌnˈlɒk] aufschließen, entsperren 2: 4 (127)

untidy [ʌnˈtaɪdi] unordentlich 2: 2 (54)

until [ənˈtɪl] bis (zeitlich) 2: 3 (90) **not ... until** erst, wenn ... 2: 3 (90)

up [ʌp] hinauf, hoch 1 **up a hill** einen Hügel hinauf, hoch 2: 3 (88)

upset [ʌpˈset] bestürzt; aufgebracht, verärgert 2: 2 (61)

upset sb. [ʌpˈset], **upset, upset** jn. erschüttern; jn. aufregen, ärgern 2: 2 (61)

upside down [ʌpsaɪd ˈdaʊn] verkehrt herum, auf dem Kopf 1

upstairs [ʌpˈsteəz] (nach) oben (die Treppe hinauf) 2: 4 (127)

us [ʌs], [əs] uns 1

use [juːz] benutzen, verwenden 1

useful [ˈjuːsfl] nützlich, hilfreich 1

user [ˈjuːzə] der (Be-)Nutzer, die (Be-)Nutzerin 1

usually [ˈjuːʒuəli] normalerweise, meistens 1

V

vacuum [ˈvækjuəm] Staub saugen 2: 5 (150)

vacuum cleaner [ˈvækjuəm kliːnə] der Staubsauger 2: 5 (150)

°**Valentine's Day** [ˈvæləntaɪnz deɪ] der Valentinstag

vampire [ˈvæmpaɪə] der Vampir 2: 1 (16)

vanilla [vəˈnɪlə] die Vanille 1

vegan [ˈviːɡən]:
1. vegan 1
2. der Veganer, die Veganerin 1

vegetables (pl) [ˈvedʒtəblz] das/die Gemüse 1

vegetarian [vedʒəˈteəriən], infml auch **veggie**:

1. vegetarisch 1
2. der Vegetarier, die Vegetarierin 1

veggie [ˈvedʒi] siehe **vegetarian**

°**verse** [vɜːs] der Vers, die Strophe (Lied)

vertical [ˈvɜːtɪkl] senkrecht, vertikal 2: 5 (151)

very [ˈveri] sehr 1

vet [vet] der Tierarzt, die Tierärztin 1

video [ˈvɪdiəʊ] das Video; Video- 1

view [vjuː]:
1. der (An-)Blick, die (Aus-)Sicht 1
2. **view sth.** etwas anschauen 1

village [ˈvɪlɪdʒ] das Dorf 1

villain [ˈvɪlən] der Verbrecher, die Verbrecherin; der Schurke, die Schurkin 2: 2 (57)

°**Virgo** [ˈvɜːɡəʊ] die Jungfrau (Sternzeichen)

visit [ˈvɪzɪt]:
1. besuchen 1
2. der Besuch 1

visitor [ˈvɪzɪtə] der Besucher, die Besucherin; der Gast 1

visitor information centre [vɪzɪtər ɪnfəˈmeɪʃn sentə] die Touristeninformation, das Fremdenverkehrsbüro 1

visual [ˈvɪʒuəl] visuell, optisch 2: 4 (131)

vocab [ˈvəʊkæb] siehe **vocabulary**

vocabulary [vəˈkæbjələri], infml auch **vocab** der Wortschatz, das Vokabular; das Vokabelverzeichnis 1

°**voice** [vɔɪs] die Stimme

°**voice-over** [ˈvɔɪs əʊvə] der Filmkommentar, die Off-Stimme

W

wait (for) [weɪt] warten (auf) 2: (10/11) **Wait a minute.** Warte mal. / Einen Moment. 2: (10/11) **I can't wait!** Ich kann es kaum erwarten! 2: (10/11)

walk [wɔːk]:
1. der Spaziergang 1
2. (zu Fuß) gehen, wandern 1 **walk around** umhergehen (in) 2: 1 (28) **walk the dog** mit dem Hund rausgehen, mit dem Hund Gassi gehen 2: 5 (154) °**walk over** hinübergehen, rübergehen

walking [ˈwɔːkɪŋ] das Wandern 1

walking boot [ˈwɔːkɪŋ buːt] der Wanderstiefel 2: 2 (57)

wall [wɔːl] die Wand, die Mauer 1 **on the wall** an der Wand; an der Wand 1

°**wanna** [ˈwɒnə] (infml) wollen (= want to)

want [wɒnt] wollen 1 **want to do sth.** etwas tun wollen 1

wanted [ˈwɒntɪd] gesucht; polizeilich gesucht 2: 2 (49)

war [wɔː] der Krieg 2: 2 (59)

wardrobe [ˈwɔːdrəʊb] der Kleiderschrank 1

warm [wɔːm] warm 1

was [wɒz], [wəz] siehe **be**

wash [wɒʃ] (sich) waschen 2: 5 (150)

washing [ˈwɒʃɪŋ] die Wäsche 2: 5 (150) **do the washing** die Wäsche erledigen, Wäsche waschen 2: 5 (150)

watch (sth.) [wɒtʃ] (sich etwas) anschauen; (etwas) beobachten 1

water [ˈwɔːtə] das Wasser 1

watermelon [ˈmelən] die Wassermelone 1

wave [weɪv]:
1. **wave (to sb.)** (jm. zu)winken 1
2. das Winken 1
give sb. a wave jm. zuwinken 1

way [weɪ]:
1. der Weg 1
one-way ticket die einfache Fahrkarte (= ohne Rückfahrt) 2: 1 (19)
2. die Art und Weise 1
(in) this way auf diese Art/Weise 1 **in different ways** unterschiedlich (Adv.), auf unterschiedliche Art/Weise 1
3. die Richtung 2: 1 (27)
that way da entlang, in jene(r) Richtung 2: 1 (27) **the wrong way** (in) die falsche Richtung 2: 1 (27) **this way** hier entlang, in diese(r) Richtung 2: 1 (27)

we [wiː] wir 1 **we're (= we are)** wir sind 1

wear [weə], **wore, worn** tragen, anhaben (Kleidung) 1

weather [ˈweðə] das Wetter, die Witterung 1

web [web] das Netz; das Internet 2: 3 (91) **surf the web** im Internet surfen 2: 3 (91)

website [ˈwebsaɪt] die Website 1

wedding [ˈwedɪŋ] die Hochzeit 1

wedding present [ˈwedɪŋ preznt] das Hochzeitsgeschenk 1

wedding ring [ˈwedɪŋ rɪŋ] der Ehering 1

Wednesday [ˈwenzdeɪ], [ˈwenzdi] der Mittwoch 1

week [wiːk] die Woche 1

weekday [ˈwiːkdeɪ] der Werktag, der Wochentag 1

weekend [wiːkˈend] das Wochenende 1 **at the weekend** am Wochenende 1

weird [wɪəd] seltsam, komisch 1

welcome [ˈwelkəm]:
1. **Welcome to ...** Willkommen in/an ... 1
2. **You're welcome.** Bitte, gern geschehen. / Nichts zu danken. 1

well [wel]:
1. gut (Adv.) 1
Well done. Gut gemacht! 1
2. gesund 2: 3 (92)
Get well soon! Gute Besserung! 2: 3 (92)
3. **Well, ...** Nun, .../ Also, .../ Na ja, ... 1

went [went] siehe **go**

were [wɜː], [wə] siehe **be**

°**wet** [wet] nass

°**whale** [weɪl] der Wal

what [wɒt]:
1. was 1

2. welche(r, s) 1
What about a ...? Wie wäre es mit einer/einem ...? 1 **What about you?** Und du?/Was ist mit dir? 1 **What's your name?** Wie heißt du? 1
wheelchair [ˈwiːltʃeə] der Rollstuhl 1
when [wen]:
1. wann 1
2. wenn *(zeitlich)* 1
3. als *(zeitlich)* 2:1 (16)
where [weə] wo; wohin 1 **Where are you from?** Wo kommst du her? 1
which [wɪtʃ] welche(r, s) 1 **Which clubs ...?** Welche AGs ...? 1
while [waɪl]:
1. während 2:2 (59)
2. **a while** eine Weile, einige Zeit 2:3 (92)
whipped cream [wɪpt ˈkriːm] die Schlagsahne, die geschlagene Sahne 1
white [waɪt] weiß 1
who [huː]:
1. wer 1
2. wen; wem 2:2 (52)
°**3. someone who ...** jemand, der/die ...
whose [huːz] wessen 2:2 (59)
why [waɪ] warum 1 **that's why** deswegen, darum 2:5 (153)
wife [waɪf], *pl* **wives** die (Ehe-)Frau 1
will [wɪl]: **I'll (= I will) be ...** ich werde ... sein 2:5 (148)
win [wɪn], won, won gewinnen 1
wind [wɪnd] der Wind 1
window [ˈwɪndəʊ] das Fenster 1
windsurfing [wɪndsɜːfɪŋ] das Windsurfing 1
windy [ˈwɪndi] windig 1
winner [ˈwɪnə] der Gewinner, die Gewinnerin/der Sieger, die Siegerin 1
winter [ˈwɪntə] der Winter 1
wish [wɪʃ]:
1. (sich) wünschen 2:4 (115)
2. der Wunsch 2:4 (115)
Best wishes Viele Grüße *(Briefschluss)* 2:4 (115) **make a wish** sich etwas wünschen 2:4 (115)
with [wɪð]:
1. mit 1
2. bei 1
with me/us/... bei mir/uns/... 1
°**without** [wɪˈðaʊt] ohne 1
wives [waɪvz] *Plural von* **wife**

wok [wɒk] der Wok *(chinesischer Kochtopf)* 1
woman [ˈwʊmən], *pl* **women** die Frau 1
women [ˈwɪmɪn] *Plural von* **woman**
won [wʌn] *siehe* **win**
wonderful [ˈwʌndəfl] wunderbar 2:1 (21)
°**wonderland** [ˈwʌndəlænd] das Wunderland
won't [wəʊnt]: **they won't (= will not) believe ...** sie werden ... nicht glauben 2:5 (148)
°**woof** [wʊf] Wau
word [wɜːd] das Wort 1 **words (of a song)** *(pl)* der (Song-)Text 2:4 (122)
°**wordbank** [ˈwɜːdbæŋk] die Wortbank *(die Sammlung von Wörtern zu einem Thema)*
wore [wɔː] *siehe* **wear**
work [wɜːk]:
1. funktionieren 1
2. arbeiten 1
work long days lange arbeiten, lange Arbeitstage haben 1 **work sth. out** etwas herausfinden, etwas erarbeiten, etwas verstehen 2:2 (64) °**work on sth.** an etwas arbeiten
3. die Arbeit 1
at work bei der Arbeit, am Arbeitsplatz 1
world [wɜːld] die Welt 2:2 (59) **the best place in the world** der beste Ort der Welt/auf der Welt 2:2 (59)
world war [wɜːld ˈwɔː] der Weltkrieg 2:2 (59)
°**worm** [wɜːm] der Wurm
worn [wɔːn] *siehe* **wear**
worried (about) [ˈwʌrid] beunruhigt, besorgt (wegen) 1
worry [ˈwʌri]:
1. die Sorge 1
2. **worry (about)** sich Sorgen machen (wegen, um) 1
Don't worry. Mach dir keine Sorgen. 1
worse [wɜːs] schlechter, schlimmer 2:3 (85) **for better or (for) worse** was auch immer geschieht, in guten wie in schlechten Zeiten *(beim Ehegelöbnis)* 2:4 (127)
worst [wɜːst] der/die/das Schlechteste, Schlimmste; am schlechtesten, am schlimmsten 2:3 (86)
would [wʊd]: **Would you like ...?** Möchtest du ...? 1 **I'd (= I would) like/**

love ... Ich hätte (liebend) gern .../Ich möchte (liebend gern)... 1 **I'd (= I would) love/like to meet ....** Ich würde mich (liebend) gerne mit ... treffen. 1
write [raɪt], wrote, written schreiben 1 °**write sth. down** etwas aufschreiben
writer [ˈraɪtə] der Autor, die Autorin; der Verfasser, die Verfasserin 2:5 (147)
wrong [rɒŋ] falsch 1 **be wrong** Unrecht haben 1 **Something is wrong.** Irgendetwas ist nicht in Ordnung./Irgendetwas stimmt nicht. 2:3 (93) **What's wrong?** Was ist los?/Was/Wo ist das Problem? 2:3 (93) °**go wrong** schiefgehen
wrote [rəʊt] *siehe* **write**

Y

°**Yay!** [jeɪ] *(infml)* Hurra!
°**yeah** [jeə] *(infml)* ja
year [jɪə] das Jahr; der Jahrgang 1
yellow [ˈjeləʊ] gelb 1
yes [jes] ja 1
yesterday [ˈjestədeɪ] gestern 2:1 (24)
yet [jet]: **... yet?** ... schon ...? 2:4 (119) **not ... yet** noch nicht ... 2:4 (119)
yoga [ˈjəʊɡə] das Yoga 1
yoghurt [ˈjɒɡət] der Joghurt 2:4 (115)
you [juː]:
1. du; dich; dir; ihr; euch; Sie; Ihnen 1
2. man 2:1 (26)
your [jɔː], [jə] dein/e; euer/eure; Ihr/e 1
yours [jɔːz] deine, deiner, deins; eurer, eure, eures; Ihrer, Ihre, Ihres 1
yourself [jəˈself] du/dir/dich (selbst) 2:2 (49)
youth [juːθ] die Jugend; der Jugendliche 1
youth centre [ˈjuːθ sentə] das Jugendzentrum 1

Z

zero [ˈzɪərəʊ], *pl* **zeros** die Null, die Nullen 1
zip wire [ˈzɪp waɪə] die Seilrutsche 2:3 (78/79)
zoo [zuː] der Zoo 1

Das *German-English Dictionary* enthält den **Lernwortschatz** deines Schulbuchs.
Es kann dir eine erste Hilfe sein, wenn du vergessen hast, wie etwas auf Englisch heißt.
Wenn du wissen möchtest, wo das englische Wort zum ersten Mal in deinem Schulbuch vorkommt,
dann kannst du im *English-German Dictionary* (Seiten 277–298) nachschlagen.

Im Dictionary werden folgende **Abkürzungen und Symbole** verwendet:

infml = informal (umgangssprachlich)   *pl = plural* (Mehrzahl)
sb. = somebody (jemand)   *sth. = something* (etwas)
jd. = jemand   jm. = jemandem   jn. = jemanden

A

**abbiegen (rechts/links), nach rechts/
links abbiegen** turn left/right [tɜːn]
Abend evening [ˈiːvnɪŋ]
  am Abend in the evening
Abendessen dinner [ˈdɪnə]
  zum Abendessen for dinner
abends in the evening [ˈiːvnɪŋ]
  9 Uhr abends *(21 Uhr)* 9 p.m. [piːˈem]
aber but [bʌt], [bət]
Abenteuer adventure [ədˈventʃə]
A bis Z: (von) A bis Z (from) A to Z
  [eɪ tu zed]
Abfall rubbish [ˈrʌbɪʃ]
abhängen hang out [hæŋ aʊt]
abschließen *(z. B. Tür)* lock [lɒk]
abwechseln: sich abwechseln take
  turns [tɜːn] **sich dabei abwechseln,
  etwas zu tun** take it in turns
  (to do sth.)
Achse axis [ˈæksɪs]
acht eight [eɪt]
achtzehn eighteen [eɪˈtiːn]
achtzig eighty [ˈeɪti]
addieren add [æd]
Adresse address [əˈdres]
Affe monkey [ˈmʌŋki]
AG *(in der Schule)* school club
  [skuːl klʌb]
aktiv active [ˈæktɪv]
akustisch acoustic [əˈkuːstɪk]
Aktivist, Aktivistin activist [ˈæktɪvɪst]
Aktivität activity [ækˈtɪvəti]
albern stupid [ˈstjuːpɪd]
alle(s) all [ɔːl] **alle 30 Minuten**
  every 30 minutes [ˈevri]
allein alone [əˈləʊn]
allergisch (gegen) allergic (to)
  [əˈlɜːdʒɪk]
alles everything [ˈevriθɪŋ]
Alphabet alphabet [ˈælfəbet]
als as [æz], [əz] *(zeitlich)* when [wen]
also so [səʊ] **Also, ...** Well, ... [wel]
alt old [əʊld] **Wie alt bist du?**
  How old are you?
Alternative; alternativ alternative
  [ɔːlˈtɜːnətɪv]
am: am Anfang at first [æt], [ət]
  am Arbeitsplatz at work
  am besten best [best]
  am Ende (von) at the end (of)
  am größten biggest [ˈbɪɡɪst]
  am Meer by the sea [baɪ]
  am Montag on Monday [ɒn]
  am Morgen in the morning [ɪn]
  am Nachmittag in the afternoon

  am nächsten Tag the next day
  am oberen Ende (von) at the top (of)
  am Strand on the beach
  am Telefon on the phone
  am Wochenende at the weekend
an at [æt], [ət] **an sein (eingeschaltet
  sein)** be on [biː ɒn]
andere(r, s) other [ˈʌðə]
  die anderen the others
  ein/e andere(r, s) another [əˈnʌðə]
anders different [ˈdɪfrənt]
Anfang start [stɑːt]; beginning
  [bɪˈɡɪnɪŋ]
  am Anfang at first [æt], [ət]
anfangen (mit) start [stɑːt]
anfassen, berühren touch [tʌtʃ]
Angst: Angst haben be scared (of)
  [skeəd]
anhaben *(Kleidung)* wear [weə]
anhalten stop [stɒp]
anhören: sich etwas anhören listen
  to sth. [ˈlɪsn]
ankommen arrive [əˈraɪv]
Ankunft arrival [əˈraɪvl]
anlächeln: jn. anlächeln smile at sb.
  [smaɪl]
Anprobe *(im Geschäft)* changing room
  [ˈtʃeɪndʒɪŋ ruːm]
anprobieren *(Kleidung)*, **(etwas)
  anprobieren** try sth. on [traɪ]
Anruf (phone) call [ˈfəʊn kɔːl]
anrufen call [kɔːl]; phone [fəʊn]
Ansage announcement [əˈnaʊnsmənt]
anschauen: etwas/jn. anschauen
  look at sth./sb. [lʊk] **sich etwas
  anschauen** watch sth. [wɒtʃ]
Anspitzer sharpener [ˈʃɑːpnə]
Anspruch: in Anspruch nehmen
  take [teɪk]
Anteil share [ʃeə]
Antwort answer [ˈɑːnsə] **Antwort auf
  die Frage** the answer to the question
antworten answer [ˈɑːnsə]
Anweisung instruction [ɪnˈstrʌkʃn]
Anzug *(Herrenanzug)* suit [suːt]
anziehen: sich anziehen get dressed
  [drest] **etwas anziehen** *(Kleidung)*,
  aufsetzen *(Hut)* put sth. on [pʊt]
App app [æp]
April April [ˈeɪprəl]
Arbeit work [wɜːk] **bei der Arbeit,
  am Arbeitsplatz** at work
Hausarbeit, (lästige) Pflicht chore
  [tʃɔː]
arbeiten work [wɜːk] **lange arbeiten**
  work long days [lɒŋ]

Architekt, Architektin architect
  [ˈɑːkɪtekt]
Ärger trouble [ˈtrʌbl] **Ärger kriegen**
  be in trouble
ärgern annoy [əˈnɔɪ]
ärgerlich annoying [əˈnɔɪɪŋ]
arm poor [pɔː], [pʊə]
Art way [weɪ] **auf diese Art**
  (in) this way, like this [laɪk] **auf
  unterschiedliche Art** in different ways
  eine Art (von) ... a kind (of) ... [kaɪnd],
  sort (of) [sɔːt]
Artikel article [ˈɑːtɪkl]
Arzt, Ärztin doctor [ˈdɒktə]
atmen, ein-/ausatmen breathe
  (in/out) [briːð]
auch also [ˈɔːlsəʊ]; too [tuː]
  auch aus Berlin from Berlin too
auf at [æt], [ət]; in [ɪn]; on [ɒn]
  auf dem Bild, auf dem Foto in the
  picture **auf dem Kopf** upside down
  [ʌpsaɪd ˈdaʊn] **auf den Tisch** onto
  the table [ˈɒntu], [ˈɒntə] **auf dem
  Land** in the country **auf der Weide**
  in the field **auf einmal** suddenly
  [ˈsʌdənli] **auf Englisch** in English
  Auf Wiedersehen! Goodbye. [ɡʊdˈbaɪ]
aufbewahren keep [kiːp]
Aufführung show [ʃəʊ]
Aufgabe exercise [ˈeksəsaɪz]
aufgeregt excited [ɪkˈsaɪtɪd]
aufhören (mit) stop [stɒp]
auflisten list [lɪst]
Aufmerksamkeit attention [əˈtenʃn]
Aufnahme *(Ton-, Bild-)* recording
  [rɪˈkɔːdɪŋ]
aufnehmen record [rɪˈkɔːd]
aufpassen auf look after [lʊk]
aufräumen tidy [ˈtaɪdi] **etwas
  aufräumen** clean sth. up [kliːn]
aufregend exciting [ɪkˈsaɪtɪŋ]
aufschlagen *(Buch)* open [ˈəʊpən]
  Schlagt eure Bücher auf Seite 10 auf.
  Open your books at page 10.
aufstehen *(aus dem Bett)* get up
  [get ˈʌp] **sich hinstellen** stand up
  [stænd ˈʌp]
aufwachsen grow up [ɡrəʊ ʌp]
aufzeichnen record [rɪˈkɔːd]
Auge eye [aɪ]
August August [ɔːˈɡʌst]
aus from [frɒm]
aus ... (heraus/hinaus) out of [aʊt]
Ausdruck phrase [freɪz]
Außerirdische/r; außerirdisch alien
  [ˈeɪliən]

Ausflug, Reise trip [trɪp]
ausruhen: sich ausruhen relax [rɪˈlæks]
Ausrüstung equipment [ɪˈkwɪpmənt]
ausschneiden: etwas ausschneiden cut sth. out [kʌt]
aussehen look [lʊk]
Aussprache pronunciation [prənʌnsiˈeɪʃn]
außerhalb (von) outside [aʊtˈsaɪd]
aussteigen *(aus einem Zug/Bus)* get off (a train/bus) [get ɒf]
Ausstellung show [ʃəʊ]
auswählen choose [tʃuːz]
Auto car [kɑː]
Automat machine [məˈʃiːn]
Autoscheinwerfer car light [ˈkɑː laɪt]

B

babysitten babysit [ˈbeɪbisɪt]
backen bake [beɪk]
Bäckerei bakery [ˈbeɪkəri]
Backofen oven [ˈʌvn]
Backpulver baking powder [ˈbeɪkɪŋ paʊdə]
Badeanzug swimsuit [ˈswɪmsuːt]
Badewanne bath [bɑːθ]
Bad(ezimmer) bathroom [ˈbɑːθruːm]
Badminton badminton [ˈbædmɪntn]
Bahnhof (train) station [ˈtreɪn steɪʃn]
Bahnsteig platform [ˈplætfɔːm]
bald soon [suːn]
Balkon balcony [ˈbælkəni]
Ball ball [bɔːl]
Ballon balloon [bəˈluːn]
Banane banana [bəˈnɑːnə]
Band band [bænd]
Bank *(Geldinstitut)* bank [bæŋk]
Bargeld cash [kæʃ]
Basketball basketball [ˈbɑːskɪtbɔːl]
Basteln crafts *(pl)* [krɑːfts]
Bauarbeiter/in, Bauunternehmer/in builder [ˈbɪldə]
Baum tree [triː]
beängstigend scary [ˈskeəri]
beantworten answer [ˈɑːnsə]
bedeuten mean [miːn]
Bedeutung meaning [ˈmiːnɪŋ]
beenden end [end]; finish [ˈfɪnɪʃ]
Beförderung transport [ˈtrænspɔːt]
beginnen start [stɑːt]
Behälter case [keɪs]
bei at [æt], [ət]; with [wɪð]
　bei der Arbeit at work
　bei ihrer Mutter (zu Hause/daheim) at her mum's (house)
beibringen: jm. beibringen, etwas zu tun teach sb. to do sth. [tiːtʃ]
beide both [bəʊθ]
Bein leg [leg]
Beispiel example [ɪgˈzɑːmpl]
　zum Beispiel for example
　wie zum Beispiel like [laɪk]
bekommen get [get]
belebt busy [ˈbɪzi]
Beleg receipt [rɪˈsiːt]
beliebt (bei) popular (with) [ˈpɒpjələ]
bellen: (jn. an)bellen bark (at sb.) [bɑːk]

benutzen use [juːz]
Benutzer/in user [ˈjuːzə]
beobachten: (etwas) beobachten watch (sth.) [wɒtʃ]
bequem comfortable [ˈkʌmftəbl]
Bereich area [ˈeəriə]
bereit ready [ˈredi]
Berg mountain [ˈmaʊntən]
berichten (über) report (on) [rɪˈpɔːt]
berühmt (für, wegen) famous [ˈfeɪməs]
beschäftigt: (viel) beschäftigt busy [ˈbɪzi] **du bist beschäftigt** you're busy
beschreiben describe [dɪˈskraɪb]
Beschreibung description [dɪˈskrɪpʃn]
beschützen (vor) protect (from/against) [prəˈtekt]
besondere(r, s) special [ˈspeʃl]
besonnen calm [kɑːm]
besorgen: (sich etwas) besorgen get sth. [get]
besorgt (wegen) worried (about) [ˈwʌrid]
besprechen discuss [dɪˈskʌs]
besser better [ˈbetə]
beste(r, s) best [best] **der beste Sohn überhaupt / der beste Sohn, den man sich wünschen kann** the best son ever [ˈevə]
Bestie beast [biːst]
Bestimmungsort destination [destɪˈneɪʃn]
bestürzt upset [ʌpˈset]
Besuch visit [ˈvɪzɪt]
besuchen visit [ˈvɪzɪt]
Besucher/in visitor [ˈvɪzɪtə]
beten pray [preɪ]
Betrieb business [ˈbɪznəs]
Bett bed [bed] **ins Bett gehen** go to bed
beunruhigt worried (about) [ˈwʌrid]
beurteilen rate sth. [ˈreɪt]
bevor before [bɪˈfɔː] **bevor (du liest)** before (you read)
bewegen: sich bewegen move [muːv]
bewerten: etwas bewerten rate sth. [ˈreɪt]
bewölkt cloudy [ˈklaʊdi]
Bibliothek library [ˈlaɪbrəri]
Bild picture [ˈpɪktʃə] **auf dem Bild** in the picture [ɪn]
Bildschirm screen [skriːn]
Bildschirmpräsentation slide show [ˈslaɪd ʃəʊ]
Bildunterschrift caption [ˈkæpʃn]
billig cheap [tʃiːp]
Biologie biology [baɪˈɒlədʒi]
bis to [tu], [tə] **Bis bald!** See you soon. [ˈsiː juː], [ˈsiː jə] **Bis dann.** See you. **bis jetzt, bis hierher** so far [səʊ fɑː] **Bis später.** Speak later. [ˈleɪtə]
bis *(zeitlich)* until/till [ənˈtɪl]
bisschen: ein bisschen a little [ˈlɪtl]
bitte please [pliːz] **Bitte schön. / Hier, bitte.** Here you are. [hɪə juː ˈɑː] **Bitte, gern geschehen.** You're welcome. [ˈwelkəm]
bitten: jn. bitten, etwas zu tun ask sb. to do sth. [ɑːsk] **jn. um etwas bitten** ask sb. for sth.

blasen blow [bləʊ]
blau blue [bluː]
Blazer *(das Jackett, oft Teil der Schuluniform)* blazer [ˈbleɪzə]
bleiben stay [steɪ]
Bleistift pencil [ˈpensl]
Bleistift(an)spitzer pencil sharpener [ˈpensl ʃɑːpnə]
blind blind [blaɪnd]
Blindenhund guide dog [ˈgaɪd dɒg]
blöd stupid [ˈstjuːpɪd]
bloß just [dʒʌst]; only [ˈəʊnli]
Blume flower [ˈflaʊə]
Blüte flower [ˈflaʊə]
Bockwurst sausage [ˈsɒsɪdʒ]
Boden ground [graʊnd]
Bohne: die weißen Bohnen in Tomatensoße baked beans *(pl)* [beɪkt ˈbiːnz]
Bonbon sweet [swiːt]
Bowling bowling [ˈbəʊlɪŋ]
Boxen boxing [ˈbɒksɪŋ]
boxen box [bɒks]
braten fry [fraɪ] **gebraten** fried [fraɪd]
Brathähnchen chicken [ˈtʃɪkɪn]
Bratwurst sausage [ˈsɒsɪdʒ]
brauchen need [niːd]; *(Zeit)* take [teɪk]
braun brown [braʊn]
Braut bride [braɪd]
Bräutigam bridegroom [ˈbraɪdgruːm]
Brautjungfer bridesmaid [ˈbraɪdzmeɪd]
brav good [gʊd]
Brief letter [ˈletə] **der kurze Brief** note [nəʊt]
Brille glasses *(pl)* [ˈglɑːsɪz]
bringen bring [brɪŋ]; take [teɪk] **jn. dazu bringen, etwas zu tun** make sb. do sth. [meɪk]
britisch British [ˈbrɪtɪʃ]
Brot bread [bred]
Brücke bridge [brɪdʒ]
Bruder brother [ˈbrʌðə]
Buch book [bʊk]
buchen book [bʊk]
Buchseite page (p.) [peɪdʒ]
Bücherei library [ˈlaɪbrəri]
Büchse tin [tɪn]
Buchstabe letter [ˈletə]
buchstabieren spell [spel]
Bühne stage [steɪdʒ]
bunt colourful [ˈkʌləfl]
Burg castle [ˈkɑːsl]
Bürger/in citizen [ˈsɪtɪzn]
Büro office [ˈɒfɪs]
Bürste brush [brʌʃ]
bürsten brush [brʌʃ]
Bus bus [bʌs] **im Bus** on the bus **mit dem Bus** by bus
Bushaltestelle bus stop [ˈbʌs stɒp]
Butter butter [ˈbʌtə]

C

Café cafe [ˈkæfeɪ]
Campingplatz campsite [ˈkæmpsaɪt]
Cash cash [kæʃ]
Cent cent [sent]

Chaos mess [mes]
Charakter character [ˈkærəktə], personality [pɜːsəˈnæləti]
chatten (mit) chat [tʃæt]
Chemikalie; chemisch chemical [ˈkemɪkl]
clever smart [smɑːt]
Code code [kəʊd]
codieren code [kəʊd]
Cola cola [ˈkəʊlə]
Comic comic [ˈkɒmɪk]
Computer computer [kəmˈpjuːtə]
cool cool [kuːl]
Cousin/e cousin [ˈkʌzn]
Cricket *(Mannschaftssportart)* cricket [ˈkrɪkɪt]
Curry *(Gewürz/Gericht)* curry [ˈkʌri]
Custard *(Vanillesoße)* custard [ˈkʌstəd]

D

da there [ðeə] **da drüben** over there
Dachgeschoss top floor [tɒp ˈflɔː]
daher so [səʊ]
dahin there [ðeə]
damit so that [səʊ ðæt]
danach then [ðen]
Dank: Vielen Dank. Thank you very much. [ˈθæŋk juː] **Danke (schön).** Thank you. [ˈθæŋk juː]; thanks [θæŋks] **Danke vielmals.** Thank you very much. [mʌtʃ]
dankbar: (jm. für etwas) dankbar sein be grateful (to sb. for sth.) [ˈɡreɪtfl]
danken: Nichts zu danken. You're welcome. [ˈwelkʌm] **sich bei jm. bedanken** thank sb.
dann then [ðen]
das
1. *(Artikel)* the [ðə]
2. *(Relativpronomen)* that [ðæt]
das (dort) that [ðæt] **das (da)** that's (= that is)
dasselbe the same [seɪm]
Datei file [faɪl]
Datum date [deɪt] **Datum des Geburtstags** birthday date [ˈbɜːθdeɪ]
dauern take [teɪk]
Decke (zum Zudecken) blanket [ˈblæŋkɪt]
dein/e your [jɔː], [jə]
Dekoration decoration [dekəˈreɪʃn]
dekorieren decorate [ˈdekəreɪt]
denken think [θɪŋk] **daran denken (etwas zu tun)** remember (to do sth.) [rɪˈmembə] **Ich denke, …** I think … **an jn./etwas denken** think of sb./sth. [θɪŋk]
Delfin dolphin [ˈdɒlfɪn]
der
1. *(Artikel)* the [ðə]
2. *(Relativpronomen)* that [ðæt]
derselbe the same [seɪm]
Design design [dɪˈzaɪn]
Dessert dessert [dɪˈzɜːt]
deutlich clear [klɪə] **deutlich sprechen** speak clearly [spiːk ˈklɪəli]
Deutsch; deutsch German [ˈdʒɜːmən]
Deutsche German [ˈdʒɜːmən]
Deutschland Germany [ˈdʒɜːməni]

Dezember December [dɪˈsembə]
Dia slide [slaɪd]
die
1. *(Artikel)* the [ðə]
2. *(Relativpronomen)* that [ðæt]
die dort those [ðəʊz]
Diele hall [hɔːl]
Dienstag Tuesday [ˈtjuːzdeɪ]
diese (hier) these [ðiːz]
diese(r, s) this [ðɪs]
dieselbe(n) the same [seɪm]
Ding thing [θɪŋ] **Dinge, die Menschen gebrauchen/ benutzen können** things that people can use [θɪŋ] **Dinge zum Essen** things to eat
Direktor, Direktorin head teacher [ˈhed tiːtʃə]
diskutieren discuss [dɪˈskʌs]
Donnerstag Thursday [ˈθɜːzdeɪ]
Dorf village [ˈvɪlɪdʒ]
dort there [ðeə] **dort drüben** over there [ˈəʊvə]
dorthin there [ðeə]
Dose tin [tɪn]
Drache dragon [ˈdræɡən]
dramatisch dramatic [drəˈmætɪk]
dran: jd. ist dran it is sb.'s turn [tɜːn] **Wann bin ich dran (etwas zu tun)?** When is (it) my turn (to do sth.)?
draußen; nach draußen outside [aʊtˈsaɪd]
drehen turn [tɜːn] **Dreh etwas auf den Kopf.** Turn it upside down. [ʌpsaɪd ˈdaʊn] **etwas umdrehen** turn sth. (over)
drei three [θriː]
dreißig thirty [ˈθɜːti]
dreizehn thirteen [θɜːˈtiːn]
drinnen; nach drinnen inside [ɪnˈsaɪd]
dritte(r, s) third (3rd) [θɜːd]
Drohne drone [drəʊn]
du you [juː] **du bist** you're (= you are) [jɔː] **du bist beschäftigt** you're busy [ˈbɪzi]
du/dir/dich (selbst) yourself [jəˈself]
dürfen: ich darf nicht I mustn't [mʌsnt] **Darf ich …?** May I …?
dunkel dark [dɑːk]
dumm stupid [ˈstjuːpɪd]
durch through [θruː]
Durchsage announcement [əˈnaʊnsmənt]
durstig sein, Durst haben be thirsty [ˈθɜːsti]
Dusche shower [ˈʃaʊə]
duschen: (sich) duschen have a shower [ˈʃaʊə]

E

echt, wirklich real [rɪəl]
Eckladen corner shop [ˈkɔːnə ʃɒp]
Ehemann husband [ˈhʌzbənd]
ehrlich honest [ˈɒnɪst]
Ei egg [eɡ]
Eidechse lizard [ˈlɪzəd]
eigene(r, s): mein/ein eigenes Zimmer my own room [əʊn]
Eimer *(Mülleimer)* bin [bɪn]

ein(e) *(Artikel)* a [ə]; *(vor Vokalen)* an [ən] **ein paar** some [sʌm], [səm]
ein paar, einige a few [fjuː]
ein bisschen, ein wenig some; a little [ˈlɪtl]; a bit [ə ˈbɪt] **noch ein(e)** another [əˈnʌðə]
einander, sich (gegenseitig) each other [iːtʃ ˈʌðə]
einfach just [dʒʌst]
einfach easy [ˈiːzi]
Einfluss (auf) effect (on) [ɪˈfekt]
Einführung introduction [ɪntrəˈdʌkʃn]
einige some [sʌm], [səm]
Einkäufe shopping [ˈʃɒpɪŋ] **Einkäufe erledigen** do the shopping, be at the shops [ʃɒp]
Einkaufen shopping [ˈʃɒpɪŋ]
einkaufen shop (for sth.) [ʃɒp] **einkaufen gehen** do the shopping [ˈʃɒpɪŋ]; go shopping
Einkaufsliste shopping list [ˈʃɒpɪŋ lɪst]
Einkaufszentrum shopping centre [ˈʃɒpɪŋ sentə]
einladen (zu, nach) invite (to) [ɪnˈvaɪt]
Einladung (zu, nach) invitation (to) [ˌɪnvɪˈteɪʃn]
Einleitung introduction [ɪntrəˈdʌkʃn]
einmal: noch einmal again [əˈɡen] **einmal** once [wʌns] **einmal pro Monat** once a month [mʌnθ]
eins one [wʌn]
einsammeln collect [kəˈlekt]
einschlafen fall asleep [əˈsliːp]
einschließen include [ɪnˈkluːd]
einsteigen (in einen Zug, Bus) get on (a train/bus) [ɡet ɒn]
Eintrittskarte ticket [ˈtɪkɪt]
einverstanden: mit etwas einverstanden sein agree [əˈɡriː]
Einzel-, einzelne(r,s) single [ˈsɪŋɡl]
Einzugsfeier house-warming (party) [ˈhaʊs wɔːmɪŋ]
Eis *(Speiseeis)* ice cream [ˈaɪs kriːm]
Eisenbahn train [treɪn]
Elefant elephant [ˈelɪfənt]
elektrisch, Elektro- electric [ɪˈlektrɪk]
Elektronik; elektronische Geräte electronics [ɪlekˈtrɒnɪks]
elf eleven [ɪˈlevən]
Eltern parents *(pl)* [ˈpeərənts]
Ende end [end] **das obere Ende** top [tɒp] **am oberen Ende** at the top (of) **das untere Ende** bottom [ˈbɒtəm]
Endung *(Text, Geschichte)* ending [ˈendɪŋ]
enden end [end] finish [ˈfɪnɪʃ]
Energie power [ˈpaʊə]
energiegeladen energetic [enəˈdʒetɪk]
England England [ˈɪŋɡlənd]
Englisch; englisch English [ˈɪŋɡlɪʃ] **auf Englisch** in English [ɪn]
Enkel grandson [ˈɡrænsʌn]
Enkelin granddaughter [ˈɡrændɔːtə]
entdecken discover [dɪˈskʌvə]
Entschuldigung. Sorry./I'm sorry. [ˈsɒri] **Entschuldigung, … / Entschuldigen Sie, …** Excuse me, … [ɪkˈskjuːz miː]
entspannen: sich entspannen relax [rɪˈlæks]

enttäuscht (von) disappointed (in/with) [dɪsəˈpɔɪntɪd]
er he [hiː] **er ist** he's (= he is) **er ist nicht** he isn't (= is not)
Erbse pea [piː]
Erdbeere strawberry [ˈstrɔːbəri]
Erdboden ground [graʊnd]
Erde earth [ɜːθ]
Erdgeschoss ground floor [graʊnd ˈflɔː]
Erdkunde geography [dʒiˈɒɡrəfi]
Ereignis event [ɪˈvent]
Erfahrung experience [ɪkˈspɪəriəns]
erforschen research [rɪˈsɜːtʃ]
erfolgreich successful [səkˈsesfl]
Erholung rest [rest]
erinnern: sich erinnern an remember [rɪˈmembə] **sich daran erinnern, etwas getan zu haben** remember doing sth.
erkennen: jn./etwas erkennen an … know sb./sth. by … [nəʊ]
erklären: jm. etwas erklären explain sth. to sb. [ɪkˈspleɪn]
Erklärung explanation [ekspləˈneɪʃn]
Erlebnis experience [ɪkˈspɪəriəns]
ernähren feed [fiːd]
erschrecken scare sb. [skeə]
erst only [ˈəʊnli]
erstaunlich amazing [əˈmeɪzɪŋ]
erste(r, s) first [fɜːst] **als Erstes** first
erzählen tell [tel]
es it [ɪt] **es ist** (bei Sachen und Tieren auch: er ist; sie ist) it's (= it is)
   es ist … / es gibt … there's [ðeəz]
   es sind … / es gibt … there are [ˈðeər ɑː] **es sollte …** it should [ʃʊd]
   Es macht mir nichts aus … I don't mind [maɪnd]
Essen cooking [ˈkʊkɪŋ]; food [fuːd]; meal [miːl]
essen eat [iːt] **Dinge zum Essen** things to eat
Esslöffel tablespoon [ˈteɪblspuːn]
Esszimmer dining room [ˈdaɪnɪŋ ruːm]
Etage floor [flɔː] **die oberste Etage** top floor [tɒp ˈflɔː]
Etui case [keɪs]
etwas some [sʌm], [səm]; something [ˈsʌmθɪŋ]
euer/eure your [jɔː], [jə]
Euro euro, euros (pl) [ˈjʊərəʊ]

F

Fach subject [ˈsʌbdʒɪkt]
Fähigkeit skill [skɪl]
Fahne flag [flæg]
Fähre ferry [ˈferi]
fahren go [gəʊ]; travel [ˈtrævl] **mit dem Fahrrad fahren** ride a bike [raɪd] **Rad fahren** cycle [ˈsaɪkl] **Skateboard fahren** skateboard [ˈskeɪtbɔːd] **mit dem Auto fahren** drive [draɪv]
Fahrkarte ticket [ˈtɪkɪt]
Fahrrad bike [baɪk]
Fahrt journey [ˈdʒɜːni]
Fakt fact [fækt]
fallen, hinfallen fall [fɔːl]
falls if [ɪf]

falsch wrong [rɒŋ]
falscher Freund (Übersetzungsfalle) false friend [fɔːls ˈfrend]
falsche Richtung, (in) die falsche Richtung the wrong way [rɒŋ weɪ]
falten fold [fəʊld]
Familie family [ˈfæməli]
Familienname family name [ˈfæməli neɪm]
Fan fan [fæn]
fantasievoll imaginative [ɪˈmædʒɪnətɪv]
Farbe colour [ˈkʌlə] **Welche Farbe hat …?** What colour is …?
farbig colourful [ˈkʌləfl]
fast nearly [ˈnɪəli]
fasten fast [fɑːst]
Fasten brechen break the fast [breɪk ðə fɑːst]
faul lazy [ˈleɪzi]
Favorit/in favourite [ˈfeɪvərɪt]
Februar February [ˈfebruəri]
Federball badminton [ˈbædmɪntən]
Federmäppchen pencil case [ˈpensl keɪs]
Feedback (Rückmeldung) feedback (no pl) [ˈfiːdbæk]
Fehler mistake [mɪˈsteɪk]
Feier ceremony [ˈserəməni]
feiern celebrate [ˈselɪbreɪt]
Feld field [fiːld]
Fenster window [ˈwɪndəʊ]
Ferien holidays (pl) [ˈhɒlədeɪz]
Fernsehen, Fernseher TV [tiːˈviː]
fertig ready [ˈredi]
Fertigkeit skill [skɪl]
Feuer fire [ˈfaɪə]
Feuerwehrauto fire engine [ˈfaɪər endʒɪn]
Feuerwehrmann, Feuerwehrfrau firefighter [ˈfaɪəfaɪtə]
Feuerwerkskörper firework [ˈfaɪəwɜːk]
fies mean [miːn]
Figur (aus einer Geschichte) character [ˈkærəktə]
Film film [fɪlm] **die sechs besten Filme** the top six films [tɒp]
Filmstar star [stɑː]
finden find [faɪnd] **Ich finde, …** I think … [θɪŋk]
Finger finger [ˈfɪŋgə]
Fisch fish, (pl) fish [fɪʃ] **Fisch mit Pommes frites** fish and chips [fɪʃ ən ˈtʃɪps] **Imbissstube, die Fisch mit Pommes frites verkauft** fish and chip shop [ʃɒp]
Flagge flag [flæg]
Flasche bottle [ˈbɒtl]
Fleisch meat [miːt]
fleißig hard-working [hɑːd ˈwɜːkɪŋ]
fliegen fly [flaɪ]
Flughafen airport [ˈeəpɔːt]
Flugzeug plane [pleɪn]
Flur hall [hɔːl]
Fluss river [ˈrɪvə] **am Fluss** by the river [baɪ ðə ˈrɪvə]
folgen follow [ˈfɒləʊ]
Folie slide [slaɪd]
Forschungen research [rɪˈsɜːtʃ]
fort away [əˈweɪ]

Fortbewegungsmittel transport [ˈtrænspɔːt]
fortfahren continue [kənˈtɪnjuː] **mit etwas fortfahren** continue to do sth. [duː]
fortsetzen: (sich) fortsetzen continue [kənˈtɪnjuː]
Foto photo [ˈfəʊtəʊ] **auf dem Foto** in the photo **ein Foto machen** take a photo
Fotografie, Fotografieren photography [fəˈtɒgrəfi]
Fotograf/in photographer [fəˈtɒgrəfə]
Frage question [kwestʃən] **Antwort auf die Frage** the answer to the question [ˈɑːnsə] **eine Frage stellen** ask a question **Habt ihr / Hast du (irgendwelche) Fragen?** Do you have any questions?
fragen ask [ɑːsk]
Frau woman, (pl) women [ˈwʊmən], [ˈwɪmɪn] **Frau Lee** (Anrede für verheiratete Frauen) Mrs Lee [ˈmɪsɪz] (allgemeine Anrede für Frauen) Ms Lee [mɪz] **Ehefrau** wife [waɪf]
frech rude [ruːd]
frei free [friː] **freie Zeit** free time [taɪm]
Freitag Friday [ˈfraɪdeɪ], [ˈfraɪdi]
Freizeit free time [ˈfriː taɪm]
Fremdenverkehrsbüro tourist information centre [tʊərɪst ɪnfəˈmeɪʃn sentə]
fressen eat [iːt]
freuen: Freut mich, dich/euch/Sie kennenzulernen. Nice to meet you. [naɪs] **sich auf etwas freuen** look forward to sth.
Freund/in friend [ˈfrend] **Das hier sind meine Freunde/Freundinnen.** These are my friends. [ðiːz] **ihre Freunde/Freundinnen** her friends [hɜː], [hə] **seine Freunde/Freundinnen** his friends [hɪz] **(feste) Freundin** girlfriend [ˈgɜːlfrend] **einen Freund / eine Freundin / Freunde finden** make a friend/friends [meɪk ə frend]
freundlich friendly [ˈfrendli]; kind [kaɪnd]
Frieden peace [piːs]
frieren be cold [kəʊld]
Friseur/in hairdresser [ˈheədresə]
frittieren fry [fraɪ] **frittiert** fried [fraɪd]
froh happy [ˈhæpi]; glad [glæd]
früh early [ˈɜːli]
Frühling spring [sprɪŋ]
Frühstück breakfast [ˈbrekfəst]
fühlen: sich fühlen feel [fiːl]
führen lead [liːd]
Füller pen [pen]
für for [fɔː] **für 30 Sekunden** for 30 seconds
fünf five [faɪv]
fünfzehn fifteen [fɪfˈtiːn]
fünfzig fifty [ˈfɪfti]
fürchterlich terrible [ˈterəbl]
Fuß foot [fʊt]
Fußball football [ˈfʊtbɔːl]

Fußboden floor [flɔ:]
Fußgelenk ankle [ˈæŋkl]
Futter food [fu:d]
füttern feed [fi:d]

G

ganz quite [kwaɪt] **ganz (still)**
perfectly (still) [ˈpɜːfɪktli]
die ganze Familie all the family
gar nichts not ... at all [nɒt ət ɔːl]
Garage garage [ˈgærɑːʒ]
Garten garden [ˈgɑːdn]
Gast visitor [ˈvɪzɪtə]
Gebäude building [ˈbɪldɪŋ]
geben give [gɪv] **es gibt ...** there's
(= there is) ... [ˈðeəz]; there are ...
[ˈðeər ɑː] **es gibt keine ...** there
aren't any ... [ˈeni] **Was gibt es zum
Mittagessen?** What's for lunch?
[lʌntʃ]
geboren: er wurde geboren he was
born [ˈbɔːn]
Geburtstag birthday [ˈbɜːθdeɪ] **an
meinem Geburtstag** on my birthday
Datum des Geburtstags birthday
date [deɪt] **Herzlichen Glückwunsch
zum Geburtstag!** Happy birthday!
[ˈhæpi] **Ich habe im April Geburtstag.**
My birthday is in April. **Wann hast du
Geburtstag?** When's your birthday?
Gedankenkarte mind map
[ˈmaɪnd mæp]
Gedicht poem [ˈpəʊɪm]
geduldig patient [ˈpeɪʃnt]
gefährlich dangerous [ˈdeɪndʒərəs]
Gefühl feeling [ˈfiːlɪŋ]
gegen against [əˈgenst]
Gegend: ländliche Gegend country
[ˈkʌntri] **Gegend** area [ˈeəriə]
Gegenteil opposite [ˈɒpəzɪt]
geheim secret [ˈsiːkrət]
Geheimnis secret [ˈsiːkrət]
gehen go [gəʊ] **ins Bett gehen** go to
bed [bed] **nach Hause gehen**
go home [həʊm] **Wie geht's? /
Wie geht es dir/euch/Ihnen?**
How are you? [haʊ] **(zu Fuß) gehen**
walk [wɔːk] **mit dem Hund Gassi
gehen** walk the dog [wɔːk ðə dɒg]
Geist ghost [gəʊst]
gelangen, (hin)kommen (nach) get to
[get tu]
gelangweilt bored [bɔːd]
gelb yellow [ˈjeləʊ]
Geld money [ˈmʌni]
Geldautomat cash machine
[ˈkæʃ məʃiːn]
Gelee jelly [ˈdʒeli]
gemein mean [miːn]
Gemüse vegetables (pl) [ˈvedʒtəblz]
gemütlich comfortable [ˈkʌmftəbl]
genießen enjoy [ɪnˈdʒɔɪ] **es genießen,
etwas zu tun** enjoy doing sth.
genug enough [ɪˈnʌf]
Geografie geography [dʒiˈɒgrəfi]
Geräusch noise [nɔɪz]
gerade (eben) just [dʒʌst]
gerade; (Haare glatt) straight [streɪt]

geradeaus (weiter) straight on
[streɪt ɒn]
Gericht (Mahlzeit) dish [dɪʃ]
gern: ich hätte gern ... I'd (= I would)
like ... [laɪk] **Ich hätte liebend gern ... /
Ich möchte liebend gern ...** I'd
(= I would) love ... [lʌv] **Ich würde
mich (liebend) gerne mit ... treffen.**
I'd (= I would) like/love to meet ...
Geruch smell [smel]
Geschäft shop [ʃɒp]
Geschäft business [ˈbɪznəs]
Geschäftsfrau business woman
[ˈbɪznəs wʊmən]
geschehen: (jm.) geschehen happen (to
sb.) [ˈhæpən] **Bitte, gern geschehen.**
You're welcome. [ˈwelkʌm]
Geschenk present [ˈpreznt]; gift [gɪft]
Geschichte (Erzählung) story [ˈstɔːri];
vergangene Zeiten history [ˈhɪstri]
so/solch eine Geschichte a story
like this [laɪk]
Geschirrspülmaschine dishwasher
[ˈdɪʃwɒʃə]
Gesicht face [feɪs]
Gespenst ghost [gəʊst]
Gespräch talk [tɔːk]; conversation
[kɒnvəˈseɪʃn]
gesellig sociable [ˈsəʊʃəbl]
Gestaltung design [dɪˈzaɪn]
Gestank smell [smel]
gestern yesterday [ˈjestədeɪ]
gesund healthy [ˈhelθi]
Gesundheit health [helθ]
Getränk drink [drɪŋk]
Gewerbegebiet estate [ɪˈsteɪt]
Gewinn prize [praɪz]
gewinnen win [wɪn]
Gewinner/in winner [ˈwɪnə]
als Gewinner/in as the winner
Gewürz spice [spaɪs]
Gitarre guitar [gɪˈtɑː]
Glas(gefäß) jar [dʒɑː]
Glasur icing [ˈaɪsɪŋ]
glauben think [θɪŋk] **Ich glaube, ...**
I think ... **(an etwas) glauben** believe
[bɪˈliːv]
gleich the same [seɪm]
global, weltweit global [ˈgləʊbl]
Glück: Glücks- lucky [ˈlʌki]
Glück haben be lucky
Glück, Zufriedenheit happiness
[ˈhæpinəs]
glücklich happy [ˈhæpi]; lucky [ˈlʌki]
glücklicherweise luckily [ˈlʌkɪli]
Glückszahl lucky number
[lʌki ˈnʌmbə]
Gold gold [gəʊld]
goldfarben gold [gəʊld]
Gott god [gɒd]
graben dig [dɪg]
Gramm gram (g) [græm]
Grad degree [dɪˈgriː]
Grad, Stufe, Niveau level [ˈlevl]
grau grey [greɪ]
Grillen barbecue [ˈbɑːbɪkjuː]
Grillfest barbecue [ˈbɑːbɪkjuː]

groß big [bɪg] **der/die/das größte,
am größten** biggest **groß (Person),
hoch (Gebäude)** tall [tɔːl]
großartig amazing [əˈmeɪzɪŋ];
awesome [ˈɔːsəm]; great [greɪt]
Größe size [saɪz]; (bei Menschen)
height [haɪt]
Großbritannien (Great) Britain [ˈbrɪtn]
Großeltern grandparents (pl)
[ˈgrænpeərənts]
Großstadt city [ˈsɪti]
großzügig generous [ˈdʒenərəs]
grün green [griːn]
grün/umweltfreundlich werden
go green [gəʊ]
Gruppe group [gruːp]
gruselig scary [ˈskeəri]
gut good [gʊd]; (Adv.) well [wel]
Es geht mir gut. I'm OK. [əʊˈkeɪ]
etwas gut können; gut in etwas sein
be good at sth. / at doing sth.
Gut gemacht. Well done. [dʌn]
gut umgehen können mit ... be good
with ... **Mir geht es gut.** I'm fine.
[faɪn] **so gut** so good [səʊ] **Gute
Besserung! / Werde bald gesund!**
Get better/well soon!

H

Haar, Haare hair [heə]
haben have [hæv] **er/sie/es hat**
he/she/it has [hæz], [həz]
Hähnchen chicken [ˈtʃɪkɪn]
halb sieben half past six [hɑːf]
Halle hall [hɔːl]
Hallo. Hello. [həˈləʊ]; Hi. [haɪ]
Hallo allerseits! Hello everybody!
[ˈevribɒdi]
Hals neck [nek]
halten stop [stɒp]
halten: behalten keep [kiːp] **etwas
halten** hold [həʊld]
Hamburger (Frikadelle) burger [ˈbɜːgə]
Hamster hamster [ˈhæmstə]
Hand hand [hænd] **Hand/Hände
hochstrecken** put your hand/hands
up [pʊt]
handeln, sich verhalten act [ækt]
Handschuh glove [glʌv]
Handy phone [fəʊn]
hart hard [hɑːd]
Hass hate [heɪt]
hassen hate [heɪt]
Haupt- main [meɪn]
Hauptgericht main course [ˈkɔːs];
main dish [dɪʃ]
Hauptstadt capital (city) [ˈkæpɪtl]
Haus house [haʊs]
nach Hause gehen go home [həʊm]
im Haus inside the house [ɪnˈsaɪd]
wieder zu Hause back at home [bæk]
zu Hause at home
Hausaufgabe(n) homework
[ˈhəʊmwɜːk] **Hausaufgaben machen**
do your homework **Was haben wir
als Hausaufgabe(n) auf?** What's for
homework? [wɒts fɔː]
Hausmüll rubbish [ˈrʌbɪʃ]
Hausschuhe slippers [slɪpə]

Haustier pet [pet]
heben lift [lɪft]
Heftseite page (p.) [peɪdʒ]
Heim home [həʊm]
heiraten marry [ˈmæri]
heiß hot [hɒt] **heiße (Trink-)-Schokolade** hot chocolate [ˈtʃɒklət]
heißen: Wie heißt du? What's your name? [wɒts jɔː ˈneɪm]
hektisch busy [ˈbɪzi]
Held/in hero [ˈhɪərəʊ]
helfen help [help]
Helm helmet [ˈhelmɪt]
heraus, hinaus out [aʊt]
herausfinden find out (about) [ˌfaɪnd ˈaʊt] **etwas herausfinden** work sth. out [wɜːk]
Herausforderung challenge [ˈtʃælɪndʒ]
Herbst autumn [ˈɔːtəm]
Herr Lee Mr Lee [ˈmɪstə]
herrschen (über) rule [ruːl]
herstellen make [meɪk]
herunter down [daʊn]
hervorheben highlight [ˈhaɪlaɪt]
Herzog duke [djuːk]
heute today [təˈdeɪ] **heute Morgen/Abend** this morning/evening [ðɪs] **heute Nacht/Abend** tonight [təˈnaɪt]
hier here [hɪə] **Hier, bitte.** Here you are. **hier herüber; hier drüben** over here [ˈəʊvə]
hierher here [hɪə]
Highlight (Höhepunkt) highlight [ˈhaɪlaɪt]
Hilfe help [help]
hilfreich helpful [ˈhelpfl]; useful [ˈjuːsfl]
hilfsbereit helpful [ˈhelpfl]
hinauf up [ʌp]
hinaus out [aʊt]
hinsetzen: sich hinsetzen sit down [sɪt ˈdaʊn]
hinter behind [bɪˈhaɪnd]
hinunter down [daʊn] **hinunter von** off [ɒf]
hinzufügen add [æd]
Hobby hobby [ˈhɒbi]
hoch up [ʌp]; high [haɪ]
Hochgenuss treat [ˈtriːt]
Hochzeit wedding [ˈwedɪŋ]
Hockey hockey [ˈhɒki]
Höhe height [haɪt]
hoffen hope [həʊp]
höflich polite [pəˈlaɪt]
holen: (sich etwas) holen get sth. [get]
Honig honey [ˈhʌni]
hören hear [hɪə]
Horoskop horoscope [ˈhɒrəskəʊp]
Hose trousers (pl) [ˈtraʊzəz]
Hotdog (heißes Würstchen in einem Brötchen) hot dog [ˈhɒt dɒg]
Hügel hill [hɪl]
Huhn chicken [ˈtʃɪkɪn]
Hund dog [dɒg]
Hunger: Ich habe Hunger. I'm hungry. [ˈhʌŋgri]
hungrig hungry [ˈhʌŋgri]
Husten cough [kɒf]

Hut hat [hæt]

ich I [aɪ] **Ich bin** I'm (= I am) [æm] **Ich bin's.** It's me. **Ich nicht!** (= Ich bin/war/habe/… es/das nicht!) Not me! [nɒt]
Idee idea [aɪˈdɪə]
ihm, ihn him [hɪm]
Ihnen (höfliche Anrede) you [juː]
ihnen them [ðem], [ðəm]
ihr (Plural von „du") you [juː] **ihr seid** you're (= you are) [jɔː]
Ihr/e … (besitzanzeigend zur höflichen Anrede „Sie") your [jɔː], [jə]
ihr/e … (vor Nomen; besitzanzeigend)
  1. (zu „she") her … [hɜː], [hə]
  2. (zu „it") its … [ɪts]
  3. (zu „they") their … [ðeə]
immer always [ˈɔːlweɪz]
immer noch still [stɪl]
in at [æt], [ət]; in [ɪn] **in den Urlaub** on holiday [ˈhɒlədeɪ] **in der Nähe von** near [nɪə] **in der Schule** at school [skuːl] **in der Stadt** in town [taʊn] **in die Stadt / ins Zimmer (hinein)** into town / into the room [ˈɪntu], [ˈɪntə]
Indien India [ˈɪndiə]
Informatik computing [kəmˈpjuːtɪŋ]
Information information [ɪnfəˈmeɪʃn]
informieren: sich informieren (über) find out (about) [faɪnd ˈaʊt]
innen; nach innen inside [ɪnˈsaɪd]
innerhalb (von) inside [ɪnˈsaɪd]
insbesondere especially [ɪˈspeʃəli]
Insekt insect [ˈɪnsekt]
intelligent smart [smɑːt]
interessant interesting [ˈɪntrəstɪŋ]
interessiert (an) interested (in) [ˈɪntrəstɪd]
Internet internet [ˈɪntənet]
irgendetwas anything [ˈeniθɪŋ]
irgendjemand anybody [ˈenibɒdi]; anyone [ˈeniwʌn]
irgendwo(hin) somewhere [ˈsʌmweə]

Ja. Yes. [jes] **Na ja, …** Well, … [wel]
Jachthafen marina [məˈriːnə]
Jacke, Jackett jacket [ˈdʒækɪt]
Jahr year [jɪə] **Ich bin elf Jahre alt.** I'm eleven years old. [jɪəz]
Jahreszeit season [ˈsiːzn]
Jahrgang year [jɪə]
Januar January [ˈdʒænjuəri]
jede(r, s) every [ˈevri] **jede(r, s) einzelne** each [iːtʃ]
jede(r,s) (beliebige), jegliche(r,s) any [ˈeni]
jeder everybody [ˈevribɒdi]
jemals ever [ˈevə]
jemand somebody [ˈsʌmbədi]; someone [ˈsʌmwʌn]
jene (dort) those [ðəʊz]
jetzt now [naʊ]
jeweils each [iːtʃ]
Joghurt yoghurt [ˈjɒgət]

jonglieren juggle [ˈdʒʌgl]
Jugend youth [juːθ]
Jugendliche kid [kɪd]; youth [juːθ]
Jugendzentrum youth centre [ˈjuːθ sentə]
Juli July [dʒuˈlaɪ]
Junge boy [bɔɪ] **Ich bin kein Junge.** I'm not a boy. [nɒt]
Juni June [dʒuːn]

Kaffee coffee [ˈkɒfi]
Kakao cocoa [ˈkəʊkəʊ]; hot chocolate [hɒt ˈtʃɒklət]
Kalender calendar [ˈkælɪndə]
kalt cold [kəʊld] **kalt werden** get cold [get]
Kälte cold [kəʊld]
Kamera camera [ˈkæmərə]
kämpfen (für) fight (for) [faɪt]
Kaninchen rabbit [ˈræbɪt]
Kanne (Tee/Kaffee) pot [pɒt]
Kantine canteen [kænˈtiːn]
Kappe cap [kæp]
kaputt broken [ˈbrəʊkən]
Karaoke karaoke [kæriˈəʊki]
Karneval carnival [ˈkɑːnɪvl]
Karotte carrot [ˈkærət]
Karte card [kɑːd]
Karton carton [ˈkɑːtn]
Kartoffel potato, (pl) potatoes [pəˈteɪtəʊ]
Käse cheese [tʃiːz]
Kassenzettel receipt [rɪˈsiːt]
Kasten case [keɪs]
Katze cat [kæt]
kaufen buy [baɪ]; shop (for sth.) [ʃɒp]
Kebab kebab [kɪˈbæb]
Kegeln bowling [ˈbəʊlɪŋ]
kein/e no [nəʊ] **es gibt keine …** there aren't any … [ˈeni]
Keks biscuit [ˈbɪskɪt]
kennen know [nəʊ]
kennenlernen meet [miːt] **Freut mich, dich/euch/Sie kennenzulernen.** Nice to meet you. [naɪs]
Kerker dungeon [ˈdʌndʒən]
Kerze candle [ˈkændl]
Kette chain [tʃeɪn]
Kilometer kilometre (km) [ˈkɪləmiːtə]
Kind kid [kɪd]; child [tʃaɪld]
Kino cinema [ˈsɪnəmə] **im Kino** at the cinema
Kiosk kiosk [ˈkiːɒsk]
Kissen cushion [ˈkʊʃn]
kitschig cheesy [ˈtʃiːzi]
klar clear [klɪə]
Klasse class [klɑːs]
Klassenarbeit test [test]
Klassenlehrer/in class teacher [ˈklɑːs tiːtʃə]
Klassenzimmer classroom [ˈklɑːsruːm]
klassisch classical [ˈklæsɪkl]
Klavier piano [piˈænəʊ]
Kleber glue [gluː]
Klebestift glue stick [ˈgluː stɪk]
Klebstoff glue [gluː]
Kleid dress [dres]
Kleiderschrank wardrobe [ˈwɔːdrəʊb]

Kleidertausch(party) clothes swap [ˈkləʊðz swɒp]
Kleidung clothes (pl) [kləʊðz]
Kleidungsstücke clothes (pl) [kləʊðz]
klein little [ˈlɪtl]; (Person; Körpergröße) short [ʃɔːt]; small [smɔːl]
  kleine Mahlzeit snack [snæk]
klettern (auf) climb [klaɪm]
klicken (auf) click (on) [klɪk]
klingen (sich gut /... anhören) sound [saʊnd]
klopfen knock [nɒk]
Klub club [klʌb]
klug clever [ˈklevə]
Knöchel ankle [ˈæŋkl]
Koch, Köchin cook [kʊk]
Kochbuch recipe book [ˈresəpi]
kochen cook [kʊk]; (in Wasser) boil [bɔɪl]
Kochen cooking [ˈkʊkɪŋ]
Kochrezept recipe [ˈresəpi]
komisch weird [wɪəd]
Komma (Dezimalzeichen) point [pɔɪnt]
  1,6 (eins Komma sechs) 1.6 (one point six)
kommen come [kʌm] **Wo kommst du her?** Where are you from?
können can [kæn], [kən] **etwas gut können** be good at sth. / at doing sth. [æt], [ət] **gut umgehen können mit ...** be good at ... [ɡʊd] **Ich kann ... sehen.** I can see ... **Ich kann ... nicht sehen.** I can't (= cannot) see ... [kɑːnt] **Könnte ich ...?** Could I ...? [kəd]
Konsole console [kənˈsəʊl]
Kontakt contact [ˈkɒntækt]
kontaktfreudig sociable [ˈsəʊʃəbl]
Kontrolle check [tʃek]
kontrollieren check [tʃek]
Konzert concert [ˈkɒnsət]
Kopf head [hed] **Dreh/Stell es auf den Kopf.** Turn it upside down. [ʌpsaɪd ˈdaʊn]
Kopfhörer headphones (pl) [ˈhedfəʊnz]
Kopfschmerzen haben have a headache [ˈhedeɪk]
Körper body [ˈbɒdi]
korrekt correct [kəˈrekt]
Korridor corridor [ˈkɒrɪdɔː]
Kosten cost [kɒst]
kosten cost [kɒst]
kostenlos free [friː]
köstlich delicious [dɪˈlɪʃəs]
Kostüm costume [ˈkɒstjuːm]; (Damenkostüm) suit [suːt]
Kraft power [ˈpaʊə]; strength [streŋθ]
krank ill [ɪl]
Krankenhaus hospital [ˈhɒspɪtl]
Krankenpfleger, Krankenpflegerin nurse [nɜːs]
Krankenwagen ambulance [ˈæmbjələns]
Krankheit disease [dɪˈziːz]; illness [ˈɪlnəs]; sickness [ˈsɪknəs]
Krawatte tie [taɪ]
kreativ creative [kriˈeɪtɪv]
Kreis circle [ˈsɜːkl]
Krieg war [wɔː]
Küche kitchen [ˈkɪtʃɪn]

Kuchen cake [keɪk]
Kugelschreiber pen [pen]
Kultur culture [ˈkʌltʃə]
kümmern: sich kümmern um look after [ʊk]
Kunde, Kundin customer [ˈkʌstəmə]
Kunst art [ɑːt] **darstellende Kunst** drama [ˈdrɑːmə]
Künstler, Künstlerin artist [ˈɑːtɪst]
Kunsthandwerk crafts (pl) [krɑːfts]
Kunststoff plastic [ˈplæstɪk]
Kunststück trick [trɪk]
Kurs class [klɑːs]; course [kɔːs]
kurz short [ʃɔːt] **kurze Hose, Shorts** shorts (pl) [ʃɔːts]

L

Lächeln smile [smaɪl]
lächeln smile [smaɪl] **lachen (über)** laugh (at) [lɑːf]
Laden shop [ʃɒp]
Lamm(fleisch) lamb [læm]
Lampe lamp [læmp]; light [laɪt]
Land country [ˈkʌntri] **auf dem Land** in the country
Land (Grund und Boden) land [lænd]
Landkarte map [mæp]
lang(e) long [lɒŋ] **30 Sekunden lang** for 30 seconds [fɔː] **(für) eine lange Zeit** (for) a long time [taɪm] **lange arbeiten, lange Arbeitstage haben** work long days [wɜːk] **lange schlafen** sleep late [sliːp leɪt]
langsam slow [sləʊ] **zu langsam** too slow [tuː]
langweilig boring [ˈbɔːrɪŋ]
Lärm noise [nɔɪz]
lassen: lass(t) uns let's (= let us) [lets]
lassen leave [liːv]
Laufen (Sport) running [ˈrʌnɪŋ]
laut loud [laʊd] **lauter sprechen** speak more loudly [mɔː]
leben live [lɪv]
Leben life [laɪf]
Lebensmittel food [fuːd]
lecker delicious [dɪˈlɪʃəs]
leeren empty [ˈempti]
legen: (etwas wohin) legen put [pʊt]
lehren teach [tiːtʃ]
Lehrer/in teacher [ˈtiːtʃə]
leicht easy [ˈiːzi]
leidtun: Er tut mir leid. I'm / I feel sorry for him. [ˈsɒri]
leihen: (aus)leihen borrow [bɒrəʊ]
Leinwand screen [skriːn]
leise quiet [ˈkwaɪət]
leiten lead [liːd]
lernen learn [lɜːn]; study [ˈstʌdi]
lesen read [riːd]
Leser/in reader [ˈriːdə]
letzte(r,s): als letztes last [lɑːst] **(der/die/das) Letzte** the last one [lɑːst wʌn]
Leute people (pl) [ˈpiːpl]; (Anrede) guys (pl) [gaɪz]
Licht light [laɪt]
Liebe love [lʌv]
Liebe/r ... Dear ... [dɪə]

lieben love [lʌv] **Ich hätte liebend gern ... / Ich möchte liebend gern ...** I'd (= I would) love ... **Ich würde mich liebend gerne mit ... treffen.** I'd (= I would) love to meet ... [miːt]
Liebling favourite [ˈfeɪvərɪt]; love [lʌv]
Lieblings- favourite [ˈfeɪvərɪt]
Lied song [sɒŋ]
Liedtext lyrics [ˈlɪrɪks]
liegen lie [laɪ]
lila purple [ˈpɜːpl]
Limonade lemonade [leməˈneɪd]
Lineal ruler [ˈruːlə]
links, nach links left [left]
Liste file [faɪl]; list [lɪst]
listen list [lɪst]
lockig curly [ˈkɜːli]
Löffel spoon [spuːn]
lösen (Rätsel, Problem) solve [sɒlv]
Löwe lion [ˈlaɪən]
lüften (Geheimnis) solve [sɒlv]
lustig (be) funny [ˈfʌni] **Was ist lustig an ...?** What's funny about ...?

M

machen do [duː]; make [meɪk]
Macht power [ˈpaʊə]
Mädchen girl [gɜːl]
magisch magical [ˈmædʒɪkl]
Mahlzeit meal [miːl]
  kleine Mahlzeit snack [snæk]
  warme Mahlzeit hot meal [hɒt]
Mai May [meɪ]
Mal time [taɪm]
malen paint [peɪnt]
Mama mum [mʌm]
man you [juː]
Manager/in manager [ˈmænɪdʒə]
manchmal sometimes [ˈsʌmtaɪmz]
Marke: Produktmarke brand [brænd]
markieren highlight [ˈhaɪlaɪt]
Markt market [ˈmɑːkɪt]
März March [mɑːtʃ]
Maske mask [mɑːsk]
Mathe(matik) maths [mæθs]
Mauer wall [wɔːl]
Maus mouse, (pl) mice [maʊs], [maɪs]
Mechaniker, Mechanikerin mechanic [mɪˈkænɪk]
Meer sea [siː] **am Meer** by the sea
Mehl flour [ˈflaʊə]
mehr more [mɔː] **mehr als 50** over 50 [ˈəʊvə]
Meile (ca. 1,6 km) mile [maɪl]
  mit 30 Meilen pro Stunde at 30 miles per hour [pər ˈaʊə] **Meilen pro Stunde** miles per hour (mph)
mein/e my [maɪ]
meinen (sagen wollen) mean [miːn]; (denken, glauben) think [θɪŋk] **Ich meine, ...** I think ...
Meinung opinion [əˈpɪnjən] **meiner Meinung nach** in my opinion
meiste(r, s): die meisten Schulen most schools [məʊst]
meistens usually [ˈjuːʒuəli]
Melone melon [ˈmelən]
Mensa canteen [kænˈtiːn]
Menschen people (pl) [ˈpiːpl]

Messer knife, *(pl)* knives [naɪf], [naɪvz]
Metall, aus Metall metal [ˈmetl]
Meter metre [ˈmiːtə]
mich me [miː]
Milch milk [mɪlk]
Milliliter millilitre (ml) [ˈmɪliliːtə]
Mindmap mind map [ˈmaɪnd mæp]
Mini- mini [ˈmɪni]
Minidrohne mini-drone [mɪni ˈdrəʊn]
Minute minute [ˈmɪnɪt]
mir me [miː]
mischen mix [mɪks]
Mischung mixture [ˈmɪkstʃə]
mit with [wɪð]
mitbringen bring [brɪŋ]
Mitglied member [ˈmembə]
mitkommen come [kʌm]
Mitleid: Mitleid haben mit jm. be/feel sorry for sb. [ˈsɒri]
mitnehmen take [teɪk]
Mittagessen lunch [lʌntʃ] **Was gibt es zum Mittagessen?** What's for lunch?
Mittagszeit lunchtime [ˈlʌntʃtaɪm] **zur Mittagszeit** at lunchtime
Mitte centre [ˈsentə]; middle [ˈmɪdl]
Mitteilung message [ˈmesɪdʒ]
Mittwoch Wednesday [ˈwenzdeɪ], [ˈwenzdi]
mobben bully [ˈbʊli]
Mobber/in bully [ˈbʊli]
möchten: Ich möchte ... I'd (= I would) like ... [laɪk]
Moderator, Moderatorin presenter [prɪˈzentə]
modern modern [ˈmɒdn]
mögen like [laɪk] **sehr mögen** love [lʌv]
Möhre carrot [ˈkærət]
Moment moment [ˈməʊmənt] **in diesem Moment** at the moment
Monat month [mʌnθ]
Mond moon [muːn]
Montag Monday [ˈmʌndeɪ], [ˈmʌndi] **an jedem Montag** on Mondays
montags on Mondays [ˈmʌndeɪ], [ˈmʌndi]
Morgen morning [ˈmɔːnɪŋ] **am Morgen** in the morning
morgen tomorrow [təˈmɒrəʊ]
morgens in the morning [ˈmɔːnɪŋ] **4 Uhr (früh) morgens** 4 a.m. [eɪˈem]
Moschee mosque [mɒsk]
Möwe seagull [ˈsiːgʌl]
müde tired [ˈtaɪəd]
multikulturell multicultural [mʌltiˈkʌltʃərəl]
Münze coin [kɔɪn]
Museum museum [mjuˈziːəm]
Musik music [ˈmjuːzɪk]
musikalisch musical [ˈmjuːzɪkl]
Musiker, Musikerin musician [mjuˈzɪʃn]
Musikgruppe band [bænd]
Muslim, Muslima; muslimisch muslim [ˈmʊzlɪm]
müssen must [mʌst] **etwas tun müssen** need to do sth. [niːd] **Ich muss Schluss machen.** *(am Telefon / Briefschluss)* I must go.

Müll rubbish [ˈrʌbɪʃ] **Tüten/Säcke voller Müll** bags of rubbish [bægz]
Mülleimer bin [bɪn]
Mut bravery [ˈbreɪvəri]
mutig brave [breɪv]
Mutprobe dare [deə]
Mutter mother [ˈmʌðə]
Mutti mum [mʌm]
Mütze cap [kæp]; hat [hæt]

N

na: Na ja, ... Well, ... [wel]
nach
 1. *(örtlich)* to [tu], [tə] **nach draußen** outside [aʊtˈsaɪd] **nach (dr)innen** inside [ɪnˈsaɪd]
 2. *(zeitlich)* after [ˈɑːftə] **nach der Schule** after school
Nachbar/in neighbour [ˈneɪbə]
nachdem: nachdem (du liest) after you read [ˈɑːftə]
nachher, danach afterwards [ˈɑːftəwədz]
Nachmittag afternoon [ɑːftəˈnuːn] **am Nachmittag** in the afternoon
nachmittags in the afternoon [ɑːftəˈnuːn] **4 Uhr nachmittags (16 Uhr)** 4 p.m. [piːˈem]
Nachname family name [ˈfæməli neɪm]
Nachricht message [ˈmesɪdʒ]
Nachrichten news [njuːz]
nachschauen look sth. up [lʊk ˈʌp]
nachschlagen: etwas nachschlagen look sth. up [lʊk ˈʌp]
nächste(r, s) next [nekst] **Als nächstes ...** Next ...
Nacht night [naɪt]
Nachtisch dessert [dɪˈzɜːt] **zum/als Nachtisch** for dessert
Nacken neck [nek]
nahe (bei) near [nɪə]
Nähe: in der Nähe von near [nɪə]
Name name [neɪm]
Nase nose [nəʊz]
natürlich of course [əv ˈkɔːs]
Naturwissenschaft science [ˈsaɪəns]
Naturwissenschaftler/in scientist [ˈsaɪəntɪst]
neben next to [ˈnekst tə]
nehmen, in Anspruch nehmen take [teɪk]
nein no [nəʊ]
nennen call [kɔːl]
nett friendly [ˈfrendli]; kind [kaɪnd]; nice [naɪs]
neu new [njuː]
neugierig (auf) curious (about) [ˈkjʊəriəs]
neun nine [naɪn]
neunzehn nineteen [naɪnˈtiːn]
neunzig ninety [ˈnaɪnti]
nicht not [nɒt]
nicht mehr not (...) any more [nɒt ˈenimɔː]
Nichte niece [niːs]
nichts nothing [ˈnʌθɪŋ]
nie never [ˈnevə]
niedlich cute [kjuːt]

niemals never [ˈnevə]
niemand no one [ˈnəʊ wʌn]; nobody [ˈnəʊbədi] **niemand anders, niemand sonst** no one else [ˈnəʊ wʌn els]
noch: (immer) noch still [stɪl] **noch drei** three more [mɔː] **noch ein/e** another [əˈnʌðə] **noch einmal** again [əˈgen] **noch nicht** not ... yet [nɒt jet]
Norden north [nɔːθ]
nördlich; Nord- north [nɔːθ]
Nordosten; nordöstlich north-east [nɔːθˈiːst]
Nordwesten; nordwestlich northwest [nɔːθˈwest]
normal normal [ˈnɔːml]
normalerweise usually [ˈjuːʒuəli]
Note: Schulnote mark [mɑːk]
Notiz note [nəʊt]
Notizen: (sich) Notizen machen *(zur Vorbereitung)* make notes **(sich) Notizen machen** *(beim Lesen oder Zuhören)* take notes
November November [nəʊˈvembə]
Nudeln noodles *(pl)* [nuːdlz]
Null *(im gesprochenen Englisch)* oh [əʊ]
Nummer number [ˈnʌmbə]
nun now [naʊ] **Nun, ...** Well, ... [wel]
nur just [dʒʌst]; only [ˈəʊnli] **Es sind nur wir.** It's just us.
Nutzer/in user [ˈjuːzə]
nützlich helpful [ˈhelpfl]; useful [ˈjuːsfl]

O

ob if [ɪf]
oben at the top (of) [tɒp]
Obergeschoss top floor [tɒp ˈflɔː]
oberhalb (von) above [əˈbʌv]
Objekt *(Gegenstand)* object [ˈɒbdʒɪkt]
Obst fruit [fruːt]
oder or [ɔː]
öffnen open [ˈəʊpən]
oft often [ˈɒfn], [ˈɒftən]
Ohr ear [ɪə]
Oktober October [ɒkˈtəʊbə]
Öl oil [ɔɪl]
Oma grandma [ˈgrænmɑː]
Onkel uncle [ˈʌŋkl]
online; Online- online [ˌɒnˈlaɪn]
Opa grandpa [ˈgrænpɑː]
optisch visual [ˈvɪʒuəl]
orange orange [ˈɒrɪndʒ]
Orange orange [ˈɒrɪndʒ]
ordentlich tidy [ˈtaɪdi]
Ordner file [faɪl]
organisieren organize [ˈɔːgənaɪz]
Ort place [pleɪs]

P

paar: ein paar some [sʌm], [səm]
Päckchen packet [ˈpækɪt]
Packung carton [ˈkɑːtn]; packet [ˈpækɪt]
Palast palace [ˈpæləs]
Papa dad [dæd]
Papagei parrot [ˈpærət]
Papier paper [ˈpeɪpə] **Stück Papier** piece of paper [piːs]

Paprika pepper [ˈpepə]
Park park [pɑːk]
Parkour *(akrobatischer Hindernislauf in der Stadt)* parkour [pɑːˈkʊə]
Partner/in partner [ˈpɑːtnə]
Party party [ˈpɑːti]
passieren happen (to sb.) [ˈhæpən]
passiv passive [ˈpæsɪv]
Pasta *(italienische Bezeichnung für Teigwaren)* pasta [ˈpæstə]
Pause break [breɪk]; rest [rest]
  Pause machen take a rest [teɪk]
peinlich embarrassing [ɪmˈbærəsɪŋ]
Penny *(kleinste britische Münze)* penny (p), *(pl)* pence [ˈpeni], [pens]
Peperoni pepper [ˈpepə]
perfekt perfect [ˈpɜːfɪkt]
Person person [ˈpɜːsn]
Persönlichkeit personality [pɜːsəˈnæləti]
Pfannkuchen pancake [ˈpænkeɪk]
Pfeffer pepper [ˈpepə]
Pferd horse [hɔːs]
pflücken; (aus)wählen pick [pɪk]
Pfund *(britische Währung)* pound (£) [paʊnd]
Philosophie philosophy [fəˈlɒsəfi]
Picknick picnic [ˈpɪknɪk] **ein Picknick machen** have a picnic [hæv]
Pier pier [pɪə]
Plan plan [plæn]
planen plan [plæn] **planen, etwas zu tun** plan to do sth. [duː]
Planet planet [ˈplænɪt]
Plastik plastic [ˈplæstɪk]
Platz place [pleɪs]; *(Sitzplatz)* seat [siːt]; space [speɪs]
Plätzchen biscuit [ˈbɪskɪt]
Playlist playlist [ˈpleɪlɪst]
plötzlich suddenly [ˈsʌdənli]
Pokal trophy [ˈtrəʊfi]
Polizei police *(pl)* [pəˈliːs]
Polizeibeamter, Polizeibeamtin police officer [pəˈliːs ɒfɪsə]
Pommes frites chips *(pl)* [tʃɪps] **Fisch mit Pommes frites** fish and chips
Pool(billiard) pool [puːl]
Popcorn popcorn [ˈpɒpkɔːn]
Popstar star [stɑː]
positiv positive [ˈpɒzətɪv]
Post *(Teil eines Blogs)* post [pəʊst]
posten *(im Internet veröffentlichen)* post [pəʊst]
Poster poster [ˈpəʊstə]
Postkarte postcard [ˈpəʊstkɑːd]
praktisch practical [ˈpræktɪkl]
Praline chocolate [ˈtʃɒklət]
Präsentation presentation [preznˈteɪʃn]
präsentieren: (jm.) etwas präsentieren present sth. (to sb.) [prɪˈzent]
Preis *(Kosten)* cost [kɒst]; *(Gewinn)* prize [praɪz] **(Kauf-)Preis** price [praɪs] **Preis** *(die Auszeichnung)* award [əˈwɔːd]
Preisverleihung prize ceremony [ˈpraɪz serəməni]
preiswert cheap [tʃiːp]

pro per [pɜː], [pə] **Meilen pro Stunde** miles per hour (mph) [maɪlz]
  pro Stunde per hour [ˈaʊə]
probieren taste [teɪst]; *(ausprobieren)* try [traɪ]
Problem problem [ˈprɒbləm] **Was/Wo ist das Problem?** What's wrong?
professionell, Profi- professional [prəˈfeʃnl]
Programmieren coding [ˈkəʊdɪŋ]
programmieren *(Computer)* code [kəʊd]
Programmierer, Programmiererin programmer [ˈprəʊgræmə]
Projekt project [ˈprɒdʒekt]
Prozent per cent (%) [pə ˈsent]
prüfen check [tʃek]
Prüfung check [tʃek]
Publikum audience [ˈɔːdiəns]
Puderzucker icing sugar [ˈaɪsɪŋ ʃʊgə]
Pulver powder [ˈpaʊdə]
Punkt point [pɔɪnt]
Punktestand score [skɔː]
pünktlich on time [ɒn taɪm]
pusten blow [bləʊ]
putzen clean [kliːn] **(sich) die/deine Zähne putzen** brush your teeth [brʌʃ]
Puzzle jigsaw (puzzle) [ˈdʒɪgsɔː]

Q

Quiz quiz, *(pl)* quizzes [kwɪz], [ˈkwɪzɪz]
  ein Quiz machen do a quiz [duː]

R

Rad: Rad fahren cycle [ˈsaɪkl]
Radfahren cycling [ˈsaɪklɪŋ]
Radiergummi rubber [ˈrʌbə]
Ratespiel quiz, *(pl)* quizzes [kwɪz]
  ein Ratespiel machen do a quiz [duː]
Rätsel puzzle [ˈpʌzl]
rauben steal [stiːl]
Raum *(Zimmer)* room [ruːm]; space [speɪs]
Recherche(n) research [rɪˈsɜːtʃ]
recherchieren (do) research [rɪˈsɜːtʃ]
Recht: Recht haben be right [raɪt]
rechteckig square [skweə]
rechts; nach rechts right [raɪt]
Rechtschreibung spelling [ˈspelɪŋ]
Rede talk [tɔːk]
reden (mit) talk (to) [tɔːk] **reden über** talk about [əˈbaʊt]
Redewendung phrase [freɪz]
Referat presentation [preznˈteɪʃn]
  ein Referat halten give a presentation [gɪv]
Regal shelf, *(pl)* shelves [ʃelf], [ʃelvz]
Regel rule [ruːl]
Regen rain [reɪn]
Regenbogen rainbow [ˈreɪnbəʊ]
regnen rain [reɪn]
regnerisch rainy [ˈreɪni]
Reihe line [laɪn]; turn [tɜːn] **Wann bin ich an der Reihe (etwas zu tun)?** When is (it) my turn (to do sth.)?
Reihenfolge order [ˈɔːdə]
Reinigungskraft cleaner [ˈkliːnə]

Reis rice [raɪs]
Reise journey [ˈdʒɜːni]; tour [tʊə]
Reisen travel [ˈtrævl]
reisen travel [ˈtrævl]
reiten *(ein Pferd / auf einem Pferd)* ride a horse [raɪd]
reservieren book [bʊk]
Respekt respect [rɪˈspekt]
Restaurant restaurant [ˈrestrɒnt]
retten save [seɪv]
Rezept recipe [ˈresəpi]
richtig right [raɪt]; true [truː]
riechen smell [smel]
Rindfleisch beef [biːf]
Ring ring [rɪŋ]
Roboter robot [ˈrəʊbɒt]
Roller scooter [ˈskuːtə]
Rollstuhl wheelchair [ˈwiːltʃeə]
romantisch romantic [rəʊˈmæntɪk]
rosa pink [pɪŋk]
Rücken back [bæk]
Rückfahrkarte, Hin- und Rückfahrkarte return [rɪˈtɜːn]
Rückseite back [bæk]
Rucksack rucksack [ˈrʌksæk]
Ruf call [kɔːl]
Ruhe rest [rest]
ruhen rest [rest]
ruhig quiet [ˈkwaɪət]; calm [kɑːm]
rühren stir [stɜː]
rumhängen hang out [hæŋ aʊt]
rund round [raʊnd]
Rundfahrt (durch) tour (of) [tʊə]
Rundgang (durch) tour (of) [tʊə]

S

Saal hall [hɔːl]
Saft juice [dʒuːs]
sagen say [seɪ]; tell [tel]
Saison season [ˈsiːzn]
Salat *(als Gericht oder Beilage)* salad [ˈsæləd]
Salz salt [sɔːlt]
sammeln collect [kəˈlekt]
Sammlung collection [kəˈlekʃn]
Samstag Saturday [ˈsætədeɪ], [ˈsætədi]
Sandwich sandwich [ˈsænwɪtʃ], [ˈsænwɪdʒ]
Sänger/in singer [ˈsɪŋə]
Säulendiagramm bar chart [ˈbɑː tʃɑːt]
Satz sentence [ˈsentəns]
sauber clean [kliːn]
sauber machen clean (sth. up) [kliːn]
Saubermachen clean-up [ˈkliːn ʌp]
Säubern clean-up [ˈkliːn ʌp]
schade a shame [ʃeɪm]
Schaf sheep [ʃiːp]
Schal scarf [skɑːf]
Schale bowl [bəʊl]
Schande a shame [ʃeɪm]
scharf nachdenken think hard [θɪŋk hɑːd]
schauen look [lʊk]
Schauspiel drama [ˈdrɑːmə]
Schauspieler/in actor [ˈæktə]
schauspielern act [ækt]
Scheinwerfer spotlight [ˈspɒtlaɪt]
Scherz joke [dʒəʊk]
scheu shy [ʃaɪ]

schick smart [smɑːt]
schicken send [send]
Schild sign [saɪn]
Schinken ham [hæm]
Schirmmütze cap [kæp]
Schlaf sleep [sliːp]
schlafen be asleep [əˈsliːp]; sleep [sliːp]
Schlafzimmer bedroom [ˈbedruːm]
schlagen hit [hɪt]
Schlagwort keyword [ˈkiːwɜːd]
Schlange snake [sneɪk]
schlau clever [ˈklevə]
schlecht bad [bæd] **der/die/das schlechteste, schlimmste; am schlechtesten, am schlimmsten** worst [wɜːst] **schlecht riechen** smell [smel]
schlechter worse [wɜːs]
schließen close [kləʊz]
schließlich in the end [end]
schlimm bad [bæd]; **schlimmer** worse [wɜːs]
Schlittschuhbahn ice rink [ˈaɪs rɪŋk]
Schloss palace [ˈpæləs]
Schluss end [end] **Ich muss Schluss machen.** *(am Telefon / Briefschluss)* I must go. [mʌst ɡəʊ] **zum Schluss** in the end
Schlüssel; Schlüssel- key [kiː]
schmecken taste [teɪst]
schmücken decorate [ˈdekəreɪt]
schmutzig dirty [ˈdɜːti]
Schnee snow [snəʊ]
schneebedeckt snowy [ˈsnəʊi]
schneien snow [snəʊ]
schockiert shocked [ʃɒkt]
Schokolade chocolate [ˈtʃɒklət] **heiße (Trink-)Schokolade** hot chocolate [hɒt]
schon already [ɔːlˈredi] **... schon ...?** ... yet [jet]
schön nice [naɪs]
Schönheit beauty [ˈbjuːti]
schrecklich horrible [ˈhɒrəbl]; terrible [ˈterəbl]
schreiben write [raɪt]
Schreibtisch desk [desk]
Schreibweise spelling [ˈspelɪŋ]
schreien scream [skriːm]
Schritt step [step]
schüchtern shy [ʃaɪ]
Schuh shoe [ʃuː]
Schule school [skuːl] **Hast du nach der Schule Zeit?** Are you free after school? **in der Schule** at school **nach der Schule** after school **weiterführende Schule** secondary school [ˈsekəndri]
Schüler/in student [ˈstjuːdnt]
Schulfach subject [ˈsʌbdʒɪkt]
Schulheft exercise book [ˈeksəsaɪz bʊk]
Schulleiter, Schulleiterin head teacher [ˈhed tiːtʃə]
Schulmensa canteen [kænˈtiːn]
Schulsport PE (= physical education) [piːˈiː], [fɪzɪkl edʒuˈkeɪʃn]
Schulsprecher/in head student [hed ˈstjuːdnt]

Schuluniform school uniform [skuːl ˈjuːnɪfɔːm]
Schulversammlung assembly [əˈsembli]
Schüssel bowl [bəʊl]
schützen (vor) protect (from/against) [prəˈtekt]
schwarz black [blæk]
Schweinefleisch pork [pɔːk]
schwer difficult [ˈdɪfɪkəlt]; hard [hɑːd]
Schwester sister [ˈsɪstə]
schwierig difficult [ˈdɪfɪkəlt]; hard [hɑːd]
Schwierigkeiten trouble [ˈtrʌbl] **in Schwierigkeiten sein** be in trouble
Schwimmen swimming [ˈswɪmɪŋ]
schwimmen swim [swɪm]
Schwimmer/in swimmer [ˈswɪmə]
Sciencefiction science fiction [saɪəns ˈfɪkʃn]
sechs six [sɪks]
sechzehn sixteen [sɪksˈtiːn]
sechzig sixty [ˈsɪksti]
See *(Meer)* sea [siː] **an der See** by the sea [baɪ]
Seebrücke pier [pɪə]
sehen look [lʊk]; see [siː]
Sehenswürdigkeit sight [saɪt]
sehr lot [lɒt]; much [mʌtʃ]; very [ˈveri]
Seilrutsche zip wire [ˈzɪp waɪə]
sein be [biː]; **bist, sind, seid** are [ɑː] **(er/sie/es) ist** is [ɪz]
sein/e its [ɪts]
Seite page (p.) [peɪdʒ]; *(z. B. Straßenseite)* side [saɪd]
seit Stunden for hours [fɔː ˈaʊəs]
Sekunde second [ˈsekənd] **für 30 Sekunden** for 30 seconds [fɔː]
selbst even [ˈiːvn]
selbstverständlich of course [əv ˈkɔːs]
selten *(Adj.)* rare [reə]; *(Adv.)* rarely [ˈreəli]
seltsam funny [ˈfʌni]; weird [wɪəd]; strange [streɪndʒ]
senden send [send]
senkrecht vertical [ˈvɜːtɪkl]
September September [sepˈtembə]
shoppen shop (for sth.) [ʃɒp]
Show show [ʃəʊ]
sicher *(gefahrlos)* safe [seɪf]; *(ohne Zweifel)* sure [ʃʊə], [ʃɔː]; *(selbstsicher)* confident [ˈkɒnfɪdənt]
sichern save [seɪv]
Sie *(höfliche Anrede)* you [juː] **Sie sind** you're (= you are)
sie
1. *(weibliche Person)* her [hɜː], [hə]; she [ʃiː] **sie ist** she's (= she is)
2. *(bei Dingen und Tieren)* it [ɪt]
3. *(Plural)* them [ðem], [ðəm]; they [ðeɪ] **sie sind** they're (= they are) **sie sind nicht** they aren't
sieben seven [ˈsevn]
siebzehn seventeen [sevnˈtiːn]
siebzig seventy [ˈsevnti]
sieden boil [bɔɪl]
Sieger/in winner [ˈwɪnə]
Silber silver [ˈsɪlvə]

silberfarben silver [ˈsɪlvə]
Singen singing [ˈsɪŋɪŋ]
singen sing [sɪŋ]
Situation situation [sɪtʃuˈeɪʃn]
sitzen sit [sɪt]
Sitzplatz seat [siːt]
Skateboard (fahren) skateboard [ˈskeɪtbɔːd]
Skateboardfahren skateboarding [ˈskeɪtbɔːdɪŋ]
Skatepark skatepark [ˈskeɪtpɑːk]
Slideshow slide show [ˈslaɪd ʃəʊ]
SMS text [tekst] **jm. eine SMS schicken** text sb.
Snack snack [snæk]
so like this [laɪk]; so [səʊ]
sodass so that [səʊ ðæt]
Sofa sofa [ˈsəʊfə]
Software software [ˈsɒftweə]
so gut wie as good as [æz ɡʊd æz]
sogar even [ˈiːvn]
Sohn son [sʌn]
so(lch) (ein/e) such a [sʌtʃ]
Sommer summer [ˈsʌmə]
Sonne sun [sʌn] **Die Sonne scheint.** It's sunny. [ˈsʌni]
Sonnenaufgang sunrise [ˈsʌnraɪz]
sonnenbaden sunbathe [ˈsʌnbeɪð]
Sonnenuntergang sunset [ˈsʌnset]
sonnig sunny [ˈsʌni]
Sonntag Sunday [ˈsʌndeɪ], [ˈsʌndi]
sonst or [ɔː]
Sorte (von) kind (of) [kaɪnd]
Soße sauce [sɔːs]
Spaghetti spaghetti [spəˈɡeti]
sparen save [seɪv]
Sparkonto savings account [ˈseɪvɪŋz əkaʊnt]
Sparschwein piggy bank [ˈpɪɡi bæŋk]
Spaß fun [fʌn] **Spaß haben** have fun [hæv] **Spaß machen** be fun [biː]
spät: (zu) spät late [leɪt]
später later [ˈleɪtə]
Spaziergang walk [wɔːk]
Speisekarte menu [ˈmenjuː]
Spiegel mirror [ˈmɪrə]
Spiel game [ɡeɪm]; match [mætʃ]
spielen play [pleɪ]
Spieler/in player [ˈpleɪə]
Spielkarte playing card [ˈpleɪɪŋ kɑːd]
Spielstand score [skɔː]
Spielzeug toy [tɔɪ]
Spitze top [tɒp] **an der Spitze (von)** at the top (of) [æt], [ət]
Sport sport [spɔːt]; *(Schulsport)* PE (= physical education) [piːˈiː], [fɪzɪkl edʒuˈkeɪʃn]
Sportart sport [spɔːt]
Sporthalle sports hall [ˈspɔːts hɔːl]
Sportler/in sportsperson [ˈspɔːtspɜːsn]
sportlich sporty [ˈspɔːti]
Sprechen speaking [ˈspiːkɪŋ]
sprechen (mit) speak (to) [spiːk] **deutlich sprechen** speak clearly [ˈklɪəli] **lauter sprechen** speak more loudly [mɔː] **sprechen über** speak about [əˈbaʊt]
springen jump [dʒʌmp]
Staatsbürger/in citizen [ˈsɪtɪzn]

Stadion stadium [ˈsteɪdiəm]
Stadt city [ˈsɪti]; town [taʊn]
Stadtplan map [mæp]
Stadtzentrum town centre [taʊn ˈsentə]
Standuhr clock [klɒk]
Star star [stɑː]
stark strong [strɒŋ]
Stärke strength [streŋθ]
Start start [stɑːt]
stattfinden take place [teɪk pleɪs]; be on [bi: ɒn]
Staub saugen vacuum [ˈvækjuəm]
stecken: (etwas wohin) stecken put [pʊt]
stehen stand [stænd]
stehlen steal [stiːl]
stellen: (etwas wohin) stellen put [pʊt] **sich (hin)stellen** stand [stænd] **stellen, legen, setzen** set [set]
sterben (an) die (of) [daɪ]
Sternzeichen star sign [ˈstɑː saɪn]
Stichwort keyword [ˈkiːwɜːd]
Stiefbruder stepbrother [ˈstepbrʌðə]
Stiefel boot [buːt]
Stiefmutter stepmother [ˈstepmʌðə]; stepmum [ˈstepmʌm]
Stiefschwester stepsister [ˈstepsɪstə]
Stiefsohn stepson [ˈstepsʌn]
Stieftochter stepdaughter [ˈstepdɔːtə]
Stiefvater stepdad [ˈstepdæd]; stepfather [ˈstepfɑːðə]
Stift pen [pen]
still quiet [ˈkwaɪət]; *(lautlos)* silent [ˈsaɪlənt]
Stock(werk) floor [flɔː] **das oberste Stockwerk** top floor [tɒp ˈflɔː]
Stolz pride [praɪd]
Strand beach [biːtʃ] **an den/zum Strand** to the beach [tu], [tə]
Straße *(in Ortschaften)* street [striːt]
Straßenmusik street music [ˈstriːt mjuːzɪk]
Streetdance *(Tanzstil)* street dance [ˈstriːt dɑːns]
stricken knit [nɪt]
Stück piece [piːs] **Stück Papier** piece of paper [ˈpeɪpə]
Struktur structure [ˈstrʌktʃə]
Student/in student [ˈstjuːdnt]
studieren study [ˈstʌdi]
Stufe step [step]
Stuhl chair [tʃeə]
Stunde hour [ˈaʊə]; *(Unterrichtsstunde)* lesson [ˈlesn] **pro Stunde** per hour [pɜː], [pə]
stundenlang for hours [fɔː ˈaʊəs]
Stundenplan timetable [ˈtaɪmteɪbl]
suchen, Ausschau halten nach look for [lʊk fɔː]
Superheld/in superhero, *(pl)* superheroes [ˈsuːpəhɪərəʊ]
Supermarkt supermarket [ˈsuːpəmɑːkɪt]
Suppe soup [suːp]
Surfing surfing [ˈsɜːfɪŋ]
süß cute [kjuːt]; sweet [swiːt]
Süßigkeiten sweets *(pl)* [swiːts]
Sweatshirt sweatshirt [ˈswetʃɜːt]

T

Tag day [deɪ]
Tageszeitung newspaper [ˈnjuːspeɪpə]; paper [ˈpeɪpə]
Talent gift [gɪft]
Tante aunt [ɑːnt]
Tante-Emma-Laden corner shop [ˈkɔːnə ʃɒp]
Tanz dance [dɑːns]
Tanzen dancing [ˈdɑːnsɪŋ]
tanzen dance [dɑːns]
Tänzer/in dancer [ˈdɑːnsə]
Tapferkeit bravery [ˈbreɪvəri]
Tasche bag [bæg]; *(an Kleidungsstücken)* pocket [ˈpɒkɪt]
Tätigkeit activity [ækˈtɪvəti]
tatkräftig energetic [enəˈdʒetɪk]
Tatsache fact [fækt]
Taufe christening [ˈkrɪsnɪŋ]
Tausch swap [swɒp]
tauschen swap [swɒp]
tausend thousand [ˈθaʊznd]
Technik technology [tekˈnɒlədʒi], *(infml auch)* tech
Technikunterricht technology [tekˈnɒlədʒi], *(infml auch)* tech
Technologie technology [tekˈnɒlədʒi], *(infml auch)* tech
Tee tea [tiː]
Teelöffel teaspoon [ˈtiːspuːn]
Teil part (of) [pɑːt]; piece [piːs]; share [ʃeə]
teilen share [ʃeə]
Telefon phone [fəʊn] **am Telefon** on the phone [ɒn]
Telefonanruf (phone) call [ˈfəʊn kɔːl]
telefonieren phone [fəʊn]
Telefonnummer phone number [ˈfəʊn nʌmbə]
Tennis tennis [ˈtenɪs]
Terrarium terrarium [teˈreəriəm]
Test test [test]; quiz, *(pl)* quizzes [kwɪz], [ˈkwɪzɪz] **einen Test machen** do a quiz [duː]
testen test [test]
teuer expensive [ɪkˈspensɪv]
Text text [tekst]
Theater theatre [ˈθɪətə]
Theater spielen act [ækt]
Thema topic [ˈtɒpɪk]
Ticket ticket [ˈtɪkɪt]
Tier animal [ˈænɪml]; *(Haustier)* pet [pet]; *(Bestie)* beast [biːst]
Tierarzt/Tierärztin vet [vet]
Tipp tip [tɪp]
Tisch table [ˈteɪbl]
Tischtennis table tennis [ˈteɪbl tenɪs]
Titel title [ˈtaɪtl]
Tochter daughter [ˈdɔːtə]
Toilette toilet [ˈtɔɪlət]
tolerant (gegenüber) tolerant (of) [ˈtɒlərənt]
toll great [greɪt]
Tomate tomato, *(pl)* tomatoes [təˈmɑːtəʊ]
Tomatensauce tomato sauce [təˈmɑːtəʊ sɔːs]
Topf pot [pɒt]
Torte cake [keɪk]

tot dead [ded]
töten kill [kɪl]
Tour tour [tʊə]
Tourist/in tourist [ˈtʊərɪst]
Touristeninformation tourist information centre [tʊərɪst ɪnfəˈmeɪʃn sentə]
Tradition tradition [trəˈdɪʃn]
traditionell traditional [trəˈdɪʃənl]
tragen wear [weə]
Trainer/in trainer [ˈtreɪnə]
trainieren train [treɪn]
Training training [ˈtreɪnɪŋ]
Trampolin trampoline [ˈtræmpəliːn]
Trampolinspringen/-turnen- trampolining [ˈtræmpəliːnɪŋ]
Traum dream [driːm]
träumen (von etwas) dream (of/about sth.) [driːm]
traurig sad [sæd]
Trauzeuge *(des Bräutigams)* groomsman [ˈgruːmzmən]
treffen: treffen auf hit [hɪt] **(sich) treffen** meet [miːt]
Treppe stairs *(pl)* [steəz]
Tretroller scooter [ˈskuːtə]
Trick trick [trɪk]
Trifle *(englischer Nachtisch)* trifle [ˈtraɪfl]
trinken drink [drɪŋk]
Trophäe trophy [ˈtrəʊfi]
trotzdem still [stɪl]
Tschüs. Bye. [baɪ]; See you. [siː]; Speak later. [spiːk ˈleɪtə]
T-Shirt T-shirt [ˈtiː ʃɜːt]
tun do [duː] **(etwas wohin) tun** put [pʊt] **du hast (viel) zu tun** you're busy [ˈbɪzi] **es genießen, etwas zu tun** enjoy doing sth. [ɪnˈdʒɔɪ] **etwas dauernd/immer wieder tun** keep doing sth. **etwas tun müssen** have to do sth. **etwas weiterhin tun** continue to do sth. [kənˈtɪnjuː] **wie man etwas tut/tun kann/tun soll** how to do sth. [haʊ]
Tür door [dɔː]
Turm tower [ˈtaʊə]
Turmuhr clock [klɒk]
Tüte: Tüten voller Müll bags of rubbish [bægz]
typisch (für) typical (of) [ˈtɪpɪkl]
Tyrann/in bully [ˈbʊli]
tyrannisieren bully [ˈbʊli]

U

üben practice [ˈpræktɪs]
über
1. *(räumlich)* over [ˈəʊvə]
2. *(mehr als)* **über 50** over 50
3. about [əˈbaʊt] **über mich/dich/...** about me/you/...
über eine Brücke/Straße ... across a bridge/street ... [əˈkrɒs]
über above [əˈbʌv]
überall everywhere [ˈevriweə]
überhaupt nicht(s) not ... at all [nɒt ət ɔːl]
überprüfen check [tʃek]
Überprüfung check [tʃek]

überraschen surprise [səˈpraɪz]
überrascht surprised [səˈpraɪzd]
Überraschung surprise [səˈpraɪz]
Überschrift heading [ˈhedɪŋ]; title [ˈtaɪtl]
Übung(en) exercise [ˈeksəsaɪz]; practice [ˈpræktɪs]
Übungsheft exercise book [ˈeksəsaɪz bʊk]
Uhr clock [klɒk]
Uhrzeit time [taɪm]
umarmen: (jn./einander) umarmen hug (sb.) [hʌg]
um: um 8 Uhr at 8 o'clock [æt], [ət]
umdrehen turn [tɜːn]
umhergehen (in) walk around [wɔːk əˈraʊnd]
Umkleideraum changing room [ˈtʃeɪndʒɪŋ ruːm]
umrühren stir [stɜː]
umsteigen change trains [tʃeɪndʒ treɪn]
umweltbewusst green [griːn]
umweltfreundlich werden go green [gəʊ griːn]
umziehen (nach) move (to) [muːv]
unabhängig (von) independent (of/from) [ɪndɪˈpendənt]
und and [ænd], [ənd] **Und du?** What about you? [əˈbaʊt]
Unfall; Zufall accident [ˈæksɪdənt]
unfreundlich unfriendly [ʌnˈfrendli]
unheimlich scary [ˈskeəri]
unhöflich rude [ruːd]
Uniform uniform [ˈjuːnɪfɔːm]
unordentlich messy [ˈmesi]
Unordnung mess [mes]
Unrecht: Unrecht haben be wrong [rɒŋ]
uns us [ʌs], [əs]
unser/e our [ˈaʊə]
unsichtbar invisible [ɪnˈvɪzəbl]
unten: nach unten (die Treppe hinunter) downstairs [daʊnˈsteəz]
unter under [ˈʌndə]; below [bɪˈləʊ]
unter der Erde underground [ˈʌndəgraʊnd]
unterhalten: sich unterhalten (mit) chat (with) [tʃæt]
unterirdisch underground [ˈʌndəgraʊnd]
Unterricht class [klɑːs]
im Unterricht in class
unterrichten teach [tiːtʃ]
Unterrichtsstunde lesson [ˈlesn]
Unterschied difference [ˈdɪfrəns]
unterstreichen highlight [ˈhaɪlaɪt]
Unterstützung support [səˈpɔːt]
untersuchen research [rɪˈsɜːtʃ]
unter Wasser, Unterwasser- underwater [ʌndəˈwɔːtə]
Urlaub holiday [ˈhɒlədeɪ] **im/in den Urlaub** on holiday

V

Vanille vanilla [vəˈnɪlə]
Vampir vampire [ˈvæmpaɪə]
Vater father [ˈfɑːðə]
Vati dad [dæd]

vegan vegan [ˈviːgən]
Veganer/in vegan [ˈviːgən]
Vegetarier/in vegetarian [vedʒəˈteəriən], (infml auch) veggie [ˈvedʒi]
vegetarisch vegetarian [vedʒəˈteəriən], (infml auch) veggie [ˈvedʒi]
Verabredung date [deɪt]
verärgert upset [ʌpˈset]; annoyed [əˈnɔɪd]
verbinden (mit) link [lɪŋk]
Verbindung connection [kəˈnekʃn]
verboten no [nəʊ]
Verbrecher, Verbrecherin villain [ˈvɪlən]
verdienen (Geld) earn [ɜːn]
Verein club [klʌb]
Vereinigtes Königreich the United Kingdom (the UK) [junaɪtɪd ˈkɪŋdəm], [juː ˈkeɪ]
vergangene(r,s) past [pɑːst]
vergessen forget [fəˈget]
vergessen: nicht vergessen remember [rɪˈmembə]
vergleichen compare [kəmˈpeə]
verirren: Hast du dich verirrt? Are you lost? [lɒst]
verkaufen sell [sel]
Verkäufer, Verkäuferin shop assistant [ˈʃɒp əsɪstənt]
Verkaufsbude kiosk [ˈkiːɒsk]
Verkaufsstand kiosk [ˈkiːɒsk]
verkehrt herum upside down [ʌpsaɪd ˈdaʊn]
Verkleidung costume [ˈkɒstjuːm]
verlassen leave [liːv]
verlässlich reliable [rɪˈlaɪəbl]
verlaufen: Hast du dich verlaufen? Are you lost? [lɒst]
verletzen, wehtun hurt [hɜːt]
verlieren lose [luːz]
Verlies dungeon [ˈdʌndʒən]
vermischen mix [mɪks]
vermissen miss [mɪs]
vermisst missing [ˈmɪsɪŋ]
verpassen miss [mɪs]
verrückt crazy [ˈkreɪzi]
verschieden different [ˈdɪfrənt]
verschneit snowy [ˈsnəʊi]
verspäten: Ich habe mich verspätet. I'm late. [leɪt] **Verspäte dich nicht.** Don't be late.
Versprechen promise [ˈprɒmɪs]
verstehen understand [ʌndəˈstænd]; **etwas verstehen** work sth. out [wɜːk]
versuchen try [traɪ]
Vertrauensschüler/in head student [hed ˈstjuːdnt]
verwenden use [juːz]
verwundert puzzled [ˈpʌzld]
Verzierung decoration [dekəˈreɪʃn]
Video; Video- video [ˈvɪdiəʊ]
viel/e a lot of [ə ˈlɒt əv], lots of [ˈlɒts əv]; many [ˈmæni]; much [mʌtʃ] **wie viele?** how many? [haʊ]
vielleicht maybe [ˈmeɪbi]
vier four [fɔː]
viertel nach 7 quarter past 7 [ˈkwɔːtə pɑːst ˈsevn]

viertel vor 7 quarter to 7 [ˈkwɔːtə tu ˈsevn]
vierzehn fourteen [fɔːˈtiːn]
vierzig forty [ˈfɔːti]
violett purple [ˈpɜːpl]
visuell visual [ˈvɪʒuəl]
Vogel bird [bɜːd]
Vokabelverzeichnis vocabulary [vəˈkæbjələri], (infml auch) vocab [ˈvəʊkæb]
Vokabular vocabulary [vəˈkæbjələri], (infml auch) vocab [ˈvəʊkæb]
voll(er) full (of ...) [fʊl]
völlig (still) perfectly (still) [ˈpɜːfɪktli]
von from [frɒm]; of [ɒv], [əv]
vor
1. (zeitlich) before [bɪˈfɔː]
vor der Schule / der Unterrichtsstunde before school / the lesson [skuːl], [ˈlesn] **vor langer Zeit** a long time ago [ə lɒŋ taɪm əˈgəʊ]
2. (räumlich) in front of [ɪn ˈfrʌnt əv]
Voraussage prediction [prɪˈdɪkʃn]
vorbei an past [pɑːst]
vorbeikommen: vorbeischauen (bei jm.) come round (to sb.) [raʊnd]
vorbereiten: sich vorbereiten (auf) prepare (for) [prɪˈpeə]
Vorderseite front [frʌnt]
Vorhersage prediction [prɪˈdɪkʃn]
vormittags: 9 Uhr vormittags 9 a.m. [eɪˈem]
Vorname first name [ˈfɜːst neɪm]
vorschlagen suggest [səˈdʒest]
vorsichtig careful [ˈkeəfl]
vorstellen: (jm.) etwas vorstellen present sth. (to sb.) [prɪˈzent] **sich etwas vorstellen** imagine sth. [ɪˈmædʒɪn]
Vortrag talk [tɔːk]
vorüber an past [pɑːst]
Vorwahl(nummer) code [kəʊd]

W

waagerecht horizontal [hɒrɪˈzɒntl]
wach awake [əˈweɪk]
Wackelpudding jelly [ˈdʒeli]
wählen choose [tʃuːz]
wahr true [truː]
wahrscheinlich probably [ˈprɒbəbli]
wahr werden come true [kʌm truː]
während during [ˈdjʊərɪŋ]; as [æz], [əz]
Wald forest [ˈfɒrɪst]
Wand wall [wɔːl] **an der/die Wand** on the wall [ɒn]
Wandern hiking [ˈhaɪkɪŋ]; walking [ˈwɔːkɪŋ]
wandern hike [haɪk]; walk [wɔːk]
Wanduhr clock [klɒk]
wann when [wen]
warm hot [hɒt]; warm [wɔːm] **warm werden** get warm [get]
warten (auf) wait (for) [weɪt]
warum why [waɪ]
was what [wɒt] **Was ist mit dir?** What about you? [əˈbaʊt]
Was (Wie viel) kostet ...? How much is...? [haʊ mʌtʃ ɪz]

Was (Wie viel) kosten ...? How much are ...? [haʊ mʌtʃ ɑː]
waschen: sich waschen wash [wɒʃ]
Wasser water [ˈwɔːtə]
Wassermelone water melon [ˈmelən]
Website website [ˈwebsaɪt]
Wechselgeld change [tʃeɪndʒ]
Weg journey [ˈdʒɜːni]; way [weɪ]
weg away [əˈweɪ]
Wegbeschreibung directions (pl) [dəˈrekʃnz]
weg von off [ɒf]
weglassen: etwas weglassen cut sth. out [kʌt]
wehen blow [bləʊ]
Weide field [fiːld] **auf der Weide** in the field
Weihnachten Christmas [ˈkrɪsməs]
Weihnachtstag Christmas Day [krɪsməs ˈdeɪ]
weil because [bɪˈkɒz]
Weise: Art und Weise way [weɪ] **auf diese Weise** (in) this way **auf unterschiedliche Weise** in different ways [ˈdɪfrənt]
weit (entfernt) far [fɑː]
weiß white [waɪt]
weitere more [mɔː] **drei weitere** three more [θriː]
weitermachen continue [kənˈtɪnjuː] **(mit) etwas weitermachen** continue to do sth. [duː]
welche(r, s) which? [wɪtʃ]; what [wɒt]
Welt world [wɜːld]
Weltraum space [speɪs]
Wendung phrase [freɪz]
wen, wem who [huː]
wenn
  1. **(falls)** if [ɪf] **Was wäre, wenn?** What if? [wɒt]
  2. *(zeitlich)* when [wen]
wenigstens at least [æt liːst]
wer who [huː]
werden get [get]; become [bɪˈkʌm]
Werken design and technology [dɪzaɪn ən tekˈnɒlədʒi]
Werktag weekday [ˈwiːkdeɪ]
Werkunterricht design and technology [dɪzaɪn ən tekˈnɒlədʒi]
wessen whose [huːz]
Wetter weather [ˈweðə]
Wettkampf competition [kɒmpəˈtɪʃn]; match [mætʃ]
wichtig important [ɪmˈpɔːtnt]
wichtigste(r, s) main [meɪn]
wie (ähnlich/so wie) like [laɪk]
wie how [haʊ] **Wie alt bist du?** How old are you? **Wie geht es dir/euch/Ihnen?** How are you? **Wie heißt du?** What's your name? [wɒts] **Wie ist ...? / Wie sieht ... aus?** What's ... like? **wie viele?** how many? **Wie wäre es mit ...?** How about ...? **Wie wäre es mit einer/einem ...?** What about a ...? **Wie spät ist es?** What time is it? [wɒt taɪm ɪz ɪt]
wiederholen repeat [rɪˈpiːt]

Willkommen in/an ... Welcome to ... [ˈwelkəm]
Wind wind [wɪnd]
windig windy [ˈwɪndi]
Windsurfen windsurfing [wɪndsɜːfɪŋ]
winken: (jm. zu)winken wave (to sb.) [weɪv]
Winter winter [ˈwɪntə]
wir we [wiː] **Es sind nur wir.** It's just us. [ʌs], [əs] **wir sind** we're (= we are) **wir sind nicht** we aren't **wir waren** we were [wɜː], [wə]
wirklich really [ˈriːəli], [ˈrɪəli]
Wirkung: Auswirkung (auf) effect (on) [ɪˈfekt]
wissen know [nəʊ]
Wissenschaftler/in scientist [ˈsaɪəntɪst]
Witterung weather [ˈweðə]
Witz joke [dʒəʊk]
witzig funny [ˈfʌni]
wo where [weə] **Wo kommst du her?** Where are you from?
Woche week [wiːk]
Wochenende weekend [wiːkˈend] **am Wochenende** at the weekend
Wochentag weekday [ˈwiːkdeɪ]
wohltätige Organisation charity [ˈtʃærəti]
wohnen live [lɪv]
Wohnsiedlung estate [ɪˈsteɪt]
Wohnung flat [flæt]; apartment [əˈpɑːtmənt]
Wohnzimmer living room [ˈlɪvɪŋ ruːm]
Wolke cloud [klaʊd]
wolkig cloudy [ˈklaʊdi]
wollen want [wɒnt] **etwas tun wollen** want to do sth. [duː]
Wort word [wɜːd]
Wörternetz mind map [ˈmaɪnd mæp]
Wortschatz vocabulary [vəˈkæbjələri], *(infml auch)* vocab [ˈvəʊkæb]
wunderbar wonderful [ˈwʌndəfl]
wünschen: sich wünschen wish [wɪʃ]
Wurst: Würstchen sausage [ˈsɒsɪdʒ]
würzig spicy [ˈspaɪsi]
wütend angry [ˈæŋgri]

Y

Yoga yoga [ˈjəʊgə]

Z

Zahl number [ˈnʌmbə]
zahlen: (etwas be)zahlen pay (for sth.) [peɪ]
Zahn tooth, *(pl)* teeth [tuːθ], [tiːθ]
Zahnspange: Zahnklammer braces (pl) [ˈbreɪsɪz]
Zauberei magic [ˈmædʒɪk]
Zauberkasten magic set [ˈmædʒɪk set]
zaubern do magic [duː ˈmædʒɪk]
Zaubertrick magic trick [ˈmædʒɪk trɪk]
zehn ten [ten]
Zeichen mark [mɑːk]; sign [saɪn]
zeichnen draw [drɔː]
Zeichnen drawing [ˈdrɔːɪŋ]
zeigen show [ʃəʊ]
Zeile line [laɪn]

Zeit time [taɪm] **(für) eine lange Zeit** (for) a long time [lɒŋ] **einige Zeit** a while [waɪl]
Zeit verbringen (mit) / Geld ausgeben (für) spend time/money [spend taɪm], [spend ˈmʌni]
Zeitschrift magazine [mægəˈziːn]
Zeitung newspaper [ˈnjuːspeɪpə]; paper [ˈpeɪpə]
Zeitungshändler newsagent [ˈnjuːzeɪdʒənt]
Zensur mark [mɑːk]
Zentrum centre [ˈsentə]
zerbrechen: etwas zerbrechen break sth. [breɪk]
zerbrochen broken [ˈbrəʊkən]
Zeremonie ceremony [ˈserəməni]
Zettel piece of paper [piːs ɒv ˈpeɪpə]
Ziege goat [gəʊt]
ziehen (nach) move (to) [muːv]
ziemlich quite [kwaɪt]
Ziel destination [destɪˈneɪʃn]
Ziffer number [ˈnʌmbə]
Zimmer room [ruːm]
Zirkus circus [ˈsɜːkəs]
Zitrone lemon [ˈlemən]
Zoo zoo [zuː]
zu: um zu to [tu], [tə]
zubereiten prepare [prɪˈpeə]
Zucker sugar [ˈʃʊgə]
Zuckerguss icing [ˈaɪsɪŋ]
zuerst (at) first [fɜːst]
Zug train [treɪn]
Zuhause home [həʊm]
zuhören listen [ˈlɪsn]
Zuhörer/-innen audience [ˈɔːdiəns]
Zukunft, zukünftige(r,s) future [ˈfjuːtʃə]
zumachen close [kləʊz]
zumindest at least [æt liːst]
zurück back [bæk]
zurücklassen leave [liːv]
zurzeit at the moment [ˈməʊmənt]
zusammen together [təˈgeðə]
zusammenfügen match [mætʃ]
Zuschauer/-innen audience [ˈɔːdiəns]
zustimmen agree [əˈgriː]
zuverlässig reliable [rɪˈlaɪəbl]
zuversichtlich confident [ˈkɒnfɪdənt]
zu viel des Guten too much of a good thing [tuː mʌtʃ ɒv ə gʊd θɪŋ]
zwanzig twenty [ˈtwenti]
zwei two [tuː]
zweite(r, s) second (2nd) [ˈsekənd]
Zwiebel onion [ˈʌnjən]
zwischen between [bɪˈtwiːn]
zwölf twelve [twelv]
zwölfte(r, s) twelfth (12th) [twelfθ]

Irregular verbs

infinitive	simple past	past participle	
(to) babysit	babysat	babysat	babysitten
(to) be	I / he / she / it **was**; you / we / they **were**	been	sein
(to) become	became	become	werden
(to) begin	began	begun	anfangen, beginnen
(to) blow	blew [uː]	blown	pusten, blasen; wehen
(to) break	broke	broken	zerbrechen
(to) bring	brought	brought	(mit)bringen
(to) build [ɪ]	built [ɪ]	built [ɪ]	bauen
(to) buy	bought	bought	kaufen
(to) catch	caught	caught	(ein)fangen; erwischen; nehmen (z. B. einen Zug, einen Bus)
(to) choose	chose	chosen	(aus)wählen
(to) come	came	come	(mit)kommen
(to) cost	cost	cost	kosten
(to) cut	cut	cut	(aus)schneiden
(to) do	did	done [ʌ]	tun, machen
(to) draw	drew	drawn	zeichnen
(to) drink	drank	drunk	trinken
(to) drive [aɪ]	drove [əʊ]	driven [ɪ]	fahren
(to) eat [iː]	ate [et, eɪt]	eaten [iː]	essen; fressen
(to) fall	fell	fallen	(hin)fallen
(to) feed	fed	fed	füttern; ernähren
(to) feel	felt	felt	fühlen, sich fühlen
(to) fight	fought	fought	(be)kämpfen
(to) find	found	found	finden
(to) fly	flew	flown	fliegen
(to) forget	forgot	forgotten	vergessen
(to) get	got	got	bekommen; (sich etw.) holen; werden
(to) give [ɪ]	gave	given [ɪ]	geben
(to) go	went	gone	gehen, fahren
(to) grow (up)	grew (up)	grown (up)	(auf)wachsen
(to) hang out [æ]	hung out [ʌ]	hung out [ʌ]	rumhängen, abhängen
(to) have	had	had	haben; etw. essen
(to) hear [ɪə]	heard [ɜː]	heard	hören
(to) hide	hid	hidden	(sich) verstecken
(to) hit	hit	hit	treffen auf, schlagen, stoßen gegen
(to) hold	held	held	halten
(to) hurt	hurt	hurt	verletzen; wehtun
(to) keep	kept	kept	(be)halten; aufbewahren
(to) know [nəʊ]	knew [njuː]	known [nəʊn]	wissen; kennen
(to) leave	left	left	lassen, zurücklassen, verlassen
(to) lose [uː]	lost	lost	verlieren
(to) make	made	made	machen, herstellen
(to) mean	meant	meant	bedeuten, meinen

infinitive	simple past	past participle	
(to) **meet**	**met**	**met**	treffen; (sich) treffen
(to) **pay**	**paid**	**paid**	(be)zahlen
(to) **put**	**put**	**put**	legen, stellen, stecken
(to) **read** [iː]	**read** [e]	**read** [e]	lesen
(to) **ride** [aɪ]	**rode**	**ridden** [ɪ]	reiten; *(Rad)* fahren
(to) **run**	**ran**	**run**	rennen, laufen
(to) **say**	**said** [sed]	**said** [sed]	sagen
(to) **see**	**saw**	**seen**	sehen
(to) **sell**	**sold**	**sold**	verkaufen
(to) **send**	**sent**	**sent**	senden, schicken
(to) **set**	**set**	**set**	stellen, legen, setzen
(to) **show**	**showed**	**shown**	zeigen
(to) **sing**	**sang**	**sung**	singen
(to) **sit**	**sat**	**sat**	sitzen; sich setzen
(to) **sleep**	**slept**	**slept**	schlafen
(to) **speak** [iː]	**spoke**	**spoken**	sprechen
(to) **spend**	**spent**	**spent**	*(Geld)* ausgeben, *(Zeit)* verbringen
(to) **stand**	**stood**	**stood**	stehen; sich (hin)stellen
(to) **steal**	**stole**	**stolen**	stehlen, rauben
(to) **swim**	**swam**	**swum**	schwimmen
(to) **take**	**took**	**taken**	(mit)nehmen; bringen; dauern
(to) **teach**	**taught**	**taught**	lehren, unterrichten
(to) **tell**	**told**	**told**	sagen; erzählen, berichten
(to) **think**	**thought**	**thought**	denken, glauben, meinen
(to) **throw**	**threw**	**thrown**	werfen
(to) **understand**	**understood**	**understood**	verstehen
(to) **upset**	**upset**	**upset**	jn. erschüttern; jn. aufregen, ärgern
(to) **wear** [eə]	**wore** [ɔː]	**worn** [ɔː]	tragen, anhaben *(Kleidung)*
(to) **win**	**won** [ʌ]	**won** [ʌ]	gewinnen
(to) **write** [aɪ]	**wrote**	**written** [ɪ]	schreiben

Text file: answers for the puzzles

p. 37   1 Kennedy Space Center, Florida
        2 The Statue of Liberty, New York
        3 The White House, Washington, DC
        4 The Empire State Building, New York

p. 137   **puzzle time:** 1c, 2e, 3a, 4b, 5f, 6d
         e-postcard: **1** tip = $6, **2** tip = $11

p. 169   **pocket money puzzle:** £7 / £23 (7+7+5+4)
         e-postcard: Hudson **has** the most money.

Viele englische Wörter ähneln deutschen Wörtern: *a cowboy* = ein Cowboy. Beachte aber die Unterschiede 1–3!

(1) Nomen werden im Deutschen großgeschrieben, aber im Englischen klein.
(2) Manche Wörter haben im Deutschen andere Endungen, aber einen ähnlichen Stamm, z. B. planen – *(to) plan*.
(3) Die Aussprache kann sich unterscheiden. Höre dir die blau markierten Wörter in der App an und sprich sie nach.

active / activity	culture	melon	skateboard
address	curry	milk	skatepark
allergic (to)	dance / (to) dance	millilitre	smart
alphabet	December	minute	snack
alternative	decoration	modern	sofa
app	drama	moment	software
April	drink / (to) drink	Monday	song
article	electric	museum	sport
August	elephant	music	star
badminton	end / (to) end	name	stop
balcony	England / English	November	story
ball	family	number	street dance
banana	fan	object	student
band	February	October	summer
barbecue	feedback	online	Sunday
basketball	film	orange	supermarket
biology	(to) find	parkour	surfing
blazer	fish	partner	sweatshirt
bowling	football	party	(to) swim
(to) bring	friend / friendly	pasta	swimmer
British	garage	perfect	test / (to) test
browser	garden	person	text / (to) text
burger	gold	photo	ticket
bus	group	picnic	tip
butter	hamster	plan / (to) plan	title
cafe	happy	playlist	toilet
camera	hello	pool	tomato
card	highlight	popcorn	top
character	hockey	post	tourist
check	hot dog	poster	tradition
chocolate	house	problem	trainer / training
circus	hungry	project	trick
city	idea	respect	uniform
class	information	restaurant	vanilla
classroom	insect	ring	vegan
clever	internet	robot	vegetarian / veggie
club	January	room	video
coffee	July	rucksack	warm
comic	June	salad	website
computer	karaoke	sandwich	wind
console	kebab	sauce	winner
cool	kilometre (km)	school	winter
corridor	kiosk	(to) send	word
cost / (to) cost	lamp	September	yoga
cousin	market	shopping centre	yoghurt
creative	maths	silver	zoo

Titelbild
Cornelsen / Personen am Strand: Anja Poehlmann, Strandhäuschen: Shutterstock.com / JoolsW

Illustrationen
Cornelsen / Harald Ardeias: S. 15 1–5; S. 16; S. 18 A–F + un. re.; S. 19 ob. li. + un.; S. 24 A–I; S. 26–27; S. 33 1–6; S. 35 un. re.; S. 40 un.; S. 45 un.; S. 52–53 alle; S. 57 un.; S. 60–61 1–7; S. 66 A–D; S. 74 ob. re.; S. 76 alle; S. 80 A; S. 82 un. re.; S. 86 A–C; S. 88 un. mi.; S. 89 ob. re.; S. 90 ob. re.; S. 91 2 + 3; S. 92–93 re.; S. 98 un. re.; S. 100 1–8; S. 108 mi. re.; S. 109 A–D, 1–6; S. 111 1–6; S. 114 mi. re.; S. 120 mi. re. + un. re.; S. 121 mi. re.; S. 122 ob.; S. 123 un.; S. 124 ob.; S. 126 un.; S. 127 re.; S. 128 mi. re.; S. 132 ob. re.; S. 138 ob. re.; S. 139 A + B; S. 142 un. re.; S. 143 un. re.; S. 150 ob.; S. 156 un. re.; S. 157 ob. re.; S. 174 un. re.; S. 176–178 alle; S. 179 un.; S. 180–181 alle; S. 216 **Cornelsen/Inhouse/ Josephine Bienert-Köhler:** S. 56 A–D; S. 59 Ethel Ellis; S. 68 ob. li.; S. 70 mi.; S. 102 un.; S. 172 mi. re.; S. 187 ob. re.; S. 190 ob. re.; S. 193 ob. re.; S. 196 re.; **Cornelsen / Carlos Borrell Eiköter:** S. 104 ob. re. + un. li.; S. 105 mi. li.; Umschlaginnenseite hinten (U3): Karte Europa; **Cornelsen / Julie Colthorpe, Berlin:** S. 184 mi. re.; **Cornelsen/ Karen Donnelly:** S. 70 un. mi.; **Cornelsen / Michael Fleischmann:** S. 248 dangerous; S. 268 dishwasher; **Cornelsen/ Klara Luise Frankenberg:** S. 184 ob. re.; **Cornelsen / Jeongsook Lee:** S. 261 sheep; **Cornelsen / Irina Zinner:** S. 4–10 Möwe; S. 14 Möwe; S. 17 Möwe; S. 19 Möwe; S. 21 Möwe; S. 24; S. 24 Möwe; S. 28 Möwe; S. 30–31 Möwen; S. 42 + 44 Möwen; S. 49 Möwe; S. 51 Möwe; S. 54 un. re.; S. 55 Möwen; S. 58 Möwen; S. 64–65 Möwen; S. 73 Möwe; S. 75 Möwen; S. 82 Möwe; S. 83 Möwe; S. 85–86 Möwen; S. 87 Möwe; S. 90 Möwe; S. 94 Möwe; S. 96 Möwe; S. 97 Möwen; S. 106 Möwe; S. 110 un. re.; S. 116 Möwen; S. 117 Möwen; S. 119 Möwe, S. 120 Möwe; S. 121 Möwe; S. 128 Möwe; S. 130 Möwe; S. 131 Möwe; S. 140–141 Möwen; S. 143 Möwen; S. 148 Möwen; S. 149 Möwen; S. 152 Möwen; S. 156 Möwe; S. 162–163 Möwen; S. 171 Möwe; S. 183 Möwe; S. 194 Möwe; S. 197 un. re.; S. 198–204 Möwen; S. 206 Möwe; S. 207–209 Möwen; S. 220 Möwe; S. 223–228 Möwen

Abbildungen
Umschlaginnenseite vorn (U2): Siehe S. 12, 16, 26; **S. 1 ob. :** Siehe S. 30, 31, 32; **S. 4 – 8** ob. li.: Cornelsen / Anja Poehlmann; **S. 10** mi. re.: Cornelsen / Anja Poehlmann, Emoticon: Shutterstock.com / Yefym Turkin; **S. 11** mi.: Cornelsen / Anja Poehlmann; Emoticons: Shutterstock.com / Yefym Turkin; **S. 12** ob. li.: Shutterstock.com / Maksim Zaytsev, ob. re.: Shutterstock.com / Bobo Ling, mi. li.: Cornelsen / Anja Poehlmann, mi. re.: Shutterstock. com / wavebreakmedia; **S. 13** mi. li.: Shutterstock.com / Linda George, mi. re.: Shutterstock.com / A_Lein, un. li.: Shutterstock.com / malik965, mi. re.: Cornelsen / Anja Poehlmann; **S. 14** ob. re.: Shutterstock.com / vovidzha; **S. 15** mi. re.: Cornelsen / Anja Poehlmann; **S. 17** mi.: Shutterstock.com / Radha Design; **S. 18** Regenbogen: Shutterstock. com / sebastian ignacio coll, Emoticon: Shutterstock.com / Yefym Turkin; **S. 19** ob. re.: Cornelsen / Grasshopper Films; **S. 20** ob. re. + un. re.: Cornelsen / Anja Poehlmann, mi. re.: mauritius images / alamy stock photo / Benedicte Desrus; **S. 21** mi. re.: Shutterstock.com / Viorel Sima, un. mi.: Shutterstock.com / UfaBizPhoto; **S. 22** ob. re.: Cornelsen / Anja Poehlmann, un. li.: stock.adobe.com / Stafeeva; **S. 23** mi. re.: Cornelsen / Anja Poehlmann, un. re.: Cornelsen / Junge (li.): Anja Poehlmann, Frau (re.): Shutterstock.com / SpeedKingz; **S. 25** ob. + mi. re.: Anja Poehlmann; **S. 29** ob. re.: Cornelsen / Inhouse / Mara Leibowitz, mi. re.: Cornelsen / Grasshopper Films; **S. 32** ob. li.: Cornelsen / Anja Poehlmann, 1: Shutterstock.com / Rainer Lesniewski, 2: Shutterstock.com / FotoAndalucia, 3: Shutterstock.com / Naypong Studio, 4: Shutterstock.com / Laenz, 5 holidays: Shutterstock.com / Arsenie Krasnevsky, the journey: Shutterstock.com / XXLPhoto, Daumen: Shutterstock.com / Cosmic_Design; **S. 33** mi. re.: Cornelsen / Anja Poehlmann; **S. 34** ob. re.: Shutterstock.com / Dubova; **S. 35** ob. re.: Cornelsen / Anja Poehlmann; **S. 36** ob. li.: stock.adobe.com / Анна Бортникова, un. li.: Shutterstock.com / James Kirkikis, mi. li.: stock.adobe. com / Backyard Productions LLC 2018 / steheap, mi. re.: Shutterstock.com / D MacDonald, un. re.: stock.adobe. com / Blake Alan; **S. 37** mi. li.: Shutterstock.com / Rashevskyi Viacheslav, USA-Landkarte: stock.adobe.com / Racer57, USA-Flagge: stock.adobe.com / M-KOS, mi. re.: Shutterstock.com / Travel Stock, un. li.: NASA / Charisse Nahser, mi. li.: Shutterstock.com / TZIDO SUN, mi. re.: mauritius images / Manfred Vollmer, un. re.: stock.adobe. com / ManuPadilla; **S. 38** ob. re.: Shutterstock.com / Sue Martin, Piddocks in their holes: mauritius images / alamy stock photo / Nature Photographers Ltd, Barnacles: stock.adobe.com / Kelly Castro, Spiny crab: Shutterstock. com / Vojce, Strawberry anemone: Shutterstock.com / Becky Gill, Starfish: stock.adobe.com / Thitaree Sarmkasat / sewcream; **S. 39** ob. re.: stock.adobe.com / Copyright: Dmitry Naumov / Dmitry Naumov; **S. 41** un. re.: Cornelsen / Anja Poehlmann; **S. 46–47** A–D: Cornelsen / Anja Poehlmann; **S. 49** ob. li.: Shutterstock.com / 2xSamara.com, un. re.: Cornelsen / Oliver Meibert; **S. 50** ob. : Cornelsen / Anja Poehlmann, Emoticons: Shutterstock.com / Yefym Turkin; **S. 51** ob. : Cornelsen / Anja Poehlmann, Emoticons: Shutterstock.com / Yefym Turkin; **S. 54** Marek: Shutterstock.com / Dean Drobot, Ivy: Shutterstock.com / Luis Molinero, Cal: Shutterstock.com / sirikorn

thamniyom, Dimitra: Shutterstock.com/Nicolette Kapp; **S. 55** ob. re.: Shutterstock.com/Gleb Usovich; **S. 59** Maya Angelou: Imago Stock & People GmbH/Dwight Carter/Hallmark Entertainment/Courtesy: Everett Collection Hallmark Entertainment/Courtesy Everett Collection, Annie Lennox: mauritius images/alamy stock photo/Allstar Picture Library Ltd, Bertrand Russell: mauritius images/alamy stock photo/Pictorial Press Ltd, Alan Turing: mauritius images/alamy stock photo/Alpha Historica; **S. 62** 1–12: Shutterstock.com/Spread-thesign; **S. 63** ob. re.: Cornelsen/Inhouse/Mara Leibowitz, mi. re.: Cornelsen/Grasshopper Films; **S. 66** ob. : Cornelsen/Anja Poehlmann; **S. 67** ob. li.: Cornelsen/Anja Poehlmann, un. mi.: Shutterstock.com/Laugesen Mateo, **S. 69** ob. re.: Cornelsen/Anja Poehlmann; **S. 70** un. li.: stock.adobe.com/Carballo; **S. 71** ob. li.: Imago Stock & People GmbH/PA Images/Doug Peters/EMPICS Entertainment, ob. re.: mauritius images/alamy stock photo/michael melia; USA-Landkarte: stock.adobe.com/Racer57, USA-Flagge: stock.adobe.com/M-KOS, un. re.: Shutterstock.com/Pixel-Shot; **S. 72** mi. re.: Shutterstock.com/AnnGaysorn; **S. 73** un. re.: Cornelsen/Anja Poehlmann; **S. 78** A: Shutterstock.com/delcarmat, B: mauritius images/alamy stock photo/Paul Briden, **S. 79** C: Shutterstock.com/Kiian Oksana, D: Shutterstock.com/JurateBuiviene; **S. 80** B: Shutterstock.com/SpeedKingz, C: mauritius images/alamy stock photo/Nigel Cattlin, D: Shutterstock.com/FenlioQ, E: Shutterstock.com/Mr.Alex M, F: Shutterstock.com/Aleksandr Rybalko, G: Shutterstock.com/CKP1001, H: Shutterstock.com/michelangeloop; **S. 81** ob. re.: Cornelsen/Anja Poehlmann, un. mi.: Cornelsen/Oliver Meibert; **S. 82** mi. re.: Cornelsen/Anja Poehlmann; **S. 84** ob. re.: Cornelsen/Anja Poehlmann, un. mi.: stock.adobe.com/stockaboo; **S. 86** mi.: Cornelsen/Anja Poehlmann; **S. 87** ob. re.: Shutterstock.com/Phonlamai Photo; **S. 88** mi. re.: Cornelsen/Anja Poehlmann; **S. 89** Emoticons: Shutterstock.com/Yefym Turkin; **S. 91** 1: Shutterstock.com/Tero Vesalainen, 4: Shutterstock.com/Oleksiy Mark; **S. 95** ob. re.: Cornelsen/Inhouse/Mara Leibowitz, mi. + un. re.: Cornelsen/Grasshopper Films LTD; **S. 96** mi. li.: stock.adobe.com/pairhandmade, mi.: Shutterstock.com/ViDI Studio; **S. 99** Emoticons: Shutterstock.com/Yefym Turkin; **S. 101** mi. re.: Cornelsen/Anja Poehlmann, un. li.: Shutterstock.com/Krakenimages.com; **S. 102** mi. re.: stock.adobe.com/Scanrail, Zeina: mauritius images/Westend61, Asim: mauritius images/alamy stock photo/Zoonar GmbH, Laura: Imago Stock & People GmbH/YAY Images, Emoticon: Shutterstock.com/Yefym Turkin; **S. 103** mi.: Depositphotos/Sean Prior, USA-Landkarte: stock.adobe.com/Racer**57**, USA-Flagge: stock.adobe.com/M-KOS, un. re.: Imago Stock & People GmbH/YAY Images; **S. 104** A: mauritius images/alamy stock photo/david a eastley, B: Shutterstock.com/Daniel Lange, C: Shutterstock.com/Roy Pedersen, D: Shutterstock.com/Marius_Comanescu, E: stock.adobe.com/Lance Bellers; **S. 107** ob. re.: Cornelsen/Anja Poehlmann; **S. 112** A: stock.adobe.com/Fevziie, B: Leszczynsk; **S. 113** C: stock.adobe.com/JOHN LEIGH/thecoach1, D: mauritius images/Steve Vidler; **S. 115** A: Shutterstock.com/Gyrohype, B: Shutterstock.com/Adisa, C: Shutterstock.com/Grigor Unkovski, D: Shutterstock.com/azure1, E: Shutterstock.com/kulyk, F: Shutterstock.com/MAHATHIR MOHD YASIN, G: Shutterstock/Evgeny Karandaev, H: Shutterstock.com/KPad, un. li. + mi. re.: Cornelsen/Anja Poehlmann; **S. 116** ob. re.: Cornelsen/Anja Poehlmann; **S. 117** mi. re.: Cornelsen/Anja Poehlmann; **S. 118** alle: Cornelsen/Anja Poehlmann; **S. 124** Emoticons: Shutterstock.com/Yefym Turkin; **S. 125** ob. : Shutterstock.com/Wedding and lifestyle, A: Shutterstock.com/Lital Israeli, B: stock.adobe.com/Sergei Grigorenko/alexbard, C: Shutterstock.com/Rawpixel.com; **S. 126** Sunita: Cornelsen/Anja Poehlmann, Meera: Shutterstock.com/JacquiMoore, Emoticon: Shutterstock.com/Yefym Turkin; **S. 129** ob. re.: Cornelsen/Inhouse/Mara Leibowitz, mi. re. + un. re.: Cornelsen/Grasshopper Films; **S. 130** 1: Imago Stock & People GmbH/Sylvio Dittrich, 2: Imago Stock & People GmbH/Sylvio Dittrich; **S. 132** mi.: stock.adobe.com/grafikplusfoto; **S. 133** un. re.: Cornelsen/Anja Poehlmann, Emoticons: Shutterstock.com/Yefym Turkin; **S. 134** ob. li.: Shutterstock.com/Rawpixel.com; **S. 135** Daumen: Shutterstock.com/Cosmic_Design, mi. li.: stock.adobe.com/Gorodenkoff Productions OU/Gorodenkoff, mi. re.: Shutterstock.com/Halfpoint; **S. 136** mi. re.: dpa Picture-Alliance/ZUMAPRESS.com/London News Pictures via ZUMA/Hugo Michiels, un. re.: Cornelsen/Anja Poehlmann; **S. 137** ob. li.: stock.adobe.com/vm**2002**, ob. re.: stock.adobe.com/Ildi Papp/Ildi, USA-Landkarte: stock.adobe.com/Racer57, USA-Flagge: stock.adobe.com/M-KOS, un. re.: StockFood/Lawton, Becky/PhotoCuisine; **S. 138** 1: Shutterstock.com/tanaban chuenchay, 2: Shutterstock.com/Pressmaster, 3: www.coulorbox.de, 4: Shutterstock.com/Lukas Gojda, 5: Shutterstock.com/Botond Horvath, 6: Shutterstock.com/Irina Yusupova, 7: Shutterstock.com/lazyllama, 8: Shutterstock.com/GCapture; **S. 142** ob. re.: Shutterstock.com/stockfour; **S. 144** A: Shutterstock.com/Gorodenkoff, B: Shutterstock.com/Basyn, C: mauritius images/Westend61 RF, D: Shutterstock.com/M_Agency; **S. 145** E: Shutterstock.com/megaflop, F: Shutterstock.com/Roman Chazov, G: Shutterstock.com/Jacob Lund, H: stock.adobe.com/hedgehog94; **S. 146** ob. re.: Cornelsen/Anja Poehlmann; **S. 147** ob. re.: Shutterstock.com/Pinkcandy, un. li.: Shutterstock.com/serhii.suravikin, 1: stock.adobe.com/amin268, 2: stock.adobe.com/Skellen, 3: stock.adobe.com/spiral media, 4: stock.adobe.com/motorama, 5: Shutterstock.com/ Oleksandr Drypsiak; **S. 148** mi. li.: Shutterstock.com/4zevar; **S. 149** A: Shutterstock.com/

HONGYAN, fish: Shutterstock.com / MaraZe, sausages: Shutterstock.com / Einsteinstudio, eggs: Shutterstock.com / Nattika, lamb: Shutterstock.com / TheBusinessMan, pork: Shutterstock.com / GSDesign, strawberries: Shutterstock.com / Tim UR, apples: Shutterstock.com / Roman Samokhin, melon: Shutterstock.com / Boonchuay1970, raspberry: Shutterstock.com / Andriy Lipkan, oranges: Shutterstock.com / Valentyn Volkov, mango: Shutterstock.com / Valentyn Volkov, banana: Shutterstock.com / bergamont, lemon: Shutterstock.com / Maks Narodenko, cherry: Shutterstock.com / Serg64, popcorn: Shutterstock.com / Jiri Hera, cupcakes: Shutterstock.com / Wealthylady, muffins: Shutterstock.com / Binh Thanh Bui, ice cream: Shutterstock.com / stockcreations, donuts: Shutterstock.com / Sergey Skleznev, jelly: Shutterstock.com / cigdem, butter: Shutterstock.com / bigacis, cheese: Shutterstock.com / Tanya Sid, joghurt: Shutterstock.com / pogonici, milk: Shutterstock.com / New Africa, cream: Shutterstock.com / grey_and, aubergine: Shutterstock.com / PixaHub, broccoli: Shutterstock.com / smspsy, carrot: Shutterstock.com / Valentina Razumova, cabbage: Shutterstock.com / JIANG HONGYAN, cucumber: Shutterstock.com / Maks Narodenko, garlic: Shutterstock.com / Maks Narodenko, chili: Shutterstock.com / PixaHub, peas: Shutterstock.com / WIPHARAT CHAINUPAPHA, peppers: Shutterstock.com / DronG, onions: Shutterstock.com / Yeti studio, lettuce: Shutterstock.com / PotaeRin, potatoes: Shutterstock.com / Anna Kucherova, tomato: Shutterstock.com / Tim UR; **S. 221** beautician: Shutterstock.com / Rido, care worker: Shutterstock.com / Pixel-Shot, call centre agent: Shutterstock.com / Bojan Milinkov, cashier: Shutterstock.com / hedgehog94, dentist: Shutterstock.com / Drazen Zigic, electrician: Shutterstock.com / Phovoir, engineer: Shutterstock.com / Chaosamran_Studio, lawyer: Shutterstock.com / Gorodenkoff, paramedic: Shutterstock.com / Gorodenkoff, plumber: Shutterstock.com / amedeoemaja, salesperson: Shutterstock.com / George Rudy, secretary: Shutterstock.com / DC Studio, factory: Shutterstock.com / Gorodenkoff, farm: Shutterstock.com / Fotokostic, garage + laboratory: Shutterstock.com / Gorodenkoff; **S. 222** ob. li.: Shutterstock.com / Dean Clarke, ob. mi.: Shutterstock.com / gabriel12, ob. re.: stock.adobe.com / dusanpetkovic1, mi. li.: stock.adobe.com / 682A_IA, mi.: Shutterstock.com / Christian Mueller, mi. re.: stock.adobe.com / Heliosphile, un. li.: stock.adobe.com / nowaczykfoto.pl / Mirek, un. mi.: stock.adobe.com / Mihail, un. re.: Shutterstock.com / Bacho; **S. 229** ob. re.: Shutterstock.com / Laurie Barr; **S. 230** mi.: Shutterstock.com / HitToon; **S. 233** campsite: Shutterstock.com / Modvector, hill: Shutterstock.com / tgavrano, river: Shutterstock.com / Zoa.Arts, plane: Shutterstock.com / Isometrixus; **S. 234** ghost: Shutterstock.com / Rvector, mask: Shutterstock.com / danielmarin, eye: Shutterstock.com / Piotr Krzeslak; **S. 235** flag: Shutterstock.com / Magcom; **S. 236** rainbow: Shutterstock.com / spline_x, piano: stock.adobe.com / yurakrasil; **S. 237** equipment: Shutterstock.com / Alexander Raths, glove: Shutterstock.com / Tung Phan, sign: stock.adobe.com / Lance Bellers; **S. 238** get on (a train / bus): Shutterstock.com / BlueRingMedia, onto the platform: stock.adobe.com / Elena; **S. 239** hug: Shutterstock.com / Iris vector; **S. 241** braces: Shutterstock.com / Maria Shalamova, straight: stock.adobe.com / demimerzie, strong: Shutterstock.com / kristinblack; **S. 242** moon: Shutterstock.com / robert_s; **S. 244** nurse: Shutterstock.com / Minerva Studio, become: stock.adobe.com / Krakenimages.com; **S. 245** planet: NASA / NOAA / DSCOVR, helmet: Shutterstock.com / Rvector; **S. 246** dolphin: Shutterstock.com / Pannochka, ear: Shutterstock.com / dean bertoncelj, dress: Shutterstock.com / Yuyula; **S. 247** to die: stock.adobe.com / MR. PITUK LOONHONG / Pituk; **S. 248** machine: stock.adobe.com / coward_lion, ambulance: stock.adobe.com / nspooner, jump: Shutterstock.com / NicoElNino, ankle: stock.adobe.com / Csaba Deli; **S. 249** fall asleep: Shutterstock.com / Ollyy, blanket: stock.adobe.com / rgvc, fire engine: stock.adobe.com / GWatkins; **S. 250** broken: stock.adobe.com / Алексей Синельников, presenter: Shutterstock.com / aslysun; **S. 252** zip wire: Shutterstock.com / Marcel Jancovic, dungeon: stock.adobe.com / vectorpocket, dragon: stock.adobe.com / lightgirl; **S. 253** castle: Shutterstock.com / meunierd; **S. 254** camera: Shutterstock.com / Skylines; **S. 255** magazine: stock.adobe.com / BillionPhotos.com, forest: stock.adobe.com / The Nico Studio, key: stock.adobe.com / vectorfusionart, trophy: stock.adobe.com / Tartila, turn right / left: Shutterstock.com / Andramin; **S. 256** bird: Shutterstock.com / Ron Mertens, row: stock.adobe.com / Delphine Poggianti / Delphotostock, clocks: stock.adobe.com / wongstock; **S. 259** bonfire: Shutterstock.com / Brilliant Eye, candle: Shutterstock.com / irin-k, fireworks: Shutterstock.com / solarseven, a firework: Shutterstock.com / Kostsov; **S. 257** screen: Shutterstock.com / A-R-T; **S. 260** flower: stock.adobe.com / ecco, baked beans: Shutterstock.com / Kumpol Chuansakul, juice: Shutterstock.com / Digital Genetics, pot: stock.adobe.com / fotofabrika, teapot: stock.adobe.com / aleksandra_1981, pot of yoghurt: Shutterstock.com / oksana2010, tin: stock.adobe.com / Sergey, mosque: Shutterstock.com / naulicrea; **S. 261** soup: stock.adobe.com / AtlasStudio / Atlas; **S. 262** so far: Shutterstock.com / Peera_stockfoto; **S. 263** colourful: Shutterstock.com / mffoto, christening: stock.adobe.com / Jimena, bride / groom: Shutterstock.com / LORA MARCHENKO, suits: Shutterstock.com / Bildagentur Zoonar GmbH; **S. 265** slippers: stock.adobe.com / Coprid, jacket: stock.adobe.com / Olga, rain jacket: Shutterstock.com / gopfaster, scarf: Shutterstock.com / Yury Gulakov; **S. 267** firefighter: stock.adobe.com / toa555; **S. 268** bar chart: Shutterstock.com / Ico Maker; **S. 269** horizontal: stock.adobe.com / 2006 Adobe

Textquellen
S. 70 ob.: Shel Silverstein, 'Hug O'War', in: *Where the Sidewalk Ends – the poems and drawings of Shel Silverstein.* New York: Harper Collins Publishers, 1974

Liedquellen
S. 142: *Long-Legged Sailor:* traditionell und gemeinfrei
S. 168: *Money on my mind* by Ash, Ben/Smith, Samuel. Sony/ATV Music Publishing (Germany) GmbH, Berlin; Stellar Songs Limited/EMI Music Publishing Germany GmbH, Hamburg

Typical tasks	Häufige Arbeitsanweisungen
Act out the conversation / song / story.	Führt das Gespräch / das Lied / die Geschichte vor.
Answer the questions / partner B's questions.	Beantworte die Fragen / Partner Bs Fragen.
Ask and answer questions.	Stelle und beantworte Fragen.
Before you read / listen / watch ...	Bevor du liest / (zu-)hörst / anschaust ...
Brainstorm ideas (with a partner).	Sammle spontane Einfälle / Gedanken.
Check the spelling / your answers / ideas (with a partner).	Überprüfe deine Rechtschreibung / Antworten / Ideen (mit einem/r Partner/in).
Choose the correct answer / word.	Wähle die richtige Antwort / das richtige Wort aus.
Collect ideas / words / phrases.	Sammle Ideen / Wörter / Ausdrücke.
Compare the pictures / your answers / ... with a partner.	Vergleiche die Bilder / deine Antworten / ... mit einem/r Partner/in.
Complete the table / list / sentences / ...	Vervollständige die Tabelle / Liste / Sätze / ...
Copy the table / list / notes.	Schreibe die Tabelle / die Liste / Notizen ab.
Correct the false / wrong sentences / answers.	Berichtige die falschen Sätze / Antworten.
Describe the picture / your room / ...	Beschreibe das Bild / dein Zimmer / ...
Discuss with a partner.	Diskutiere mit einem/r Partner/in.
Find the answers / the correct / right / wrong words.	Finde die Antworten / die richtigen / falschen Wörter.
Finish the sentences.	Vervollständige die Sätze.
Give feedback.	Gib Feedback / eine Einschätzung.
Interview your partner.	Stelle deinem/r Partner/in Fragen.
Look at the board / at page ...	Schaue an die Tafel / auf Seite ...
Look at the photos / pictures / map / title.	Sieh dir die Fotos / Bilder / Karte / die Überschrift an.
Listen and check / practise / repeat / guess.	Höre zu und überprüfe / übe / wiederhole / rate.
Listen to the story / conversation / dialogue.	Höre dir die Geschichte / das Gespräch / den Dialog an.
Make a poster / quiz.	Erstelle ein Poster / Quiz.
Make groups (of six / ... students).	Bildet Gruppen (zu je sechs / ... Schüler/-innen).
Make sentences / notes / lists / a mind map.	Fertige Sätze / Notizen / Listen / eine Mindmap an.
Match the sentence parts / what the friends say.	Verbinde die Satzhälften / das, was die Freunde sagen.
Practise with a partner.	Übe mit einem/r Partner/in.
Put the sentences / dialogue in the correct order.	Bringe die Sätze / den Dialog in die richtige Reihenfolge.
Read the conversation / text / story / article.	Lies den Dialog / Text / die Geschichte / den Artikel.
Stand up when you hear ...	Wenn du ... hörst, stehe auf.
Swap (cards) with a partner.	Tausche (die Karten) mit einem/r Partner/in.
Take turns.	Wechselt euch ab.
Talk to a partner. / Talk in groups.	Sprich mit einem/r Partner/in / deiner Gruppe.
Tell your partner / the class.	Erzähle / Sage es deinem/r Partner/in / der Klasse.
True or false? / True, false or not in the text?	Wahr oder falsch? / Wahr, falsch oder nicht im Text?
Say the four / ... sentences.	Sage die vier / ... Sätze.
Say which one looks interesting / you like best.	Sage welcher/s interessant aussieht / dir am besten gefällt.
Use your notes / the words in a).	Benutze deine Notizen / die Wörter aus Aufgabe a).
Watch part / scene 1 / the whole film (again).	Sieh dir Teil / Szene 1 / den ganzen Film (nochmal) an.
Work alone / with a partner / in groups.	Arbeite allein / mit einem/r Partner/in / in Gruppen.
Write the correct answers / sentences / questions / words.	Schreibe die richtigen Antworten / Sätze / Fragen / Wörter (auf).
Write (more) about ...	Schreibe (mehr) über ...